Knowledge and Skepticism

Topics in Contemporary Philosophy

Editors

Joseph Keim Campbell, Washington State University

Michael O'Rourke, University of Idaho

Harry S. Silverstein, Washington State University

Editorial Board Members

Kent Bach, San Francisco State University

Michael Bratman, Stanford University

Nancy Cartwright, London School of Economics

Richard Feldman, University of Rochester

John Martin Fischer, University of California, Riverside

Nicholas F. Gier, University of Idaho

Philip J. Ivanhoe, Boston University

Michael McKinsey, Wayne State University

John Perry, Stanford University

Stephen Schiffer, New York University

Brian Skyrms, University of California, Irvine

Holly Smith, Rutgers University

Judith Jarvis Thomson, Massachusetts Institute of Technology

Peter van Inwagen, University of Notre Dame

Knowledge and Skepticism

edited by
Joseph Keim Campbell, Michael O'Rourke, and Harry S. Silverstein

A Bradford Book
The MIT Press
Cambridge, Massachusetts
London, England

MIT Press books may be purchased at special quantity discounts for business or sales promotional use. For information, please email special_sales@mitpress.mit.edu or write to Special Sales Department, The MIT Press, 55 Hayward Street, Cambridge, MA 02142.

This book was set in Stone Serif and Stone Sans on 3B2 by Asco Typesetters, Hong Kong. Printed and bound in the United States of America.

Library of Congress Cataloging-in-Publication Data

Inland Northwest Philosophy Conference (7th : 2004 : Pullman, Wash., and Moscow, Idaho)
Knowledge and skepticism / edited by Joseph Keim Campbell, Michael O'Rourke, and Harry S. Silverstein.
  p. cm. — (Topics in contemporary philosophy)
"A Bradford book."
Includes bibliographical references (p.) and index.
ISBN 978-0-262-01408-3 (hardcover : alk. paper)—ISBN 978-0-262-51396-8 (pbk. : alk. paper)
1. Knowledge, Theory of—Congresses. 2. Skepticism—Congresses. I. Campbell, Joseph Keim, 1958–. II. O'Rourke, Michael, 1963–. III. Silverstein, Harry S., 1942–. IV. Title.
BD161.I56 2010
121—dc22
                                                                    2009037402

10 9 8 7 6 5 4 3 2 1

In memory of John Pollock
Philosopher, teacher, friend

Contents

Acknowledgments

Earlier versions of the essays in this volume were presented at the seventh annual Inland Northwest Philosophy Conference (INPC), held between April 30 and May 2, 2004, in Pullman, Washington, and Moscow, Idaho. For their financial and administrative support of the conference, we thank the philosophy departments at Washington State University (David Shier, Chair) and the University of Idaho (Douglas Lind, Chair), the College of Liberal Arts at Washington State University (Erich Lear, Dean), the College of Letters, Arts, and Social Sciences at the University of Idaho (Joe Zeller, Dean), the Research Offices at both universities, and the administrative managers of both departments, Dee Dee Torgeson and Heather Branstetter. We are also grateful for a grant from the Idaho Humanities Council, a state-based affiliate of the National Endowment for the Humanities, to help fund the Public Forum.

All presenters at INPC 2004 were encouraged to submit their work for publication in this volume and, after a process of peer evaluation, only a few were selected. We regret that we had to turn down numerous quality essays, due to space limitations. We thank the following referees: Louise Antony, Ralph Baergen, Elizabeth Brake, Anthony Brueckner, Peter Burkholder, John Carroll, Michael Depaul, Richard Feldman, J. M. Fritzman, John Greco, Michael Huemer, Charlie Huenemann, Philip J. Ivanhoe, Thomas Kelly, Hilary Kornblith, Ann Levey, Timothy McGrew, Patrick Rysiew, Russell Wahl, Lisa Warenski, and Brian Weatherson. We also thank the members of the editorial board.

Finally, our special thanks to Delphine Keim Campbell, Rebecca O'Rourke, and Lorinda Knight for their continued understanding and support.

Introduction: Framing Knowledge and Skepticism

Joseph Keim Campbell, Michael O'Rourke, and Harry S. Silverstein

There are two main questions in epistemology: What is knowledge and do we have any of it? The former question asks after the nature of a concept, and this has two sides, namely, its intrinsic nature and its extrinsic nature. Within the analytic tradition, attention to intrinsic nature has focused on the proper analysis of knowledge into its constituent elements. Attention to extrinsic nature concerns how knowledge relates to the broader world of which it is a part. The latter question involves grappling with the skeptic, who believes that no one knows anything.[1] Among the arguments for skepticism, the Ancient Trilemma and the simply named "argument for skepticism" stand out. The former impeaches the structural integrity of justification, while the latter challenges our ability to rule out alternatives which the skeptic argues must be ruled out if we are to have knowledge. In order to affirm our possession of knowledge, a defender of knowledge must rebut these arguments, or at least undermine their intuitive appeal.

The present collection of essays addresses various aspects of these questions, and is organized into two sections around our two principal themes, knowledge and skepticism. The first section is somewhat more expansive than the second, and can in turn be divided into three sets of essays. The first three chapters, by David Hemp, Peter J. Graham, and Joe Salerno, examine the intrinsic nature of knowledge, and specifically, aspects of what distinguishes knowledge from true belief. The next set of chapters, by Duncan Pritchard, Kent Bach, and Robert J. Stainton, concern the extrinsic examination of knowledge. In particular, they examine *contextualist* accounts of knowledge, according to which the standards that determine what it is to *know* vary according to context. The final set of chapters concerns *types* of knowledge, and in particular, perceptual, introspective, and rational knowledge. Joseph T. Tolliver and George Pappas discuss perceptual knowledge, Fred Dretske discusses introspective knowledge delivered by our internal pain sensors, and John L. Pollock provides a detailed argument for rationally derived principles that extend our knowledge of probabilities in important ways.

The second section comprises four papers which address skepticism from a variety of perspectives. Leora Weitzman critiques anti-individualist replies to skepticism about the external world. Joseph Cruz argues that skepticism endorses questionable epistemic principles, and Catherine Z. Elgin gives reasons to disregard skepticism altogether. Lastly, Peter S. Fosl supplies a compelling interpretation of David Hume as a "skeptical naturalist," adopting a view that is similar to Academic and Pyrrhonian skepticism in important ways.

Knowledge

As its name suggests, epistemology principally concerns knowledge (*epistēmē*), with other topics emerging out of work that aims at clarifying this concept. Full clarification requires that we understand the concept as it is in itself and as it is in relation to certain other concepts. The former requirement dictates that we identify the constituent elements of the concept and their relationships, given that it is complex. This is conceptual analysis, and it illuminates the *intrinsic* nature of knowledge. The latter requirement is synthetic, pressing us to consider the location of this concept in complex networks of related concepts, such as the context of the knower and the judgments and actions the knower performs. This type of synthesis reveals the *extrinsic* nature of knowledge.

The Intrinsic Nature of Knowledge

The Platonic analysis From the time of Plato to the middle of the last century, there was a veritable consensus about the intrinsic nature of knowledge: Knowledge is justified true belief. More formally, according to the Platonic analysis, a person S knows some proposition p iff p is true, S believes that p, and S is justified in believing that p. Plato was primarily interested in distinguishing *knowledge* from *true belief*.[2] For instance, say that you believe that tonight's winning lottery number will be 1-2-8, and it turns out that you are correct. Did you *know* that 1-2-8 would be the winning number, or was it just a lucky guess? Differentiating between genuine knowledge and mere true belief—such as lucky guesses—was and still is an important part of the epistemological enterprise. One thing that a theory of knowledge is supposed to do is to determine when we really know something as opposed to when we merely believe something that happens to be true.

Justification According to the Platonic analysis, what distinguishes knowledge from mere true belief is *justification*. Plato also adopts the *evidentialist view of justification*, which holds that *S* is justified in believing that *p* provided that *S* has evidence for *p*, that is, reasons for believing that *p* which are in some sense available to *S* (Dretske 1970; Wittgenstein 1969, par. 18). On this view, *S* knows that he has a hand, for instance, in part because he can *see* that he has a hand. *S*'s perceptual experience provides evidence for his belief. By contrast, what evidence did you have that 1-2-8 would be the winning lottery number? There was just a belief, perhaps joined with a firm conviction—but nothing more.

Each of the three elements in the Platonic analysis is arguably complex, admitting of further analysis. Belief falls within the province of the philosophy of mind, and truth within the philosophy of language; but justification falls squarely within epistemology, and investigation into its nature has been an important epistemological pursuit. Metaphor can provide some illumination here. This was evident to Plato, who got at justification with the metaphors "account" and "tether."[3] Another common metaphor used to illuminate justification is *support*, as it is justification that supports the belief, or perhaps more appropriately, that supports the agent in maintaining the belief. Theoretical progress requires getting behind the metaphors, though, and this has been a point of emphasis in epistemology at least since Plato.

Theorizing about justification traditionally begins with a consideration of *justifications*, that is, those structures typically associated with beliefs that qualify them as knowledge when they are true. If we think of specific justifications as structures, it makes sense to ask after their constituents and the relationships among them. We call these constituents 'justifiers' because of their role in justifying beliefs. One principal question about justifiers concerns whether or not they are all *available* to the believer, yielding the internalism/externalism distinction. Another important question concerns the *source* of the justification they convey to the beliefs they justify: Is a justifier rooted in a foundation that does not itself require justification, or does it emerge from the network of related justifiers themselves in some fashion? Work on this question, which centers on the relationships among justifiers, has revolved around the foundationalism/coherentism distinction.[4] We will consider each of these distinctions in turn.

Internalism and externalism If a belief *B* is justified, then it can be said to have a justification, which we have suggested is a complex structure comprising interrelated justifiers. There is little agreement about the nature of justifiers in the literature. According to evidentialism, justifiers are other justified beliefs. Generally, these beliefs justify B by virtue of their content, or what they are *about*—if they are justified, there is good reason to believe that their content is true, and it is through the relation between their content and the content of B that they convey justification to it. Other candidate justifiers have been proposed and defended, including visual and other experiences (Russell 1940), reliable belief-forming processes (Goldman 1986), and properly functioning cognitive faculties (Plantinga 1993).

An important question about justifiers concerns their relation to the believing agent. Are all the things that justify a candidate belief themselves available to the believer, thereby bringing knowledge more squarely under the control of the knower? This question divides proponents of justification into two camps, the *internalists* and the *externalists*. Justification internalists believe that the justifiers for any given belief are accessible to the knowing subject, while justification externalists deny this. More specifically, internalists contend that knowing subjects have access to what justifies their beliefs *from the inside*, whereas externalists contend that a subject may be justified in believing something without having any access to its justifiers.

How do externalist and internalist theories of justification differ? Compare two subjects, S and S', both of whom believe they have a hand. S is a normal person in the actual world who sees his hand and believes that he has a hand on the basis of this visual experience. S' is in the *Matrix* world; his brain is stimulated to produce the visual experience of a hand independently of his actually having a hand. We may suppose that S and S' have identical subjective experiences with the same degree of detail and vivacity. Thus, "from the inside" things seem the same. Yet the subjects are causally connected to their worlds—and to their beliefs—in very different ways. According to justification internalism, since the difference between S and S' cannot be identified "from the inside," their level of justification is the same. That is, S is justified in believing that he has a hand iff S' is justified in believing that he has a hand. According to justification externalism, justification depends exclusively or primarily on external factors, and so the externalist may claim that S is justified in believing that he has a hand while S' is not (cf. Nozick 1981; DeRose 1999b).

Foundationalism and coherentism   An adequate understanding of the justificational structure of knowledge requires that we identify the relationships among justifiers. Justification distinguishes beliefs that are more likely true from those that are not. A justification *supports* a belief by enabling it to withstand critical scrutiny, where this support is a type of propping-up or buttressing in the face of potential doubt. This way of looking at justification finds comfortable expression in evidentialism, where a justified belief is supported—propped up, as it were—by other beliefs. In what follows, we begin by casting the foundationalism/coherentism distinction in terms of evidentialism, taking justifiers to be beliefs.

What of these supporting beliefs? To support another belief, they must also be supported in some fashion. The Ancient Trilemma pursues this question to skeptical ends. According to this trilemma, a justifier J must (1) be self-justifying or ultimately justified by that which is self-justifying, (2) be justified by a sequence of justifiers that eventually loop back to J itself, or (3) be justified by a sequence of justifiers that goes on without end. As we will see in the next section, skeptics argue that these three alternatives are all unworkable, but defenders of knowledge have marshaled responses. The dominant responses are *foundationalism*, which rejects the first horn of the trilemma, and *coherentism*, which rejects the second. Foundationalism divides justified beliefs into *basic* and *non-basic* beliefs. All justified beliefs are ultimately justified by basic beliefs, but basic beliefs are not justified in terms of other beliefs. Foundationalism holds that each justified basic belief B has some justification conferring property ψ. Versions of foundationalism differ, however, in how they characterize the features of ψ, as well as in other matters.

Traditional foundationalism holds that basic beliefs are self-evident. An example of a self-evident belief might be a belief about a personal experience. Reports about the content of one's experiences are often thought to be infallible, incorrigible or indubitable and, thus, they seem to provide evidence for their own truth. Descartes' "I am, I exist!" (1984, Second Meditation) is often claimed to be self-evident, for example, because it is apparently indubitable. There are good reasons, though, to doubt that any belief is self-evident (see Pollock and Cruz 1999); so traditional foundationalism has fallen out of favor among contemporary philosophers. According to *modest foundationalism*, basic beliefs need not be self-evident. A modest foundationalist might hold that basic beliefs are *prima facie justified*, that is, that they are justified provided that there is no reason to deny them. Or a modest foundationalist might hold that basic beliefs are justified, but that they are not justified in terms of other beliefs. Perhaps, for instance, a basic belief is justified because it is the result of a cognitive faculty that is properly functioning (Plantinga 1993), or because it is the result of a reliable belief-forming process like visual perception (Goldman 1986). Thus, many forms of modest foundationalism are *externalist* theories that deny the evidentialist view of justification that originally gave rise to the Ancient Trilemma.

Coherentism rejects the second horn of the trilemma, which holds that beliefs cannot be justified by circular reasoning (Lehrer 1974; BonJour 1985). According to the coherentist, S is justified in believing that p provided that p is part of a system of coherent beliefs (Klein 2000). Thus, being part of a system of coherent beliefs is what justifies a given belief, but making out what counts as "coherence" and just how this can be truth-conducive has proven elusive. As a result, coherentism is not endorsed by many contemporary philosophers, and many former coherentists are now foundationalists (Lehrer 1990; BonJour 2002).

Gettier examples   Long tradition supported the view that knowledge is justified true belief, but consensus around this analysis dissolved in the 1960s through the influence of what are known, after their author, as *Gettier examples*. Suppose that Nogot is a student in Jones's philosophy class and that he claims to own a Mustang. Nogot shows Jones a copy of a car title for a Mustang with his name on it, etc. (You may include whatever it is that you think would secure Jones's justification.) Thus, Jones forms the justified belief that Nogot owns a Mustang, and then let's have Jones reason to a new belief that is entailed by the former belief: "Someone in my philosophy class owns a Mustang." As it turns out, Nogot does not own a Mustang (the documents are false, etc.) but another student, Havit, does own a Mustang. Thus, Jones's *belief* that "Someone in my philosophy class owns a Mustang" is justified (since it is entailed by a justified belief), and true (since Havit owns a Mustang); yet Jones does not *know* that "Someone in this philosophy class owns a Mustang."[5]

Gettier examples are generally regarded as counterexamples to any analysis that relies on internalist justification to distinguish knowledge from mere true belief (e.g., the Platonic analysis). Justification does this, one might say, by establishing that what one knows is not a matter of luck. The question is what to say in light of such examples. It is also generally accepted that what is missing in the Gettier examples is a proper connection between the belief that p and the fact that p. In our case, Jones begins with a false belief and then deduces a true belief on that basis, rendering her acceptance of a *true* belief a matter of luck.

There are two kinds of solutions to the Gettier problem. First, one might think that the basis of the Platonic analysis is correct but incomplete. Thus, knowledge is justified true belief that satisfies some additional condition. Second, one might scrap *justification* altogether and replace it with something that is independent of the knowing agent, such as *warrant*. According to this response, knowledge is *warranted* true belief and justification is not essential to knowledge.

Rejecting justification In light of all the work that has been done on justification, it might seem extreme to scrap it, but this reveals just how damaging the Gettier examples have been to the Platonic analysis. If we reject justification, much of what we have said in connection with it is rendered moot; however, this is not true of the internalism/externalism debate, which we can recharacterize in terms of *knowledge*. So characterized, the distinction subsumes the more limited internalism/externalism distinction made out with respect to justification, while also accommodating those who reject justification. *Knowledge internalists* contend that what distinguishes a true belief as knowledge is accessible "from the inside," while *knowledge externalists* reject this claim. Internalists about knowledge typically believe that justification is a condition of knowledge, available "from the inside" to the knowing agent. Thus, knowledge internalists also tend to be justification internalists, endorsing either the Platonic analysis or, more likely, the Platonic analysis plus some condition that works as a response to the Gettier examples.

Knowledge externalists, though, do not have to be justification externalists. Some are, taking justification to be a necessary part of knowledge, but only if it is externalistically understood. Such philosophers start with the Platonic analysis but replace justification with some essentially externalist concept, such as *warrant*. For these externalists, knowledge is "warranted true belief" (Plantinga 1993). In addition to those who believe that justification is warrant externalistically understood, there are knowledge externalists who believe that justification is essential to knowledge but believe that it must be supplemented with an externalist element (Sosa 2007), as well those who recommend dispensing with justification altogether in order to arrive at the correct theory of knowledge (Goldman 1975).

The Extrinsic Nature of Knowledge

Knowledge and action Historically, the epistemological enterprise has been a footnote to Plato, working out the details associated with the "justified true belief" analysis of knowledge. But an adequate understanding of knowledge cannot be achieved in isolation from the various contexts within which knowledge operates. Knowledge orients us to the world, enabling us to exert control over our judgments and our actions. If we charge ahead armed with mere belief, we assume risks that threaten the success of our ventures. Knowledge also supports the proper organization and management of information we receive from the world. We seek knowledge because it makes us more effective and efficient managers of our selves and our surroundings.

Invariantism and contextualism   Relations with reflection, judgment, and action must be preserved in an adequate account of knowledge. Other extrinsic relations are also critical, such as the relation between knowledge and the context within which it is attributed; of particular importance to epistemology is the question of whether or not knowledge is *invariant* across contexts. Called "invariantism" and "contextualism" in Unger (1984), these types distinguish concepts that demand satisfaction of the same conditions across all contexts, from those that allow for contextual variation in the conditions determining what falls under the concept. Exploiting semantic machinery developed for explaining context-sensitive words, such as indexicals, epistemologists have examined whether knowledge is invariant or contextual by investigating the truth conditions for sentences containing the term 'know'.

Traditional theories of knowledge have assumed that 'know' is univocal, expressing only one relation regardless of context of use. This invariantist perspective has been challenged by epistemologists who contend that 'know' is context sensitive. These contextualists maintain that 'know' expresses different relations in different contexts. The allure of contextualism is rooted in its support for a response to the skeptic, who uses a variety of scenarios to cast doubt on knowledge. By insisting on high standards for knowledge, the skeptic argues that we can't be sure of anything we claim to know—and so we don't actually know anything at all. Contextualism proposes that we can exploit the semantics of 'know' and do justice to skepticism and common sense at the same time. 'Know', we are told, expresses a relation in normal, low-standards contexts that we bear to many propositions, thereby implying that we know these things after all. In the more demanding, high-standards contexts introduced by the skeptic, though, 'know' expresses a second relation that we rarely, if ever, bear to propositions. Thus, contextualism vindicates commonsense and skeptical intuitions by demonstrating that both are true, relative to different contexts and the way that truth-conditions of sentences using 'know' vary in those contexts.

One invariantist response is that one can do justice to these intuitions without resorting to a semantic solution; indeed, an invariantist may well suggest that contextualists here confuse a pragmatic phenomenon with a semantic one. For example, an anti-skeptical invariantist might argue that "A knows he has a hand" is true in a normal, low-standards context and remains true when we move to a skeptical, high-standards context. It may *appear* to be false in the latter context, but in fact it is just conversationally inappropriate, and this pragmatic fact underwrites our willingness to take the skeptic seriously. Calling this a "warranted assertibility maneuver" (or "WAM"), DeRose (1999a) has argued that it does not help the invariantist respond to contextualism. He puts forward three pragmatic conditions on "good" WAMs and proceeds to argue that no invariantist WAM can meet them. The anti-skeptical WAM just considered fails, for instance, because the invariantist knowledge-ascription is simply false and is not "conversationally inappropriate" in the skeptical context. Thus, DeRose argues that invariantist responses of this type fail, leaving only the contextualist response to the skeptic as a viable option.

Types of Knowledge

After identifying the intrinsic and extrinsic attributes of knowledge in general, it is only natural to be curious about the specific types of knowledge that can be identified. This is reflected in many epistemology texts and anthologies that include sections devoted to various categories of knowledge. For example, Dancy (1985) devotes a section to "forms" of knowledge, Greco and Sosa (1999) several chapters to "varieties," and both Bernecker and Dretske (2000) and Moser (2002) address "sources."

Each of these classifications is associated with its characteristic question. One classifies knowledge into "forms" or "varieties" in response to an inquiry into *what* we can know, while "sources" emerge if we are seeking to answer *whence* knowledge comes. Questions like these are motivated by an interest in conceptual taxonomy, that is, of typing knowledge into kinds; but they are not obviously univocal. Consider the question, for example, "Where does knowledge come from?" This could be asking after any of the following, among others:

1. Does knowledge depend on something *outside* the knower? (That is, does it come from without, or just from within?)
2. What is the (causal) *path* by which one comes to know anything? (For example, can our senses—or perhaps only reason—deliver knowledge?)
3. What is the *type of content* that can be known? (That is, does knowledge arise only if the content of what is believed is of a certain type, e.g., scientific, philosophical, or mathematical?)
4. What justifies what is *known*? (That is, where does knowledge come from, as opposed to mere true belief?)

This polysemy is exhibited by the other questions as well, and as one might expect, it generates a lengthy and quite heterogeneous list of types of knowledge—propositional, procedural, introspective, perceptual, memorial, testimonial, experiential, rational, inductive, deductive, intuitive, self-, ethical, religious, scientific, mathematical, logical, probabilistic, apodictic, a priori, a posteriori, conceptual, empirical, and the list goes on. Perhaps this should not be surprising, since there are a variety of things that might interest us when we seek to classify knowledge into kinds. But failure to note the different classificatory criteria can result in a collection of types that does not represent the full range along any particular epistemic dimension.

It is worth taking a closer look at the list of types just offered. As most of the categories are types of *propositional* knowledge, the distinction between this and procedural knowledge—*know-that* versus *know-how*—is antecedent to the rest of the list. Certain categories pertain most closely to the type of content, or what that content is about—most notably, conceptual and empirical. Under these as genera, we find various species, such as ethical, religious, scientific, mathematical, and logical. Self-knowledge could also be classified as a species here, although depending on context, this might concern less the topic of knowledge than the *mode* of knowledge, that is, the way in which one comes to know. Understood in this way, it could be typed causally and/or logically. If causally, self-knowledge would fall in alongside introspective, perceptual, memorial, experiential, rational, and testimonial knowledge, as these all identify causal pathways along which we acquire knowable content. If we took 'mode' logically, however, then self-knowledge in human agents would correspond to inductive, deductive, and intuitive knowledge, as these concern the logical origin of what is known. The remaining four categories—probabilistic, apodictic, a priori, and a posteriori—classify knowledge by virtue of the strength and source of the justification associated with it.

Between these very general categories—topic, mode of knowledge, and mode of justification—arise associations that have proven illuminating for epistemologists. For example, introspective knowledge and self-knowledge are typically associated with one another, as are rational and a priori knowledge. Historically, the categories of *a posteriori*, probabilistic, empirical, inductive, and scientific knowledge have been joined, if not collapsed. The same can be said of *a priori*, apodictic, conceptual, deductive, and logical knowledge. A proper cross-categorical analysis of the elements of our list is well beyond the scope of this essay, but it is important to note the presence of affinities that have, in many instances, underwritten the conflation of conceptually distinct categories in the presentation of knowledge.

Skepticism

The Argument for Skepticism

The Ancient Trilemma provides a compelling argument for skepticism, provided that none of the solutions to it proves to be adequate. Yet it seems that there is an easy general response, namely, to reject the evidentialist theory of justification. Here we consider a more powerful skeptical argument, one that is problematic for modest foundationalists as well as others.

The *argument for skepticism* is actually an argument-schema that potentially undermines *any* ordinary knowledge claim. Consider, for instance, S's belief that he has a hand. That S has a hand entails that S is not a brain-in-a-vat, for brains-in-vats do not have hands. Thus, if S knows that he has a hand, and S knows the entailment noted above, then S can deduce that he is not a brain-in-a-vat. It seems to follow, then, that S knows that he is not a brain-in-a-vat.

Yet how can S know that he is not a brain-in-a-vat? For one thing, even if S were a brain-in-a-vat his available evidence would (putatively) be the same as it is now. Thus, his available evidence is consistent with the supposition that he is a brain-in-a-vat. Brains-in-vats have hand-like sensations as well as feelings of solidity when "touching" the various "objects" which are "around them." Were a brain-in-a-vat to be asked whether he had a hand, the subsequent answer would (presumably) be "yes." If a brain-in-a-vat's "hand" itched, presumably he'd "scratch it" and get relief; and a brain-in-a-vat could (apparently) "pinch himself" to see whether he is dreaming. The experiences and evidence of people in the real world and brains-in-vats are, ex hypothesi, simply the same. What can possibly ground a distinction between them in a sense that is relevant to what the various subjects do or do not know?

Before considering responses to the argument for skepticism, it might be worthwhile to discuss its structure in more detail. Let S be the knowing subject, O an ordinary belief, and H a skeptical hypothesis, for instance, the suggestion that S is a brain-in-a-vat (DeRose 1999b):

1. S does not know that not-H.
2. If S does not know that not-H, then S does not know that O.
3. Therefore, S does not know that O.

Note that the skeptic need not offer one hypothesis to undermine *all* of our beliefs. Consider the belief that we have brains. It is difficult to see how this belief would be undermined by the brain-in-a-vat hypothesis since brains-in-vats have (or rather, simply *are*) brains. Likewise the hypothesis that we are in the *Matrix* world would undermine most of our ordinary beliefs, but it is unclear that it would undermine our belief that we have a body, or our belief that we have hands, or even (for instance) Neo's belief that he loves Trinity. For folks in the *Matrix* have both hands and bodies, and some of them are apparently in love with others. All the skeptic needs to claim is that for any belief there is a skeptical hypothesis that undermines it. We might believe that we have brains—but then again we might be utterly disembodied souls being misled by an evil genius.

The Commonsense Response

G. E. Moore (1959) offers a commonsense response to the argument for skepticism. Moore simply denies the skeptical conclusion and claims that, contrary to the opinion of many philosophers, we *do* know that we are not brains-in-vats. In fact, there is an argument readily available which proves that S knows that he is not a brain-in-a-vat. Here it is:

1. *S* knows that he has a hand.
2. *S* knows that if he has a hand, then he is not a brain-in-a-vat.
3. Therefore, *S* knows that he is not a brain-in-a-vat.

What makes Moore's response so appealing is that it accepts much of what the skeptic accepts, but manages to draw a different conclusion.

For instance, Moore agrees with the skeptic that knowledge is *closed under known entailment*. Both accept the following principle:

Principle of Deductive Epistemic Closure

From *S* knows that *P* and *S* knows that *P* entails *Q*, deduce *S* knows that *Q*.

It is hard to see how deduction could increase knowledge unless something like the above principle is true. Another interesting element in Moore's response to the skeptic is the concept of a *Moorean fact*, namely, "one of those things that we know better than we know the premises of any philosophical argument to the contrary" (Lewis 1996). *S*'s knowledge that he has a hand would be an instance of this sort of fact. Thus, Moore's argument has some serious advantages over the argument for skepticism.

Externalist Responses

The externalist also has an easy answer to the skeptic. One difference between *S* and less fortunate folks like *S′*, who is a brain-in-a-vat, is the causal relations holding between the worlds they inhabit and their relevant beliefs. *S*'s belief that he has a hand is caused, in part, by his seeing an actual hand, whereas the same belief held by *S′* is caused not by his seeing a hand but by a nefarious surgeon who is bent on fooling *S′*. But the causal relation between S's hand and his true belief that he has a hand is not something to which S has access. Thus, if S knows that he has a hand on this basis, knowledge externalism is true (Goldman 1986; Plantinga 1993). Some philosophers are unimpressed with this response, arguing that the difference between the situations of S and S' is, relative to them, a matter of luck and something over which neither of them has any control; but knowledge should be immune to luck. Ernest Sosa (2007) has developed an interesting version of virtue epistemology in an attempt to deal with these and other externalist problems.

Denying Closure and Relevant Alternatives

Two other, interrelated approaches are worth noting. The first is relatively straightforward: Deny the principle of deductive epistemic closure. Here is an apparent counterexample to the principle, from Fred Dretske:

You take your son to the zoo, see several zebras, and, when questioned by your son, tell him they are zebras. Do you know they are zebras? Well, most of us would have little hesitation in saying that we know this. We know what zebras look like, and, be-sides, this is the city zoo and the animals are in a pen clearly marked "Zebras." Yet, something's being a zebra implies that it is not a mule and, in particular, not a mule cleverly disguised by the zoo authorities to look like a zebra. Do you know that these animals are not mules cleverly disguised by the zoo authorities to look like zebras? (Dretske 1970, 138)

This lack of knowledge, it seems, does not undermine one's knowledge that the "Zebras" are in fact zebras. There are serious problems with denying closure, however, for as we noted earlier, some kind of closure principle is essential to deductive reasoning (Hawthorne 2004). Furthermore, anyone who denies closure is forced to accept a variety of "abominable conjunc-tions" (DeRose 1995), such as: "I know that that animal is a zebra and I know that zebras are not mules, but I don't know that that animal is not a cleverly disguised mule."

A related response to the skeptic is the *relevant alternatives view*. The rele-vant alternatives view offers the basis for a compelling analysis: S knows that p only if S is able to rule out all of the *relevant alternatives* to p. The short response to the skeptic is that skeptical hypotheses—being a brain-in-a-vat, living in the *Matrix* world, and so on—are not relevant alternatives to ordinary beliefs. Thus, one need not rule out such alternatives to our ordinary beliefs in order to know those beliefs. One virtue of the relevant alternatives view is that it affords a response to the argument for skepticism without rejecting the principle of deductive epistemic closure (Stine 1976).

The Two-'Knows' View and Contextualism

According to the two-'knows' view (Malcolm 1951), the word 'know' is *ambiguous*, for there is both an ordinary and a philosophical sense of the term, and the ordinary sense is weaker than the philosophical sense. I know that I have a hand in the ordinary sense of 'know', but do I *really* know it? Do I know that I have a hand in some stronger, more philosophically motivated sense of 'know'? If not, then the argument for skepticism trades on this ambiguity, falling prey to the fallacy of equivocation.

On the other hand, one might think that the word 'know' always *means* the same thing but that contextualism can be adopted as a way of responding to the argument for skepticism because other aspects of context use vary. There are different specific forms of this response. For instance, one might hold that "*S* knows that *p*" means "*S* is able to rule out all relevant alternatives to *p*," but also hold that the standards for what counts as a relevant alternative vary from one context to the next. One may ignore alternatives unless they are explicitly noted (Lewis 1996), say, or perhaps the standards are raised whenever someone mentions a knowledge-claim (DeRose 1995). In any case, the philosophical context created by the skeptic might cause us to lose knowledge that we have in ordinary contexts. Ordinarily, then, skepticism is false—for we know a lot of claims in ordinary contexts—yet whenever the argument for skepticism is raised, the skeptic wins! For in raising the argument, the skeptic simultaneously raises the standards for knowledge to a level that is impossible to satisfy.

Concessive Responses to Skepticism

One notable group of responses to the argument for skepticism, which we have not considered, is of course the one that is inspired by the skeptic—by one who believes that the conclusion of the argument for skepticism is true (cf. Stroud 1984). There are problems with articulating the skeptic's position. Since the skeptic's belief is (apparently) based on an argument, why not think that it is known? For this reason, some argue that skepticism is incoherent. One might escape this worry, however, by endorsing a slightly more modest form of skepticism: We know *very little*, that is, much less than common sense and experience would suggest (Unger 1979).

Another potential inconsistency is even more pressing. Here it is not a worry about skeptical claims, but rather a worry about the skeptic's beliefs in relation to his actions. For the skeptic believes that he knows nothing, yet his actions suggest that he favors some beliefs over others. His reasons for doing so suggest a *prima facie* theory of justification, if not a theory of knowledge. Interestingly, this problem has been around for as long as skepticism itself (cf. Burnyeat and Frede 1997). The answer is still a matter of controversy, as some of the chapters in this volume attest (e.g., those by Elgin and Fosl).

Recall that we are considering responses to the argument for skepticism. One might agree with the skeptic that there is no adequate response to the argument for skepticism, and yet still *not* be a skeptic. Consider, by way of comparison, that at one time most philosophers believed that there was no adequate response to Zeno's Paradox, but only a handful of them denied the existence of motion. Of course, how much of a concession to the argument for skepticism one might make without thereby becoming a skeptic needs to be addressed, but the list of philosophers who fall strongly on the concession side is long and growing (see Wittgenstein 1969; Strawson 1985; Nagel 1986).

Studies in Knowledge and Skepticism

Chapters 1 to 3: The Intrinsic Nature of Knowledge

The first three chapters of this volume, as noted above, concern the intrinsic nature of knowledge. In chapter 1, "Knowledge and Conclusive Evidence," David Hemp provides a defense of Dretske's (1971) claim that when knowledge is based on evidence, this evidence must be conclusive. More specifically, Hemp defends:

DC: If one knows, on the basis of evidence E, that p, then E shows that p.

Hemp begins by discussing a variety of puzzles about knowledge as well as some notable contextualist solutions to these puzzles. Next, he considers related responses from two kinds of invariantist theories. Finally, he develops related problems about conclusive evidence and shows that similar contextualist and invariantist responses are available. This is the basis for his defense of DC. Hemp concludes that by endorsing DC, both contextualists and invariantists can improve their solutions to the puzzles he surveyed in the first sections of his essay.

As noted above, traditional theoretical developments of justification have focused on a taxonomy driven by two distinctions, internalism/externalism and foundationalism/coherentism. In "Theorizing Justification," Peter J. Graham develops an alternative taxonomy that is grounded in a different pair of distinctions. The first distinction concerns the connection between the concepts of justification and truth: Is a belief justified just in case it is objectively more likely to be true (actual-result), or just in case it is held in a way that properly aims it at truth (proper-aim)? The second distinction concerns how we can know if a candidate epistemic principle confers justification: Fundamentalists hold that this knowledge is philosophical (i.e., a priori and necessary), while nonfundamentalists take it to be empirical (i.e., a posteriori and contingent). These distinctions are orthogonal to one another, carving the epistemic space into four theoretical quadrants. Graham gives these four theories the following names: Cartesianism (actual-result fundamentalism), intuitionism (proper-aim fundamentalism), reliabilism (actual-result nonfundamentalism), and pragmatism (proper-aim nonfundamentalism). After developing each theory, Graham proceeds to compare this new taxonomy to the standard one, which dominates work on justification. He concludes by arguing that the new taxonomy is (1) conceptually superior, properly emphasizing "modest" foundationalism and the varieties of internalism, among other things, and (2) empirically superior, capturing more of the contemporary debate surrounding justification.

In "Truth Tracking and the Problem of Reflective Knowledge," Joe Salerno focuses on the idea that the ability to track the truth of a proposition p distinguishes knowledge that p from mere true belief that p. This idea is formulated as the counterfactual condition that one would not have believed that p if p were false, and it figures prominently into certain externalist accounts of knowledge, such as those defended by Nozick (1981) and DeRose (1995). Vogel (2000) has argued that this condition is too strong, ruling out certain types of things we can know. In particular, it rules out our ability to reflect on our beliefs and each come to know, "I do not falsely believe that p" (call this 'RB'), since in Vogel's view reflective beliefs of this type do not track the truth. Salerno agrees with Vogel that we can know this, but denies that it fails to track the truth. Among other complaints, Salerno criticizes Vogel's logical regimentation of RB, arguing for a regimentation that better reflects the logic of the situation and better expresses the truth condition of the claim. Once this correction is made, though, Vogel's argument falls apart, since this formulation of RB tracks the truth. Thus, externalist accounts of knowledge that embed the tracking condition can accommodate reflective knowledge.

Chapters 4 to 6: The Extrinsic Nature of Knowledge

The second set of chapters concerns the extrinsic nature of knowledge, and more specifically, prospects for contextualism. In "Contextualism, Skepticism, and Warranted Assertibility Maneuvers," Duncan Pritchard marshals a linguistic defense of the invariantist use of WAMs against DeRose's (1999a) challenge. In particular, he contends that the invariantist can identify a WAM that meets DeRose's three pragmatic conditions. Turning away from third-person to first-person ascriptions, he focuses in particular on what he calls "simple self-ascriptions," or simple assertions (e.g., "I am in my study") that are taken to be knowledge-claims. He argues that an invariantist WAM built around these not only meets DeRose's conditions, but stands as the most plausible explanation of their epistemic character. Pritchard then extends this result to cover explicit first- and third-person knowledge-ascriptions, concluding that invariantism is as viable an option as contextualism.

Kent Bach, in his chapter "Knowledge In and Out of Context," also defends what is called "moderate," or non-skeptical invariantism, against the challenge of contextualism. Bach's version, though, does not rely on WAMs. Contextualism appeals to intuitions about cases in which (1) the standards prevailing in the attributor's context are relatively high compared to normal, low-standards contexts, such as the subject's, (2) the attributor's and the subject's evidence is the same or at least of equal strength, and (3) intuitively, a 'know'-attribution made of the subject in a normal, low-standards context is true but the one made of the subject by the attributor in a high-standards context is false.[6] According to Bach, contextualist intuitions about these examples can be explained away, and so they do not support the view that 'know' is context sensitive, and that the truth conditions of knowledge-ascribing sentences vary with the context of utterance. Bach's approach involves embracing the apparent conflict between skepticism and common sense, explaining this in terms of the rise in the "threshold of confidence" for settled belief that is required by the attributor in high-standards contexts. This leads the attributor to "demand more evidence than knowledge requires," due often to practical concerns that are rational and understandable. Thus, knowledge is found in both low- and high-standards contexts, even though the attributor may be unable to recognize it when the standards are high.

Weighing in on the side of the "spirit" of contextualism is Robert J. Stainton, with "Contextualism in Epistemology and the Context-Sensitivity of 'Knows'." As Stainton sees it, contextualists seek to achieve three goals: (1) to explain the allure of skeptical arguments while confirming the truth of ordinary knowledge-attributions, (2) to make knowledge-attributions depend for their content, in part, on the standards that are operative in the attributor's context, and (3) to preserve the principle of deductive epistemic closure. Certain foes of contextualism argue that its reliance on the context-sensitivity of 'know' is ill-conceived. Stainton argues that contextualist goals can be achieved and the "spirit" of contextualism saved even if these foes are correct and 'know' is univocal and not context sensitive, assuming that independent problems "not having to do specifically with the context-sensitivity of the word 'know'" can be resolved. The trick to this solution is to see the truth conditions of knowledge-attributions as varying from context to context, not because 'know' is context sensitive, but rather because of "free pragmatic determinants" of content. That is, if it turns out that there are pragmatically generated elements of content that are not bound to context-sensitive words or syntactically generated locations—and Stainton presents several arguments in favor of this view—then the truth conditions of a knowledge-attribution could vary from context to context, even if 'know' is not context sensitive. Thus, assuming that there are free pragmatic determinants of content and contextualism isn't otherwise troubled, the contextualists get what they most want and those who oppose contextualism on semantic grounds get what they want as well.

Chapters 7 to 10: Types of Knowledge

To classify this last set of essays in the first section, we push procedural knowledge into the background and focus on propositional knowledge. In particular, we carve knowledge according to its causal modes, specifically perception, introspection, and reason. The first two chapters, by Pappas and Tolliver, address perceptual knowledge of the external world, while the third, by Dretske, addresses introspective knowledge of pain. The final chapter in this section, by Pollock, focuses on rational knowledge, and in particular, on the rational derivation of principles that sanction the defeasible extension of our knowledge of probabilities.

In "Locke's Account of Sensitive Knowledge," George Pappas considers textually based, as well as more broadly philosophical, criticisms of Locke's theory of sensitive knowledge. Arguably, Locke is committed to the claims that (1) sensitive knowledge is inferential, (2) this inference depends on the resemblance between our ideas and features of the external world, and (3) this resemblance must be known with certainty. Given that such certain knowledge is doubtful, Locke's theory is suspect. Since the inference is based on a questionable inductive principle, Locke's theory is problematic even if he is not committed to the certainty claim, according to Pappas. Part of the broader problem lies with Locke's indirect realism, which questions any essential link between *idea* and *quality*. Berkeley alleged that Locke's theory ultimately leads to skepticism. Pappas avoids this result by rejecting Locke's commitment to inferential knowledge along with his acceptance of (1).

In "Revelations: On What Is Manifest in Visual Experience," Joseph T. Tolliver critiques the *Doctrine of Revelation* according to which, for instance: "The intrinsic nature of canary yellow is fully revealed by a standard visual experience as of a canary yellow thing." When combined with the Lockean intuition that the experience of colors is necessary for knowledge of those colors, this suggests that the experience of something as of canary yellow is both necessary and sufficient for knowledge of the nature of that color. Tolliver notes that the Lockean intuition rubs against Locke's own view of colors as secondary qualities, for the latter is favorable to color dispositionalism, which suggests that colors are dispositional properties. More importantly, he makes a strong case against Revelation. For one thing, it entails that no one familiar with canary yellow is ignorant of any fact about the intrinsic nature of the color. Tolliver thus distinguishes between a color and a *manifest color*—which is a mode of presentation of the color. Revelation is false, but a related thesis about manifest colors is true, which explains Revelation's initial appeal.

In his chapter, "Knowing It Hurts," Fred Dretske focuses our attention on knowing about pain, and in particular on the type of pain that "really hurts," namely, pain of which we are aware. After restricting his attention to those who have the requisite concepts, including PAIN and AWARENESS, and so can think of themselves as being in pain, he asks his primary question: What is it about pain that "confers epistemological authority on those who feel it?" The cornerstone of his view is the self-intimation principle (SI): "If S understands what awareness is (i.e., is capable of holding beliefs and making judgments to the effect that she is aware of things), and S is aware of x, S knows she is aware of x." Epistemic authority is conferred on those who feel pain because awareness is "epistemologically transparent." He goes on to argue that the truth of SI does not depend on any analytic connection between the awareness and belief—these are distinct concepts that are nevertheless bound together for those who understand them. Rather, its truth is tied to the fact that one must reliably tell that one is aware of something in order to understand what awareness is—that is, in order to possess the concept AWARENESS, you must be able to tell that you are aware of something and therefore know it, if in fact you are aware of it. This solves the epistemological problem by converting it into a developmental one, namely: How is it that we come to have this concept, given this constraint on its possession? Thus, Dretske reminds us that "questions about how we know P are sometimes best approached by asking how we manage to believe P."

John L. Pollock begins his chapter, "Reasoning Defeasibly about Probabilities," by introducing the Problem of Sparse Probability Knowledge.

When we are working with probabilistic data, we often find ourselves desiring to know more than our empirical investigation combined with the probability calculus can yield. Simply put, "we lack direct knowledge of most probabilities." In practice, "probability practitioners" make certain undefended assumptions (e.g., of statistical independence) and rely on certain underived but plausible inferences to shore up their knowledge of probabilities. Pollock argues that these moves are justified, given the theory of nomic probability. This theory, developed in Pollock (1990), is built around a possible-worlds semantics that analyzes objective indefinite probabilities in terms of relative proportions of physically possible instances of properties. This theory lies midway between a fully empirical account of objective probabilities and a purely logical account, making "the values of probabilities contingent rather than logically necessary," but also making "our limited empirical investigations much more fruitful by giving them the power to license defeasible, non-deductive inferences to a wide range of further probabilities that we have not investigated empirically." These inferences are sanctioned by what Pollock calls "Principles of Probable Probabilities," derived with the help of combinatorial mathematics. While these principles do not support deductive inferences from probabilities to probabilities, they are underwritten by the fact that the "second-order probability of their yielding correct results is 1," thereby making it defeasibly reasonable to employ them in augmenting our knowledge of probabilities.

Chapters 11 to 14: Considering Skepticism

The second section of essays addresses skepticism from a variety of angles. In "Anti-Individualism, Self-Knowledge, and Why Skepticism Cannot Be Cartesian," Leora Weitzman considers an anti-individualist approach to skepticism about the external world. Her argument begins with an assumption that every Cartesian skeptic should endorse: Individuals have atomic concepts. Yet given the anti-individualist view of concept-formation, any such concept would be impossible unless there were instantiations—things in the external world that exemplified the concepts. Weitzman shows that the anti-individualist can only support a weaker claim, for there is no reason to think that our atomic concepts require the existence of physical objects, or of things that exist in the external world, or even of things that exist apart from the thinking self. All that follows is that they exist outside of our introspective awareness. This result questions the kind of inner world/outer world dichotomy that is essential to Cartesian skepticism. Left standing is a skepticism between Descartes's and Hume's, that is, a skepticism about a reality beyond the thinking self.

Joseph Cruz offers a unique way of looking at the argument for skepticism in "Is There a Reason for Skepticism?" According to Cruz, skepticism rests on a tension between apparently unassailable epistemic principles. For instance, in arguing for skepticism, Descartes seems to endorse the following principle:

(DE) If S possesses total evidence e, and if e does not discriminate between two or more conflicting conclusions, then it is not rational for S to believe one of those conclusions.

Yet this conflicts with a number of epistemic principles regarded as salient, such as this one articulated by Robert Audi (2001): "If a person has a clear sensory impression that x is F (or of x's being F) and on that basis believes that x is F, then this belief is prima facie justified." Given this analysis of the argument for skepticism, Cruz considers two promising responses to the skeptic. First, if the principles are essential to good reasoning, then one may adopt a pragmatic resignation to skepticism. Second, if the principles are questionable, we have an even more powerful response. Cruz concludes that one principle about discriminating evidence is so strong that it challenges skepticism itself.

In keeping with the title of her chapter—"Skepticism Aside"—Catherine Z. Elgin does not so much respond to the argument for skepticism as explain why we may disregard it. Elgin argues that skepticism is inconsistent with practice, for action requires a disbelief in, or more precisely—following L. Jonathan Cohen's distinction between belief and acceptance—a non-acceptance of, skepticism. Given that theory is inseparable from practice, it follows that it may be epistemically responsible to *assume* that skepticism is false. Thus, we may set the problem of skepticism aside. There is also an interesting discussion of the role of epistemic principles in the argument for skepticism, making Elgin's paper a nice complement to Cruz's.

In "Hume's Skeptical Naturalism," Peter S. Fosl discusses the relationship between Hume's skepticism and his naturalism. He notes that there is a prima facie case to be made that these two views are inconsistent with one another, which is one reason that many commentators have failed to get Hume's position right. For this reason, commentators have emphasized one view to the exclusion of the other. This is a mistake, according to Fosl, who situates Hume's naturalism within the broader skeptical tradition of the ancient Pyrrhonians and Academics. In the end, Fosl presents an original, non-dogmatic interpretation of Hume's view that is aptly called "skeptical naturalism."

Notes

1. Following Unger (1979), we might more carefully state that the skeptic knows *very little if anything*.

2. See the *Theaetetus* (in Plato 1961, 845–919, esp. 918 [210a]).

3. The former is developed in the *Theaetetus* (Plato 1961, 914–918 [206c–210b]), while the latter is found in the *Meno* (Plato 1961, 382–383 [97e–98a]).

4. While foundationalism and coherentism have dominated the discussion, there are really three responses to the Ancient Trilemma. *Infinitism* arises when one rejects the third horn of the trilemma. According to the infinitist, a belief may be justified even if it is justified by an infinite string of reasons; see Klein 2000.

5. This example is taken from Lehrer 1974, although it is structurally similar to examples that appear in the original paper, Gettier 1963.

6. In characterizing contextualism as dependent primarily on the attributor's context, Bach follows the dominant tendency. For more, see DeRose 1999a.

References

Audi, R. 2001. *The Architecture of Reason*. Oxford: Oxford University Press.

Bernecker, S., and F. Dretske, eds. 2000. *Knowledge*. Oxford: Oxford University Press.

BonJour, L. 1985. *The Structure of Empirical Knowledge*. Cambridge, Mass.: Harvard University Press.

BonJour, L. 2002. *Epistemology: Classic Problems and Contemporary Responses*. Lanham, Md.: Rowman & Littlefield.

Burnyeat, M., and M. Frede, eds. 1997. *The Original Sceptics: A Controversy*. Indianapolis, Ind.: Hackett.

Dancy, J. 1985. *Introduction to Contemporary Epistemology*. Oxford: Blackwell.

DeRose, K. 1995. "Solving the Skeptical Problem." *Philosophical Review* 104: 1–52.

DeRose, K. 1999a. "Contextualism: An Explanation and Defense." In J. Greco and E. Sosa, eds., *The Blackwell Guide to Epistemology*. Oxford: Blackwell.

DeRose, K. 1999b. "Introduction: Responding to Skepticism." In K. DeRose and T. Warfield, eds., *Skepticism: A Contemporary Reader*. Oxford: Oxford University Press.

DeRose, K., and T. Warfield, eds. 1999. *Skepticism: A Contemporary Reader*. Oxford: Oxford University Press.

Descartes, R. 1984. *Meditations on First Philosophy*. In J. Cottingham, R. Stoothoff, and D. Murdoch, eds. *The Philosophical Writings of Descartes*, vol. 2. Cambridge: Cambridge University Press.

Dretske, F. 1970. "Epistemic Operators." *Journal of Philosophy* 67: 1007–1023. Reprinted in DeRose and Warfield (1999); references are to the latter edition.

Gettier, E. 1963. "Is Justified True Belief Knowledge?" *Analysis* 23: 121–123.

Goldman, A. 1975. "Innate Knowledge." In S. Stich, ed., *Innate Ideas*. Berkeley and Los Angeles: University of California Press.

Goldman, A. 1976. "Discrimination and Perceptual Knowledge." *Journal of Philosophy* 73: 771–791.

Goldman, A. 1979. "What Is Justified True Belief?" In G. Pappas, ed., *Justification and Knowledge*. Dordrecht: D. Reidel.

Goldman, A. 1986. *Knowledge and Cognition*. Cambridge, Mass.: Harvard University Press.

Greco, J., and E. Sosa, eds. 1999. *The Blackwell Guide to Epistemology*. Oxford: Blackwell.

Hawthorne, J. 2004. *Knowledge and Lotteries*. Oxford: Oxford University Press.

Klein, P. 2000. "Why Not Infinitism?" In R. Cobb-Stevens, ed., *Epistemology: Proceedings of the Twentieth World Congress in Philosophy*, vol. 5. Bowling Green, Ohio: Philosophy Documentation Center.

Lehrer, K. 1974. *Knowledge*. Oxford: Oxford University Press.

Lehrer, K. 1990. *Theory of Knowledge*. Boulder, Col.: Westview Press.

Lewis, D. 1996. "Elusive Knowledge." *Australasian Journal of Philosophy* 74: 549–567.

Long, A., and D. Sedley, trans. and eds. 1987. *The Hellenistic Philosophers*, vol. 1. Cambridge: Cambridge University Press.

Malcolm, N. 1952. "Knowledge and Belief." *Mind* 61: 178–189.

Moore, G. E. 1959. *Philosophical Papers*. London: George Allen & Unwin.

Moser, P., ed. 2002. *The Oxford Handbook of Epistemology*. Oxford: Oxford University Press.

Nagel, T. 1986. *The View from Nowhere*. Oxford: Oxford University Press.

Nozick, R. 1981. *Philosophical Explanations*. Cambridge, Mass.: Harvard University Press.

Plantinga, A. 1993. *Warrant and Proper Function*. Oxford: Oxford University Press.

Plato. 1961. *Plato: The Collected Dialogues*. E. Hamilton and H. Cairns, eds. Princeton: Princeton University Press.

Pollock, J., and J. Cruz. 1999. *Contemporary Knowledge*, 2nd ed. Lanham, Md.: Rowman & Littlefield.

Russell, B. 1940. *An Inquiry into Meaning and Truth*. Oxford: Oxford University Press.

Sosa, E. 2007. *A Virtue Epistemology*. Oxford: Oxford University Press.

Stine, G. 1976. "Skepticism, Relevant Alternatives, and Deductive Closure." *Philosophical Studies* 29: 249–261.

Strawson, P. F. 1985. *Skepticism and Naturalism: Some Varieties*. London: Methuen.

Stroud, B. 1984. *The Significance of Philosophical Skepticism*. Oxford: Clarendon Press.

Unger, P. 1979. *Ignorance: A Case for Skepticism*. Oxford: Oxford University Press.

Unger, P. 1984. *Philosophical Relativity*. Minneapolis: University of Minnesota Press.

Vogel, J. 2000. "Reliabilism Leveled." *Journal of Philosophy* 97: 602–623.

Wittgenstein, L. 1969. *On Certainty*. New York: Harper.

I Knowledge

1 Knowledge and Conclusive Evidence

David Hemp

In "Conclusive Reasons," Fred Dretske argues that when knowledge is based on evidence, this evidence must be conclusive.[1] The present essay uses recent work on epistemic contextualism[2] to defend a version of Dretske's claim. Advocates of epistemic contextualism usually defend it by arguing that it can solve certain puzzles about knowledge.[3] In what follows, I will argue (1) that there are parallel puzzles about conclusive evidence and (2) that, by appealing to similarities between the two sets of puzzles, we can defend a version of Dretske's claim.

Sections 1 to 4 describe three puzzles that motivate epistemic contextualism and some ways of solving them. Sections 5 and 6 argue that there are exactly parallel puzzles about conclusive evidence and that solutions to these puzzles run parallel to the solutions described in sections 1 to 4. Section 7 uses similarities between the two sets of puzzles to defend a version of Dretske's claim. The gist of the defense is that, by endorsing the claim, both contextualists and their opponents can significantly improve their solutions to the puzzles described in sections 1 to 4.

1 A Puzzle about Importance

One puzzle about knowledge that contextualists can solve is generated by pairs of cases[4] like the following:

Case A: A couple, Mary and John, have just woken to discover that their son, Joe, is ill. They have no reason to think he is seriously ill, but they decide to take his temperature anyway. When they do, they get a reading that says that his temperature is normal. The thermometer that they are using has always been reliable in the past, and they have no reason to think it is malfunctioning now, so when Mary gets this reading, she says "We know, on the basis of this reading, that Joe's temperature is normal."

Case B: Mary and John have once again woken to discover that Joe is ill. But this time, it is possible that the illness is serious: there is a child at Joe's school who has measles. As before, they take his temperature with a thermometer which has always been reliable in the past, and as before, they get a normal reading. But this time, Mary is not satisfied. This time, she says "We *don't* know, on the basis of this reading, that Joe's temperature is normal. The thermometer could be malfunctioning. We ought to check with another one."

On the assumption that Joe's temperature is normal in cases A and B, and that there are no unusual features of either case that are not mentioned in the above descriptions, it is natural to say that the knowledge-claims that Mary makes in the two cases are both true. The fact that it is natural to say this is puzzling. For the thermometer reading seems to provide just as much evidence for Joe's temperature being normal in case A as it does in case B. Why is it natural to say that this evidence is sufficient for knowledge in A, and natural to say that it is not sufficient for knowledge in B?

Contextualists can explain this by saying that the standards for knowledge are higher in B than they are in A. More exactly, they can say that the standards that a piece of evidence must meet, in order to be sufficient for knowledge, are higher in B than in A. A natural way for them to explain this shift in standards is to say that it is more important for Mary to be right about Joe's temperature in B. They can flesh out this explanation by appealing to a version of the relevant alternatives theory of knowledge.[5]

According to the relevant alternatives theory, S's evidence for P is strong enough for knowledge only if it rules out all relevant alternatives to P. *Subject-sensitive* versions of the theory say that the range of relevant alternatives to P varies with the context of the subject, S, who is said to know P; *speaker-sensitive* versions say that it varies with the context of the speaker who says that S knows P.[6] By appealing to an appropriately formulated speaker-sensitive version of the theory, contextualists can give a more detailed account of why the standards for knowledge are higher in case B than in A.

To see this, consider a speaker-sensitive version of the theory on which the range of relevant alternatives to P increases as it becomes more important for the speaker to be right about P. This version of the theory implies that the range of relevant alternatives to the proposition that *Joe's temperature is normal* is larger in case B than it is in A. Because of this, advocates of the theory can say that the possibility of the thermometer malfunctioning is a relevant alternative to this proposition in B, but not in A. Consequently they can say that the thermometer reading rules out all relevant alternatives to this proposition in A but not B, and can thereby explain why the evidence provided by this reading seems strong enough for knowledge in A but not B.[7]

2 A Puzzle about Skeptical Possibilities

Another puzzle that contextualists can solve[8] is generated by pairing case A with the following case:

Case C: As in case A, Mary and John have woken to discover that Joe is ill and have no reason to think that the illness is serious. They take his temperature with a thermometer that has always been reliable and get a normal reading. But this time, John raises doubts about the reliability of the thermometer. He says: "Isn't it possible that the thermometer is malfunctioning? It could be failing to register temperatures above 98 degrees—perhaps the mercury sticks when it gets to 98 degrees. I know it hasn't malfunctioned before, but the malfunction may have developed since the last time we used it. I know it isn't very likely that that's happened—but isn't it possible?" After thinking for a second, Mary says "Yes, I suppose that is possible. And given that it's possible, I suppose we don't really *know*, just on the basis of the thermometer reading, that Joe's temperature is normal."

On the assumption that Joe's temperature is normal in cases A and C, and that there are no unusual features of either case that are not mentioned in the above descriptions, it is again natural to say that the knowledge-claims that Mary makes in these two cases are both true. The fact that it is natural to say this is again puzzling, since John and Mary's evidence seems just as good in C as it is in A. As before, contextualists can explain why it is natural to say that this evidence is sufficient for knowledge in A but not C by saying that the standards for knowledge are higher in C. And as before, they can flesh out this explanation by appealing to a speaker-sensitive version of the relevant alternatives theory of knowledge.

To see this, consider a speaker-sensitive version of the theory on which alternatives to *P* that are not ordinarily relevant become relevant when they become salient to the speaker.[9] Advocates of this theory can say (1) that in case A, the possibility of the thermometer malfunctioning in the way that John describes is not a relevant alternative to the proposition that Joe's temperature is normal, but (2) that in case C, this possibility is made salient to the speaker (Mary), and so becomes a relevant alternative to this proposition. By saying this they can explain why it is natural to say that Mary and John's evidence is sufficient for knowledge in A but not C. In A, their evidence rules out all relevant alternatives to the proposition that Joe's temperature is normal, but in C it no longer does this.

3   A Puzzle about Lotteries

A third puzzle about knowledge that contextualists can solve[10] is generated by pairing case A with the following case:

Case D: Mary and John have bought a ticket for a lottery with a £100,000 jackpot. As they wait for the draw, Mary says "If the ticket wins, we can pay off the mortgage and go on holiday this year." John replies "Yes, but the ticket won't win. The chance of it winning is tiny—one in a million, at best." Mary says "It's true that the chance of it winning is very low, but we don't *know*, just on the basis of that fact, that it won't win. If we did then we could know the same thing about each of the other tickets; but one of those tickets will win."

In what follows, I will use 'the chance fact' to refer to the fact that the chance of Mary and John's ticket winning is, at best, one in a million. When Mary says, in case D, that she and John don't know, on the basis of the chance fact, that their lottery ticket won't win, her claim seems true. And when she says in case A that she and John do know, on the basis of the thermometer reading, that Joe's temperature is normal, her claim also seems true. The fact that both claims seem true is puzzling, for the probability of the lottery ticket not winning, given the chance fact, seems higher than the probability of Joe having a temperature, given the thermometer reading. This difference in probability suggests that Mary and John's evidence is weaker in case A than it is in case D. So it is puzzling that this evidence seems sufficient for knowledge in A but not D.

Again, contextualists can solve this puzzle by saying that the standards for knowledge are higher in D than they are in A. And again, they can flesh out this explanation by appealing to a speaker-sensitive version of the relevant alternatives theory. They can say (1) that in case A, the possibility of the lottery ticket winning is not salient to the speaker, and so is not a relevant alternative, but (2) that in case D, the possibility of it winning is salient to the speaker, and so is a relevant alternative. By saying this, they can say that the range of relevant alternatives is larger in D than it is in A, and can thus explain why stronger evidence is needed for knowledge in D.[11]

4 Invariantist Solutions

There are ways for opponents of contextualism to solve the puzzles that we have described. Opponents of contextualism are called invariantists,[12] because they think that the standards for knowledge do not vary with context. Following DeRose,[13] we can distinguish *skeptical* and *nonskeptical* invariantists. Skeptical invariantists think that the standards for knowledge are always maximally high, and thus that our knowledge-ascriptions are almost always false; nonskeptical invariantists think that these standards are always relatively low, and thus that many of our knowledge-ascriptions are true.[14]

Both skeptical and nonskeptical invariantists can endorse versions of the relevant alternatives theory of knowledge. Skeptical invariantists will say that in all contexts, all alternatives are relevant, while nonskeptical invariantists will say that, in all contexts, a relatively small range of alternatives is relevant. Although skeptical and nonskeptical invariantists cannot say that there is contextual variation in the range of relevant alternatives, they can say that there is such variation in the range of *salient* alternatives—that is, in the range of alternatives that are salient to the speaker. By appealing to this variation, skeptical and nonskeptical invariantists can use their versions of the relevant alternatives theory to generate noncontextualist solutions to the puzzles we have described.[15]

To see this, focus first of all on the puzzle about importance described in section 1. Contextualists solve this puzzle by saying (i) that in case A, the possibility of the thermometer malfunctioning is not a relevant alternative, but (ii) that in case B it is. Invariantists cannot say that the range of relevant alternatives varies with context, so they cannot endorse this solution. But, by appealing to salient alternatives, they can endorse a similar solution.

The central claims of this solution are (i) that in case A, the possibility of the thermometer malfunctioning is not salient to Mary, but (ii) that in case B, it is. Both (i) and (ii) are plausible. In case A, there is no reason to think that Joe could be seriously ill, so sensibly enough, Mary does not give any thought to the possibility of the thermometer malfunctioning. But in case B, there is a significant chance that Joe has measles, so in this case Mary does focus on the possibility of a malfunction.

Because the possibility of a malfunction is not salient in case A, we can say (1) that in case A, the thermometer reading rules out all salient alternatives to the proposition that Joe's temperature is normal. And because the possibility of malfunction *is* salient in case B, we can say (2) that in case B, the thermometer reading does *not* rule out all salient alternatives to the proposition that Joe's temperature is normal. By appealing to (1) and (2), skeptical and nonskeptical invariantists can give solutions to the puzzle about importance. The skeptical invariantist can say that Mary's claim in case A is false, but seems true because it pragmatically implies (1), and the nonskeptical invariantist can say that Mary's claim in B is false, but seems true because it pragmatically implies (2).[16]

Advocates of both solutions need to explain how it is that Mary's claim pragmatically implies the thing that it is meant to imply. There are various ways of doing this;[17] I will not go into the details of these here. The most important thing to note, for now, is that both solutions are quite similar to the contextualist's. Contextualists can solve the puzzle about importance by saying that the range of relevant alternatives is larger in B than it is in A; invariantists can solve it by saying the same thing about the range of salient alternatives.

Corresponding to these "salient alternatives" solutions to the puzzle about importance, there are solutions to the puzzles about skeptical possibilities and lotteries. Again, these solutions work by replacing the contextualist's talk of relevance with talk of salience. Contextualists solve the puzzle about skeptical possibilities by saying that the possibility of the thermometer malfunctioning is *relevant* in C, but not in A; invariantists can solve it by saying that this possibility is *salient* in C, but not in A. Similarly, invariantists can solve the puzzles about lotteries by saying that the possibility of the lottery ticket winning is salient in D, but not A.[18]

Although invariantists can solve the above puzzles by appealing to variation in the range of "salient alternatives," they are not obliged to do so. Another way in which they can solve the puzzles is by endorsing an appropriately formulated *subject-sensitive* version of the relevant alternatives theory. To see this, consider a subject-sensitive version of this theory on which (i) the range of relevant alternatives to P increases with the importance of the *subject* being right about P, and (ii) possibilities that would not ordinarily be relevant alternatives to P become relevant when they become salient to the subject. Because the speaker in cases A to D is also the subject of the knowledge-claims made in those cases, advocates of this theory can give solutions to the puzzles of sections 1 to 3 that run exactly parallel to the contextualist solutions that we have described.[19]

I will not say anything here about whether the above invariantist solutions are better than their contextualist rivals; I will just argue that there are exactly parallel contextualist and invariantist solutions to certain puzzles about conclusive evidence. The next two sections will outline these puzzles, and the contextualist and invariantist solutions to them. The final section will use similarities between the two sets of puzzles to defend a version of Dretske's claim regarding conclusive evidence.

5   Conclusive Evidence

Corresponding to the puzzles about knowledge we have described, there are puzzles about conclusive evidence. By 'conclusive evidence', I mean evidence that *shows* that something is the case. We can clarify this definition by distinguishing evidence that *shows* that p from evidence that merely *suggests* that p. In what follows, I will say something about both kinds of evidence.

Consider the following claim:

E1:   Evidence collected by the Spirit probe suggests that there were once oceans on Mars.

E1 is qualified—it does not say that the evidence collected by the Spirit probe *proves* that Mars once had oceans, or even that it *strongly supports* this claim—it only says that this evidence provides *some* support for the claim. One way of strengthening E1 is to modify it as follows:

E2:   Evidence collected by the Spirit probe strongly suggests that there were once oceans on Mars.

E2 is less qualified than E1, but is still qualified. For, it still leaves open the possibility that the evidence described is misleading. It is consistent with E2, that there were never oceans on Mars. This would be consistent with E2 even if E2 said, "The Spirit probe's evidence *very* strongly suggests that there were once oceans on Mars."

Now consider this claim:

E3:   Evidence collected by the Spirit probe *shows* that there were once oceans on Mars.

E3 is not qualified. It does not leave open the possibility that the evidence described is misleading. If E3 is true, then there were once oceans on Mars. The claim that there were never such oceans is not consistent with E3.

Evidence which only suggests that p leaves open the possibility that p is false. For that reason, such evidence is inconclusive, even if it is very strong. Evidence which shows that p is different; it does not leave open the possibility of p's falsity. For that reason, such evidence is conclusive: it settles the matter of whether p is true.

Claims like E3 are very common. It is not at all unusual to hear people saying things like this:

E4: Medical evidence shows that smoking causes cancer.

E5: A new survey shows that 49 percent of Labour voters in Britain are anti-Europe.

E6: This dent on the car shows that it has been in an accident.

E7: This rash shows that the patient has measles.

Claims which say that evidence *proves*, or *establishes*, or *demonstrates* something are also common. The following are all examples:

E8: DNA evidence proves that Hanratty was guilty.

E9: Forensic evidence establishes that Iraqi prisoners were tortured.

E10: Carbon dating demonstrates that the Turin Shroud is a fraud.

In claims like E4 to E10, the terms 'proves', 'establishes', and 'demonstrates' seem to mean roughly the same as 'shows'. Substitution of one of these terms for one of the others does not seem to significantly alter the meaning of claims like E4 to E10. Sometimes, claims like E4 to E7 can sound a little less plausible if we replace 'shows' with 'proves' or with 'demonstrates'. But it is natural to put this down to pragmatics rather than semantics—that is, we could say that the replacement of 'shows' with 'proves' or 'demonstrates' changes, not the meaning of the sentence, but the things that it pragmatically implies.

It can be argued that claims like E4 to E10 are not strictly speaking true. To see this, note first of all that, for each of E4 to E10, there are logically possible worlds in which the evidence referred to is present, but the proposition referred to is false. When we focus on these worlds, we sometimes become hesitant about endorsing E4 to E10, preferring instead to endorse weaker claims like "DNA evidence *strongly suggests* that Hanratty was guilty." Some may take this fact to show that, although claims like E4 to E10 often *seem* true, they are all, strictly speaking, false.[20]

For our purposes, it does not matter if claims like E4 to E10 are all strictly speaking false. All that matters to us is that such claims often seem to be true. By focusing on situations in which they seem true, we can generate puzzles about conclusive evidence that are exactly parallel to the puzzles that motivate epistemic contextualism. The next section will describe these puzzles; section 7 will use them to defend a version of Dretske's claim.

6   Three Puzzles about Conclusive Evidence

Corresponding to the puzzle about importance that we described in section 1, there is a puzzle about conclusive evidence. It is generated by two cases—A* and B*—that are exactly parallel to cases A and B. Case A* starts in the same way as case A, with Mary and John waking to discover that Joe is ill, and taking his temperature with a thermometer that has always been reliable in the past. As in case A, they have no reason to think that Joe is seriously ill. When Mary gets a normal thermometer reading, she says "This reading *shows* that Joe's temperature is normal" (using 'shows' in the sense described in section 5). As in case A, the claim that she makes seems to be true; to say that the reading only *suggests* that his temperature is normal seems too weak.

Case B* is like case A*, but this time it is possible that Joe has measles. Mary takes his temperature with a thermometer that has always been reliable, and gets a normal reading, but this time, she says "This thermometer reading *doesn't* show that Joe's temperature is normal. The thermometer might be malfunctioning: we ought to check with another one." Her claim seems to conflict with the claim that she makes in case A*. But, in spite of this, the claim seems true; given the possibility that Joe is seriously ill, it seems right for her to say what she does.

Why do Mary's claims in cases A* and B* both seem true? One natural way of explaining this is to endorse a contextualist theory of conclusive evidence, on which there is contextual variation in the standards that a piece of evidence has to meet in order to show that *p*. Advocates of this theory can say that Mary's claims both seem true because the "standards for showing" are higher in B* than they are in A*. In A*, the thermometer reading shows that Joe's temperature is normal, but in B*, stronger evidence is needed to show this.

As before, advocates of this form of contextualism can explain why more evidence is needed in B* by saying that it is more important for Mary and John to be right in B*. And, as before, they can flesh out this explanation by appealing to a relevant alternatives theory, on which evidence shows that *p* only if it rules out all relevant alternatives to *p*. If one endorses a speaker-sensitive version of this theory, then one can say that the range of relevant alternatives to *p* increases as the importance of the speaker being right about *p* increases. By saying this, one can explain, just as before, why it is natural to say that Mary and John's evidence is strong enough to show that Joe's temperature is normal in A*, but not strong enough to show this in B*.

There is also a puzzle about conclusive evidence that corresponds to section 2's puzzle about skeptical possibilities. It is generated by a case—C*—that is exactly parallel to case C. In C*, as in C, Mary and John have no reason to think that Joe's illness is serious. They take his temperature with a thermometer that has always been reliable, and this thermometer gives a normal reading. John then raises doubts about the reliability of the thermometer, stressing that it is possible that it is sticking at 98 degrees, and Mary agrees that this is possible. But this time, instead of saying that they don't *know*, on the basis of the reading, that Joe's temperature is normal, Mary says that the reading doesn't *show* that his temperature is normal. Once again, it is natural to say that her claim is true, but also puzzling that it seems true, since the thermometer reading seems to provide just as much evidence in C* as it does in A*.

As before, we can solve this puzzle by endorsing contextualism about conclusive evidence and using a speaker-sensitive relevant alternatives theory to flesh our explanation out. More exactly, we can say (1) that in case A*, the possibility of the thermometer sticking is not a relevant alternative to the proposition that Joe's temperature is normal, but (2) that in case C*, this possibility is made salient to the speaker (Mary), and so becomes a relevant alternative to this proposition. By saying this, we can explain why Mary and John's evidence seems strong enough to show that Joe's temperature is normal in case A*, but not strong enough to show this in case C*. In A*, it rules out all relevant alternatives to the proposition that Joe's temperature is normal, but in C*, it no longer does this.

By appealing to another case, we can generate a third puzzle about conclusive evidence, which is parallel to the puzzle about lotteries. Case D* is like case D, except that this time Mary says that the chance fact does not *show* that their ticket will not win (and defends this claim as before, by stressing that, if it did show this, then similar facts would show the same thing with respect to all of the tickets). As before, her claim seems true, and as before, its apparent truth is puzzling; for the probability of their ticket not winning, given the chance fact, seems higher than the probability of Joe having a temperature, given the thermometer reading. This difference in probability suggests that Mary and John's evidence is weaker in case D* than it is in case A*. So it is puzzling that this evidence seems conclusive in A* but not D*.

Again, we can solve this puzzle by saying that the standards for conclusiveness are higher in D* than they are in A*. And again, we can flesh out this explanation by appealing to a speaker-sensitive version of the relevant alternatives theory. We can say (1) that, in case A*, the possibility of the lottery ticket winning is not salient to the speaker and so is not a relevant alternative, but (2) that in D*, the possibility of its winning is salient to the speaker, and so is a relevant alternative. By saying this, we can argue that the range of relevant alternatives is larger in D* than it is in A*, and can thus explain why the standards for conclusiveness are higher in D* than they are in A*.

Overall, there seem to be contextualist solutions to the puzzles of this section that run exactly parallel to the contextualist solutions to the puzzles of sections 1 to 3. There also seem to be invariantist solutions of this kind. One way of generating such solutions is to replace the contextualist's claims about relevant alternatives with parallel claims about salient alternatives. Another is to replace the contextualist's speaker-sensitive relevant alternatives theory with a subject-sensitive theory, on which the range of relevant alternatives to a proposition, P, varies with the context of the subject who has been said to have or lack conclusive evidence for P.

Because the puzzles about conclusive evidence run exactly parallel to the puzzles about knowledge, it is very plausible that one should solve the former in the same way as one solves the latter. Those who endorse a contextualist solution to the puzzles about knowledge should endorse a parallel contextualist solution to the puzzles about conclusive evidence, and likewise for invariantist solutions. By appealing to this fact about the two sets of puzzles, we can defend a version of Dretske's claim about knowledge and conclusive evidence. The gist of the defense is that, by endorsing the relevant version of Dretske's claim, we can improve both contextualist and invariantist solutions to section 1 to 3's puzzles about knowledge.

7   Defending Dretske's Claim

The version of Dretske's claim that this section will defend can be stated as follows (where 'shows' is used in the sense described in section 5):

(DC)   If one knows, on the basis of evidence E, that p, then E shows that p.

In what follows, I will defend (DC) by arguing (1) that it is intuitively plausible, (2) that it does not lead to an unacceptable form of skepticism and (3) that acceptance of it significantly improves both contextualist and invariantist solutions to section 1 to 3's puzzles about knowledge.

In defense of (1), consider cases in which it seems right to say (a) that some subject, S, knows, on the basis of evidence E, that p. In such cases, it generally also seems right to say (b) that E shows that p. After reflecting on ways in which E might be misleading, we can become hesitant about endorsing (b). But when we do, we tend to become similarly hesitant about endorsing (a), as we can see by focusing on the following examples.[21]

Suppose that you have just walked into your office, and have seen the voicemail light on your phone flashing. Ordinarily, it will seem right to say (a_1) that you *know*, on the basis of this flashing light, that you have new voicemail, and (b_1) that this flashing light *shows* that you have new voicemail. After reflecting on the possibility that the light is malfunctioning, you may start to become hesitant about endorsing (b_1). But if you do, you will become similarly hesitant about endorsing (a_1); so it is natural to say that (a_1) implies (b_1).

Now suppose that you have just read, in a reliable newspaper, that a senior government official is about to resign. Ordinarily, it will seem right to say (a_2) that you *know*, on the basis of this newspaper report, that this official is about to resign, and (b_2) that this report *shows* that the official is about to resign. After reflecting on the possibility that the report in question is mistaken, you may start to become hesitant about endorsing (b_2). But, if you do, then you will become similarly hesitant about endorsing (a_2); so again, it is natural to say that (a_2) implies (b_2).

Finally, suppose that you have just arrived at a restaurant, and have seen your friend's car parked outside. Ordinarily, it will seem right to say (a_3) that you *know*, on the basis of the car's presence, that your friend is in the restaurant, and (b_3) that the car's presence *shows* that your friend is in the restaurant. After reflecting on the possibility that your friend has lent his car to someone else, you may become hesitant about endorsing (b_3). But in this case, you will also be hesitant about endorsing (a_3); so it is once again natural to say that (a_3) implies (b_3).

Examples of this kind show that (DC) is intuitively plausible. But many will still think that it should be rejected. Their reasons can be given by focusing on this pair of entailment principles:

(EP_1) Evidence E shows/proves/establishes that p only if E entails that p.

(EP_2) Subject S knows that p on the basis of evidence E only if E entails that p.

When (DC) is conjoined with (EP_1), which is very plausible, it entails (EP_2), which seems to lead to an unacceptable form of skepticism.

By appealing to the results of section 6, we can show that (DC) does not lead in this way to an unacceptable form of skepticism. To see this, note first of all that one should not think that (DC) leads in this way to skepticism unless one endorses (EP_1). If one endorses (EP_1), then one should endorse a skeptical invariantist solution to section 6's puzzles about conclusive evidence, and should thus endorse a parallel skeptical invariantist solution to section 1 to 3's puzzles about knowledge. But one cannot endorse this kind of solution to section 1 to 3's puzzles without accepting the skepticism that is entailed by (EP$_2$); so if one thinks that (DC) leads to skepticism in the way just described, then one should not think that the skepticism it leads to is unacceptable.

The above points make it natural to endorse (DC). Endorsement of it becomes more natural when we realise that it can be used to improve both contextualist and invariantist solutions to section 1 to 3's puzzles about knowledge. To see that it can be used to do this, focus first of all on the contextualist solutions described in sections 1 to 3.

The core claims of these contextualist solutions are (i) that one knows P on the basis of evidence E only if E rules out all relevant alternatives to P, (ii) that the range of relevant alternatives to P increases as the importance of the speaker being right about P increases, and (iii) that alternatives to P that are not ordinarily relevant become relevant when they become salient to the speaker. If advocates of these solutions endorse (DC), then they can explain why claims (i) to (iii) hold. For, as section 6 shows, advocates of these solutions are committed to endorsing parallel solutions to the puzzles about conclusive evidence, the core claims of which are (i′) that E shows that P only if E rules out all relevant alternatives to P, (ii′) that the range of relevant alternatives to P increases as the importance of the speaker being right about P increases, and (iii′) that alternatives to P that are not ordinarily relevant become relevant when they become salient to the speaker. When claims (i′) to (iii′) are conjoined with (DC), they entail claims (i) to (iii): So by endorsing (DC), contextualists can explain why claims (i) to (iii) hold.

The above reasoning shows that, by endorsing (DC), contextualists can improve their solutions to the puzzles described in sections 1 to 3. Similar reasoning shows the same thing with respect to invariantist solutions to these puzzles.[22] Because of this, both contextualists and invariantists have reason to endorse (DC). Since contextualism and invariantism exhaust the options, (DC) is a claim that all of us have reason to endorse.

We may also have reasons to reject (DC), which may defeat the reason just described. But in light of (DC)'s intuitive plausibility, and of the fact that it does not lead to an unacceptable form of skepticism, it seems unlikely that this is so. In any case, it seems fair to conclude that there are good reasons to endorse (DC). Opponents of (DC) who want to attack these reasons need to provide us with objections to (DC) that the arguments of this essay do not undermine.

8 Summary

Sections 1 to 4 described three puzzles that motivate epistemic contextualism and some ways of solving them. Sections 5 and 6 argued that there are exactly parallel puzzles about conclusive evidence and that solutions to these puzzles run parallel to the solutions described in sections 1 to 4. Section 7 used similarities between the two sets of puzzles to defend a version of Dretske's claim that, when knowledge is based on evidence, this evidence must be conclusive. It did so by arguing (1) that the claim is intuitively plausible, (2) that it does not lead to an unacceptable form of skepticism, and (3) that by endorsing it, both contextualists and invariantists can improve their solutions to the puzzles described in sections 1 to 4.

Acknowledgments

Thanks to Jessica Brown and an audience at the 2004 Inland Northwest Philosophy Conference for helpful comments on earlier drafts of this essay. Special thanks to Anastasia Panagopoulos for the reply that she gave at the INPC, and to two anonymous referees for very helpful comments on the penultimate draft.

Notes

1. Dretske 1971, 1–2.

2. By 'epistemic contextualism', I mean the doctrine that the truth conditions of knowledge-attributions vary with the context of the attributor. According to this doctrine, there is contextual variation in the standards that one must satisfy in order to know something (henceforth, the standards for knowledge).

3. Cohen (1988, 1999), DeRose (1991, 1995), and Lewis (1996) all defend contextualism in this way.

4. For contextualist solutions to this sort of puzzle, see DeRose 1991, 913–918, and Cohen 1999, 58–60. The puzzle is usually stated by reference to DeRose's bank cases (DeRose 1991, 913) or Cohen's airport case (Cohen 1999, 58), but for the purposes of this paper it is easier to use cases that differ slightly from these.

5. For classic statements of this theory see Goldman 1976 and Dretske 1981. My formulation is closer to Dretske's than to Goldman's.

6. The distinction between subject-sensitive and speaker-sensitive versions of the relevant alternatives theory is noted by DeRose (1992) and Cohen (1998). Both note that it is only speaker-sensitive versions of the theory that entail epistemic contex-

tualism. For defenses of speaker-sensitive relevant alternatives theories, see Cohen 1987 and Lewis 1996. For a defense of a relevant alternatives theory that is subject-sensitive, but not significantly speaker-sensitive, see Rysiew 2001.

7. This explanation could be improved still further by the addition of an explicit account of what it takes to rule out a relevant alternative—e.g., the account in Lewis 1996. It would also be improved by an explanation of how the notion of importance is to be understood, but the notion is clear enough for the explanation to have some value as it stands.

8. For contextualist solutions to this sort of puzzle, see Cohen 1987, DeRose 1995, and Lewis 1996.

9. Cohen (1987) and Lewis (1996) both defend theories of this kind.

10. For contextualist solutions to this sort of puzzle, see Cohen 1987, DeRose 1996, and Lewis 1996.

11. Cohen (1987, 106ff.) seems to endorse a solution of this kind to the lottery puzzle, though his statement of this puzzle differs slightly from ours.

12. The term comes from Unger (1984).

13. DeRose 1992, 915–916.

14. We can also distinguish a range of positions that fall between skeptical and nonskeptical invariantism, but the distinctions between these positions are not important to the arguments of this section.

15. Rysiew (2001) describes a solution of this kind in some detail. The solutions that I describe are modeled on Rysiew's.

16. To say that S's claim that p *pragmatically implies* that q is to say that, while S does not strictly and literally *say* that q by claiming that p, she does *convey* or *impart* that q by doing so. In the terminology of Grice (1975), it is to say that S's claim that p *implicates* that q.

17. Nonskeptical invariantists can do it by appealing to Grice's maxim of Relation; see Grice 1975 and Rysiew 2001, 491ff. Skeptical invariantists can do it by focusing on cases of hyperbole; see Schaffer 2004.

18. In offering solutions of this kind, invariantists do not presuppose that there is any special link between salience and relevance. Even if there is no link between salience and relevance, it is plausible (i) that the possibility of the thermometer malfunctioning is salient in C but not in A, and (ii) that the possibility of the lottery ticket winning is salient in D but not in A.

19. The possibility of solving the puzzles in this subject-sensitive way is discussed at length in chapter 4 of Hawthorne 2004, and in Stanley 2005.

20. Others may deny this, by claiming that some logically possible worlds are irrelevant to the truth of claims like E4 to E10. I will not try to decide between these two positions here; the decision between them does not have any bearing on the arguments of sections 6 and 7.

21. These examples are similar to examples given in Dretske 1971, 2–9, but unlike Dretske's examples, they are not being used to defend a counterfactual constraint on knowledge.

22. This reasoning again focuses on the fact that, when the core claims of invariantist solutions to the puzzles about conclusive evidence are conjoined with (DC), they entail the core claims of the parallel invariantist solutions to the puzzles about knowledge. From this fact it follows that, by appealing to (DC), invariantists can explain the truth of the core claims of their solutions to the puzzles about knowledge, and can thus improve these solutions.

References

Cohen, S. 1988. "How to Be a Fallibilist." In J. Tomberlin, ed., *Philosophical Perspectives 2*. Atascadero, Calif.: Ridgeview.

Cohen, S. 1998. "Contextualist Solutions to Epistemological Problems: Scepticism, Gettier and the Lottery." *Australasian Journal of Philosophy* 76: 289–306.

Cohen, S. 1999. "Contextualism, Skepticism, and Reasons." In J. Tomberlin, ed., *Philosophical Perspectives 13*. Oxford: Wiley-Blackwell.

DeRose, K. 1992. "Contextualism and Knowledge Attributions." *Philosophy and Phenomenological Research* 52: 913–929.

DeRose, K. 1995. "Solving the Skeptical Problem." *Philosophical Review* 104: 1–52.

DeRose, K. 1996. "Knowledge, Assertion, and Lotteries." *Australasian Journal of Philosophy* 74: 568–580.

Dretske, F. 1971. "Conclusive Reasons." *Australasian Journal of Philosophy* 49: 1–22.

Dretske, F. 1981. "The Pragmatic Dimension of Knowledge." *Philosophical Studies* 40: 363–378.

Goldman, A. 1976. "Discrimination and Perceptual Knowledge." *Journal of Philosophy* 73: 771–791.

Grice, H. P. 1975. "Logic and Conversation." In D. Davidson and G. Harman, eds., *The Logic of Grammar*. Encino, Calif.: Dickensen.

Harman, G. 1968. "Knowledge, Inference, and Explanation." *American Philosophical Quarterly* 5: 164–173.

Hawthorne, J. 2004. *Knowledge and Lotteries*. Oxford: Oxford University Press.

Lewis, D. 1996. "Elusive Knowledge." *Australasian Journal of Philosophy* 74: 549–567.

Rysiew, P. 2001. "The Context-Sensitivity of Knowledge Attributions." *Noûs* 35: 477–514.

Schaffer, J. 2004. "Skepticism, Contextualism, and Discrimination." *Philosophy and Phenomenological Research* 69: 138–156.

Stanley, J. 2005. *Knowledge and Practical Interests*. Oxford: Oxford University Press.

Unger, P. 1984. *Philosophical Relativity*. Minneapolis: University of Minnesota Press.

2 Theorizing Justification

Peter J. Graham

Just as there are many theories of the concept of *knowledge*—some that require justification and some that do not—so too there are many theories of the concept of *justification*. Any epistemology textbook or anthology would lead one to believe that the major disagreements over its analysis are internalism versus externalism and foundationalism versus coherentism. But these disagreements are not exhaustive. Equally or even more important are disagreements between actual-result versus proper-aim conceptions of justification, and between fundamentalist versus nonfundamentalist conceptions of justification. These latter disagreements determine four positions: Cartesianism, reliabilism, intuitionism, and pragmatism.

Our topic is epistemic justification. Epistemic justification is distinct from moral or practical justification. A subject may be morally obligated to believe something that is not epistemically justified for her. It may also be practically rational for a subject to believe something without evidence for its truth. Correspondingly, a subject may have plenty of evidence in favor of believing something that morally or practically she should not believe. Furthermore, a subject may have inquired whether P and found little evidence for P. Belief in P would then not be justified. Likewise, a subject may have conducted no inquiry whether P, but for all that possess plenty of evidence in favor of P. Belief in P would then be justified. Inquiry is one thing; justification is another.

Paradigm cases of epistemically justified belief include belief based on good inferences, belief in self-evident truths, belief based on perceptual representations or immediate introspective awareness, and so on. Beliefs formed, sustained, or held in certain ways count as well-formed, reasonable, supported by evidence, and so forth (Goldman 1979; Feldman and Conee 1985). Justification is the property that makes a belief justified. Our goal is to carve a good deal of the debate about justification at its joints.

We shall not discuss knowledge. Epistemic justification may or may not be a necessary condition upon knowledge. I do not assume that whatever justification is, it is a property that converts true belief (absent Gettier cases) into knowledge (*pace* Bach 1985, among others; cf. Pollock 2001, 46). It may be that property, but I do not assume that to understand what justification is, or to understand debates about its nature, one must or should conceive of it in terms of its relation to knowledge. Though knowledge is a fundamental concept in epistemology, it is not the only concept. The concept of justification is an important epistemic concept in its own right (*pace* Alston 1999). Much work in epistemology is devoted to its analysis. The present essay advances that enterprise.

The essay has four parts: The first offers a new taxonomy of theories of justification. The second elaborates on the four positions in the new taxonomy. The third makes some points of comparison between the two taxonomies. The fourth briefly discusses evidence for theory-choice.

1 Two Taxonomies

The Standard Taxonomy

According to BonJour (among many others), foundationalism versus coherentism and internalism versus externalism mark the contemporary debate. There are thus, BonJour says, "four prima facie possible overall positions" (2003, 7). The standard taxonomy is shown in table 2.1.

A New Taxonomy

Though useful and important, this taxonomy is not exhaustive. I shall develop a new taxonomy which is driven by two different distinctions. The first concerns the conceptual connection between justification and truth; the second concerns the epistemic and modal status of epistemic principles.

There are two ways justification and truth may be connected: *Either* justification makes belief *objectively* more likely to be true, *or* justification *properly aims* belief at truth. On the first, a belief is justified just in case it is held in a way that *makes* it more likely than not to be true. On the second,

Table 2.1

	Foundations	Coherence
Internalism	Foundationalist-internalism	Coherentist-internalism
Externalism	Foundationalist-externalism	Coherentist-externalism

a belief is justified just in case it is *held* in a *proper way* or *based* on a *proper method*, insofar as truth is the *aim* or *norm*. (Compare consequentialist and nonconsequentialist theories of moral rightness.) Call the former *actual-result* justification (reliable belief is the actual result of justification), and the latter *proper-aim* justification (justification properly aims belief at truth).[1]

The second distinction concerns the epistemic and modal status of epistemic principles. All parties to the present debate agree that theorists know a priori that justification necessarily supervenes on some condition C. All parties agree that there is some C such that it is a priori necessary that a belief is prima facie justified iff it satisfies C.[2] They disagree, however, over what C is.

Fundamentalists propose a condition C such that *theorists* can know a priori whether *particular* ways of forming, sustaining, and holding beliefs (such as introspection, memory, and perception) are *necessarily* justification-conferring. According to the fundamentalist, knowledge of which particular ways of forming, sustaining, and holding beliefs are justification-conferring is, so to speak, philosophical knowledge. *Nonfundamentalists* propose a condition C such that theorists *cannot* know a priori whether particular ways of forming, sustaining, and holding beliefs are necessarily justification-conferring. According to the nonfundamentalist, knowledge of which ways of forming, sustaining, and holding beliefs are justification-conferring is empirical knowledge.

For example, suppose that perceptual representational states confer prima facie justification on the beliefs they normally cause and sustain. The fundamentalist would hold that this is necessarily true, knowable by a priori reflection on the nature of perceptual representation and perceptual belief.[3] The nonfundamentalist, on the other hand, would hold that the supposition is only contingently true, not made true by the essential nature of perceptual representation or perceptual belief. The supposition is thus not a priori necessary.[4]

The new taxonomy determines four positions.[5] I have given each position a name, shown in table 2.2.

Table 2.2

	Actual-Result	Proper-Aim
Fundamentalism	Cartesianism	Intuitionism
Nonfundamentalism	Reliabilism	Pragmatism

2 Four Theories of Justification

Each position can be stated as a *thesis*, as a necessary condition upon justification. Each thesis is a (putative) conceptual, a priori truth. I assume that
if they are a priori, they are necessary (i.e., they are not Kripke-type, a priori
contingencies).

Cartesianism: A belief is justified only if held in a way which is a priori
known or knowable to *either* necessarily make the belief true *or* make the
belief true more likely than not in all worlds. The way held confers prima
facie justification only if it is a priori knowable that it is *either* every-
instance reliable *or* all-worlds reliable.

Reliabilism: A belief is justified only if held in a way that *de facto*
makes the belief more likely than not to be true in the actual circumstances
of use. The way held confers prima facie justification only if *de facto*
reliable.

Intuitionism: A belief is justified only if held in a way that is a priori
known or knowable to necessarily constitute properly aiming belief at
truth, where 'properly aiming belief at truth' means conformity to a priori
necessary epistemic principles (to be listed below).

Pragmatism: A belief is justified only if held in a way that *de facto* constitutes properly aiming the belief at truth, where 'properly aiming belief at
truth' means conformity to our deepest held norms of proper belief-
formation (where 'our' can mean the subject, the discipline, the community, the tradition, or the species).

I intend each of these to be interpreted broadly enough so as to include *being a member of a coherent system of beliefs* to be that property which confers
justification on belief. That is, one way a belief might be held *in the right
way* is by being a member of a coherent system of beliefs.

  What would each view say about perceptual beliefs? For the Cartesian
they are justified only if perception is all-worlds reliable. For the reliabilist
they are justified only if perception is reliable in the circumstances of use.
For the intuitionist they are justified only if it is conceptually necessary
that holding beliefs on the basis of perceptual representations is among
the right ways to hold a belief insofar as truth is the aim or norm. And for
the pragmatist, perceptual beliefs are justified only if it is a deeply held

belief or norm that holding beliefs on the basis of states is among the right ways to hold belief.

Each of the positions will receive some further elucidation in what follows. A few preliminary comments on my labels, however, are in order.

By 'pragmatism' (in epistemology) I do *not* mean a thesis about the nature of *truth*. Pragmatism in metaphysics is the view that a belief is *true* if appropriately *justified*; pragmatism in epistemology is a view about what it is for a belief to *be* justified. Pragmatism in metaphysics is one thing and pragmatism in epistemology is another. I might have used 'norm relativism' for this position instead.

By 'Cartesianism' I mean a disjunctive thesis. The first disjunct is the traditional view that a belief is justified only if infallible. The second is the weaker but still high-octane requirement that a belief is justified only if necessarily more likely than not to be true. Such a belief may be false. 'Cartesianism' as I use it thus makes room for the possibility of false justified beliefs, *but only a very few*. Cartesianism so defined is consistent with fallibilism, but only to a limited extent. I might have used 'near infallibilism' for this position instead.

'Intuitionism' also labels a familiar position in ethics. Intuitionism in ethics holds that principles of right action (keep promises, do not cause unnecessary harm, etc.) are self-evident, a priori truths, not derivable from other truths. Intuitionism in ethics is one version of deontologism in ethics. Other versions of deontologism hold that principles of right action are a priori knowable, but are derived from other truths. I shall use the label 'intuitionism' in epistemology broadly so as to cover both the view that principles of "right belief" (so to speak) are self-evident, a priori truths, *not* derivable from other truths, and the view that though the principles are a priori, they are *derived* from other self-evident, a priori truths, or even from a priori evidence from cases. 'Intuitionism' as I shall use it is thus less about whether epistemic principles of right belief are derived or underived, but rather about whether they are a priori necessary truths. I might have used 'moderate rationalism' or 'deontologism' as a label for this position instead.[6]

I have stated the four positions as necessary conditions upon justification. As such they are *theses*. As theses, they are not mutually exclusive. A belief may satisfy all four conditions. Not every belief, however, is likely to satisfy all four.

A theorist is free to develop a *theory* of justification (a list of necessary and jointly sufficient conditions) by insisting that one or more of the above conditions are necessary and also jointly sufficient. "Pure" theories that are clear competitors would hold that each condition states a jointly necessary and sufficient condition. "Hybrid" theories are possible, that is, theories that embrace more than one of the four theses as necessary conditions upon justification.[7] One might embrace both the reliabilist and pragmatist, or the Cartesian and intuitionist, necessary conditions as jointly necessary and sufficient. The most natural, or the most successful, may indeed turn out to be a hybrid; I shall not discuss such theories here. For the sake of clarity and illumination, I will treat the four pure views as complete theories of prima facie epistemic justification.[8] As such they are mutually exclusive. What follows in the rest of this section will give content to these four theories and also discuss foundationalism, coherentism, internalism, and externalism.

Epistemic Principles

There are many ways of forming, sustaining and holding beliefs. Some confer justification on the beliefs which are formed or held; some do not. Ways of forming or holding beliefs that many hold to be justification-conferring, include a priori insight, introspection, deductive reasoning, memory, and so on. For each way of forming or holding a belief we can formulate a principle that states that if a belief is formed or held in that particular way, then it will be (at least *prima facie pro tanto*) justified.[9] I will list nine such principles. Though the exact formulation of each principle would require entering a number of qualifications, each principle, roughly stated, is at first glance a plausible and familiar principle.

Epistemologists do not universally accept that *all* of the principles are true; there is disagreement over *which* principles are true. The reason why they disagree has to do in part with what overall theory of epistemic justification they happen to endorse. If you are a Cartesian, as I will explain below, you will only accept the first three principles. Most non-Cartesians tend to accept most of the principles. They agree that most of them are true. They disagree over *why* they are true. In each case, if a theorist accepts a principle, she does so because she believes that the way of forming and holding beliefs governed by the principle passes the relevant condition *C*, the condition that she believes is both necessary and sufficient for a belief to be (at least *prima facie pro tanto*) justified.

Here are the principles.

(AP) If it seems to *S* upon understanding *P* that *P* is self-evident or necessary, then the belief that *P* is *prima facie pro tanto* justified.

(INT) If it introspectively seems to *S* as if *S* is occurrently having a sensory or perceptual experience such and such (or another occurrent conscious mental state), and this causes or sustains in the normal way the belief that S is experiencing such and such (or undergoing a certain mental episode), then that confers prima facie justification on S's belief.

(DED)   If S believes P and believes (P entails Q), and believes Q on the basis of inferring Q from P and (P entails Q), then S's belief that Q is conditionally justified.

(MEM)   If S seems to remember that P and this causes or sustains in the normal way S's belief that P, then that confers prima facie justification on S's belief that P.

(EIND)   If S possesses a sufficiently large and representative inductive base (of observation-based beliefs) where all (most) observed Fs are Gs, then were S to infer that all (most) Fs are Gs on that basis, then S's belief that all (most) Fs are Gs would be conditionally *prima facie pro tanto* justified by the inference.

(IBE)   If S possesses one explanation that better explains S's evidence than any other available alternative explanation, then S is *prima facie pro tanto* justified in believing that explanation on the basis of the evidence.

(PER)   If it perceptually seems to S as if some object x is F (where F is a perceptible property), and this causes or sustains in the normal way S's belief of x that it is F, then that confers *prima facie pro tanto* justification on S's belief.

(TEST)   If a subject S (seemingly) understands a (seeming) report by a (seeming) speaker that P, and if that causes or sustains in the normal way S's belief that P, then that confers *prima facie pro tanto* justification on S's belief that P.

(COH)   If the belief that P is a member of S's coherent set of beliefs R, then S's belief that P is prima facie justified to the degree that R is coherent.

The *pure* coherentist accepts only COH. Foundationalists accept some or all of the other principles. A foundationalist may also accept COH, but cannot accept only COH.[10]

I now further characterize the four positions, treating the Fundamentalist positions first.

Intuitionism

Intuitionism *qua* theory holds that a belief is (at least *prima facie pro tanto*) justified iff held in a way that is a priori knowable to be, of its very nature, a right or proper way to hold belief insofar as truth is the aim or norm. Being actually truth-conducive is not, for the intuitionist, a constraint on being the right or proper way to hold a belief. The intuitionist denies that a reason to believe P is true or likely to be true as such *makes* the belief that P, as an objective matter of fact, true or more likely to be true. The *content* of the expression 'right or proper way insofar as truth is the aim' is given by the epistemic principles from the list above. Intuitionism, then, *just is* the view that one or more of the principles are a priori necessary, where the truth of any of the principles does not depend on the *de facto* or necessary reliability of the relevant ways of holding belief. A belief is held in a right or proper way insofar as truth is the aim iff the belief satisfies an a priori necessary epistemic principle.

Intuitionists differ over which principles are true. Most practicing foundationalist intuitionists, as far as I can tell, embrace AP, DED, INT, MEM, IBE, and EIND. There is disagreement over PER and TEST.

Intuitionist coherentism is a possible option. One might hold that the proper "ground" of a belief is membership in a coherent system of beliefs, as I noted above. An intuitionist may embrace COH. A *pure* coherentist intuitionist would embrace *only* COH. Keith Lehrer, I conjecture, could be read this way.[11]

There are three ways for the intuitionist to argue for the principles. The first is direct a priori insight into the truth of the *general* principle, based on understanding. This parallels intuitionist views in ethics (Sidgwick, Ross). This is like Chisholm's "methodist." Here is Richard Feldman on enumerative induction:

[A principle governing enumerative induction] is something we can know to be true a priori; that is, we can know it simply by understanding the concepts involved.... It is part of the concept of being reasonable to use past cases as one's guide to the future. There is no possible situation in which the condition it mentions—knowledge that things have been a certain way in the past—could fail to give you a good reason to think that they will be that way in the future. There may be cases in which that belief is false, and there may be cases in which that good reason is overridden by other reasons.... But there are no cases in which information about past regularities fails to provide some reason for beliefs about the future. That is just how being reasonable works. (2003, 138)

One may argue similarly for some or all of the other principles.

The second way of arguing for the principles is similar to how some Intuitionists in ethics argue for moral principles: Generalize from particular examples to principles. This is like Chisholm's "particularist." Describe a number of cases where it is a priori intuitive that the subject has a prima facie justified belief, and a number of cases where it is a priori intuitive that the subject does not have a prima facie justified belief.[12] Then note that one of the principles explains both the presence and the lack of prima facie justification. The cases thus support the principle. The cases provide a priori evidence, and the evidential relation between the evidence and the principle is a priori. It is customary, for example, to analyze the concept of knowledge and other concepts in this way.

The third way is to argue a priori from the nature of the relevant belief-forming process or way of holding beliefs to the conclusion that forming or holding beliefs in that way is a right or proper way insofar as truth is the aim or norm. For instance, Tyler Burge (2003) has argued that perceptual states by their very nature confer justification on the beliefs they normally cause and sustain, for it is a priori that perceptual representations are veridical in normal conditions when the perceptual system is functioning normally. Forming beliefs on the basis of perceptual representations is holding beliefs in the right or proper way insofar as truth is the aim for perceptual representations are, by their very nature, veridical in normal conditions when the perceptual system is functioning normally; it is the function of a perceptual system to represent veridically. Perceptual beliefs, so held, are prima facie justified. This does not entail that most justified perceptual beliefs are true, for it does not entail that the subject must be in normal conditions to form perceptual beliefs.[13] Burge has argued in broadly similar fashion in favor of INT (1996) and TEST (1993).

Intuitionism is a view that is enjoying something of a renaissance. Intuitionists include Robert Audi (1988), Tyler Burge (1993, 2003a), Roderick Chisholm (1966, 1977), Richard Feldman (2003), Michael Huemer (2001), Christopher Peacocke (2004), John Pollock and Joseph Cruz (1999), as well as others. Intuitionists, as I noted, disagree on PER and TEST. Feldman, for example, rejects both. Audi and Huemer accept PER but not TEST, while Burge embraces both.[14]

Cartesianism

Cartesianism *qua* theory claims that a belief is prima facie justified iff held in a way that is a priori known or knowable to be either *every-instance* or *all-worlds* reliable. The cogito, other self-verifying thoughts, some beliefs about one's current conscious episodes, beliefs about some simple and obvious necessary truths, and some beliefs deduced from these beliefs by simple and obvious steps, are the best candidates for beliefs that satisfy the Cartesian test. Other beliefs may satisfy the requirement. But if the history of the subject is our guide, it is highly unlikely that others do.[15]

Cartesians typically hold that if any "processes" of belief-formation are sufficiently reliable they are restricted to a priori intuition, introspective access to current mental episodes, and some deductive reasoning. Cartesians are typically foundationalists. If they accept any of the principles, they accept AP, INT, and DED. They accept the principles related to various processes *provided that* the processes are sufficiently reliable. It is every-instance or all-worlds-reliable processes *first* and epistemic principles *second*. In what follows we will assume, for the sake of discussion, that the foundationalist version of Cartesianism holds that if any of the principles are true, *only* AP, INT, and DED are true.

Cartesian coherentism is a possible (though implausible) position. A Cartesian could (in principle) embrace COH provided that coherence necessarily conduces truth in all worlds. If truth is coherence, this is straightforward. If truth is one thing and coherence is another, it might still be necessarily true that they march in step (or so one might argue). Perhaps BonJour's (1985) "meta-justification" of coherence can be read this way; and perhaps Davidson's "A Coherence Theory of Truth and Knowledge" (1986) paper falls in here.

Since Cartesians can be coherentists, Cartesianism is one thing and its classical foundationalist variant is another. Cartesianism and Coherentism are not contradictories (*pace* Rorty 1979; Willliams 1977; and Thagard 2000, among others).

It is hard to tell who the Cartesians are across the board. Those who seem to embrace it for non-inferential justification include Timothy McGrew (1996), Richard Fumerton (1995, 2001), and Laurence BonJour (1999, 2001, 2002, 2003).[16]

Reliabilism

What unifies the nonfundamentalist camp is the rejection of a priori conceptual knowledge regarding which particular events, states, processes, or ways of holding belief necessarily confer justification. The principles, if true, are not a priori necessary truths. At best the nature of epistemic justification can only be known a priori at a rather abstract, general level. The biconditional that a belief is (at least *prima facie pro tanto*) justified iff it is satisfies *C* is a priori necessary, but whether a belief in fact satisfies *C* is only empirically knowable and only contingently true.[17]

The reliabilist claims that beliefs held in *de facto* reliable ways are (at least *prima facie pro tanto*) justified. It need not be known or knowable which ways are *de facto* reliable for those ways of holding belief to confer prima facie justification. For the reliabilist, it is not a priori necessary that *this* way or *that* way of holding belief confers prima facie justification. Which processes are reliable—and so, which processes confer justification—can only be known empirically. Epistemic principles are neither a priori nor necessary. For example, reliabilists allow that if circumstances are right, perception is a process that confers prima facie justification. A reliabilist could thus accept that principle PER is true. However, the reliabilist rejects the claim that PER is a priori necessary. If it is known that perceptual states confer justification, then that is only empirically known. PER, if true, is (according to the reliabilist) only empirically known, contingently true. Similar remarks apply to all of the other principles.[18]

Other ways of holding belief may be *de facto* reliable as well, processes that may or may not involve internal mental states with shared overlapping satisfaction-conditions with the belief that is the output. Hence other "principles" may be, for the reliabilist, empirically knowable, contingently true.

A *pure* coherentist version of reliabilism is possible (though implausible). One might hold that coherence confers justification because, as a matter of fact, a belief is more likely to be true iff it is a member of a coherent system of beliefs. Coherence might be the one and only *de facto* mark of truth or probable truth.

Reliabilists include Kent Bach (1985), Alvin Goldman (1979, 1999), John Greco (2002), Philip Kitcher (1983), Charles Landesman (2002), Frederick Schmitt (1992), and many others.

Pragmatism

Pragmatism is a proper-aim view of justification. Most justified beliefs, on this view, need not be true. Like intuitionism, pragmatism explains what is meant by 'the right way of forming or sustaining' a belief by the particular principles embraced. Pragmatists embrace principles that reflect deeply held (or even constitutive) norms or epistemic commitments of the relevant community; the relevant community may be you, or your discipline, or your community, or your tradition, or your species, etc.[19]

There are two versions of pragmatism, one more like reliabilism and the other more like intuitionism. The first holds that a belief is prima facie justified just in case it is formed or held in a way that the relevant community believes is reliable. It is like reliabilism because of its essential use of the concept of a reliable process. So if the relevant community believes, for example, that perception is reliable, then beliefs which are held on the basis of perception are prima facie justified. It is *contingent* and only *empirically* known whether perception is *believed* to be reliable. On this version, what is fundamental is the relevant community's *belief* (implicit or explicit) about the *reliability* of the way of holding beliefs. The way of holding beliefs need not *in fact* be *de facto* reliable to confer justification; it need only be *believed* to be *de facto* reliable.

The second version is more like intuitionism than reliabilism. On this version, what matters first and foremost is *not* what ways of holding beliefs the relevant community believes to be *reliable*, but rather what ways of holding beliefs are believed (by the relevant community) to be *the right* or *proper ways* to hold beliefs insofar as truth is the aim or norm. If the relevant community embraces a principle like PER, then it is true. The (contingently embraced) *principles* (of rightly held belief) themselves come first on this version of pragmatism, and not which ways are *believed* to be *reliable*. It is like intuitionism because its content comes directly from the principles. It differs because the principles are not, according to the pragmatist, a priori necessary truths.

These two versions interrelate. On the first, various principles will be embraced *because* the ways of holding beliefs are believed to be reliable. On the second, various ways of holding beliefs will be believed to be reliable *because* they are taken to be the right or proper ways of holding beliefs insofar as truth is the aim. If you are justified in believing *P* on the basis of perception, then you are justified in believing that a perceptual belief is true, and so justified in believing that perception gets things right.

Both versions, like reliabilism, allow all sorts of ways of holding beliefs to confer justification, though like intuitionism they tend to stick to the standard set. Pragmatists can either hold that inner mental states or events confer justification on belief, or disavow, like the reliabilist, such inner states or events. It all depends on which norms are embraced.[20]

A coherentist version of pragmatism is possible. Indeed, Rorty's 1979 pragmatist position was explicitly advertised as a version of coherentism. Pragmatists can be either foundationalists or coherentists.

Pragmatism is a view with a number of weighty adherents. Historical advocates include Hegel, Peirce, Dewey, and Wittgenstein. Contemporary advocates include William Alston (1989), Robert Brandom (1996), Catherine Elgin (1996), Hartry Field (2000), Richard Foley (1987, 2001), Mark Kaplan (1991), and Richard Rorty (1979).

We can now place everyone on the table (table 2.3). To sum up so far, I first claimed that the standard taxonomy is not exhaustive. I went on to develop a new taxonomy based on two contrasts: actual-result versus proper-aim, and fundamentalism versus nonfundamentalism. I defined four theses and then four 'pure' theories. I did not discuss hybrid theories,

Table 2.3

	Actual-Result	Proper-Aim
Fundamentalists	BonJour, Fumerton, McGrew	Audi, Burge, Chisholm, Feldman, Huemer, Lehrer, Peacocke, Pollock and Cruz
Nonfundamentalists	Bach, Goldman, Greco, Kitcher, Landesman, Schmitt	Dewey, Hegel, Peirce, Wittgenstein, Alston, Brandom, Elgin, Field, Foley, Goldman, Kaplan, Rorty, Williams

though they are logically possible. I then said more about each pure theory. In searching the literature one can find a number of occupants for each of the four theories, though who the Cartesians are is hard to say. This shows that a good deal (but not all) of the debate is captured by the new taxonomy. I also claimed that coherentism is compatible with each position. I now briefly raise a few points of comparison between the old and new taxonomies.

3   Connections to the Standard Taxonomy

"Modest" Foundationalism

I begin with a point about a "modest" foundationalism. The new taxonomy shows that "modest foundationalism" is seriously ambiguous as a positive thesis. This is important since "modest," "minimal," "weak," or "fallible" foundationalism is a popular position, but it is unclear what position it is. There are (at least) five different kinds of "modest" or "fallible" foundationalism. All are compatible with reliabilism, intuitionism, and pragmatism, and one is compatible with Cartesianism. We can define them by the epistemic principles they accept (as either a priori necessary or a posteriori contingent):

Reactionary foundationalism: DED, INT, AP
Conservative foundationalism: DED, INT, AP, IBE, EIND, MEM
Moderate foundationalism: DED, INT, AP, IBE, EIND, MEM, PER
Liberal foundationalism: DED, INT, AP, IBE, EIND, MEM, PER, TEST
Revolutionary foundationalism: Any number of these or more

The label 'modest foundationalism' gets applied to any view that allows for "fallible foundations." As I have described the Cartesian, even he allows for *some* false but justified beliefs. Cartesianism allows for fallibility *to a certain degree* (BonJour 2003). Hence the 'modest foundationalist' label may refer to a version of *reactionary* foundationalism that allows beliefs to be justified that are not infallible, but for all that are based on all-worlds reliable processes. This is how Michael Williams (1996, 120–121; 2001, 102–103) uses the label; 'modest foundationalism' may also be used to refer to *conservative* foundationalism. Most naturally it refers to *moderate* foundationalism. This seems to be how Feldman (2003) uses the term. And it may refer to *liberal* or *revolutionary* foundationalists, though revolutionaries are more likely to call themselves "contextual" foundationalists if they call themselves foundationalists at all.

The reason 'modest foundationalism' is ambiguous in this way is because it was introduced as a contrast to *infallible classical* Cartesian foundationalism. On this reading, *any* foundationalist view that allows for fallible foundations of *any* sort is a "modest foundationalist" view. Which fallible foundations *count*, however, is what the five foundationalisms disagree over; hence the plurality of so-called modest foundationalist views.

The standard taxonomy would not predict this plurality; the new taxonomy does. Different versions of modest foundationalism will be embraced depending on which ways of holding a belief pass the relevant condition C that justification allegedly supervenes upon. Cartesians tend toward reactionary foundationalism. Intuitionists tend to avoid the extremes (reactionary and revolutionary) but divide over the intermediate positions. Reliabilists tend to be either moderates or liberals, shying away from feactionary and conservative foundationalism. Pragmatists tend toward liberal or revolutionary foundationalisms.

Whither Coherentism?

I claimed that for each theory a *pure* coherentist version is possible. In this section, I explain why I do not find pure coherentism very plausible. The points I raise deserve much more discussion that I can provide here. I hope to elaborate elsewhere.

First, pure coherentism is the view that *only* COH is true, and that it is true because (1) one of CRIP is true, and (2) membership in a coherent system of beliefs is co-extensive with the relevant condition C that justification supervenes upon. But if any one of CRIP is correct, it is highly implausible to suppose that *only* COH is true, that *only* membership in a coherent system of beliefs meets the relevant C. Surely on any of CRIP *some* of the other principles will be true as well; hence *pure* coherentism is likely to be false.

Second, 'coherence' is notoriously vague. Either it supervenes, in large part, on inferential and explanatory relations or it does not. If it does, then it seems that COH is just shorthand for DED, EIND, and IBE. But if that is so, coherentist justification is just a species of foundationalist justification. On the other hand, if coherence really is a *distinct* kind of property from *ordinary* inferential and explanatory relations, it is hard to know what it is, and even harder still to see why it is epistemically relevant. Hence pure coherentism is either a version of foundationalism or is incoherent (unintelligible). Negative coherence (undermining beliefs) may prevent prima facie justification from converting to on-balance justification, but it is hard to see why coherence *per se* and coherence per se *alone* should be what *confers* justification.

Though there are theorists who call themselves coherentists, there are fewer than there used to be (e.g., BonJour is now a foundationalist and Rorty and Williams are now "contextualists," or pragmatist foundationalists), and some who call themselves coherentists are (arguably) simply rejecting reactionary Cartesian foundationalism (e.g., Quine, Davidson, Thagard).

The standard taxonomy would have us believe that foundationalism versus coherentism is fundamental. But if coherentism is implausible, and if there are a plethora of foundationalist theories, then a good deal of the current controversy lies on the new taxonomy.

Internalism and Externalism

The simple opposition "internalism versus externalism" in the standard taxonomy is too narrow, for there are three versions of internalism (and so three versions of externalism), where the third combines elements from the first two. (I ignore another version, "deontologism"; see note 6.) I shall define these notions and then comment on how they connect to the positions in the new taxonomy.

Ontological internalism is the view that justifiers are internal mental states. Internal mental states are accessible to introspection (for subjects that can introspect). This is the position Feldman and Conee (1985, 2001) call "mentalism."

Epistemic internalism is the view that a belief is justified only if the subject can know or justifiably believe that it is *justified*. (A *belief that P* is justified only if the subject's belief *that her belief that P is justified* is justified.) This might also be called the 'JJ Thesis': JB → JJB.

Combined internalism is the view that a belief that P is justified only if the *subject* can know or justifiably believe by introspection, a priori insight, and reasoning (if necessary) that it is justified. Combined internalism restricts justifiers to things knowable by reflection alone (a priori insight, introspection, and reasoning), and so is like ontological internalism. And combined internalism requires that for empirical beliefs to be justified they must be known by reflection alone to be justified, and so is like epistemic internalism. (But it need not require justified belief that the beliefs from reflection alone are justified; that is optional, though it usually comes along for free.) It takes an element from each view, hence "combined" internalism. It might also be called "philosophical internalism," requiring philosophical reflection on the part of the subject for all justification, including ordinary empirical justification.[21]

Reasonable externalism is the rejection of epistemic (and hence combined) internalism. The reasonable externalist does not think subjects need to justifiably *believe* that their first-*level* beliefs are justified in order for those first-level beliefs to *be* justified. Animals, children, and ordinary adults do not have such meta-beliefs or even (in many cases) the capacity for such beliefs. The reasonable externalist about justification is like the reasonable externalist about knowledge: a subject need not *know* that he knows in order to know; he need not know that the conditions necessary for knowledge obtain. Likewise for reasonable externalism about justification. To justifiably believe something, the subject need not justifiably believe that the conditions necessary for justified belief obtain; they need only obtain.

Radical externalism is the rejection of ontological (and hence combined) internalism. The radical externalist does not require that beliefs be based on or supported by other mental states to be justified. Beliefs held reliably but that come from out of the blue, as it were, may be justified for the radical externalist.

If you are an intuitionist then you must be an ontological internalist, for the epistemic principles you embrace as a priori necessary refer to internal, mental states on the left-hand sides.[22] Intuitionists that call themselves "externalists," for instance Burge (1993, 2003), are clearly ontological internalists. Burge's "externalism" is the rejection of epistemic (and hence combined) internalism.[23] No intuitionist has to be an epistemic internalist; such a variation on intuitionism, however, is possible. One might embrace epistemic norms that place in the antecedent beliefs about how one is forming one's beliefs and beliefs about whether the target belief is justified. Though one might do this, most intuitionists would not.

If you are a reliabilist you do not require internal, mental states for justification. Their presence may coincide with justification, but they are not necessary; you reject ontological internalism. You are thus a radical externalist. You also reject epistemic internalism. You are thus also a reasonable externalist.[24]

If you are a Cartesian, are you both an ontological and an epistemic internalist, hence a combined internalist? Not necessarily. There is nothing in the definition that entails either ontological or epistemic internalism. Hence there is nothing in the definition of Cartesianism that entails that an individual subject, to have a justified belief, must (be able to) justifiably believe by reflection alone that it passes the Cartesian condition on epistemic justification. The definition only requires that the belief pass the condition, that it is known or can be known by someone or other that it passes the condition, not that the subject himself knows (or can know) that it does.

However, if a belief passes the Cartesian standard then it is (most likely) based on either introspection or a priori insight or deductive reasoning or all three. For a belief that is Cartesian justified the subject will (most likely) then be in a position to know by reflection alone that it is justified. Passing the condition seems sufficient for meeting the combined internalist necessary condition. So though the position itself may not require that the subject know or be able to know that his belief is justified, if it is justified a sophisticated subject will be able to know (or justifiably believe) by reflection alone that it is justified.

The same might also be true for intuitionism. For example, a subject might be able to know by reflection alone that a belief is a perceptual belief, and might also be able to know by reflection alone that PER is true. Hence a subject might be able to know by reflection alone, given Intuitionism, that a perceptual belief is justified.

The moral here is twofold. First, that combined internalists are naturally fundamentalists, for only on *fundamentalist* views is there a possibility of knowing that an empirical belief is justified by reflection alone. But second, fundamentalists are not committed to combined internalism. At best fundamentalists are committed to ontological internalism.

If you are a pragmatist, your options are open. If you embrace the epistemic principles as they stand then you are, like the intuitionist, an ontological internalist. However you may, like the reliabilist, think that internal mental states are simply concomitant to justification and not themselves necessary. You would then be a radical externalist.[25] But if the standards of the relevant community were epistemic internalist or ontological internalist, then you would be one or the other. Pragmatists tend to think neither internalism is a priori necessary. When it comes to internalism, pragmatists can take it or leave it.

The new taxonomy thus reveals interesting facts about who is an Internalist of a certain sort and why. The new taxonomy sheds some light on what drives various internalists and externalists.

4   Evidence for Theory-Choice

How then do we decide between the four rival theories? How do we argue for a particular C in the formula: A belief is (at least *prima facie pro tanto*) justified iff it passes C? There are four ways to argue for, and so four ways to argue against, a particular C. The first two go straight to the *intension* of the concept of epistemic justification; the second two go from knowledge of the *extension* to knowledge of the intension.

I have discussed the first three already in connection with intuitionism. To support intuitionism, one must show that one or more of the epistemic principles is a priori necessary. This can be done in one of three ways. The first two are at the intensional level. The third moves from extension to intension. The first way at the intensional level is direct, a priori intuition of the truth of one or more of the epistemic principles. The second way is to derive one or more of the principles from other a priori known principles. The third way collects cases of justified and unjustified beliefs where it is a priori intuitive that the beliefs are justified or unjustified, and an epistemic principle is inferred a priori as the explanation for why the beliefs are either justified or not.

Each of these three ways of arguing a priori is available for the other three rival theories: Cartesianism, reliabilism, and pragmatism. One may argue that the Cartesian or reliabilist or pragmatist theory is a priori, underived from other truths. One may also argue that the Cartesian or reliabilist or pragmatist theory is derivable from other a priori truths. Or one may infer a priori from a priori intuitions about particular cases that either the Cartesian, reliabilist, or pragmatist theory is correct. One may also use all three forms of argument *against* any particular theory: It is self-evident that theory T is false, or it is derivable from other truths that T is false, or T is subject to counter-example.

The fourth way to argue for a particular theory is like the third. The idea is to move from extension to intension. But the fourth does not appeal to *a priori* intuitions about the applicability or inapplicability of a concept to particular cases; rather it relies upon empirical first-person and third-person judgments. From the first person, this means reflecting on how one is disposed to apply the concept to cases, where one lacks the rational intuition that the concept necessarily applies (or necessarily fails to apply). One just notes how one applies (or withholds) the concept, without having a priori intuitions about the necessary applicability or necessary inapplicability of the concept. One simply reflects from the armchair on one's use. From the third person, this amounts to anthropological observations of the use of the concept, to where and when it is applied or withheld. This is the point of view of the anthropologist. The anthropologist surveys practices and notes when the term is applied and when it is not. The anthropologist then generalizes and states principles that govern the use of the concept. In both cases, from either the first person or the third, one infers a general theory about its contours from the use of the concept, and a general theory of the intension of the concept from these contours. This approach is also like Chisholm's "particularist" (cf. Pollock 2001, 46–47).

Ideally, all four forms of evidence would point in favor of one of the four theories. One can find all four of these ways of arguing at work throughout the literature. What one finds less often is an explicit statement of the (implicit) methodology of theory-choice; the epistemology of epistemology often goes without saying (cf. Sosa 2005).

Will direct a priori reflection (our first method for theory-choice) on the two broad theoretical claims, "a belief is justified only if it is more likely than not to be true" and "a belief is justified only if properly aimed at the truth," settle whether actual-result or proper-aim accounts of justification are correct? This is not the place to settle the matter, but let me end by expressing two doubts.

First, suppose you find the actual-result view more obvious upon reflection. There will be those who find the proper-aim view more obvious instead. The fact that others reasonably disagree is a reason for thinking that it is not entirely obvious that one's initial reaction is correct. The question will, at this stage, remain open.

Second, the existence of more detailed a priori arguments, counter-examples from reflection on particular cases, and empirical investigation into the use of the concept will further drive the debate. If such evidence exists and is relevant, direct a priori reflection on the most abstract issue in the debate is highly unlikely to settle the debate. More evidence is required. Only the investigation of more concrete epistemic principles and reflecting on particular cases, I conjecture, will settle whether an actual-result or proper-aim theory is true.

Much of the debate in the theory of epistemic justification has turned on concrete cases and on arguments about the nature of memory, introspection, perception, explanatory inference, and so forth. A priori reflection and empirical inquiry play a large role in these debates. Reflection on the logical space of theories and the nature of the relevant evidence for or against any particular theory should both illuminate and advance the debate.

Acknowledgments

I began thinking about these issues while teaching at Saint Louis University, and then while on medical and research leave from the University. I am deeply grateful for the generous support from my former colleagues, especially my former Chair, Ted Vitali. I have presented versions of this paper at the University of Michigan and at the seventh Inland Northwest Philosophy Conference, at Azusa Pacific University, Pomona College, and California State University, Northridge. For comments that led to improvements, I am grateful to many: the referee for this volume, Fred Adams, Jonathan Adler, Robert Audi, Tim Black, Bill Bracken, Fred Dretske, John Greco, Richard Feldman, Dan Howard-Synder, Paul Hurley, Brian Keeley, James Jhun, Peter Kung, Adam Leite, Philip Nickel, Bonnie Paller, Matt Pugsley, Patrick Rysiew, Dion Scott-Kakures, Rivka Weinberg, Matt Weiner, and Gideon Yaffe.

Notes

1. This distinction is, I believe, the same as Audi's (1988) distinction between "ontological" (getting actual truth) and "teleological" (aiming at truth properly) conceptions of justification. He does not at the same time, however, draw attention to the fundamentalist/nonfundamentalist divide in epistemology.

2. Our topic is the *analysis* of the concept of epistemic justification. If you reject conceptual analysis then you are not a participant to the present discussion. For rejections, see Kitcher 1992, Stich 1988, and Devitt 2005; for defense of the a priori and conceptual analysis, see Casullo 2003 and Sosa 2005. Alvin Goldman is a clear case of a theorist who accepts the existence of the a priori but severely limits its scope; see Goldman 1999 and Goldman and Pust 1998.

3. This in no way implies that perceptual justification is a priori justification. What is a priori knowable is that perceptual representations empirically justify perceptual beliefs; see Peacocke 2004, 148ff.

4. In earlier versions of this essay I defined fundamentalism as the view that theorists can know by reflection alone (a priori knowledge combined with introspective knowledge and inference) whether a particular *belief* is justified. If fundamentalism (about justification) were true, philosophers would thus be those who could know whether particular *beliefs* were justified, and not just whether particular *ways* of hold-

ing beliefs conferred justification. Questions from Bonnie Paller prompted me to rethink this way of drawing the distinction. My earlier distinction is close to Richard Fumerton's distinction between the internalist-metaepistemologist and externalist-metaepistemologist (Fumerton 1995, 66–67, 171): "if externalist metaepistemologies are correct, then . . . [p]hilosophers as they are presently trained have no special *philosophical* expertise enabling them to reach conclusions about which beliefs are or are not justified." The distinction as presented in the text *allows* for the possibility that philosophers *cannot* know by reflection alone whether a particular belief is formed, sustained or held in a particular *way*, and so cannot know by reflection whether a particular *belief* is justified.

5. Previous discussions have *listed* (most of) the positions; see, for instance, Field 2000 and Cohen 1984. But that is all they have done (beyond criticizing various positions). They have not shown how the positions *agree* and how they *differ*, and how certain arguments against one view apply to others. The new taxonomy and the kinds of evidence for theory-choice I discuss below will show just that.

6. I avoid using the label 'deontologism', for that connotes the "deontological conception of justification" (as criticized by Alston, Plantinga, and others), which tends to be a theory of when a *subject* is "justified" in believing something: When a subject has reasoned well, carried out a proper inquiry, considered alternative points of view, and so forth. It is not necessarily a theory of when a *belief* is justified. "Intuitionism" as I see it is a theory of when a *belief* is justified. It is a theory that applies equally well to the beliefs of adults, higher animals, and young children. The traditional deontological conception applies to the intellectual *activities* of adults, and not to higher animals and children.

7. Alston offered a "hybrid" nonfundamentalist theory in his paper "An Internalist Externalism" (1988). On my taxonomy, he combines reliabilism (the externalism) with pragmatism (the internalism).

8. Additional conditions would have to be added to explain the relationship between prima facie and undefeated justification, and between *pro tanto* and on-balance justification. See also the following note.

9. Each principle states when a belief formed or held in a certain way enjoys *prima facie pro tanto* justification. Prima facie justification is defeasible justification; '*pro tanto*' literally means "for a little" or "just so much." In law it means something like "to that extent," or "as far as it goes." I use it to mean *some* justification as opposed to *enough* or *on-balance* justification. For example, an experience as of a red apple in the distance may confer some justification on the belief that there is a red apple but not *enough* or *on-balance* justification. The belief that there is a red apple may not be justified (on-balance) though it is partially (*pro tanto*) justified. Or one person may tell me that *P*, and my understanding her assertion may provide some justification, but it is only until another person also tells me that *P* that my justification converts from *pro tanto* to on-balance. For discussion and elaboration, see Graham 2006.

The qualification *"prima facie pro tanto"* will not matter here, but it does matter over-all in a complete theory of epistemic justification, and so at times I will make it explicit in the text.

10. Cf. Haack 1993.

11. For the intuitionist the *subject* does not have to know the principle for the principle to govern her beliefs. If PER, for example, is necessarily true, then a subject's perceptual experiences will confer prima facie justification on her beliefs even if she does not *know* that PER is true. Indeed, it will govern her beliefs even if she cannot *understand* the principle. The *theorist* must know or be able to know the principle a priori, but the *subject* whose beliefs are governed by the principle need not. The "combined internalist" (defined below) denies this: The subject, to be justified, must have (or be able to have) "philosophical" knowledge that her belief is justified in order to have justified belief.

12. It is a priori intuitive that justification is present when it is intuitive that justification, given the case, is necessarily present; and it is a priori intuitive that justification is lacking when it is intuitive that, given the case, justification is necessarily absent.

13. For comparison, see Peacocke 2004.

14. I discuss TEST in my "Liberal Fundamentalism and Its Rivals" (2006) and else-where; I discuss PER in Graham 1999.

15. This is on the assumption that metaphysical realism is true, that there is a logical or metaphysical gap between the nature of the mind and the nature of the world. If idealism is true, then perceptual beliefs may satisfy the Cartesian test for they are, in a way, simply introspective beliefs. And if an extremely strong version of content externalism is true, then perceptual beliefs may also pass the Cartesian test.

16. Though not Cartesians generally, Kitcher (1983, 1992) and Goldman (1999) both seem to impose all-worlds reliability as a constraint on a priori justification. For criticism, see Casullo 2003.

17. Goldman (1992, 1999) "rigidifies" the condition: A way of forming beliefs confers justification if and only if it is reliable in the actual world. The result is that processes which confer justification do so necessarily; but it is not known or knowable a priori which ones confer justification. The principles, then, may be necessary truths for Goldman, but they are not a priori necessary truths (i.e., they are not conceptual truths).

18. Indeed, for Goldman, even whether a belief is a priori justified is only empirically knowable, for whether the belief is a priori justified depends upon the psychological mechanism that produced it and its properties, and those are only knowable empirically. It is cognitive psychology, for Goldman, that tells us whether our beliefs

are justified or not, though it is philosophy that tells us what the general criteria are for justified belief. See Goldman 1999 and Goldman and Pust 1998.

19. The norm may be explicit or implicit. It may be possible to make mistakes about the norm, and so make mistakes about when a belief is justified. The belief that one conforms to a norm does not guarantee that one does.

20. Most pragmatists tend to hold that the *process* of justifying a claim to another is prior to the *property* of a belief's being justified (Rorty 1979, Brandom 1996; cf. Audi 1988, Foley 1987). I shall assume this is inessential. A pragmatist can hold that the reason a belief has the property is because the belief passes the norm set by the relevant community, and the reason why the subject could justify the belief to another is for the same reason. What is primary, then, is the norm. The norm explains why the belief is justified and why the subject can justify her belief to another.

21. For similar ways of defining the first two internalisms, see Alston 1998, Fumerton 1995, Heil 2002, Pryor 2001, and Schmitt 1992. I have avoided using the word 'access' in the definitions of ontological and epistemic internalism. Ontological internalism does not entail that justifiers are introspectively accessible, for certain creatures with mental states might not be able to introspect them (viz., higher animals and children). *We* can introspect our mental states, but *that* we can is not essential; what matters is the mental state, not the access. Epistemic internalism involves knowledge or justified belief (of a higher order) about whether a belief (of a lower order) is justified. Introspection is one way among others, though surely the standard way, to form beliefs about one's own beliefs. Combined internalism builds in introspective "access" as necessary. BonJour is a combined internalist. "Internalism," for BonJour, *just is* a combined internalism.

22. Possessing inductive evidence or an explanation means believing that there is such evidence for believing the explanation, etc.

23. Burge (1993) distinguishes between "entitlement" and "justification." The former he says is externalist, and the latter internalist. This is misleading. Perceptual representations, he holds, *entitle* perceptual beliefs. The nonconceptual perceptual representations are internal mental states (though they metaphysically supervene on causal-explanatory external relations to external environmental conditions). They satisfy the ontological internalist condition. The subject need not know why they confer entitlement. Hence epistemic (and also combined) internalism is false. Now the same seems true of what Burge calls "justification." A justification for Burge is a set of reasons that the subject possesses in favor of a conclusion, and the subject can tell that the reasons support the conclusion. Justifications (for Burge) are arguments; the reasons (premises) are internal mental states. Once again they satisfy the ontological internalist condition. And the subject need not know why reasons support their conclusions (i.e., the subject does not need a philosophical account or explicit understanding of why arguments justify). Epistemic internalism, again, is not required. Burge's distinction thus strikes me not as an "externalist" versus

"internalist" distinction, but just the distinction between non-inferential and inferential justification. See also Burge 2003b, 337.

24. Reliabilists are fond of pointing out that justified belief about whether a first-level belief is justified is possible on their view: A belief that a first-level belief is justified might be reliably formed, and so justified. (Likewise they point out that a subject might know that he knows.) They thus show that they can satisfy the epistemic internalist condition. But "internalists" (like BonJour, Stroud, and Fumerton) are not satisfied with that. What they want is something further, what I have called *combined* internalism: The target first-level belief must be shown to be justified by reflection alone, and they tend to impose an actual-result condition, and so it must be shown by reflection alone that the empirical belief is actually likely to be true. Reliabilists cannot claim *that* condition is met, simply by showing that certain higher-order beliefs are reliably formed.

25. Rorty's "epistemological behaviorism" (1979) rejects inner mental perceptual experiences as necessary for justification; at best they are causally relevant to perceptual belief. What matters for Rorty is the linguistic ability to justify one's beliefs to others. This involves, for example, the belief that one sees a tree. Such a belief, though it is not an experience and may not refer to an experience, is itself an inner mental state. Rorty is thus not a radical externalist.

References

Alston, W. 1988. "An Internalist Externalism." *Synthèse* 74: 265–283.

Alston, W. 1989. "A Doxastic Practices Approach to Epistemology." In M. Clay and K. Lehrer, eds., *Knowledge and Skepticism*. Boulder, Col.: Westview Press.

Alston, W. 1998. "Internalism and Externalism." In E. Craig, ed., *Routledge Encyclopedia of Philosophy*. London: Routledge.

Alston, W. 1999. "Doing Epistemology without Justification." *Philosophical Topics* 29: 1–18.

Audi, R. 1988. "Justification, Truth, and Reliability." *Philosophy and Phenomenological Research* 49: 1–29.

Bach, K. 1985. "A Rationale for Reliabilism." *Monist* 68: 246–263.

BonJour, L. 1985. *The Structure of Empirical Knowledge*. Cambridge, Mass.: Harvard University Press.

BonJour, L. 1999. *In Defense of Pure Reason*. Cambridge: Cambridge University Press.

BonJour, L. 2001. "Toward a Defense of Empirical Foundationalism." In M. DePaul, ed., *Resurrecting Old-Fashioned Foundationalism*. Lanham, Md.: Rowman & Littlefield.

BonJour, L. 2002. *Epistemology: Classic Problems and Contemporary Responses*. Lanham, Md.: Rowman & Littlefield.

BonJour, L. 2003. *Epistemic Justification: Internalism vs. Externalism, Foundations vs. Virtues*. Oxford: Blackwell.

Brandom, R. 1996. *Making It Explicit*. Cambridge, Mass.: Harvard University Press.

Burge, T. 1993. "Content Preservation." *Philosophical Review* 102: 457–488.

Burge, T. 1996. "Our Entitlement to Self-Knowledge." *Proceedings of the Aristotelian Society* 96: 91–116

Burge, T. 2003a. "Perceptual Entitlement." *Philosophy and Phenomenological Research* 67: 503–548.

Burge, T. 2003b. "Some Reflections on Scepticism: Reply to Stroud." In M. Hahn and B. Ramberg, eds., *Reflections and Replies: Essays on the Philosophy of Tyler Burge*. Cambridge, Mass.: MIT Press.

Casullo, A. 2003. *A Priori Justification*. Oxford: Oxford University Press.

Chisholm, R. 1966. *The Theory of Knowledge*. Englewood Cliffs, N.J.: Prentice-Hall.

Cohen, S. 1984. "Justification and Truth." *Philosophical Studies* 46: 279–296.

Davidson, D. 1986. "A Coherence Theory of Truth and Knowledge." In E. Lepore, ed., *Truth and Interpretation*. Oxford: Blackwell.

Devitt, M. 2005. "There Is No A Priori." In E. Sosa and M. Steup, eds., *Contemporary Debates in Epistemology*. Oxford: Blackwell.

Elgin, C. 1996. *Considered Judgment*. Princeton: Princeton University Press.

Feldman, R. 2003. *Epistemology*. Englewood Cliffs, N.J.: Prentice-Hall.

Feldman, R., and E. Conee. 1985. "Evidentialism." *Philosophical Studies* 48: 15–34.

Feldman, R., and E. Conee. 2001. "Internalism Defended." *American Philosophical Quarterly* 38: 1–18.

Field, H. 2000. "A Priority as an Evaluative Notion." In P. Boghossian and C. Peacocke, eds., *New Essays on the A Priori*. Oxford: Oxford University Press.

Foley, R. 1987. *The Theory of Epistemic Rationality*. Cambridge, Mass.: Harvard University Press.

Foley, R. 2001. *Intellectual Trust in Oneself and Others*. Cambridge: Cambridge University Press.

Fumerton, R. 1995. *Metaepistemology and Skepticism*. Lanham, Md.: Rowman & Littlefield.

Fumerton, R. 2001. "Classical Foundationalism." In M. DePaul, ed., *Resurrecting Old-Fashioned Foundationalism*. Lanham, Md.: Rowman & Littlefield.

Goldman, A. 1979. "What Is Justified Belief?" In M. Swain, ed., *Epistemic Justification*. Dordrecht: Kluwer.

Goldman, A. 1992. "Epistemic Folkways and Scientific Epistemology." In A. Goldman, *Liaisons: Philosophy Meets the Cognitive and Social Sciences*. Cambridge, Mass.: MIT Press.

Goldman, A. 1999. "A Priori Warrant and Naturalistic Epistemology." In A. Goldman, *Pathways to Knowledge*. Oxford: Oxford University Press, 2002.

Goldman, A., and J. Pust. 1998. "Philosophical Theory and Intuitional Evidence." In A. Goldman, *Pathways to Knowledge*. Oxford: Oxford University Press, 2002.

Graham, P. 1999. "Perceptual Entitlement." Paper presented at the Pacific Division of the American Philosophical Association, Berkeley, California, March 31–April 3, 1999.

Graham, P. 2006. "Liberal Fundamentalism and Its Rivals." In J. Lackey and E. Sosa, eds., *The Epistemology of Testimony*. Oxford: Oxford University Press.

Graham, P. 2007. "The Theoretical Diagnosis of Skepticism." *Synthèse* 158: 19–39.

Greco, J. 2002. *Putting Skeptics in Their Place*. Cambridge: Cambridge University Press.

Haack, S. 1993. *Evidence and Inquiry*. Oxford: Blackwell.

Heil, J. 2002. "Mind and Knowledge." In Paul Moser, ed., *Oxford Handbook of Epistemology*. Oxford: Oxford University Press.

Huemer, M. 2001. *Skepticism and the Veil of Perception*. Lanham, Md.: Rowman & Littlefield.

Kaplan, M. 1991. "Epistemology on Holiday." *Journal of Philosophy* 88: 132–154.

Kitcher, P. 1983. *The Nature of Mathematical Knowledge*. Oxford: Oxford University Press.

Kitcher, P. 1992. "The Naturalist's Return." *Philosophical Review* 101: 53–114.

Landesman, C. 2002. *Skepticism: The Central Issues*. Oxford: Blackwell.

McGrew, T. 1996. "A Defense of Classical Foundationalism." In L. Pojman, ed., *The Theory of Knowledge: Classical and Contemporary Readings*, 3rd ed. Belmont, Calif.: Wadsworth, 2003.

Nozick, R. 1986. *Philosophical Explanations*. Cambridge, Mass.: Harvard University Press.

Peacocke, C. 2004. *The Realm of Reason*. Oxford: Oxford University Press.

Pollock, J. 2001. "Nondoxastic Foundationalism." In M. DePaul, ed., *Resurrecting Old-Fashioned Foundationalism*. Lanham, Md.: Rowman & Littlefield.

Pollock, J., and J. Cruz. 1999. *Contemporary Theories of Knowledge*, 2nd ed. Lanham, Md.: Rowman & Littlefield.

Pryor, J. 2001. "Highlights of Recent Epistemology." *British Journal for the Philosophy of Science* 52: 95–124.

Rorty, R. 1979. *Philosophy and the Mirror of Nature*. Princeton: Princeton University Press.

Schmitt, F. 1992. *Knowledge and Belief*. London: Routledge.

Sosa, E. 2005. "A Defense of the Use of Intuitions in Philosophy." In M. Bishop and D. Murphy, eds., *Stich and His Critics*. Oxford: Wiley-Blackwell.

Stich, S. 1988. "Reflective Equilibrium, Analytic Epistemology, and the Problem of Cognitive Diversity." *Synthèse* 74: 391–413.

Thagard, P. 2000. *Coherence in Thought and Action*. Cambridge, Mass.: MIT Press.

Williams, M. 1977. *Groundless Belief*. Oxford: Oxford University Press.

Williams, M. 1996. *Unnatural Doubts: Epistemological Realism and the Basis of Skepticism*. Princeton: Princeton University Press.

Williams, M. 2001. *Problems of Knowledge*. Oxford: Oxford University Press.

3   Truth Tracking and the Problem of Reflective Knowledge

Joe Salerno

In "Reliabilism Leveled," Jonathan Vogel (2000) provides a strong case against epistemic theories that stress the importance of tracking/sensitivity conditions. A tracking/sensitivity condition is to be understood as some version of the following counterfactual:

(T) $\sim p \; \Box \!\!\rightarrow \sim Bp$

(T) says that s would not believe p, if p were false. Among other things, tracking is supposed to express the external relation that explains why some justified true beliefs are not knowledge. Champions of the condition include Robert Nozick (1981) and, more recently, Keith DeRose (1995). To my knowledge, the earliest formulation of the counterfactual condition is found in Fred Dretske's *conclusive reasons* condition (1971), which says, s would not have had the reason that she does for believing p, if p were false. Vogel contends that any such counterfactual condition on knowledge will render the theory of knowledge too strong. He believes that there is at least some possible reflective knowledge that cannot satisfy the counterfactual— namely, the possible knowledge that one does not believe falsely that p. The alleged impossibility of such reflective knowledge is taken by Vogel to be a decisive objection to the tracking theories advocated by Dretske, Nozick, DeRose,[1] and others.

The criticism finds its roots in Vogel's earlier work (1987), and recurs in papers by Ernest Sosa (2002, 1996). Sosa suggests that the externalist idea behind tracking is on target, but that Nozick's counterfactual is a mis-begotten regimentation of the idea. In its place Sosa offers his own counter-factual "safety" condition, which he feels properly captures the externalist idea. Sosa's counterfactual is not the topic of this paper. I mention it only to point out that the criticism that constitutes the subject of my investigation is meant to do a lot of work. In Sosa's case the criticism is meant to motivate his own counterfactual analysis, and in Vogel's case the criticism promises to be a silver bullet against a theory that has recently found renewed life in the work of Keith DeRose. It will be argued here that the criticism is misguided. My belief that I do not believe falsely that *p* can track the truth.

The Counterexample to Truth Tracking

Consider the proposition that I do not believe falsely that *p*. I should be able to know a proposition like that. Sometimes I know *p* and double-check my sources, thereby coming to know, additionally, that I do not believe falsely that *p*. Vogel's concern is that this kind of epistemic confidence cannot track the truth: If my belief that I am not mistaken were false, I would *still* believe that I'm not mistaken.

Vogel begins by translating the claim of epistemic confidence, "I do not believe falsely that *p*" as shown. Call it (EC):

(EC)   ~(B*p* & ~*p*)

Formally, (EC) reads, "it is not the case that both I believe *p* and *p* is false." The tracking condition, again, says, if *p* were false it would not be believed that *p*:

(T)   ~*p* $\square\rightarrow$ ~B*p*

Knowing (EC) then requires satisfying the following instance of (T):

(T*)   (B*p* & ~*p*) $\square\rightarrow$ ~B~(B*p* & ~*p*)

It says this: If I were to believe *p* falsely, then I would not believe that I do not believe *p* falsely.

Evaluating this counterfactual is tricky business. Nevertheless, Vogel argues that clearly it is not satisfiable, because he thinks, "If you believe *p*, you believe that you do not falsely believe *p*" (2000, 611). Formally,

(*)   B*p* $\Rightarrow$ B~(B*p* & ~*p*)[2]

Of course, if (*) is valid then (T*) is not satisfiable. In the relevantly close worlds where the antecedent of (T*) is true, you believe you are not mistaken. That is because, by (*), in *every* world where the antecedent of (*) is true, you believe you are not mistaken.

So if (*) is valid and (EC)—that is, '~(B*p* & ~*p*)'—properly regiments the claim "I do not believe falsely that *p*," then it is not possible to track the truth of this claim. Therefore, if Vogel's logical resources are in order and tracking is a necessary condition on knowledge, then, absurdly, one cannot know that one does not believe falsely that *p*.

I Believe Higher-Order Consequences of What I Believe

This is a good place to point out that both the assumption that (*) is valid and the assumption that (EC) best captures the expression of epistemic confidence are questionable. I address each of these worries in turn.

Vogel's criticism of tracking theories depends on the validity of (*). A number of concerns arise. First, it is not obvious that believing p entails having the higher-order belief that one is not mistaken in believing p. That implies that small children and other unreflective thinkers have beliefs about their own beliefs. More to the point, no contradiction flows from the assumption that there is a thinker who, for whatever reason, is able to form only first-order beliefs (i.e., beliefs that do not have the concept of belief as part of their content).[3] So we have some reason from the start to be suspicious of (*).

Second, Vogel cites as his defense of (*) the validity of a closure principle for knowledge. He writes,

any proposition p itself entails that a belief that p is not false: p entails $\sim(Bp \ \& \ \sim p)$. So, to say that you know [p] but you fail to know that you do not believe falsely that [p] would be to reject the closure principle for knowledge. (2000, 610, n. 15)

Vogel here refers to the principle stating that we know all the consequences of what we know. Call the principle (CP):

(CP) $(Kp \ \& \ p{\Rightarrow}q) \Rightarrow Kq$

There are several problems with this defense, not the least of which is that (CP) is invalid. (CP) notoriously implies that we know even the undiscovered consequences of what we know. For instance, we know (the conjunction of) the axioms of arithmetic. But then by CP, we know that Goldbach's conjecture is false (if it is false). But clearly we do not know whether Goldbach's conjecture is false. We might in the familiar way weaken the closure principle to "we know all the *known* consequences of what is known," giving (WCP): $(Kp \ \& \ K(p{\Rightarrow}q)) \Rightarrow Kq$. (WCP) is a more plausible closure principle. But it should be noted that Nozick and Dretske reject (WCP), and with it the stronger (CP). So any argument for rejecting the tracking condition that employs a closure principle at least as strong as (WCP) is not something by which Nozick or Dretske would be moved.

One might weaken (CP) by strengthening the antecedent in some way. To what extent we ought to strengthen it is an open question.[4] That we ought to strengthen it, on the other hand, is the received view among those who believe that logical entailment can extend our knowledge. But strengthening the antecedent of (CP) will destroy Vogel's argument for (*). The thought here is that weakening (CP) will enjoin an analogous weakening of (*). But Vogel's central argument depends on something at least as strong as (*).

Another problem with Vogel's appeal to knowledge closure is that the principle he is defending—namely, (*) Bp ⇒ B~(Bp & ~p)—is not a consequence of even the strongest closure principle for knowledge—namely, (CP) (Kp & p⇒q) ⇒ Kq. It is at best a consequence of some closure principle for belief. Perhaps Vogel's strategy is this. If knowledge closure is valid, then the corresponding closure principle for belief is also valid. In other words, if (Kp & p⇒q) ⇒ Kp is valid, then so is (Bp & p⇒q) ⇒ Bq. The reasoning here must be that if closure holds for knowledge, then it holds for every necessary condition on knowledge.

The important objection to this strategy is that it is simply false that closure holds of knowledge only if it holds of every necessary condition on knowledge. To think otherwise is to commit the fallacy of division.[5] So I find no plausible argument in Vogel from the validity of closure for knowledge to the validity of (*).

If we hope to avoid closure principles altogether, then we might rehabilitate Vogel's criticism another way. All we need to do is to argue that

(T*)   (Bp & ~p) □→ ~B~(Bp & ~p)

is not satisfied in all those cases where, plausibly, one knows that one is not mistaken in believing p. But consider a case where s knows p and corroborates her belief with an independent source, thereby coming to believe that she is not mistaken. It might be argued that in the closest worlds where s is mistaken (i.e., where sBp & ~p), s continues to believe that she is not mistaken. The idea here is that in the closest worlds where she is mistaken, she continues to believe that she is not mistaken, even though in the actual world she checked her work by an independent method.[6]

There is an obvious objection to this outcome. For the case at hand, it is unclear that a world where {s is mistaken but believes she is not} is closer than a world where {s is mistaken but withholds judgment about whether she is mistaken}. After all, in the actual world s double-checked (by an independent method) whether p. The result of her double-checking was that p. She thereby concluded that she was not mistaken in believing p. Arguably, the closest worlds where she is mistaken, her double-checking would not have corroborated her belief that p, and so, she loses her reason for thinking she is not mistaken. To deny this is to suggest the following strange claim: A world where independent methods give us faulty results, if any of our methods give us faulty results, is a closer world than one where our independent methods do not go haywire in this way. My point here is that it is all but clear that (T*) is unsatisfiable or that some general argument avoiding closure principles will show that (T*) is unsatisfiable.

If Vogel can show in some other way that the closest worlds where s is mistaken in believing p are worlds where one would believe that one is not mistaken, then perhaps his argument may be revived. But this is yet to be done, and as we will presently see it would not help. The reason it would not help is that '~(Bp & ~p)' is not the best formal representation of the thought that I do not believe falsely that p.

I Do Not Believe Falsely That p

We are considering the statement, "I do not falsely believe p." One might be inclined to think that this is the negation of "My belief that p is false," in which case, with Vogel, we simply negate the claim "I believe that p and p is false," giving us (EC): ~(Bp & ~p). Whether a belief of this form tracks is actually not important, because the thought-process behind this regimentation is subtly confused. The relevant formulation of "I do not falsely believe p" is not the negation of "My belief that p is false." These two statements are contraries, not contradictories. The point is developed here.

We begin by noticing that "I do not falsely believe p" (or "I am not mistaken in believing p") is ambiguous. On one reading, the claim that

(+)   I do not falsely believe p

is equivalent to

(1)   I believe p and p is not false.

Formally,

Bp & ~~p

or equivalently,

Bp & p

This reading has the trivial implication that I believe p. The second reading does not have this implication. Accordingly, it may reasonably be argued that I do not falsely believe p, if I do not believe p at all. On this reading, the claim that

(+)   I do not falsely believe that p

is equivalent to

(2) It is not the case that both I believe that p and not-p.

Formally,

$\sim$(Bp & $\sim p$)

Reading (2) does not have the implication that I believe that p. My failing to believe p is sufficient for the truth of (2).

The question is this: In the contexts in which, intuitively, I can know that I do not believe falsely that p, which reading best captures the proposition? In ordinary speech the reasonable claim that I do not believe falsely that p is an expression of epistemic confidence in one's belief that p. And it is this expression of confidence that Vogel is focusing on. For it is in the context of knowing p that it seems to him that one also knows that one is not mistaken in believing p. Here is his example:

> You see your long-time friend Omar, who is a perfectly decent and straightforward sort of person. Noticing his shiny white footwear, you say, "Nice shoes, Omar, are they new?" Omar replies, "Yes, I bought them yesterday." I think the following things are true: [a] You know Omar has a new pair of shoes. [b] You know that your belief that Omar has a new pair of shoes is true, or at least not false. (2000, 609–610)

My belief that p is not false occurs in a context where I believe p. And it is the belief that p that the thought "My belief that p is not false" is about. So arguably, "My belief that p is not false" is best represented by an expression that entails that I believe p. Bp & p is the best reading.

Ernest Sosa offers the same criticism as does Vogel against tracking theories, though he makes no appeal to (*) or closure principles. He writes,

> Consider: (a) p, and (b) I do not believe incorrectly (falsely) that p. Surely no one minimally rational and attentive who believes both of these will normally know either without knowing the other. Yet even in the cases where one tracks the truth of (a), one could never track the truth of (b). After all, even if (b) were false, one would still believe it anyhow. (1996, 276)[7]

What is important here is that Sosa is considering contexts in which p is known, and so believed. The claim that I am not wrong in thinking p must then be saying something that may serve as an expression of epistemic confidence. And so, the claim that I am not mistaken is saying, among other things, that I believe p. If I am saying something that does not imply that I believe p, then I am not saying something that expresses my epistemic confidence in my belief that p. The reading that seems most appropriate then is Reading (1), Bp & p. Reading (1) has the truth conditions that best suit it for ordinary speech, where one's claim that one is not mistaken is commonly used as an expression of epistemic confidence. At the very least, Reading (1) has the truth conditions that best suit it for the kind of case that Sosa has in mind—namely, one in which a minimally rational and attentive agent believes both p and that her belief that p has not gone wrong.

Why then do Vogel and Sosa automatically interpret the claim that I am not mistaken, with Reading (2)? I fear that they are confusing the claim that I am not mistaken with the negation of the claim that I am mistaken. But just as the claim that I am not mistaken in believing p ordinarily means something that implies that I do believe that p, so the statement that I *am* mistaken in believing p implies that I do believe p. And so, if I fail to believe p, then both claims are false. The two claims do not contradict, since the falsity of one does not preclude the falsity of the other. They are contraries, since (in addition to the joint satisfiability of their negations) they cannot both be true. The fact that they cannot both be true explains the confusion; it explains why Vogel and Sosa confuse "I do not believe falsely that p" for the negation of "I do believe falsely that p."

We may better represent the expression of confidence in one's belief as the claim that my belief is correct. This suggests that we regiment the thought as Reading (1), Bp & p. This regimentation gives us the right truth conditions. The proposition is false when and only when either p is not believed or p is false. Furthermore, Reading (1) properly formalizes "I am not mistaken" as a contrary of "I am mistaken" (formally, Bp & $\sim p$).

Reading (1), Bp & p, is a stronger claim than Reading (2), $\sim(Bp$ & $\sim p)$. The former entails the latter, but not vice versa. The former better represents the claim that one is not mistaken, and the truth that it depicts can be tracked. I will show that in a moment. Before I do, it should be noted that Vogel considered Reading (1). He claims that he chose Reading (2) over Reading (1)

to avoid complications about counterfactuals with disjunctive antecedents. Such technical hazards will arise any time one tries to apply [thesis (T)] to knowledge of conjunctions. (2000, 611 n. 17)

With all due respect, this is a terrible reason to opt for one reading over another. The correct logical characterization of a proposition (that is not a counterfactual) should be decided independently of any problems there may be with interpreting counterfactuals that embed that proposition. Otherwise, we should not interpret any apparent natural language conjunction as p & q, when evaluating a counterfactual that embeds its negation (in the antecedent place).

Back to Tracking

We seek to determine whether the belief that I am correct in believing p (i.e., Bp & p) can track the truth. The belief can track just in case the following counterfactual can be true:

(T**)   ~(Bp & p) $\Box\!\!\rightarrow$ ~B(Bp & p)

This is the relevant instance of (T). Equivalently,

(T**)   (~Bp ∨ ~p) $\Box\!\!\rightarrow$ ~B(Bp & p)

(T**) embeds the dreaded disjunctive antecedent that Vogel wished to avoid. But for the ordinary case a counterfactual with a disjunctive antecedent simplifies. That is, a counterfactual with a disjunctive antecedent, (p ∨ q) $\Box\!\!\rightarrow$ r, implies the conjunction of two counterfactuals, (p $\Box\!\!\rightarrow$ r) & (q $\Box\!\!\rightarrow$ r). For instance, "If it were to rain or frost, the game would be canceled" implies, "If it were to rain the game would be cancelled, and if it were to frost the game would be canceled." Of course there are cases that appear to invalidate the inference, but all of these are cases where one of the disjuncts is not taken to be a "real possibility,"[8] as in, "If Spain were to fight on one side or the other (i.e., with the Allies or with the Axis in World War II), she would fight with the Axis," or "If she were to run for Congress (i.e., the House or the Senate), she would run for the House." There is no reason to think that (T**) exhibits the peculiarity of these latter examples. So we should allow the inference here.[9]

The relevant counterfactual is (T**) (~Bp ∨ ~p) $\Box\!\!\rightarrow$ ~B(Bp & p). So, if it is true, then the following two counterfactuals are true:

(T**1)   ~p $\Box\!\!\rightarrow$ ~B(Bp & p)

(T**2)   ~Bp $\Box\!\!\rightarrow$ ~B(Bp & p)

(T**2) is trivially satisfied, because any world where I do not believe p is a world where I do not believe Bp & p.[10] The significant point is that (T**1) is not impossible. In fact, it seems to be exactly that on which knowledge of one's own correctness depends. It depends on whether I would have believed I am correct in thinking p, if p were false. For instance, if Omar did not have a new pair of shoes, I would not have thought that my belief that he does have a new pair shoes is correct. After all, Omar is "a perfectly decent and straightforward sort of person," and so would not have misled me. In the closest worlds where Omar does not have a new pair of shoes, I would not believe that he does (and so, I would not have thought that I have a true belief that he does). (T**1) is satisfied. Consider another case. I come to believe p and independently corroborate, thereby coming to believe that my initial belief is true, not false. In the relevantly close worlds where p is false, my independent source would not corroborate that p. And so, I would not have thought that my belief that p is true, not false. (T**1) is satisfied. The two counterfactuals, (T**1) and (T**2), are jointly satisfiable.[11] So, tracking condition (T) is satisfied in the relevant cases.

In conclusion, Vogel's proposal against truth tracking rests on a subtle confusion about how to interpret an expression of epistemic confidence. The best interpretation allows for the possibility of sensitively believing that one is not mistaken. If Vogel's argument was intended to show that any renewed interest in tracking conditions is hopeless, then Vogel's argument falls short. If Sosa's criticism was intended to motivate his own counterfactual analysis, then Sosa's analysis is ill-motivated. Whatever the shortcomings of truth-tracking proposals, they do not include the impossibility of reflective knowledge that one is not mistaken.

Acknowledgments

The author wishes to thank Berit Brogaard, Susan Brower-Toland, Alicia Finch, Dan Haybron, Joe Keim Campbell, Marion Ledwig, Steven Luper, Matt McGrath, Michael O'Rourke, Duncan Pritchard, Scott Ragland, Ernest Sosa, Kent Staley, Jim Stone, and Adam Wager for useful discussion and comments. The majority of the paper was completed with the help of a Saint Louis University Mellon Faculty Development Grant in the summer of 2003.

Notes

1. For DeRose (1995), sensitivity is not a general requirement for knowledge, although the effect of denying that one has knowledge is to require that sensitivity be met thereafter. Thus Vogel's argument threatens DeRose's position. In an ordinary (non-philosophical) context where I think that I am not mistaken in believing p and you deny that I know this, it should be possible to rise to the challenge thereby satisfying the sensitivity condition. Vogel's argument, in effect, denies that it is possible to rise to this challenge.

2. We are here interpreting Vogel's conditional (*) as a necessary material conditional, because only on this familiar interpretation is Vogel's argument valid. If (*) is treated as a material conditional, the argument is invalid. The material conditional, $Bp \to B{\sim}(Bp \ \& \ {\sim}p)$, is not sufficient to falsify (T*). The material conditional tells us only what is the case in the actual Bp-world, but to evaluate the counterfactual (T*) we need to know what is the case in the closest $Bp\&{\sim}p$-worlds. Furthermore, if

Vogel's conditional (*) is treated as a counterfactual, the argument is invalid. It is well known that strengthening the antecedent of a counterfactual does not preserve truth. In particular, $Bp \ \Box \rightarrow B\sim(Bp \ \& \sim p)$ does not entail $(Bp \ \& \sim p) \ \Box \rightarrow B\sim(Bp \ \& \sim p)$. And so, the truth of $Bp \ \Box \rightarrow B\sim(Bp \ \& \sim p)$ does nothing by way of undermining (T*), $(Bp \ \& \sim p) \ \Box \rightarrow \sim B\sim(Bp \ \& \sim p)$.

3. Thanks to Steven Luper for sharpening this point.

4. It has been emphasized repeatedly that even (WCP) is problematic as it stands. Perhaps one may know p and know that p entails q without believing (and so without knowing) q. The suggestion is that the antecedent of (WCP) be strengthened to include that the agent performs the deduction thereby coming to believe q. Other problems then arise. It might be that one knows p and knows that p entails q but in the time it takes to perform the inference from p to q the agent loses her knowledge that p. The suggestion here is that we strengthen the antecedent further to include that the agent retains her knowledge of the premise throughout. These concerns about the validity of (WCP) are developed in Hawthorne 2004 and in David and Warfield 2008.

5. This point is the thesis of Warfield (2004). Vogel recently acknowledged this lesson in his "Varieties of Skepticism" (2004).

6. It may be noted that Nozick's treatment of these counterfactuals is not the familiar Lewis semantic. For reasons we need not go into here, Nozick requires, roughly, that the *sufficiently close* worlds (not just the closest worlds) are relevant for the proper evaluation of the counterfactual. This difference does not effect the above argument, since it is sufficient for showing that the Nozick counterfactual, $p \ \Box \rightarrow q$, is false that there is a closest p-world that is not a q-world. For if there is a closest p-world that is not a q-world, then there is a sufficiently close p-world that is not a q-world. The difference becomes crucial when demonstrating the *truth* of a counterfactual. On the Lewis approach the actual truth of p and q is sufficient for $p \ \Box \rightarrow q$, since the closest p-world (i.e., the actual world) is a q-world. Not so on the Nozick approach. The closest p-world may be a q-world, but for the counterfactual, $p \ \Box \rightarrow q$, to be true, it must be that all the sufficiently close p-worlds (and not just the actual p-world) are q-worlds.

7. For another formulation of the argument, see Sosa 2002, 265.

8. See Lycan 2001, 42–46.

9. We should not get hung up on the inference. It is apparent that even if we disallow the simplification, (T**) is satisfiable, and so, the bit of reflective knowledge in question is possible. See note 11.

10. Here I merely suppose that believing a conjunction entails believing each of the conjuncts. This is more plausible than unrestricted closure principles for belief since, arguably, believing conjuncts is constitutive of believing a conjunction.

11. Notice that if counterfactuals with disjunctive antecedents do not simplify, we need to evaluate (T**),

$(\sim Bp \vee \sim p) \; \square\!\!\rightarrow \; \sim B(Bp \; \& \; p)$

as it stands, unsimplified. On the standard Lewis/Stalnaker semantic, this requires that we go to the closest $(\sim Bp \vee \sim p)$-world and determine whether it is a $\sim B(Bp \; \& \; p)$-world. The closest $(\sim Bp \vee \sim p)$-world is either the closest $\sim Bp$-world or it is the closest $\neg p$-world. If the former, the satisfiability of (T**) hangs on the satisfiability of (T**2). If the latter, the satisfiability of (T**) hangs on the satisfiability of (T**1). As we have seen (T**1) is satisfiable, and so is (T**2). But then, either way (T**) is satisfiable.

References

David, M., and T. Warfield. 2008. "Knowledge-Closure and Skepticism." In Q. Smith, ed., *Epistemology: New Philosophical Essays*. Oxford: Oxford University Press.

DeRose, K. 1995. "Solving the Skeptical Problem." *Philosophical Review* 104: 1–52.

Dretske, F. 1971. "Conclusive Reasons." *Australasian Journal of Philosophy* 49: 1–22.

Hawthorne, J. 2004. *Knowledge and Lotteries*. Oxford: Oxford University Press.

Lycan, W. 2001. *Real Conditionals*. Oxford: Oxford University Press.

Nozick, R. 1981. *Philosophical Explanations*. Cambridge, Mass.: Harvard University Press.

Sosa, E. 1996. "Postscript to 'Proper Functionalism and Virtue Epistemology.'" In J. Kvanvig, ed., *Warrant in Contemporary Epistemology: Essays in Honor of Plantinga's Theory of Knowledge*. Lanham, Md.: Rowman & Littlefield.

Sosa, E. 2002. "Tracking, Competence, and Knowledge." In P. Moser, ed., *The Oxford Handbook of Epistemology*. Oxford: Oxford University Press.

Vogel, J. 1987. "Tracking, Closure, and Inductive Knowledge." In S. Luper(-Foy), ed., *The Possibility of Knowledge: Nozick and His Critics*. Lanham, Md.: Rowman & Littlefield.

Vogel, J. 2000. "Reliabilism Leveled." *Journal of Philosophy* 97: 602–623.

Vogel, J. 2004. "Varieties of Skepticism." *Philosophy and Phenomenological Research* 68: 1–37.

Warfield, T. 2004. "When Epistemic Closure Does and Does Not Fail: A Lesson from the History of Epistemology." *Analysis* 64: 35–41.

4 Contextualism, Skepticism, and Warranted Assertibility Maneuvers

Duncan Pritchard

Contextualism and Warranted Assertibility Maneuvers

Attributer contextualists maintain that 'knows' is a context-sensitive term in the sense that sentences of the form "*S* knows that *p*" (call this the 'ascription sentence') will have different truth-values depending on the context of utterance (which will, of course, be the *attributer's* context). One interesting consequence of the contextualist thesis is that assertions of the very same ascription sentence can simultaneously express a truth and a falsehood relative to two different contexts of utterance,[1] and it is this component of the thesis that enables it to offer a compelling response to the problem of radical skepticism, by accommodating our apparently conflicting intuitions in this regard.

In particular, it offers a straightforward explanation of why it is that (1) outside of contexts[2] in which we are actively considering skeptical doubts, we are perfectly happy (*ceteris paribus*) to ascribe a great deal of knowledge to agents, and yet (2) once we begin to seriously consider skeptical doubts (and thus enter skeptical contexts) we are inclined to withdraw such ascriptions. Since we can stipulate that the epistemic position of the agents under consideration is fixed, it seems that one of these intuitions must be wrong. Either we are (in nonskeptical contexts) wrong to ascribe knowledge to agents, or (in skeptical contexts) we are wrong to withdraw such ascriptions and regard the agents in question as lacking knowledge. Contextualism tries to tread an irenic path here by maintaining that, suitably qualified, *both* of these intuitions can be accommodated. In particular, contextualists typically argue that, because of the context-sensitivity of 'knows', relative to the quotidian epistemic standards at issue in nonskeptical contexts, assertions of ascription sentences will (*ceteris paribus*) express truths; while relative to the epistemic standards at issue in skeptical contexts, assertions of those same ascription sentences will express falsehoods.[3]

There are a number of lines of criticism that have been leveled against contextualist theories of this sort,[4] but perhaps the most immediate worry one might have about the view is that it confuses changes in the conditions under which it is conversationally appropriate to assert ascription sentences with changes in the truth conditions of those sentences. That is, it might be argued by the skeptic that although it is conversationally inappropriate, in nonskeptical contexts, to deny that agents have knowledge, this is not because such denials are false. Similarly, an anti-skeptic who was not persuaded by contextualism might well contend that while it is conversationally inappropriate to ascribe knowledge to agents in skeptical contexts, nevertheless those agents do possess the knowledge that is being ascribed to them.

Keith DeRose (1999, secs. 8–10; 2002, secs. 1.2–5) has argued against this "conversational" defense of an "invariantist" (i.e., noncontextualist) construal of the term 'knows' by placing three constraints on proposals of this sort (what he calls "Warranted Assertibility Manœuvres," or "WAMs" for short). First, that it must be inappropriate to both assert the sentence in question *and* to assert its denial. Second, that the WAM must be able to explain the impropriety of the assertion in terms of the generation of a false implicature. And finally, that the false implicature should be explained in terms of a general rule of conversation rather than in terms of an *ad hoc* rule that is specific to that particular case.

To illustrate how these conditions work, DeRose contrasts a successful WAM with one that is unsuccessful. In the former case, the WAM is being employed in order to explain why assertions of sentences of the form "It's possible that P_{ind}"[5] can seem false when they are asserted by an agent who knows the proposition in question. For example, suppose I know that your umbrella is in the broom cupboard but, when asked, reply that "It's possible that your umbrella in the broom cupboard." The idea is that such an assertion is not false, but it is conversationally inappropriate because it generates a false conversational implicature to the effect that one does not know P.

This WAM meets the three conditions set down. It meets the first condition because in this case it seems just as improper to assert, "It's *not* possible that your umbrella is in the broom cupboard." And it meets the second and third conditions because it appeals to a general conversational principle—the "assert the stronger" principle—in order to explain why a false conversational implicature is being generated here (that one lacks knowledge of where the umbrella is). If you know that the umbrella is in the broom cupboard, but you merely make the logically weaker (yet true) claim that it is possible that it is there, then your assertion will generate the false conversational implicature that you do not know where the umbrella is because if you did then you would say so.

DeRose contrasts this use of a WAM with a WAM that is employed in order to defend the thesis that the truth conditions of "*S* is a bachelor" do not contain any condition to the effect that *S* is unmarried. The intuition that when one asserts this sentence about a married man one asserts something false is then explained away in terms of how assertions of this sentence in these situations are conversationally inappropriate even though what is being asserted is nevertheless true. Clearly, this WAM does not meet the three conditions that DeRose identifies. While it is indeed conversationally inappropriate to assert the sentence in question when it applies to a married man, it is not conversationally inappropriate to assert its negation (i.e., "*It is false* that *S* is a bachelor"). Indeed, such an assertion seems entirely appropriate. Second, the explanation of why this claim is conversationally inappropriate does not make appeal to the generation of a false conversational implicature. DeRose (1999, 199; cf. DeRose 2002, sec. 1.4) calls this strategy a "bare warranted assertibility manœuvre" on the grounds that it "simply explains away the problematic intuitions of falsehood by claiming that the assertions are unwarranted . . . without further explaining *why*." And even if the strategy were to incorporate a claim about how these assertions generate false conversational implicatures, it would then become susceptible to the third constraint that the conversational rules at issue should not be *ad hoc*, and it is difficult to see how the account can meet this challenge.

DeRose further argues that the invariantist response to contextualism is a version of a "bad" WAM, like the bachelor case.[6] There are two sorts of invariantism that are possible here—an *anti-skeptical* invariantism which argues that assertions of the relevant ascription sentences will (tend to) express truths in all contexts, and a *skeptical* invariantism which argues that assertions of ascription sentences will express falsehoods in all contexts.[7] In both cases, contrary intuitions will need to be explained away using a WAM.

As regards the anti-skeptical WAM that will be required, DeRose argues that it faces the following problems. First, it will have to explain not only why assertions of ascription sentences seem to be both conversationally inappropriate and express falsehoods in skeptical contexts, but also why assertions of the negations of those ascription sentences seem to be both conversationally appropriate and express truths in those same contexts. That is, it will have to explain not only why an assertion of, say, "Keith knows that he is in his study" made in a skeptical context seems to be both conversationally inappropriate and express a falsehood, but also why an assertion of "*It is false that* Keith knows that he is in his study" made in the same context seems to be both conversationally appropriate and express a truth.

Second, DeRose contends that this strategy will typically take the form of a "bare" WAM and will hence be as a result subject to the second constraint on "good" WAMs. Moreover, he argues that insofar as a further account is given, then this will tend to appeal to conversational principles that are specific to the case of 'knows', such as "If someone is close enough, for present intents and purposes, to being a knower, don't say that she doesn't know, but rather say that she knows" (DeRose 1999, 201).[8]

DeRose further maintains that similar objections will also apply to any WAM that the skeptic puts forward.[9] So while DeRose thinks that there are situations in which WAMs can be legitimately employed in order to explain away the appearance of truth (or falsity), he argues that there isn't a legitimate WAM available that can be put into service by the invariantist. His claim is thus that, as far as the linguistic data is concerned at any rate, contextualism has a considerable, if not decisive, theoretical advantage over invariantism.

The Prospects for an Anti-Skeptical WAM

I will be taking issue neither with the constraints that DeRose imposes on "good" WAMs nor with the conclusions that DeRose draws from the contrast he makes between the "good" and the "bad" WAM discussed in the last section.[10] Instead, I will be arguing that there is a WAM available that supports the invariantist thesis and which meets these three constraints. Since our anti-skeptical intuitions are clearly much stronger than our skeptical intuitions, the invariantist WAM that I will focus upon is one that supports an *anti*-skeptical version of the invariantist thesis.

The prospects for mounting a successful anti-skeptical WAM against contextualism are considerably enhanced by a feature of our use of the term 'knows' in skeptical contexts that contextualists like DeRose overlook. This is that when first faced with a skeptical argument the normal response is not to *reverse* one's assessment of an agent's epistemic position (and thus to start asserting the negations of the ascription sentences that one was previously willing to assert), but rather to simply *withdraw* those ascriptions— that is, to be reluctant to continue to assert them. More specifically, in skeptical conversational contexts it seems inappropriate and false *either* to assert that an agent has knowledge *or* to assert that the agent lacks knowledge, particularly when the agent in question is the person making the assertion.[11]

We will look at why this is the case in a moment. First, however, it is important to note that this feature of the linguistic data enables the proponent of an anti-skeptical invariantist WAM to meet DeRose's first condition on "good" WAMs. *Contra* DeRose, what is required is not an account that explains away both the apparent falsity and conversational impropriety of an assertion of an ascription sentence (i.e., "Keith knows that he is in his study") *and* the apparent truth and conversational propriety of an assertion of the negation of this ascription sentence (i.e., "*It is false that* Keith knows that he is in his study"), but only an account that explains the former. In particular, what we need is a description of what is happening in the skeptical context that explains why agents would be disinclined to assert anything of substance in that context. As we will see, the key seems to lie in how skeptical contexts explicitly consider the truth or otherwise of radical skeptical hypotheses, such as the hypothesis that one is presently a brain-in-a-vat (BIV) being "fed" one's experiences by neuroscientists.

Of course, contextualists will no doubt be inclined to simply deny this claim that agents tend to withdraw rather than reverse their assertions of ascription sentences when they enter skeptical contexts. Crucially, however, the difference between contextualists and anti-skeptical invariantists on this score does not merely reduce to a clash of intuitions, since the contextualist is under an obligation to at least *partially* accept the opposing intuition in this regard. The reason for this is that while contextualists have tended to focus on assertions of ascription sentences where knowledge is being ascribed to a third person (call these "third-person ascription sentences"), another common feature of our practices of ascribing knowledge concerns *self*-ascriptions of knowledge. Although this can be done explicitly, via sentences such as "I know that I am in my study" (call these "explicit self-ascription sentences"), more typically it is done less directly via the simple assertion of the embedded proposition, in this case via the assertion of the sentence "I am in my study" (call this a "simple self-ascription sentence").

The problem facing contextualists is that while the issue of whether we withdraw our assertions where an ascription of knowledge is explicitly involved is (by their lights) moot, the issue of whether we withdraw our assertions of simple self-ascription sentences is not moot at all (by anyone's lights). That is, in response to a mere change in the context a simple self-ascription sentence that was once assertible might well be no longer assertible, but this will not mean that the relevant contrary sentence (i.e., *"It is false that P"*) will become assertible. And given that assertions of simple self-ascription sentences are only withdrawn in response to mere changes in the context, rather than reversed, the natural question to ask is why the context-sensitivity of the propriety of assertions of ascription sentences should not simply be explained in terms of the shifting propriety conditions of the embedded proposition rather than in terms of any more robust thesis regarding the context-sensitivity of 'knows'. As DeRose puts the point (which he terms the "Generality Objection"):

Since "P" becomes unassertible in high-standards contexts even though there is no change in its content as we move into the high-standards context, and since the drift towards the unassertibility of "S knows that P" as we move into more demanding contexts is just what we would expect given that "P" displays a similar drift, why suppose the unassertibility of the knowledge claim in high contexts is due to a change in content *it* undergoes as we move into such contexts? According to the Generality Objection, there is no good reason to suppose there is such a variation in truth-conditions of knowledge attributions. (2002, sec. 1.5)

DeRose's response to this problem has been to combine his critique of the invariantist WAM with a commitment to the knowledge account of assertion. This latter thesis maintains that when one asserts a proposition, one represents oneself as knowing that proposition, such that the overriding rule of assertion is to only assert what one knows.[12] On a contextualist reading, the knowledge account of assertion takes on a relativized form such that "To be positioned to assert that P, one must know that P according to the standards for knowledge that are in place as one makes one's assertion" (DeRose 2002, sec. 2.2), where the applicable standards will, of course, be variable in the manner that contextualism maintains.

While the knowledge account of assertion is itself a contentious thesis, by combining his contextualism with this view DeRose is seemingly able to offer an ingenious solution to the Generality Objection. If to assert that *P* is to represent oneself as knowing *P*, and if the standards for knowledge are context-sensitive, then it follows that it is little wonder that the assertibility of *"P"* should be context-sensitive. In epistemically undemanding contexts, *"P"* will (tend to) be assertible, whereas in epistemically demanding contexts it won't (tend to) be assertible. And note that this result is achieved without stipulating anything about how the truth conditions for assertions of simple self-ascription sentences change merely in response to conversational factors. On the contextualist account, our willingness to withdraw assertions of sentences of this sort in response to changes in the context indicates our implicit recognition that changes in the context can affect the epistemic standards in play and thus whether or not the assertion of that sentence is conversationally appropriate.

Moreover, although DeRose himself does not appear to have noticed this, one of the immediate consequences of adopting the knowledge account of assertion is that a skeptical invariantist WAM is not going to be available. After all if one should only assert P when one knows that P then, given that knowledge is factive (in that one can only know that P where P is true), the knowledge account of assertion will straightforwardly rule out the possibility that one could properly assert P even though P is false, and this would be a central component of any skeptical invariantist WAM.[13] It seems then that DeRose has not only found a way of dealing with the Generality Objection, but has also aligned his view with an account of assertion which excludes a skeptical invariantist WAM from ever getting off the ground.

Responding to the Linguistic Data

We can take the following claims to capture the agreed-upon features of the linguistic data in this dispute:

1. Agents withdraw (but do not reverse) their assertions of simple self-ascription sentences when they move from a quotidian to a skeptical context.
2. Agents *at the very least* withdraw their assertions of third-person and explicit self-ascription sentences when they move from a quotidian to a skeptical context.
3. Agents do not assert ascription sentences (including simple and explicit self-ascription sentences) which involve skeptical hypotheses in any context.

We have already remarked on (1) and noted that while contextualists will accept (2) they will want to add that agents do more than merely withdraw their assertions, claiming instead that agents actually reverse them (i.e., assert the relevant contrary sentence). (3) has been implicit in much of what we have been discussing so far, in that all parties to this dispute grant that there is something about the assertion of an ascription sentence involving a skeptical hypothesis that entails that (*ceteris paribus*) the context is now (if it wasn't already) a *skeptical* context. Note that while it is usually the *denials* of skeptical hypotheses that will be at issue in this regard (such as when one asserts "I am not a BIV," or "*S* knows that she is not a BIV"), what is important is only that it is the truth or otherwise of a skeptical hypothesis that is in question. The thought is that the mere raising of this issue changes the context to a skeptical context.

With the agreed-upon linguistic data so characterized, the first task in hand is to determine whether there is an alternative explanation available, which does not make use of the knowledge account of assertion, as to why the propriety-conditions for assertions of simple self-ascription sentences shift in response to changes in the context. In particular, what is required is an account of why the propriety conditions for assertions of this sort are affected by the move to a context in which the truth of a skeptical hypothesis is at issue.

In order to see why the introduction of a skeptical hypothesis could affect the propriety of one's assertions, one needs to consider how the conversational propriety of assertions is constrained by the Gricean conversational maxim of evidence, which demands that agents should not make assertions if they are unable to back-up that assertion with adequate evidence (see Grice 1989, 26). What counts as 'adequate' evidence in this regard will, however, be a context-sensitive matter. In particular, as we will now see, regarding the assertion of the same sentence the evidential demands in skeptical contexts are greater than in nonskeptical contexts.

Suppose that an agent asserts, in a nonskeptical quotidian context, "I am in my study," perhaps because she wants to indicate to someone in another room of the house where she is. The maxim of evidence demands that this assertion be backed up by the appropriate evidence which, in this context, would normally only require such relevant evidence as to indicate that she is in the study *as opposed to*, for example, the kitchen. Here, basic perceptual evidence would typically suffice to rule out these "local" error-possibilities. Accordingly, the conversational implicature generated by this assertion that our agent has adequate evidence to back-up her assertion will generally be true.

Compare this example with a situation in which our agent asserts the following anti-skeptical sentence, 'I am not a brain-in-a-vat', perhaps in response to a skeptical challenge raised in an epistemology seminar. The problem with an assertion of this sort is that there are *no* adequate grounds that can be offered in support of it, since one does not possess adequate reasons for thinking that one is not a BIV (which is what ensures the enduring attraction of skeptical arguments).[14] Accordingly, this assertion will inevitably generate the false conversational implicature that one is able to adduce these grounds. As a result, such an assertion is conversationally inappropriate in *all* contexts (i.e., it is *in principle* conversationally inappropriate). And note that the same goes for assertions of the contrary sentence, 'I *am* a brain-in-a-vat'.

The interesting case, however, is the assertion of a "nonskeptical" sentence—that is, one that does not explicitly or implicitly concern a skeptical hypothesis, such as the example given above, 'I am in my study'—in a *skeptical* context, such as one in which the BIV skeptical hypothesis is at issue. Crucially, the relevant grounds that need to be offered in support of this assertion in this context are far more demanding, since now our agent needs to offer evidence in support of her assertion which supports what is asserted (that she is in her study) *as opposed to* the skeptical hypothesis under consideration (that she is a BIV). And since grounds of this sort are in principle unavailable, assertions of nonskeptical sentences in skeptical contexts will inevitably generate false conversational implicatures and thus be conversationally inappropriate. Moreover, notice that what applies to an assertion of the sentence 'I am in my study', will apply with just as much force to an assertion of the sentence 'I am *not* in my study'. Accordingly, it is little wonder that in skeptical contexts agents only withdraw assertions of simple self-ascription sentences that they would ordinarily assert in nonskeptical contexts, rather than reversing those assertions.

In any case, even setting aside the role of this conversational maxim as regards assertions of simple self-ascription sentences, asserting the denial of what one previously asserted purely in response to conversational factors would offend against what I will refer to as the "commitment" principle. In general, this is the principle that in asserting a proposition one is thereby committing oneself to that proposition, where this means that, all other things being equal, one is obliged to "stick with" what one has asserted in all subsequent contexts.[15] An assertion thus generates the conversational implicature that one has this commitment to the proposition asserted. Accordingly, the assertions of agents who lack this kind of commitment to what they assert—such that they are willing to reverse their assertions in response to mere changes in the context—will generate false conversational implicatures and so will be conversationally inappropriate.[16]

Note, however, that it does not follow from this principle that agents should be willing to continue (*ceteris paribus*) to assert what they are committed to in all subsequent contexts because, as we have seen, there can be conversational constraints in play which make even true assertions unassertible. If one is in a context in which the assertion of the sentence, 'I am in my study', carries the anti-skeptical conversational implicature that one has evidence in favor of this assertion that suffices to eliminate the skeptical error-possibilities under consideration in that context, then one ought not to make the assertion. Nevertheless, given that, *ex hypothesi*, all that has changed is the context, the agent's previous assertion of this proposition in a nonskeptical context brings with it a commitment to the proposition asserted which carries over to the current skeptical context (albeit in a tacit form).

When it comes to assertions of simple self-ascriptions of knowledge, then, there is a WAM available that can meet the three conditions that DeRose sets down on "good" WAMs but which does not employ a contextualized version of the knowledge account of assertion. It meets the first condition because the problem assertions in question are just as problematic when one deals with assertions where the sentence at issue is negated. Moreover, it meets the second and third conditions because it employs general conversational maxims and principles in order to explain the inappropriateness of the assertions in terms of the generation of false conversational implicatures.

Applying the WAM to Other Assertions of Ascription Sentences

Given this *impasse* between contextualists and anti-skeptical invariantists as regards the best interpretation of the linguistic data when it comes to assertions of simple self-ascription sentences, the issue then becomes whether we can extend this WAM so that it applies to assertions of explicit self-ascription sentences and third-person ascription sentences.

At first pass, one might think that the WAM just described as regards assertions of simple self-ascription sentences will straightforwardly apply, *a fortiori*, to assertions of explicit self-ascription sentences as well. That is, the natural thought would be that by asserting the logically stronger claim, the agent thereby incurs additional commitments and evidential burdens such that insofar as the weaker assertion is conversationally inappropriate, then the stronger assertion will be even more so. In terms of assertions of nonskeptical explicit self-ascription sentences (such as 'I know that I am in my study') in skeptical contexts, and skeptical explicit self-ascription sentences (such as 'I know that I am not a brain-in-a-vat') in any context, this is certainly true. Complications arise, however, once one notices that one cannot simply apply the WAM set out above to explain why assertions of the relevant contrary assertions are also (in certain contexts) conversationally inappropriate, such as the assertions "I do *not* know that I am in my study," or "I do *not* know that I am not a brain-in-a-vat." The reason for this is that, unlike contrary assertions in the case of simple self-ascription sentences, these contrary assertions are not assertions about the *falsity* of the embedded proposition, but merely concern the epistemic status of the agent's belief about this proposition. Accordingly, we cannot explain their conversational impropriety by citing, as we did above, the agent's lack of relevant evidential grounds in support of the assertion of the *opposing* proposition in the context in question.

Nevertheless, although the maxim of evidence does not gain a purchase on this issue of why such contrary sentences can be unassertible, the commitment principle does still have application in this case. Indeed, since the propositions expressed by explicit self-ascription sentences are logically stronger than those expressed by the counterpart simple self-ascription sentences, one would naturally expect there to be a greater level of commitment involved in the former case.[17] With such a commitment in play, while agents might not continue to assert the explicit self-ascription sentences that they previously asserted because of changes in the context, they won't assert anything that they are aware directly conflicts with their previous assertions (such as "I do not know that I am not a brain-in-a-vat"), much less will they tend to reverse their previous assertions (and thus assert, for example, "I do not know that I am in my study") merely in response to changes in the context.[18]

Of course, the contextualist response to this will no doubt be to claim that what the agent is committed to is simply the proposition at issue, and that it is part of their thesis that the proposition that is being expressed in each case is different. Accordingly, while agents should retain their commitment to the propositions expressed by assertions of explicit self-ascription sentences in quotidian contexts even when they enter skeptical contexts, this is consistent with them asserting the relevant contrary sentence in the new context because in doing so they are signaling their lack of commitment to a *different* proposition.

While there is nothing wrong with this move, it does alter the dialectical landscape somewhat. What we were promised were considerations which demonstrated that there was linguistic data which was firmly on the side of the contextualist, whereas what we have ended up with is merely the claim that there is *an* interpretation of the relevant linguistic data, that is consistent with contextualism. A supposedly knock-down argument against invariantism has thus become an argument to the effect that the relevant linguistic data alone doesn't entail the invariantist view. Intuitively, this weaker claim isn't something that the invariantist should be overly concerned about, since it simply means that the battle between contextualists and invariantists needs to be fought on other grounds, and here one would expect invariantists to be in a strong position. In any case, the invariantist cause has turned out to be a lot better off than was advertised by DeRose.

Finally, we can extend the WAM under consideration here to third-person ascription sentences, such as the nonskeptical sentence 'Keith knows that he is in his study'. Notice that the evidential burdens incurred by assertions of this sort do not merely relate to the ascription of knowledge itself, but also to the embedded proposition (in this case, that Keith is in his study), since the truth of this proposition is part of the truth conditions for this sentence as a whole. As a result, in order to properly assert this sentence, agents not only need to be able to offer relevant evidence in favor of the knowledge ascription, but also in favor of the embedded proposition. In this sense, then, assertions of third-person ascription sentences, like assertions of explicit self-ascription sentences, are logically stronger than assertions of simple self-ascription sentences and thus incur greater evidential burdens. Accordingly, the considerations offered above as regards the conversational impropriety of certain assertions of simple self-ascription sentences will have even greater force when it comes to (1) assertions of nonskeptical third-person ascription sentences (e.g., 'Keith knows that he is in his study') in skeptical contexts, and (2) assertions of skeptical third-person ascription sentences (e.g., 'Keith knows that he is not a brain-in-a-vat') in all contexts.

As with assertions of explicit self-ascription sentences, however, one cannot simply adduce the maxim of evidence in order to explain why the relevant contrary sentences in this case are not assertible, because these assertions do not entail the falsity of the embedded proposition. Just as with assertions of explicit self-ascription sentences, however, the commitment principle *will* be applicable here to account for why agents do not in skeptical contexts assert anything that directly conflicts with what they previously asserted in a nonskeptical context (e.g., 'Keith does not know that he is not a brain-in-a-vat'). Still less will they explicitly reverse their previous assertions in response to a mere conversational change (e.g., 'Keith does not know that he is in his study').

Again, contextualists can respond to this claim by maintaining that by their lights the proposition that the agent is committed to is not inconsistent with the proposition expressed in the new context by the agent's assertion of the relevant contrary sentence. But as we saw above, this move simply highlights the fact that what they are presenting here are merely grounds for the claim that there is a stand-off between invariantism and contextualism when it comes to the linguistic data, as opposed to the stronger contention which was supposed to be on offer—namely, that the linguistic data are firmly on the side of contextualism.

Concluding Remarks

So despite DeRose's claims to the contrary, there is a WAM available that can meet the three conditions that he sets down. The considerations that DeRose offers in favor of a contextualist—as opposed to an anti-skeptical and invariantist—interpretation of the linguistic data are thus indecisive, and hence whatever the other merits of the contextualist approach (and demerits of the anti-skeptical invariantist stance), one cannot evade the challenge that the anti-skeptical invariantist WAM presents contextualism via the argument that DeRose offers.

Acknowledgments

Thanks to Peter Bauman, Jessica Brown, Keith DeRose, Michael O'Rourke, and two anonymous referees for this volume who each read and commented on an earlier draft of this paper. Earlier versions of this paper were presented at the Pacific APA meeting in San Francisco in March 2003, at the NAMICONA conference on *Modalism and Mentalism* in Copenhagen in January 2004, and at the Inland Northwest Philosophy Conference on *Knowledge and Skepticism* in Moscow, Idaho, and Pullman, Washington, in May 2004. I am grateful to my audiences on these occasions, especially Kent Bach, Tim Black, Tom Blackson (who was also my commentator at the APA session), Tony Brueckner, Joe Campbell (who also chaired the Inland Northwest session), Stew Cohen (who also chaired the APA session), Mylan Engel, Mikkel Gerken, Patrick Greenough, Lars-Bo Gundersen, Vincent Hendricks, Jesper Kallestrup, Ram Neta, Patrick Rysiew (who was also my commentator at the Inland Northwest session), and Jonathan Schaffer. Finally, I have also benefited from discussions on this topic with Martijn Blaauw, and by the award of a Leverhulme Trust Special Research Fellowship that has enabled me to conduct work in this area.

Notes

1. Here, for example, is Cohen (2000, 94):

I...defend the view that ascriptions of knowledge are context sensitive. According to this view, the truth-value of sentences containing the words "know," and its cognates will depend on contextually determined standards. Because of this, such a sentence can have different truth-values in different contexts. Now when I say "contexts," I mean "contexts of ascription." . . . This view has the consequence that, given a fixed set of circumstances, a subject S, and a proposition p, two speakers may say "S knows that p," and only one of them thereby say something true. For the same reason, one speaker may say "S knows p," and another say "S does not know p," (relative to the same circumstances), and both speakers thereby say something true.

It is this feature of the view that distinguishes attributer-contextualist theories from subject-contextualist theories, as advanced, for example, by Williams (1991). For discussion of this contrast, see DeRose 1999, sec. 4, and Pritchard 2002b. Henceforth, when I use 'contextualism', I will have attributer contextualism in mind.

2. Following most attributer contextualists, by 'context' here I mean (at least primarily) *conversational* context.

3. Numerous versions of contextualism of this sort have been proposed in the recent literature, with each version of the thesis incorporating a specific account of, *inter alia*, the mechanisms that raise and lower the epistemic standards. See especially DeRose 1995, Lewis 1996, and Cohen 2000.

4. For the main discussions of contextualism in the recent literature, see Schiffer 1996, Feldman 1999, Heller 1999, Vogel 1999, Fogelin 2000, Sosa 2000, and Pritchard 2001. For a partial survey of the literature on contextualism in general, see Pritchard 2002a, secs. 5–7; 2002b.

5. The subscript here is meant to indicate that the proposition in question is to be understood in the indicative mood.

6. Interestingly, DeRose's focus when it comes to the invariantist WAM is not on how this proposal works in *skeptical* contexts at all, but on how it would function in nonskeptical contexts where the epistemic standards are "high" (such as contexts in which a lot hangs on the correctness of the knowledge ascription). Quite reasonably, DeRose (2002, sec. 1.1) motivates this focus on nonskeptical but epistemically demanding contexts by contending that we want contextualism to be motivated on grounds independent of the skeptical problem. This way of putting matters tends to assume that the considerations that indicate that an invariantist WAM is problematic when it comes to nonskeptical but epistemically demanding contexts will be just as applicable when it comes to skeptical contexts. As I argue below, however, there are good reasons for thinking that there is an invariantist WAM that meets the conditions that DeRose lays down for it when it is applied to skeptical contexts. If this is right, then that an invariantist WAM is implausible in nonskeptical "high"-standard contexts will not in itself suffice to motivate the application of its rival theory, contextualism, to the skeptical problem. Since one of the chief advantages of contextualism is meant to be its resolution of the skeptical problem, this is a major difficulty for the view. At any rate, I won't be questioning here DeRose's claim that the invariantist WAM is implausible in nonskeptical "high"-standard contexts, although I do think that this claim is problematic and that the considerations offered here will have application to assertions of ascription sentences in nonskeptical

"high"-standard contexts. In what follows, I will take DeRose's remarks about invariantist WAMs to be directly applicable to the issue of how those WAMs function in skeptical contexts.

7. Unger (1971; 1975) endorses a version of the skeptical invariantist position, and Stroud (1984, chap. 2) expresses sympathy with the general skeptical line. In later work, Unger's (1984) position evolves into a third type of position that we might term 'quasi-invariantism'. According to this view, there are no grounds for preferring an anti-skeptical contextualist thesis over a skeptical invariantist thesis.

8. DeRose has Unger's (1975) version of invariantism specifically in mind here.

9. DeRose does argue, however, that the situation is a little more complicated when it comes to the skeptical WAM proposed by Unger (1975; cf. Unger 1971) because he motivates an invariantism-based skepticism via the claim that "knowledge" is an absolute concept like "flat" or "empty." Unger's view thus raises special problems because he is adverting to conversational rules that apply to a fairly wide class of terms.

10. Both of these points have been contested. See, for example, Brown 2003, 2005, and Bach 2004.

11. Black (2002) argues for a similar claim, though on different grounds to those put forward here. The exceptions to this claim are, of course, those agents who respond to the skeptical argument with a reaction of complete defeat, and who are therefore willing to reverse their assertions in the way that DeRose envisages, though this is (in my experience of teaching skepticism, at any rate) rare. Nevertheless, it is important to note that these reactions of defeat do not immediately play into the hands of the contextualist, because such defeatism is most naturally understood as the agent in question *changing her mind* rather than as reflecting the context-sensitivity of 'knows'. That is, one who is genuinely inclined to concede defeat in the face of a skeptical argument will tend to retain this pessimistic judgment about our epistemic position in nonskeptical contexts, at least until she convinces herself that she was right all along. Accordingly, that agents are liable to change their minds does not in itself lend support to contextualism.

12. The key discussion (and defense) of the knowledge account of assertion in the recent literature (and the discussion that DeRose has in mind), is Williamson 2000a, chap. 11 (cf. Williamson 1996).

13. For more on this point, see Brown 2003, 2005.

14. At any rate, contextualists are usually happy to grant this feature of the skeptical argument. Cohen (1988, 111; 1999, 67) notes, for example, that radical skeptical hypotheses such as the BIV hypothesis are "immune to rejection on the basis of any evidence." Accordingly, one of the key difficulties facing contextualism is to explain how agents can have knowledge of the denials of skeptical hypotheses even at "low"

epistemic standards. For discussion of this issue, see Cohen 1999; 2000, 103–106, and DeRose 2000; cf. Williamson 2000b.

15. The commitment principle is closely bound up with the conversational maxim that one should only assert what one believes to be true (though note that, for Grice [1989, 26], this maxim is understood as the slightly weaker "Do not say what you believe to be false"). Since believing that P is itself a form of commitment to P—and moreover a commitment that, if genuine at all, is not easily lost—then arguably one could just as well focus on the close relationship between belief and assertion. One finds discussions of this general commitment that is incurred by assertion in a number of places, though perhaps the most famous recent discussion is Brandom 1994, chap. 4 (cf. Brandom 1995).

16. It should be noted that there is an issue here as to whether Grice would agree that this is a genuine conversational implicature, since he tends to employ this term in such a way that it excludes commitments that are trivially generated by the cooperative principle and the associated conversational maxims (see Grice 1989, 41–42). Nevertheless, Grice is not always consistent on this point and there are places where he seems willing to countenance a broader sense of conversational implicature that includes these direct implicatures. Moreover, since DeRose has argued elsewhere for a broad reading of the notion of conversational implicature, it ought not to be problematic to adopt this reading in this regard (see DeRose and Grandy 1999, notes 13 and 19).

In general, the account of a conversational implicature that 'I am employing here is more relaxed than that which Grice had in mind in his official pronouncements on this topic. For example, it is essential to Grice's conception of a conversational implicature that the assertion in question be in apparent tension with the cooperation principle, and yet many of the implicature-generating assertions that I focus on here are not so in tension (e.g., 'I am in the study', uttered in a normal conversational context). Nevertheless, this more relaxed conception of conversational implicature (at least in this respect) is quite common in the literature, and so ought not to be objectionable here.

Relatedly, a (defeasible) test that Grice offered for conversational implicature questions was whether they could be comfortably cancelled, and yet a number of the implicatures that I describe are not comfortably cancellable. To assert "P, but I am unable to offer any (relevant) evidence in support of this claim" is puzzling to say the least. Nevertheless, we should be careful about reading too much into this. As even DeRose admits (DeRose and Grandy 1999, note 13), when it comes to very direct implicatures such as this it becomes increasingly difficult to cancel them (the extreme case being the Moorean paradox where one asserts "P, but I don't believe that P"), and even Grice (1989, 46) conceded that not every implicature can be comfortably cancelled.

Interestingly, Cohen (1999, 60) has been one commentator who, in response to remarks made by Sosa, has argued that the play with implicatures will not work because such implicatures are *not* comfortably cancellable. The putative implicature of a claim to know that Cohen focuses on is that there is no need for further investigation, which is a very different implicature from those which are considered here. Accordingly, Cohen could be right that this putative implicature cannot be comfortably canceled without this generating problems for the approach sketched above. In any case, as I have just noted, even if one grants that the implicatures in question cannot be comfortably cancelled, one should be cautious about drawing any dramatic conclusions from this observation. For further critical discussion of Cohen's remarks in the respect, see Rysiew 2001, sec. 7.

17. This intuition is borne out by many of the standard discussions of assertions of explicit self-ascription sentences. Here, for example, is Austin (1961, 99; author's italics): "When I say, 'I know', I *give* others my word: I *give* others *my authority for saying* that 'S is P'." And Austin is not alone in advancing this performative thesis as regards assertions of explicit self-ascription sentences—one can find similar claims in, for example, the work of A. J. Ayer (1956, chap. 1) and Wittgenstein (1969).

18. Unless, of course, they are convinced by the skeptical argument, in which case they incur a commitment to the proposition expressed by the contrary sentence when they return to a nonskeptical context.

References

Austin, J. L. 1961. "Other Minds." In J. Urmson and G. Warnock, eds., *Philosophical Papers*. Oxford: Clarendon Press.

Ayer, A. J. 1956. *The Problem of Knowledge*. Harmondsworth: Pelican.

Bach, K. 2004. "The Emperor's New 'Knows'." In G. Preyer and G. Peter, eds., *Contextualism in Philosophy: On Epistemology, Language and Truth*. Oxford: Oxford University Press.

Black, T. 2002. "Skepticism and Warranted Assertibility Manœuvres." Typescript.

Brandom, R. 1994. *Making It Explicit*. Cambridge, Mass.: Harvard University Press.

Brandom, R. 1995. "Knowledge and the Social Articulation of the Space of Reasons." *Philosophy and Phenomenological Research* 55: 895–908.

Brown, J. 2003. "Contextualism and Warranted Assertibility Manœuvres." Typescript.

Brown, J. 2005. "Adapt or Die: The Death of Invariantism?" *Philosophical Quarterly* 55: 263–286.

Cohen, S. 1988. "How to Be a Fallibilist." *Philosophical Perspectives* 2: 91–123.

Cohen, S. 1999. "Contextualism, Skepticism, and the Structure of Reasons." *Philosophical Perspectives* 13: 57–89.

Cohen, S. 2000. "Contextualism and Skepticism." *Philosophical Issues* 10: 94–107.

DeRose, K. 1995. "Solving the Skeptical Problem." *Philosophical Review* 104: 1–52.

DeRose, K. 1999. "Contextualism: An Explanation and Defense." In J. Greco and E. Sosa, eds., *The Blackwell Guide to Epistemology*. Oxford: Blackwell.

DeRose, K. 2000. "How Can We Know That We're Not Brains in Vats?" *Southern Journal of Philosophy* 38: 121–148.

DeRose, K. 2002. "Assertion, Knowledge, and Context." *Philosophical Review* 111: 167–203.

DeRose, K., and R. Grandy. 1999. "Conditional Assertions and 'Biscuit' Conditionals." *Noûs* 33: 405–420.

Feldman, R. 1999. "Contextualism and Skepticism." *Philosophical Perspectives* 13: 91–114.

Fogelin, R. 2000. "Contextualism and Externalism: Trading in One Form of Skepticism for Another." *Philosophical Issues* 10: 43–57.

Grice, H. 1989. *Studies in the Way of Words*. Cambridge, Mass.: Harvard University Press.

Heller, M. 1999. "The Proper Role for Contextualism in an Anti-Luck Epistemology." *Philosophical Perspectives* 13: 115–130.

Lewis, D. 1996. "Elusive Knowledge." *Australasian Journal of Philosophy* 74: 549–567.

Pritchard, D. H. 2001. "Contextualism, Scepticism, and the Problem of Epistemic Descent." *Dialectica* 55: 327–349.

Pritchard, D. H. 2002a. "Recent Work on Radical Skepticism." *American Philosophical Quarterly* 39: 215–257.

Pritchard, D. H. 2002b. "Two Forms of Epistemological Contextualism." *Grazer Philosophische Studien* 64: 19–55.

Rysiew, P. 2001. "The Context-Sensitivity of Knowledge Attributions." *Noûs* 35: 477–514.

Schiffer, S. 1996. "Contextualist Solutions to Scepticism." *Proceedings of the Aristotelian Society* 96: 317–333.

Sosa, E. 2000. "Skepticism and Contextualism." *Philosophical Issues* 10: 1–18.

Stroud, B. 1984. *The Significance of Philosophical Scepticism*. Oxford: Clarendon Press.

Unger, P. 1971. "A Defense of Skepticism." *Philosophical Review* 80: 198–219.

Unger, P. 1975. *Ignorance: A Case for Scepticism*. Oxford: Clarendon Press.

Unger, P. 1984. *Philosophical Relativity*. Oxford: Blackwell.

Vogel, J. 1999. "The New Relevant Alternatives Theory." *Philosophical Perspectives* 13: 155–180.

Williams, M. 1991. *Unnatural Doubts: Epistemological Realism and the Basis of Scepticism*. Oxford: Blackwell.

Williamson, T. 1996. "Knowing and Asserting." *Philosophical Review* 105: 489–523.

Williamson, T. 2000a. *Knowledge and Its Limits*. Oxford: Oxford University Press.

Williamson, T. 2000b. "Scepticism, Semantic Externalism, and Keith's Mom." *Southern Journal of Philosophy* 38: 148–157.

Wittgenstein, L. 1969. *On Certainty*. G. E. M. Anscombe and G. H. von Wright, eds. D. Paul and G. E. M. Anscombe, trans. Oxford: Blackwell.

5 Knowledge In and Out of Context

Kent Bach

We can be willing in one context to attribute a bit of knowledge that we wouldn't attribute and might even deny in another, especially a context in which we're stumped by a skeptical argument. Apparently, our standards for knowledge sometimes go up, sometimes way up. How can this be? By claiming that the very contents of knowledge-ascribing sentences vary with contexts of use, epistemic contextualism offers one explanation. I will offer another. According to contextualism, variation in standards is built into this claimed variation in contents. According to me, the contents of knowledge attributions are invariant. The variation is in what knowledge attributions we're willing to make or accept. Sometimes our standards are too strong, sometimes they're too weak, and sometimes they're just right.

Contextualism aims both to acknowledge and to escape the force of skeptical arguments. Consider these seemingly paradoxical reflections of David Lewis's:

When we do epistemology, we make knowledge vanish. First we do know, then we do not. But I had been doing epistemology when I said that. The uneliminated possibilities were not being ignored—not just then. So by what right did I say even that we used to know? In trying to thread a course between the rock of fallibilism and the whirlpool of scepticism, it may well seem as if I have fallen victim to both at once. For do I not say that there are all those uneliminated possibilities of error? Yet do I not claim that we know a lot? Yet do I not claim that knowledge is, by definition, infallible knowledge? I did claim all three things. But not all at once! (1996, 566)

Contextualism is an ingenious way out: What counts as knowledge varies with the context in which it is attributed. More precisely, what so varies is the relation is expressed by the word 'knowledge' (or 'know'). So, depending on the context in which a sentence of the form 'S knows that p' is used, different relations between S and p are attributed.[1]

At first taste this idea is not easy to swallow. Despite the age-old difficulty of defining propositional knowledge, it still seems that the truth of a statement made using a sentence of the form 'S knows (at t) that p' depends at least on whether it is true that p, whether S believes that p, and whether S's belief that p is adequately supported *and* that it does not at all depend on any facts about the person making the statement or on the context in which he is making it.[2] Why should it? Intuitively, it does not seem that the verb 'knows' expresses different relations in different contexts. So, for example, it seems that there is a unique proposition expressed by the sentence, 'Eminem knew on December 31, 1999 that Detroit was in Michigan,' namely, the proposition that Eminem knew on December 31, 1999 that Detroit was in Michigan. There do not seem to be even two different relations expressed by 'know', such that on that date Eminem knew$_1$ this but didn't know$_2$ it. In this respect, 'know' is very different from other allegedly context-sensitive terms such as 'poor', 'tall', and 'flat'.[3] With those terms, it takes just a little reflection on usage to be convinced that they can each express different properties. You don't need to be presented with arguments to appreciate this, but with 'know' you do (assuming you are ultimately persuaded by contextualist arguments). So, at the very least, 'know' is not a typical context-sensitive term.[4]

Leaving that detail aside, notice that contextualism about 'S knows that p' does not concern the context of S (assuming the attributor is distinct from S). S's circumstance does not affect the content of a knowledge attribution, but it can affect the truth-value (for example, S may be in a Gettier situation). Indeed, a new rival to contextualism, known as Subject-Sensitive Invariantism, goes so far as to suggest that practical importance to the subject, and perhaps even mere salience to him, can affect the truth-value of a knowledge attribution. Another recent view, put forward by John MacFarlane (2005), is that the truth-value of a knowledge attribution is not absolute but relative. Here there is no suggestion that the content of the knowledge attribution varies but only that its truth-value does, and that it varies not with the context of utterance but rather with the context of assessment. These two views raise interesting questions in their own right, but it is only contextualism that implies that the *content* of a knowledge attribution can vary, specifically, with facts about the context in which it is made.[5]

In what follows, I will (1) explain why the contextualist anti-skeptical strategy is based on an illusion that the propositions expressed by knowledge-ascribing sentences are themselves context-bound, (2) point out also that contextualism underplays the significance of skepticism, (3) offer a straightforward alternative to the contextualists' interpretation of what's going on in their pet examples, (4) argue that the special features of their examples, practical interests and salience, do not directly affect people's epistemic position, (5) point out that, nevertheless, the salience of a possibility to a person can provide evidence for its relevance and that its nonsalience can function as tacit evidence for its irrelevance, and (6) suggest that what contextualists assume to be categorical knowledge attributions may really be attributions of conditional knowledge, or else conditional attributions of knowledge. Although much of the following discussion is rather critical, I think the issues raised by contextualism are highly instructive and the challenges it poses are well worth confronting. So the discussion will also be constructive.

1   Making It Explicit: The Trouble with Contextualism's Anti-Skeptical Strategy

Suppose that 'knows' is context-sensitive, as contextualists maintain. Even so, it would not follow that the propositions expressed, relative to contexts, by sentences of the form 'S knows that p' are themselves context-bound. This crucial point is generally overlooked or at least not highlighted by contextualists. The point bears repeating: Even if contextualism were true, so that a given knowledge-ascribing *sentence* could express various propositions in various contexts, those *propositions* would not themselves be context-bound. To the contrary, each such proposition could be expressed by a more elaborate knowledge-ascribing sentence in which 'knows' is explicitly indexed or relativized to whatever it is that is supposed to vary with the context. Suppose it is an epistemic standard E.[6] Then *each* such proposition would be expressible in *any* context by the same more elaborate, context-insensitive sentence of the form 'S knows-by-E (at t) that p'.[7] It just has to be spelled out.

Contextualists neglect this crucial point when they implement their strategy for explaining the lure of skeptical arguments and resolving skeptical paradoxes. This neglect fosters the false impression that somehow the different propositions (allegedly) expressible (at a given time) by a given sentence of the form 'S knows that p' cannot be considered in the same context. Contextualists exploit this impression when they compare knowledge attributions made in ordinary contexts with those made in skeptical or otherwise more stringent contexts.[8] As I will now explain, once it is clear that distinct propositions—say, the propositions that Eminem knew-by-E_1 that Detroit was in Michigan, and the proposition that

Eminem knew-by-E_2 that Detroit was in Michigan—*can* be considered in the same context, the contextualist strategy for both explaining and neutralizing the lure of skeptical arguments loses its bite.

What is the contextualist strategy?[9] Consider the claim that Moore knew he had at least one hand, which to most people seems undeniable. The skeptical paradox arises from the fact that people are also moved by skeptical arguments, such as those based on far-fetched but seemingly hard-to-rule-out possibilities. One such possibility is that Moore was a bodiless (and hence handless) brain-in-a-vat—in short, a BBIV. In light of this possibility, the skeptic proposes an argument like this:

Skeptical Argument
If Moore knew he had at least one hand, then Moore knew that he wasn't a BBIV.
Moore didn't know that he wasn't a BBIV.

Moore didn't know that he had at least one hand.

Since this argument is formally valid, the only direct way to rebut it is to reject one of its premises, but that is not the contextualists' approach. Their strategy is more subtle, aiming to expose an alleged equivocation on the word 'know'. The equivocation is not across steps of one argument, but rather across contexts. That is, the above wording of what appears to be a single Skeptical Argument masks different arguments, each expressible by the same sentences used in different contexts. Each such argument is valid, but at most one is sound, and this one has no drastic skeptical consequences. The above form of argument is sound only if 'know' is applied according to the highest epistemic standards, but those standards are operative only in a "skeptical" context, a context in which skeptical considerations and far-fetched possibilities (such as the BBIV) are raised. In an ordinary, less demanding context, where 'know' expresses a weaker relation, a different argument is on the table.[10] The argument in that context is unsound, because its second premise is false.[11]

So contextualists respect skeptical intuitions as well as commonsense, Moorean ones, but deny that these intuitions conflict. They thereby reject a more straightforward assessment: Intuitions that give rise to skeptical paradoxes really do conflict and thus do not settle questions as to the truth-values of knowledge attributions; rather, they comprise genuinely competing responses to skeptical considerations. Besides, people don't feebly capitulate to skeptical arguments like the one stated above, but tend to vacillate. They go back and forth between finding the argument hard to refute and finding its conclusion hard to swallow. Their resistance to its conclusion cannot be written off as a Humean lapse into an ordinary, nonskeptical context, for it occurs while skeptical possibilities are firmly in mind. So it seems that contextualists are not really entitled to rely on their intuition that knowledge attributions made in skeptical contexts are false.

But suppose they are so entitled. In claiming that the conclusion of the Skeptical Argument in a skeptical context is compatible with the claim made in an ordinary context that Moore knew he had hands, the contextualist has to concede that people not privy to contextualism do not realize that the relation expressed by 'know' can shift with context.[12] After all, they are taken in by the Skeptical Argument—at least enough to take it seriously, and without any sense that the subject has been changed. By allowing the skeptical argument to call into question the ordinary claim that Moore knew he had hands, they both mistakenly and unwittingly take it be one and the same thing—namely, knowledge—that is at issue from context to context. So contextualism is a kind of error theory. To be sure, people will make and accept ordinary knowledge claims once they're removed from a skeptical context (does this require a bit of amnesia?), but that only compounds the error, since they do not realize that what they're now willing to accept as true is not the same proposition as the one they rejected in the skeptical context. So the contextualist claim that people's contrasting intuitions seem to but don't really conflict, requires that people don't notice these contextual shifts in the relation that is expressed by 'knows'.

This is clear when we apply our earlier observation that even if standard knowledge-ascribing sentences are context-sensitive, the different propositions they supposedly express in different contexts are not themselves context-bound. We can make explicit two different arguments, one presented in an ordinary context and one in a skeptical context, which both take the form of the Skeptical Argument, so that both may be stated in any context, including this one. Let knowledge-by-ordinary-standards be expressed by 'knows$_o$', and knowledge-by-skeptical-standards by 'knows$_s$'. Then the two arguments take the following forms:

Skeptical Argument in an ordinary context
If Moore knew$_o$ he had at least one hand, then Moore knew$_o$ that he wasn't a BBIV.
Moore didn't know$_o$ that he wasn't a BBIV.

Moore didn't know$_o$ that he had at least one hand.

and

Skeptical Argument in a skeptical context
If Moore knew$_S$ he had at least one hand, then Moore knew$_S$ that he wasn't a BBIV.
Moore didn't know$_S$ that he wasn't a BBIV.

Moore didn't know$_S$ that he had at least one hand.

There is now no question of unwittingly shifting from one context to another and thereby confusing the Skeptical Argument in a skeptical context with the Skeptical Argument in an ordinary context. We can just look at the two arguments together, regardless of our context, and evaluate the two of them. Now assume that contextualists' intuitions about the truth-values are correct. Then the first argument is unsound, since its second premise is false. Moore *did* know$_o$ that he had at least one hand. But the second argument is sound, since its second premise is true; or at least the second argument will seem sound, and seem irrefutable, to anyone moved by skeptical considerations and unable to rebut its second premise. But the conclusion of the second argument is relatively innocuous, since it denies only that Moore *knew$_S$* (knew by the most demanding standards) that he had at least one hand.

So the contextualist strategy for resolving the skeptical paradox loses its bite once we use different phrases, 'knows by ordinary standards' and 'knows by skeptical standards' or, as above, abbreviate these phrases with the help of different subscripts. Since everything is now out on the table, we can intuit without conflict that there are lots of things we can know by ordinary standards even if we can't know them by skeptical standards—assuming, of course, that there are different knowing relations. Later (in section 3) we will see that there is no reason to concede this, but first let's look further at contextualism's attempt to marginalize skepticism.

2 Facing Up to Skepticism

In attempting to confine the plausibility of skeptical arguments to contexts in which far-fetched skeptical possibilities are raised, contextualism doesn't really do justice to those arguments, however cogent or fallacious they may be. Hilary Kornblith's title, "The Contextualist Evasion of Epistemology," is apt, for skeptical arguments purport to show that *ordinary* knowledge attributions are generally false.[13] The contextualist's attempt to marginalize these arguments by restricting them to skeptical contexts ignores the fact that skepticism denies that we have knowledge even by ordinary standards. How assiduously people *apply* epistemic standards may vary from context to context, but the skeptic denies that the standards themselves come in various strengths. When a skeptic brings up far-fetched possibilities and argues that we can't rule them out, he is not raising the standards for what it takes to belong to the extension of the word 'knowledge'. Rather, he is using these possibilities to show that it is much tougher than we realize for a belief to qualify as knowledge at all, that is, to have the one property actually and ordinarily expressed by the word 'knowledge'. He is not proposing to reform its meaning. He is recommending that we keep using it to mean what it ordinarily means but use it much more carefully, even if it turns out rarely to apply.

In light of this, must the invariantist capitulate to skepticism? No, because invariantism is a semantic thesis about 'know', not a substantive theory of knowledge. Even so, the invariantist needn't be completely neutral, and has a way of countering the lure of skeptical arguments. When we are confronted with what we ordinarily take to be far-fetched sources of error, in effect we are asked to imagine ourselves, with our current experiences, (apparent) memories, and beliefs, being plunked into a world of we know not what sort. It could be a dream world or a demon world, a BBIV or a *Matrix* world, or any of a whole host of others. Or it could be a world of just the sort we think we're in. But we're not supposed to have any prejudices about what sort of world we're being plunked into (or, as the skeptic would rather put it, about what sort of world we're actually in). Since each of these possible worlds is consistent (let's assume) with our having the perceptual and memory experiences and beliefs that we have, there is nothing to make the world as we commonly conceive of it epistemically special in any way.[14] It's just one of those countless sorts of worlds, any one of which we could be plunked into. So of course we can't tell which one we're in or whether it's at all like the world we think we're in.

This explains why skeptical arguments, as inspired by Descartes' systematic doubt, are so seductive—but it doesn't show that they are any good. Yes, it's true that if we were suddenly plunked into a world, we wouldn't be able to tell what sort of world we were in. But that's not our situation. To know in this world, it is not necessary to be able to discriminate between the different possible worlds we might be in. It is not necessary to know that we're not in a world where we would be chronically prone to undetectable and uncorrectable error, at least not if knowing this requires going out and verifying that we're not. True, a skeptical scenario would seem no less absurd if we were in it than it does in fact, but that doesn't show that it is not in fact absurd. The fact that there are possible worlds in which we would know very little does not show, or even suggest, that we are in such a world. Knowledge may not be as easy to come by as people casually suppose, but to be in a world which is stable in various fundamental respects, with which we informationally interact in clearly explicable ways, and in which we communicatively interact to transmit information successfully, such that a great many of our expectations and intentions appear to be fulfilled, is to be in a world in which there is plenty of knowledge to be had. Although our evidence does not deductively eliminate the possibility that we live in some sort of fanciful skeptical world, skeptical arguments offer no reason to suppose that we do. And, if only because of the intractable computational complexity required to maintain such a world, these worlds are far more improbable than Hume thought miracles to be.

Whether or not this is even the beginning of a good answer to the skeptic, at least it doesn't accuse of skeptic of changing the subject. It does concede to the skeptic that if we were BBIVs, we would take our epistemic position with respect to things we claim to know to be as good as we actually think it is, and no doubt the skeptic would pounce on that. However, the skeptic has a similar basis for responding to the contextualist. He could point out that if contextualists were BBIVs, they would still believe that 'know' is context-sensitive and base this belief on the same intuitions that they actually rely on. But in that case the intuition that many of our ordinary knowledge attributions are true would be mistaken. Yet 'know' would mean the same thing as it does in what we take to be the actual world.

At any rate, there is one thing that everyone can agree on: The sorts of possibilities used to support skeptical arguments have to be so sweeping that no kind or amount of further inquiry can eliminate them. It's inherent in these possibilities, as standardly laid out, that any inquiry aimed at ruling them out is vulnerable to the same or similar possibilities, so that no progress in ruling them out can ever be made. In this important respect, they are unlike the sorts of error-possibilities we take seriously in everyday life, which we can and do take effective measures to rule out. However, contextualists do not rely solely on the contrast between ordinary and skeptical contexts, between contexts in which we take much for granted and those in which everything is up for grabs. It's a key part of their strategy to invoke a different contrast, between ordinary undemanding contexts and merely *relatively* demanding ones, where people feel they need to eliminate realistic possibilities of error.

3   An Invariantist Take on the Bank and Airport Cases

Whether skepticism is refutable or merely indefensible, you don't have to be a skeptic to be an invariantist, certainly not for the purpose of rebutting contextualism. From here on I will go along with contextualists' assumption that a good many of the knowledge attributions we make are true, at least in ordinary contexts. However, I will offer a moderate (nonskeptical) invariantist alternative to their interpretation of the high-standards versions of their pet examples.

Their most well-known examples are Keith DeRose's Bank case (1992, 913) and Stewart Cohen's Airport case (1999, 58). I will assume that the reader is familiar with the details. In each case we are asked to make an intuitive comparison between a knowledge attribution made in a normal, low-standards context and one made in a high-standards but nonskeptical context. It is assumed that the subject has the same evidence in both the low- and the high-standards version of each case and that the attributor's evidence is essentially the same (identical or at least of equal strength) as the subject's. Even so, according to contextualists' intuitions, whereas the knowledge attribution made in the normal, low-standards context is true, the one made (using the same knowledge-ascribing sentence) in the high-standards context is false.[15]

Contextualists contend that these contrasting intuitions do not really conflict and can both be correct, because 'know' is context-sensitive so that the truth conditions of knowledge-ascribing sentences can vary with the context in which they are used. I think there's a simpler, more straightforward interpretation, according to which the two intuitions really do conflict, just as they seem to, and hence cannot both be accepted as correct.[16] On this interpretation, what varies with context is the attributor's threshold of confidence. In the high-standards context, it is raised; either a practical concern or (in skeptical cases) an excessive epistemic demand leads the attributor to demand more evidence than knowledge requires. In contexts where special concerns arise, whether practical or skeptical, what varies is not the truth conditions of knowledge attributions but the knowledge attributions people are prepared to make. What goes up is not the standard for the truth of a knowledge attribution, but the threshold of confidence the attributor has to reach to make such an attribution.

Consider the contextualist characterization of the high-standards Airport case, in which Mary is unwilling to assert that Smith knows that the plane will stop in Chicago. Given how important the Chicago stopover is to Mary, not only does she refrain from attributing knowledge to Smith but, unwilling to take Smith's word as based on his itinerary, she goes so far as to deny that he knows that the plane will stop in Chicago. According to the contextualist, that's because it isn't true that Smith knows this (by high standards). But the moderate invariantist has to say that if Smith knows in the normal, low-standards case, he knows in the high-standards case too, even if Mary is not prepared to say that he does. How could this be?

Mary is making a mistake, albeit a very understandable one. It is because of her own doxastic situation that she does not say, "Smith knows that the plane will stop in Chicago," and indeed goes so far as to assert its negation. Because she is not sure his itinerary is reliable, she herself does not believe, at least not confidently, that the plane will stop in Chicago. So she can't coherently attribute knowledge of it to Smith, not if knowledge implies truth. In general, you can't coherently assert that someone else knows that p if you are not confident that p and think it still needs to be verified. Not only can't Mary very well assert that Smith knows that the plane will stop in Chicago, she has to deny that she knows it, since she thinks it is not yet established. And, since Smith has no evidence that she doesn't have, she must deny that he knows it either.

Now what is essential here is not the attributor's lack of settled belief, but her raised threshold for (confidently) believing.[17] Before believing the proposition in question, at least with the confidence and freedom from doubt necessary for knowing, the attributor demands more evidence than knowledge requires. Look at what happens, in the high-standards version of the Airport case, when Mary checks further until she is satisfied that the plane will stop in Chicago. She will then believe that it will stop there and will think that she knows this. However, she still won't concede that Smith knows this and indeed will still deny that he does, given that his epistemic position is no better than hers was. Now the explanation for her denial is not that she doesn't believe it herself but, rather, that her threshold of confidence has gone up.

One's threshold for (confidently) believing a proposition is a matter of what one implicitly takes to be adequate evidence. I say "implicitly" because people generally do not reflect on such things. Even if in fact one is in a position to know something, thinking one is not in a position to know it is enough to keep one from believing it (confidently) and to lead one, if it matters enough, to look into it further. When one does look further and verifies the proposition to one's satisfaction, one implicitly takes oneself now to be in a position to know it and continues to regard one's prior, weaker position as inadequate. So one cannot consistently take someone else, who was in and still is in that weaker position, to know it. In consistency, one must regard him as not knowing it.

It might seem that I have merely described in different terms what the contextualist describes as raising the standards on knowledge attributions. However, my account does not imply a shift in their contents. I have simply pointed out a constraint on what it takes for an attributor coherently to make a knowledge attribution to someone else who has certain evidence, given the attributor's doxastic stance relative to the same evidence. Here's a way to put the difference between the contextualist view and my own. Considering that attributing knowledge that p requires confidently believing that p, I am suggesting that willingness to attribute knowledge tracks not the standards on the truth of a knowledge attribution but one's threshold of doxastic confidence. In the so-called high-standards cases, the attributor's confidence threshold goes up to the point that without additional evidence she implicitly, but mistakenly, thinks she is not in a position to know. In high-standards Airport and Bank cases, a special practical interest makes it more difficult than normal for the attributor to have a settled belief in the relevant proposition and, accordingly, raises her bar for attributing knowledge to someone else. Even so, that person knows.

Now let us consider what happens when a skeptical possibility is raised. It could be a general skeptical possibility, such as victimization by an Evil Demon, or one specific to the case, say a rumor that disgruntled travel agents are distributing inaccurate itineraries. Does merely raising such a possibility, without making it plausible, turn a true knowledge attribution into a false one? Making it salient does not do that.[18] As Patrick Rysiew (2001) has shown, making it salient can affect only the assertibility of the knowledge attribution, because attributing knowledge pragmatically conveys that a newly raised possibility has been ruled out.[19] Raising plausible possibilities, on the other hand, indicates genuine doubts or worries on the attributor's part and may lower the audience's confidence level accordingly. Moreover, if these plausible possibilities are objective ones, in which case they bear on the subject's epistemic position, and if the subject's epistemic position is not strong enough to rule them out, then the subject does not know, quite independently of the attributor's context. So the truth condition and the truth-value of a knowledge attribution is not affected by the epistemic standards that prevail in the context of attribution. All that is affected is the attributor's willingness to make it and the audience's willingness to accept it, as the result of their confidence threshold having been raised.

We are now in a good epistemic position to meet a challenge posed by DeRose for moderate invariantism in its effort to account for intuitions about ordinary and high-standards knowledge attributions. He writes,

[Invariantists] have to explain away as misleading intuitions of truth as well as intuitions of falsehood. For in the "low standards" contexts, it seems appropriate and it seems true to say that certain subjects know and it would seem wrong and false to deny that they know, while in the "high standards" context [as in the Bank case], it seems appropriate and true to say that similarly situated subjects don't know and it seems inappropriate and false to say they do know. Thus, whichever set of appearances the invariantist seeks to discredit—whether she says we're mistaken about the "high" or the "low" contexts—she'll have to explain away both an appearance of falsity and (much more problematically) an appearance of truth. (DeRose 2002, 193)

The problem here is that DeRose accepts the appearances at face value.[20] Moderate invariantists should accept intuitions about ordinary knowledge attributions at face value, but should reject DeRose's intuitions about the "high-standards" Bank case (where the cost is high of the bank not being open on Saturday). The attributor's high stakes (on Friday) when asserting or accepting as true "Keith knows that the bank is open on Saturday" do not translate into higher standards for its truth. Rather, she has good practical reason, because of the cost of him being wrong, not to take Keith's word for it that the bank is open on Saturday. Given this, she doesn't accept his statement as true without checking further; so she can't consistently accept or assert "Keith knows that the bank is open on Saturday."

Moderate invariantists should also reject the intuition that knowledge denials involving skeptical possibilities are true. The moderate invariantist should not concede that there is something right about the intuition that Moore does not know he is not a BBIV and that an utterance of 'Moore does not know that he is not a BBIV' is true, at least in an epistemic context. Rather, he should insist that Moore does know he is not a BBIV, and that the intuition that he doesn't is based on the false assumption that in a skeptical scenario Moore's epistemic situation would be no different. To be sure, Moore doesn't have evidence that he would not have if he were a BBIV, but that doesn't matter. The intuition that some people have that it does matter seems to be based on a leap, from the obvious truth that Moore, if he were a BBIV, wouldn't know it and would still believe that he is not a BBIV, to the conclusion that in fact he doesn't know he's not a BBIV.[21] If he were a BBIV, there would be lots of things he wouldn't know, even if the world were otherwise as much as possible like the actual world, and certainly if it were vastly different. His beliefs are insensitive to the difference. But he can be in a position to know things about the actual world, such as that he has hands and that he is not a BBIV, even if, were the world quite different (or if the causes of his beliefs were quite different, as in a benign-demon world), he wouldn't know very much about it. Only certain sorts of worlds and relations to the world are such that one can know things about that world. The prevalence of massive error in some possible worlds, especially in worlds remote from this one, does not show the real possibility of massive error in the actual world.

Skeptical invariantism is obviously an error theory, and so is contextualism. I gladly concede that as I have defended it, moderate invariantism is an error theory too, but only in a minimal way. According to skeptical invariantism, the knowledge attributions that people ordinarily make are almost all false. According to contextualism, people commonly fail to recognize shifts in the contents of knowledge attributions, and thereby sense contradictions that are not there; indeed, people are even confused about what they themselves mean when they use 'know' in different contexts. But the only sort of error that moderate invariantism (as I have defended it) attributes to people, other than the error of being temporarily taken in by skeptical arguments (and attributing this error is not specific to moderate invariantism), is one of excessive epistemic caution when it comes to believing things with confidence. But such caution has a practical rationale and is therefore not irrational. Sometimes it is reasonable to go beyond the call of epistemic duty.

4 Practical Interests and Knowledge

I have suggested that in the high-standards versions of the Bank and Airport cases, the attributor, having practical reasons for not accepting the proposition in question merely on the basis of the subject's evidence, understandably but mistakenly denies that the subject knows, even though (it is assumed on both sides) the subject's evidence is adequate for knowledge. Given the attributor's practical interests, he deems the subject's evidence to be inadequate. But what about the *subject's* practical interests? Can these, or some other not obviously epistemically relevant aspect of the *subject's* context, affect the truth-value of a knowledge attribution?

That's the idea behind the new "Subject-Sensitive Invariantism" (or SSI). SSI denies that the content (i.e., the truth conditions) of a knowledge attribution is affected by the context of the attributor, but it proposes that the subject's context can matter.[22] SSI is not just another form of relevant alternatives theory. It concerns practical interests, not neutral epistemic reasons. SSI says that the subject's practical interests can make a difference as to whether or not the subject knows. That is, two people can be in identical evidential positions but different epistemic positions, such that one knows a certain thing while the other does not know the counterpart of that thing, and that's because of what is at stake.[23]

Underlying SSI is the crucial assumption that one can't know that p if one has reason to make sure that p. Of course, it is uncontroversial that one can't know that p if one has epistemic reason to make sure that p, but SSI goes further. It supposes one can't know that p just because one has practical reason to make sure.[24] But why suppose this? Or, insofar as we should suppose this, why should it require turning simple invariantism into the subject-sensitive variety? If it is true that p but it makes no difference to you whether or not p, then you are in a position to know that p if you have sufficient epistemic reason to believe it.[25] So how can having some practical interest in whether or not p keep you from being in a position to know that p? How can suddenly caring enough to be disposed to guard against possibilities that ordinarily wouldn't concern you, deprive you of that knowledge?

How this is possible is obvious from the previous section's discussion of the Bank and Airport cases: Your practical interest may lead you to want to make sure that p before you act on the supposition that it holds true. As a result, you don't yet believe that p, at least not with confidence, and wish to guard against certain possibilities of error. This means that you don't yet know that p. The reason for this is not that you have insufficient epistemic reason for believing that p, but that you don't meet the doxastic condition on knowing. So cases of this sort do not support SSI.

A different situation arises if you do have a settled and confident belief that p. Even then, given the cost of being wrong you may think that you need to make sure that p, by ruling out certain possibilities of error that would ordinarily be too remote even to consider, much less bother with. But this sort of situation does not support SSI either. Rather, it shows that one can know that p even if one has reason to make sure that p, contrary to the crucial assumption underlying SSI. Again, this is because of the cost of being wrong. It is rational to check further for essentially the same reason that it is rational to make a small bet against something you know if the payoff is large enough.[26] Thinking you might be wrong is compatible with knowing. What is not compatible with knowing is having a specific reason for thinking you might be wrong. But there's nothing irrational about recognizing one's fallibility and the general possibility of error. It might be odd to say, "I know but I need to make sure," but in this case it makes sense. Similarly, it would be coherent for an observer of the situation to say, "He knows, but he ought to check further." That would ordinarily sound odd, but not in this case. So, contrary to the assumption underlying SSI, having practical reason to make sure that p is compatible with knowing that p. When it keeps one from knowing that p, this is only because it keeps one from meeting the doxastic condition on knowing.

What about salience? Can the mere fact that a counterpossibility to p is brought up, or comes to mind, keep one from knowing that p? Can this do for a subject's epistemic position what contextualists think it can do for an attributor's? Hawthorne briefly considers the possibility that salience "destroys" belief or at least weakens it enough to destroy knowledge, but he rightly sees that this is no problem for simple invariantism, since it "hardly takes us beyond the factors traditionally adverted to in accounts of knowledge, given the centrality of the belief condition to standard accounts" (2004, 173).[27] Nevertheless, there is an epistemic role for salience (of a possibility of error), but one that also comports with simple invariantism. It is a role that Hawthorne himself considers but does not pursue, that "salience destroys knowledge by providing counterevidence" (2004, 172). As we will see next, sometimes it does, but only sometimes.

5 The Significance of Salience

There is more to be said about the interaction between one's doxastic state and one's epistemic position and about how this bears on what one is prepared to say about someone else's epistemic position. Pretty much everyone, contextualist and invariantist alike, agrees that knowing that p requires that one's experience/evidence/justification rule out counterpossibilities (these can be alternatives to p or threats to the basis for one's belief that p). There is plenty of dispute about how best to formulate this, especially if one rejects the skeptic's insistence that knowing requires ruling out all such possibilities. It is common to limit the requirement to ruling out relevant alternatives, and there are different variations on this approach. Typical internal problems for such an approach include spelling out what it is to rule out an alternative, whether it is the subject or his evidence that does this, and, of course, what it is for an alternative to be relevant. It will be instructive to focus on some of David Lewis's reflections in this regard.

Lewis exhorts you to "do some epistemology [and] let your paranoid fantasies rip!" (1996, 559). Okay, let 'em rip. That's what Descartes did with his Evil Demon fantasy, and the BBIV (or the *Matrix*) scenario is just a high-tech version of that. But to imagine yourself in such a scenario is not to take seriously the possibility that you're actually in it. So-called skeptical "hypotheses" are really just fantasies. Getting yourself and your conversational partner to entertain such fantasies may change the context, but it doesn't turn them into real possibilities. It would seem, then, that they can be safely ignored. But for Lewis things are not so simple: "Our definition of knowledge requires a *sotto voce* provision. S knows that P iff S's evidence eliminates every possibility in which not-P—Psst!—except for those possibilities that we are properly ignoring" (1996, 554). Any possibility compatible with the experience (with its having the content that it has) is not eliminated.[28] But there will always be skeptical possibilities, as many and varied as you can dream up, that are compatible with your experience. So if skepticism is to be avoided, they can't count against the truth of ordinary knowledge attributions. But how can they be properly ignored without first being eliminated? For by Lewis's Rule of Attention, "a possibility not ignored at all is *ipso facto* not properly ignored" (1996, 559). So a skeptical possibility once presented cannot properly be ignored. Because it is not eliminated by one's experience, according to Lewis it inevitably "destroys knowledge." As even Lewis's fellow contextualists acknowledge, this requirement makes it too easy for the skeptic: He can prevail just by mentioning far-fetched possibilities. But there is a way around the Rule of Attention.

Suppose that it is not an experience but the person having it that eliminates a possibility (this will simplify our description of the situation). In that case, if the thought of some possibility occurs to you, you have to rule it out—you can't just disregard it. On the other hand, it would seem that you can't rule out a possibility if the thought of it doesn't occur to you. Suppose you're looking at a zebra. If it doesn't occur to you that there might be some cleverly painted mules in the vicinity, you can't very well rule out that possibility. Does this keep you from being in a position to know you're looking at a zebra? Ordinarily you don't have to rule out such a possibility—you have no reason to and there is nothing about your environment that requires you to—and the thought of it doesn't even occur to you. But what if the thought of such a possibility did occur to you? Considering how far-fetched it is, can't you just dismiss it? The mere fact that the thought of it occurs to you shouldn't make it harder to dismiss. Or should it?

Offhand, it might seem that whether or not the thought of a certain possibility occurs to us has no epistemic significance. Possibilities just occur to us, and we should take realistic ones seriously and do what it takes to rule them out. We can just dismiss the far-fetched ones if and when they occur to us. Thinking of them is a distraction and, if chronic, would be a nuisance, but that would be that. We resist making what John Hawthorne calls "anxiety-provoking" inferences (2004, 161) because we take our anxiety, and hence its source, seriously. (Of course, some people are more cautious than others, and each of us is more cautious in some areas than in others.) In fact, however, possibilities don't just occur to us at random. Insofar as our cognitive processes work efficiently and effectively toward our cognitive goals, the fact that a possibility occurs to us provides evidence that it is worth considering. Not only that, the fact that a possibility does *not* occur to us provides evidence that it is *not* worth considering.[29]

If our cognitive processes are operating well, generally the thought of a possibility contrary to something we're inclined to believe occurs to us only if it's a realistic possibility, not a far-fetched one (this is, of course, a matter of degree). This happens, for example, when we recall a bit of information but then think of a plausible alternative. I recall that it was Senator Hruska of Nebraska who said, regarding a Nixon judicial nominee who was widely regarded as mediocre, that mediocre people need to be represented on the Supreme Court. But then I wonder if it wasn't Senator Dirksen of Illinois who said that. Then I think, if it was Dirksen, who was much more well known, I wouldn't have thought it was someone as obscure as Hruska. So I rule out Dirksen and settle on Hruska. We can always conjure up wild possibilities, as in flights of skeptical or paranoid fantasy, but when we're trying to remember some bit of information, trying to identify what we're perceiving, or are engaged in normal inquiry, we take into account only those sorts of possibilities of error that sometimes arise in situations of the sort we're concerned with, and we do so because we rely on our ability to think of them when and only when they are worth taking seriously. So it is the very occurrence of the thought that gives us a reason for considering the possibility being thought of. No wonder, then, that "a possibility not ignored at all is *ipso facto* not properly ignored"! Should it occur to us, we may of course find reason to dismiss it.

Part of cognitive competence in a given area consists in reliably thinking of possibilities of error when they are worthy of consideration, and knowing when to look further before settling into a belief—and in being able to rely on this reliability. Not only that, we implicitly take the nonoccurrence of the thought of a possibility of error to be evidence, albeit highly defeasible, that this possibility is *not* worth considering. After all, we cannot *explicitly* take the *nonoccurrence* of the thought as the evidence that it is, for that would entail thinking of the very possibility in question. We cannot explicitly weigh the evidence that the nonoccurrence of the thought provides, at least not at the time. (Sometimes, in retrospect, we reason that if something was a realistic possibility, it would have occurred to us.) Instead, we rely on the reliability of our tendency to think of error-possibilities when and only when they're worth considering. We implicitly assume that if a given possibility of error deserved consideration, we would have thought of it.

Now what does this suggest about knowledge attributions and the possibilities that come to mind or get brought up in a context of attribution? Let's say that a scenario is epistemically irrelevant to a knowledge attribution if the mere possibility of its obtaining does not affect the truth of that attribution. A scenario can be epistemically irrelevant because it is just a wild skeptical fantasy, whether global or specific to the case, or because, despite the fact that it is something the attributor has practical reasons or bad skeptical reasons for ruling out, it has no bearing on the truth of the knowledge attribution. However, considering what is in fact an epistemically irrelevant scenario gives the attributor reservations about believing the proposition in question and puts the attributor in the position of having to deny that he knows. And, as we saw in section 3, this is enough to put him in the position of refraining from asserting that the subject knows and even of falsely denying that the subject knows. As we can now see, what does this, and what can unsettle the attributor's own belief, is the consideration of a possibility that epistemically is not worth considering.

6   Conditional Knowledge and Conditional Attributions

In section 3 above, I offered an invariantist interpretation of the Bank and Airport cases. This invariantist account does not accept the contextualist intuition that when the standards go up, knowledge attributions that would ordinarily be true are not true, and that the corresponding knowledge denials are true. Instead, it proposes to explain why we are willing to make the knowledge attribution in one context but not in another. Now, partly relying on some ideas from the last two sections, I would like to suggest, without endorsing, two other possible ways of dealing with contextualist data.

Perhaps knowledge is not as easy to come by as we have been assuming. Moderate invariantism does not make a specific claim as to how easy, but in going along with contextualist stipulations I did assume that in the low-standards versions of the Bank and Airport cases the subject really did know. This might be stretching things a bit. You hardly have to be a skeptic to acknowledge that there are plenty of down-to-earth sources of error that we don't guard against most of the time. So perhaps much of what passes for categorical knowledge is really conditional knowledge. That is, when it seems that a person knows that p, it may really be that the person knows that p, if C, where C is a normality condition that is implicitly taken for granted.[30] So, for example, if you've left your car in your driveway, you know that it is in your driveway, provided it hasn't been moved since. You implicitly assume that your car hasn't been stolen, towed away, hit by a runaway truck, etc.[31] And if your knowledge about your car's whereabouts is conditional, perhaps so is Smith's knowledge that his plane will stop in Chicago. Perhaps Smith doesn't categorically know this. Perhaps what he knows is that his plane will stop in Chicago provided the itinerary is accurate, the flight won't be diverted from Chicago because of bad weather (the most likely counterpossibility), and the plane won't crash or be hijacked, etc. Being not a theory of knowledge but a view about the semantics of 'know' (and its cognates and synonyms), moderate invariantism can be neutral about how much of what people are said to know they really do know, and about how much of this is really conditional in content.

Now it might seem extreme to suppose that most of what ordinarily passes for categorical knowledge is really conditional in content. So consider a more modest suggestion. Yes, this knowledge is categorical in content, but its being knowledge is contingent on a normality condition.[32] So whereas the previous idea was that much of what passes for categorical knowledge (that p) is really conditional in content (that p, if C), here the idea is that the knowledge that p is conditional.[33] If so, then many of our ordinary knowledge *attributions*, insofar as they can be deemed true, are best interpreted as conditional on the implicit assumption that things are normal. For example, an utterance of 'Smith knows that the plane will stop in Chicago' is not categorically true, but true only if understood as a loose, casual way of saying, "Provided things are normal, Smith knows that the plane will stop in Chicago." Sometimes, the attributor may even intend this normality condition to be understood, even though it is not part of the explicit, literal content of the attribution.[34]

Each of these suggestions offers an alternative to the contextualist way of explaining how the intuitions that generate the skeptical paradox do not really conflict. Even if the contextualist is correct that they don't, this might not be a matter of 'know' expressing different relations in high-standards and low-standards contexts. On the first suggestion, there is indeed a difference in content between knowledge attributions made using the same knowledge-ascribing sentence in the two contexts, but this difference consists instead in what knowledge is attributed. In low-standards contexts it is conditional knowledge (that p, if C), even though the sentence ('S knows that p') does not make that condition explicit, whereas in high-standards contexts it is unconditional knowledge that p. Alternatively, perhaps the "low-standards" attribution is itself conditional and the "high-standards" one is not. And allowances could be made for intermediate cases by different degrees of strengthening of the condition—either in what is known or in the condition on knowing it.

One complication arises from questions raised by the extended version of what John Hawthorne (2004) calls the "lottery" puzzle. The puzzle, which is not limited to lotteries, is to explain how one can know an "ordinary" proposition but fail to know a related "lottery" proposition, that is, the highly likely proposition that a certain counterpossibility doesn't obtain.[35] The ordinary proposition could be, for example, that your car is in your driveway and the lottery proposition that your car has not been stolen (since you parked it). The puzzle is both to explain and to reconcile the intuitions (preferably without giving up closure) that you know the first but don't know the second and, in particular, to account for the fact that even if do know that your car is in your driveway, you are not entitled to infer from this that your car has not been stolen. The complication, as illustrated by this example, arises from the conflict between two intuitions—that you know your car is in your driveway, and that you do not know it has not been stolen.[36] Taking the intuitions at face value suggests that, somehow, it easier to know that your car is in your driveway than that it has not been stolen. This suggestion seems very odd, especially assuming closure, since it seems that you could not know that your car is in your driveway unless you know that it hasn't been stolen.

With this complication in mind, let's apply the two ideas offered above to this complication. The first idea was that much of what passes for categorical knowledge is really conditional in content. In this example, what you know is not that your car is in your driveway but merely that it is in your driveway if it has not been stolen (pretend that there are no other plausible error possibilities). Insofar as it is reasonable to act on what you know, it is reasonable to act on the supposition that your car is in your driveway even though you don't know that categorically, provided it is reasonable to suppose that your car has not been stolen. For example, if you soon have to get somewhere by car and you're not far from home, it would be reasonable to walk home with the intention of taking your car. However, it would be unreasonable, in order to reduce your premium, to cancel the theft coverage on your auto insurance policy on the grounds that you know that your car is in your driveway (and generally know the whereabouts of your car). This is partially explained by the fact that reasonably acting on the supposition that your car has not been stolen is not predicated on an outright conviction that your car has not been stolen. That proposition is not a lottery proposition with respect to itself. That is, even if knowledge that p if C can pass for knowledge that p, when it is reasonable to assume C, knowledge that C if C obviously cannot pass for knowledge that C.

Now let's apply the second of the above ideas. Saying that S knows that his car is in his driveway could be predicated on the condition that his car hasn't been stolen; but saying that S knows that his car hasn't been stolen couldn't be predicated on the condition that his car hasn't been stolen. Consider that when we evaluate a knowledge attribution and, indeed, when we consider making one and judge whether someone knows a certain proposition, we ask questions of this form: Would S have believed that p even if not-p? As DeRose (1995) makes clear, the possibilities of error that we take into account can vary. In some contexts, and quite apart from the subject's situation, we consider more remote possibilities than in other contexts. That is, sometimes we implicitly assume much less than we do on other occasions, so that more is, so to speak, up for grabs. This is virtually forced upon us when we shift our focus from whether S knows that p to whether S knows that not-e, where e is some possibility of error. For if *we* previously took for granted that not-e when we were otherwise inclined to attribute to S knowledge that p, we can't very well take for granted that not-e when e itself comes into consideration. So if that attribution were implicitly conditional on the supposition that not-e, then naturally we would regard it as true so long as we implicitly assumed that not-e. We would not so regard it, hence would not be inclined to make it, if we no longer implicitly assumed that not-e and regarded this as unsettled. In making this shift, we haven't used 'know' to express a stricter relation than before. Rather, we have gone from presupposing more to presupposing less in regard to the satisfaction of the conditions for S's knowing that p.

The moral of the last two paragraphs is that the data cited by contextualists as being best explained by the supposition that knowledge attributions are context-sensitive, might be better explained in this way: A great many of the knowledge attributions that we are willing to make and to accept are either attributions of implicitly conditional knowledge or are themselves implicitly conditional (insofar as they can be taken to be true). Whether or not either of these ideas is right, they at least suggest alternative ways of accommodating contextualist data without resorting to a contextualist semantics for 'know'.

7 Summing Up

Epistemic contextualism says that in different contexts, 'knows' expresses different relations and simple knowledge-ascribing sentences express different propositions. However, as pointed out in section 1, even if this is correct the propositions thus expressed would not themselves be context-bound. Indeed, they could be made fully explicit by using more elaborate sentences that specify the operative standards (or whatever it is that is supposed to vary with context). Then it would be obvious that these propositions could be compared and evaluated in any context, thus eliminating the surreptitious semantic shiftiness on which contextualism bases its anti-skeptical strategy, and also, as suggested in section 2, neutralizing the contextualist attempt to marginalize skeptical arguments by confining them to skeptical contexts. Even if we cannot consider skeptical arguments in ordinary contexts, since entertaining far-fetched possibilities *ipso facto* puts us in a skeptical context, the propositions that make up these arguments and so the arguments themselves are not context-bound. Either they are sound or they are not, independently of the contexts in which we consider them. However cogent or fallacious these arguments may be, skeptics intend them to show that *ordinary* knowledge attributions are generally false.

Section 3 offered a straightforward invariantist interpretation of the data in the contextualist's high-standards scenarios and in skeptical contexts. What goes up is not the truth condition of the relevant knowledge attribution, but rather the attributor's threshold of confidence. In the problematic scenarios, either a practical consideration or an overly demanding epistemic one raises that threshold and leads the attributor to demand more evidence than knowledge requires. Accordingly, he can't coherently attribute knowledge to someone else even if they have it. Indeed, he must go so far as to deny that they know, since he regards their evidence as being as inadequate for them as it is for himself.

This observation is relevant also to Subject-Sensitive Invariantism, a recent rival to contextualism. A crucial assumption underlying SSI, as pointed out in section 4, is that one can't know that p if one has reason to make sure that p. But this is not because the stakes or salience have raised the evidential bar for knowledge. What is raised, rather, is the subject's confidence threshold for believing. Even if you're in a position to know that p, you don't, because you don't confidently believe that p. Before you can confidently do that you need to check further, until you are satisfied that you have made sure that p.

Section 5 suggested a new twist on Lewis's observation that because what is salient or at stake can differ in the different contexts in which a given knowledge-attributing sentence is used, there is concomitant variation in the sorts of error possibilities that need to be eliminated and in the ones that can be "properly ignored." I pointed out a common but commonly overlooked way in which the consideration or non-consideration of possibilities of error is relevant to having knowledge. In forming beliefs and seeking knowledge, we implicitly rely on our reliability to think of and thereby consider possibilities of error when and only when they are worth considering. Part of what makes beliefs justified is that the cognitive processes whereby they are formed and sustained, at least in areas of cognitive competence, are sensitive to realistic possibilities of error (so-called relevant alternatives). The very occurrence of the thought of such a possibility gives one prima facie reason to take it seriously; and the fact that a particular error-possibility does not come to mind is evidence for its irrelevance. But this fact is evidence that we cannot explicitly consider, since to do so would be to bring the possibility to mind. To the extent that we can trust our ability to know when there are no further error possibilities epistemically worth considering, we don't have to consider them in order to be justified in treating them as not worth considering. This applies equally when we attribute knowledge to others.

Section 6 suggested alternative ways of dealing with the apparently conflicting intuitions that motivate both contextualism and the straightforward alternative that was suggested in section 3. It could be that the contextualist is correct in supposing that the relevant intuitions do not really conflict, while being wrong about why. Perhaps, when a given knowledge-ascribing sentence is used, there is a difference in content between knowledge attributions made in what contextualists describe as high-standards contexts and in low-standards contexts, but it is not a matter of 'know' expressing a different relation. Instead, maybe what is attributed in low-standards contexts is conditional knowledge (although the condition is not made explicit), whereas in high-standards contexts unconditional knowledge is attributed. Alternatively, perhaps "low-standards" attributions are themselves conditional and "high-standards" attributions are not. Either way, the explanation for the difference in intuitive truth-value is that only in the high-standards cases does this condition have to be discharged. Knowledge may not be as difficult to achieve as skeptics imagine or as easy to come by as contextualists allow (in so-called low-standards contexts), but there is nothing shifty in the semantics of 'know'.

Acknowledgments

Many thanks to Tim Black, Jessica Brown, Mark Heller, David Hunter, Ray Elugardo, John MacFarlane, Patrick Rysiew, and Jonathan Schaffer for very helpful comments on a predecessor of this paper, "The Emperor's New 'Knows'," not all of which I could take into account. Tim commented on that paper at the 2004 Inland Northwest Philosophy Conference, and Mark and Jonathan commented on it at the 2004 Bellingham Summer Philosophy Conference.

Notes

1. For this reason, from a contextualist perspective it is misleading to speak of knowledge attributions without qualification. Although I will persist in using the phrase 'knowledge attribution', it would be more accurate, when discussing contextualism, to use more a cumbersome phrase such as 'literal assertive utterance of a "knows"-ascribing sentence'.

2. I will not dwell on the fact that contextualists are not very clear on the semantic nature of this alleged context-sensitivity. Is it indexicality, vagueness, relativity, ambiguity, semantic underdetermination, or what? They sometimes casually speak of 'knows' as an indexical term (not that 'know' behaves like 'I' or 'now'), but sometimes they liken 'know' to relational terms ('local', 'enemy') or gradable adjectives ('tall', 'flat'). Jason Stanley (2004) has forcefully argued that 'know' does not fit any of these models. Perhaps a better model is provided by adjectives like 'eligible' and 'qualified', which connote a threshold that varies, depending on what a person is being said to be eligible or qualified for, but this is not a dependence on facts about the speaker or the context of utterance, at least not in any obvious way. At any rate, contextualists have not yet produced, much less defended, a plausible semantic model for 'know'.

3. That is, even without being ambiguous and even without being understood differently by different people, each such term can be used literally to express any of a range of properties, depending on which standard of application is operative in the context of utterance. It is not that there are different standards of wealth, tallness, or flatness, but rather that there are different standards for applying 'rich', 'tall', and 'flat'. For each term, the particular property thus expressed corresponds to a range on the same scale, and the operative standard determines which range that is.

4. This difference between 'know' and other clearly context-sensitive terms was first pointed out by Stephen Schiffer. As he explains, according to contextualism skeptical puzzles arise because "people uttering certain knowledge sentences in certain contexts systematically confound the propositions that their utterances express with the propositions that they would express by uttering those sentences in certain other

contexts" (1996, 325). Schiffer finds this implausible (whether the claim is that 'know' is ambiguous, indexical, relative, or vague), because contextualism imputes to people (i.e., those not privy to contextualism) a certain semantic blindness about 'know'. Somehow this semantic blindness does not impede their understanding of 'know'; and somehow they do not notice shifts in its use, even when they themselves use it more or less stringently.

5. Here I am going along with the pretense that contextual variability is context-dependence, as if it were context itself that determines the semantic value of a contextually variable expression. In my view, however, it is more accurate to say that the speaker's intention is what determines it and a mistake to count the intention as an element of the context. So, strictly speaking, 'contextualism' is a misnomer. For more on the uses and abuses of context, see "Context *ex machina*" (Bach 2005).

6. Contextualists differ as to what shifts—strength of justification, extent of relevant alternatives, or range of possible worlds in which the truth is tracked (this difference is investigated by Jonathan Schaffer (2005), who argues that what shifts are relevant alternatives). I'll ignore this difference here. Also, it is not obvious that standards, however conceived, form a linear ordering, but assuming that they do simplifies the discussion, as when contextualists speak of epistemic standards being raised or lowered.

7. Since what varies is the standard E, the content of 'knows' as it occurs in the locution 'knows-by-E' is fixed. The idea is that once the locus of contextual variation is identified and the appropriate relativization is made explicit, there is no further need to treat the content of 'knows' itself as contextually variable.

8. Mark Heller is a clear exception. As he explains, when uneliminated possibilities are brought up and the standards are raised, "It is misleading to describe this as a loss of knowledge. Even after the skeptic changes the standards on us, S still has the property that she had before the change of standards. There is no property that she loses" (1999a, 121).

9. The strategy discussed here is developed most fully and clearly by Keith DeRose (1995), and the illustrative argument used here is essentially the same as his.

10. Here we are contrasting skeptical contexts with ordinary, Moorean ones, but the same point applies to more demanding but nonskeptical contexts, in which it is appropriate to raise realistic, as opposed to far-fetched, skeptical possibilities. We will consider those later.

11. The first premise is still true, although its content is not the same as in the skeptical context, since 'knows' now expresses a weaker relation. This assumes a principle of epistemic closure—namely, that knowing that p entails knowing what p entails, or at least what p is known to entail. Closure is accepted by most contextualists, Mark Heller (1999b) excepted.

12. Where the BBIV possibility is not considered, the proposition expressed by the sentence 'Moore didn't know that he wasn't a BBIV' is false. However, in an ordinary context one cannot use that sentence without transforming the context into a skeptical one, in which case one is not expressing the intended proposition, that Moore didn't know-by-ordinary-standards that he wasn't a BBIV. Even so, that proposition, though not expressible by that sentence in a context that is and remains ordinary, is still false.

13. A number of philosophers, including Richard Feldman (1999, 2001), Peter Klein (2000), and Ernest Sosa (2000), as well as Kornblith (2000), have registered this complaint.

14. Here I am ignoring the Putnamesque complication that the contents of our ordinary knowledge attributions would be different.

15. For the sake of discussion, we're assuming that in the low-standards versions of these cases, the relevant attributions are true. You don't have to be a skeptic to think that these standards may be too low, and that the subject does not have knowledge even without the attributor raising the standards. If you think that, then add further stipulations on the low-standards version of the case or else pick a different example, such as one involving ordinary perceptual identification or recollection of a simple fact.

16. In my view there is a general reason not to rely too heavily on seemingly semantic intuitions, namely that they are often responsive to pragmatic factors (Bach 2001); but that is not the problem in the present case.

17. It is interesting to note that when introducing skeptical invariantism, Peter Unger (1971) focused not on the strength of the subject's epistemic position but on the strength of the subject's belief. He did not stress the skeptic's ultra-high standards so much as the strength of the doxastic condition on knowledge, arguing that it requires "absence of doubt or doubtfulness." The idea, I take it, is that the belief be settled (and this assumes that beliefs can be unsettled).

18. Of course, the very fact of its being raised, or its coming to mind and staying there, may make it seem plausible, especially if one doesn't know how to eliminate it. For more on this idea, see section 5 and also Hawthorne 2004, 170–172.

19. As Jessica Brown (2006) points out, before drawing conclusions from their examples contextualists need to control separately for salience and for practical interest. She argues that salience alone does not raise the standards, at least not in the clear way that practical interest does, and she uses this observation to develop a nonskeptical version of invariantism. Her version is a modification of Patrick Rysiew's (2001), who thinks it is salience which affects the knowledge attributions people are willing to make and which bears not on the truth or falsity of the attributions, but on what they pragmatically convey. Brown, like Rysiew, employs warranted assertibility maneuvers or "WAMs," as DeRose (2002) calls them. But these

are sophisticated WAMs, not lame ones of the sort that DeRose thinks moderate invariantism is stuck with. My defense of moderate invariantism in the face of contextualist examples does not rely on WAMs at all.

20. Nichols, Stich, and Weinberg (2003) offer strong evidence that epistemic intuitions are not nearly as universal or robust as contextualists dogmatically assume.

21. Here I am ignoring possible content-externalist differences in his beliefs, and hence in what he represents his evidence to be. It is an interesting question whether issues concerning content-internalism and externalism have any bearing on the debate between epistemic internalists and externalists.

22. The difference between contextualism and SSI is relevant to a new argument for contextualism recently put forward by Keith DeRose (2002), based on Tim Williamson's knowledge account of assertion (2000, chap. 11). As DeRose sums up this argument,

> The knowledge account of assertion provides a powerful argument for contextualism: If the standards for when one is in a position to warrantedly assert that *P* are the same as those that comprise a truth-condition for 'I know that *P*', then if the former vary with context, so do the latter. In short: The knowledge account of assertion together with the context-sensitivity of assertability yields contextualism about knowledge. (2002, 171)

Evidently, for '*P*' to be warrantedly assertible by someone is for that person to know that *P*, since that is the truth condition for one's utterance of 'I know that *P*'. Unfortunately, this "powerful argument for contextualism" applies only to first-person cases, in which attributor and subject are the same (as in DeRose's examples). In such a case, obviously, what makes '*P*' warrantedly assertible by the attributor (i.e., that the *attributor* knows that *P*) is not the truth condition for his utterance of '*S* knows that *P*', since *S* is someone else. So this argument seems not to discriminate between contextualism and SSI. For that reason, I won't consider it further.

Also, although I cannot go into detail on this here, it seems unnecessary to posit what Williamson calls a "knowledge rule" on assertion. It seems to me that the only relevant rule on assertion is belief, since an assertion is essentially the expression of a belief; there is a separate knowledge rule or, rather, norm on belief itself. So the knowledge rule has no independent status—it's the relative product of the belief rule on assertion and the knowledge norm on belief.

23. Jeremy Fantl and Matthew McGrath (2002), John Hawthorne (2004), and Jason Stanley (2005) have argued for this claim in rather different ways and defend different versions of SSI (Hawthorne calls it "sensitive moderate invariantism"). Although these differences are interesting and important, they will not be discussed here, for the point I wish to make is independent of these differences. However, one difference should be noted. In Fantl and McGrath's view and in Hawthorne's (insofar as he actually endorses it), it is what the subject thinks is at stake that matters, whereas in Stanley's view, what matters is what the stakes actually are (even if the subject is unaware of them). The latter view implies, contrary to what I assume

in the text, that there need be no difference in doxastic threshold between the two people being compared. However, I just don't share Stanley's intuition about the relevant cases. It seems to me that one can know something even if, unbeknownst to one, there is good practical reason (because of the cost of being wrong) to make sure. It seems coherent to suppose that a person can know something even if he would be well advised to make sure of it.

24. I am following common usage in contrasting 'practical' with 'epistemic' reasons, but obviously it is misleading, and indeed prejudicial against SSI, to use 'epistemic' here. After all, if, as SSI says, practical reasons can affect whether or not one is in a position to know, they *would* be epistemic (or at least could be).

25. Sufficient on whatever the correct account of knowledge might be. This may include both evidence one possesses and, to allow for Gettier cases, evidence one does not possess.

26. Hawthorne observes that "for pretty much any proposition of which we are convinced, we will be inclined to accept a bet against it given the right odds and reckon ourselves perfectly rational in doing so" (2004, 176 n.), but he does not pursue the possibility that "the sketched connection [based on the assumption underlying SSI] between knowledge and practical reasoning is only roughly correct."

27. Hawthorne adds, "From this perspective, the only mistake made by the simple moderate invariantist is to suppose that belief of the suitable type is invariably present in the puzzle cases we have been considering" (2004, 173), but *we* have not been supposing this.

28. According to Lewis, an experience or memory that P "eliminates W iff W is a possibility in which the subject's experience or memory has content different from P" (1996, 553). Notice that on this conception of elimination, it is the experience, and not the person having it, that eliminates a possibility.

29. This is a kind of default reasoning, whereby we jump safely to conclusions without having to verify the many implicit assumptions that we make, so long as we can rely on our ability to think of those and only those possibilities that are worth considering. I have previously defended this conception of default reasoning (Bach 1984) and used it to defend a form of reliabilism about justified belief (Bach 1985).

30. It is not part of this suggestion that the conditional proposition that is known be explicitly believed. Rather, the idea is that the normality condition is implicitly assumed.

31. The "etc." here goes proxy for other improbable but far-fetched ways in which the normal course of events can be broken, but it does not include skeptical and other fantastic possibilities, such as your car exploding spontaneously or being hoisted by a deranged crane operator on a nearby construction project.

32. One suggestion along these lines, and consistent with the idea of the previous section, is Harman and Sherman's (2004) proposal, that one can know something without knowing the assumptions on which it rests, provided those assumptions are true and one justifiably takes them for granted.

33. This idea comports with any fallibilist theory of knowledge which allows that one can know that p even if there are realistic situations in which someone believing the same thing on the basis of the same evidence would not know that p. In most cases, the belief that p, however well justified, would be false. The rare cases in which it is still true that p are Gettier situations. Such cases are possible on a conception of knowledge that is not only fallibilist but externalist as well.

34. As I have pointed out in other connections (Bach 2001, 2005), a great many of our everyday utterances are to be taken as not fully explicit; that is, they should be treated as if they contained words or phrases that they do not actually contain. Even when all its constituent expressions are used literally, such an utterance as a whole is not literal, although intuitively it may seem to be (see Bach 2002).

35. Lotteries raise these questions: How can you know that your ticket won't win, when you can't know of each of the other tickets that it won't win? And if you can't know that your ticket won't win, how you can you know (as it may seem that you can) that you won't get rich soon? Personally, I find the straight lottery cases unproblematic: You don't know that your ticket won't win, and you don't know that you won't get rich soon.

36. Note that this is not an alternative to your car being in your driveway, since your car could have been taken on a joy ride and returned to your driveway. But in that case you would be in a Gettier situation and wouldn't know that your car is in your driveway.

References

Bach, K. 1984. "Default Reasoning: Jumping to Conclusions and Knowing When to Think Twice." *Pacific Philosophical Quarterly* 65: 37–58.

Bach, K. 1985. "A Rationale for Reliabilism." *Monist* 62: 248–263.

Bach, K. 2001. "Speaking Loosely: Sentence Nonliterality." In P. French and H. Wettstein, eds., *Midwest Studies in Philosophy*, vol. 25: *Figurative Language*. Oxford: Blackwell.

Bach, K. 2002. "Seemingly Semantic Intuitions." In J. Keim Campbell, M. O'Rourke, and D. Shier, eds., *Meaning and Truth*. New York: Seven Bridges Press.

Bach, K. 2005. "Context *ex Machina*." In Z. Szabó, ed., *Semantics vs. Pragmatics*. Oxford: Oxford University Press.

Brown, J. 2006. "Contextualism and Warranted Assertibility Manoeuvres." *Philosophical Studies* 130: 407–435.

Cohen, S. 1999. "Contextualism, Skepticism, and the Structure of Reasons." *Philosophical Perspectives* 13: 57–89.

DeRose, K. 1992. "Contextualism and Knowledge Attributions." *Philosophy and Phenomenological Research* 52: 913–929.

DeRose, K. 1995. "Solving the Skeptical Problem." *Philosophical Review* 104: 1–52.

DeRose, K. 2002. "Assertion, Knowledge, and Context." *Philosophical Review* 111: 167–203.

Fantl, J., and M. McGrath. 2002. "Evidence, Pragmatics, and Justification." *Philosophical Review* 111: 67–94.

Feldman, R. 1999. "Contextualism and Skepticism." *Philosophical Perspectives* 13: 91–114.

Feldman, R. 2001. "Skeptical Problems, Contextualist Solutions." *Philosophical Studies* 103: 61–85.

Harman, G., and B. Sherman. 2004. "Knowledge, Assumptions, and Lotteries." *Philosophical Issues* 14: 492–500.

Hawthorne, J. 2004. *Knowledge and Lotteries*. Oxford: Oxford University Press.

Heller, M. 1999a. "The Proper Role of Contextualism in Anti-Luck Epistemology." *Philosophical Perspectives* 13: 115–129.

Heller, M. 1999b. "Relevant Alternatives and Closure." *Australasian Journal of Philosophy* 77: 196–208.

Klein, P. 2000. "Contextualism and the Real Nature of Academic Skepticism." *Philosophical Issues* 10: 108–116.

Kornblith, H. 2000. "The Contextualist Evasion of Epistemology." *Philosophical Issues* 10: 24–32.

Lewis, D. 1996. "Elusive Knowledge." *Australasian Journal of Philosophy* 74: 549–567.

MacFarlane, J. 2005. "The Assessment Sensitivity of Knowledge Attributions." In T. Gendler and J. Hawthorne, eds., *Oxford Studies in Epistemology*. Oxford: Oxford University Press.

Nichols, S., S. Stich, and J. Weinberg. 2003. "Meta-Skepticism: Meditations on Ethno-Epistemology." In S. Luper, ed., *The Skeptics*. Aldershot: Ashgate.

Rysiew, P. 2001. "The Context-Sensitivity of Knowledge Attributions." *Noûs* 35: 477–514.

Schaffer, J. 2005. "What Shifts? Thresholds, Standards, or Alternatives?" In G. Preyer and G. Peter, eds., *Contextualism in Philosophy*. Oxford: Oxford University Press.

Schiffer, S. 1996. "Contextualist Solutions to Scepticism." *Proceedings of the Aristotelian Society* 96: 317–333.

Sosa, E. 2000. "Skepticism and Contextualism." *Philosophical Issues* 10: 1–18.

Stanley, J. 2004. "On the Linguistic Basis for Contextualism." *Philosophical Studies* 119: 119–146.

Stanley, J. 2005. *Knowledge and Practical Interests*. Oxford: Oxford University Press.

Unger, P. 1971. "A Defense of Skepticism." *Philosophical Review* 80: 198–218.

Williamson, T. 2000. *Knowledge and Its Limits*. Oxford: Oxford University Press.

6 Contextualism in Epistemology and the Context-Sensitivity of 'Knows'

Robert J. Stainton

The central issue of this essay is whether contextualism in epistemology is genuinely in conflict with recent claims that 'know' is not in fact a context-sensitive word. To address this question, I will first rehearse three key aims of contextualists and the broad strategy they adopt for achieving them. I then introduce two linguistic arguments to the effect that the lexical item 'know' is not context sensitive, one from Herman Cappelen and Ernie Lepore, one from Jason Stanley. I find these and related arguments quite compelling. In particular, I think Cappelen and Lepore (2003, 2005a) show pretty definitively that 'know' is not like 'I'/'here'/'now', and Stanley (2004) shows that 'know' is not like 'tall'/'rich'.[1] One could try to find another model for 'know'. Instead, I consider whether one can rescue "the spirit of contextualism in epistemology"—that is, achieve its aims by deploying a strategy of appealing to speaker context—even while granting that 'know' isn't a context-sensitive word at all. My conclusion, in a nutshell, is this: *If* there are pragmatic determinants of what is asserted/stated, *and* contextualism can overcome independent problems not having to do specifically with the context-sensitivity of the word 'know', *then* the spirit of contextualism can be salvaged. Even though, for reasons sketched by the aforementioned authors, 'know' doesn't actually belong in the class of context-sensitive words.

The Spirit of Contextualism

At a minimum, contextualists have three multifaceted aims. First, they wish to respond to skepticism by "splitting the difference" between (apparently true) knowledge claims made in ordinary contexts, and (apparently false) knowledge claims, about the same topic, made in the face of skeptical arguments. The idea is that two such claims aren't actually in conflict, despite the same words being used about the same knower, because the speakings implicitly state different things—and this because the shift in context has changed the standards for knowledge, and standards are implicitly part of any claim to know. This allows ordinary speakers to make true knowledge attributions, while also explaining the genuine pull of skepticism. (And let me stress: The aim is to secure *true* assertions of knowledge, not just ones which, though strictly speaking false, are reasonable or practical, or which merely convey something true, etc. See DeRose 1999, 187–188.) Gail Stine (1976, 254) puts the general desideratum nicely:

It is an essential characteristic of our concept of knowledge that tighter criteria are appropriate in different contexts. It is one thing in a street encounter, another in a classroom, another in a law court—and who is to say it cannot be another in a philosophical discussion? . . . We can point out that some philosophers are very perverse in their standards (by *some* extreme standard, there is some reason to think there is an evil genius, after all)—but we cannot legitimately go so far as to say that their perversity has stretched the concept of knowledge out of all recognition—in fact they have played on an essential feature of the concept. On the other hand, a skeptical philosopher is wrong if he holds that *others* are wrong in any way—i.e., are sloppy, speaking only loosely, or whatever—when they say we know a great deal.

Yet, in letting in contextual standards, we do not want to say that 'know' is ambiguous, between a "high-standard" and a "low-standard" sense. First, this postulates ambiguities without adequate warrant. Second, there don't seem to be just two standards, there seem to be many. And they seem to vary along many different dimensions—how strongly the proposition must be believed, what degree of felt certainty is required, how well the proposition must be justified and by what means, how important for successful action the truth of the believed proposition is, and so forth. (For a taste of the complexities here, see Unger 1986.)

Second, contemporary contextualists want the *attributor's* standards to play a part in what is asserted, when we make knowledge claims. It isn't just the standards of the person who is said to know, but also the standards of the person attributing knowledge that can make two assertions of the same form—for instance, 'Keith knows that the bank is open'—said about the same knower who is in exactly the same circumstances, express different propositions. Thus, for example, Keith's spouse can utter these words, when the issue is whether to bother making a trip to the bank, and speak truly; but the philosopher facing up to skepticism, in uttering these very words, and without Keith's own standards changing, can speak falsely. (This point is stressed by, among others, DeRose 1992, 113; see also his 1999.)

Finally, contextualism aims to save the epistemic deductive closure principle (Stine 1976, 249). It says:

(1)   The Principle of Deductive Epistemic Closure: For any agent *S*, if *S* knows that p, and *S* knows that if p then q, then *S* knows that q.

This principle seems to be in trouble insofar as one wants to have it be the case that an agent can know that the bank is open, know that if the bank is open then there is an external world, yet not know that there is an external world.

There are other theorists who share these three aims. What distinguishes contextualism, as I understand it, is a distinctive *strategy* that contextualists adopt for achieving them. They take knowledge claims to be context sensitive. And sensitive not just to the context of the person spoken about (the putative knower), but also to the context of the person speaking. This idea is captured nicely by the following quotations:

A. "...the sentence '*S* knows p' will have different truth conditions in different contexts of attribution" (Cohen 1991, 23).
B. "[Contextualism is] a theory according to which the truth conditions of sentences of the form '*S* knows that p' or '*S* does not know that p' vary in certain ways according to the context in which the sentences are uttered" (DeRose 1992, 110).
C. "Contextualism is the view that...the truth-values of sentences containing 'know', and its cognates depend on contextually determined standards. Because of this, sentences of the form '*S* knows *P*' can, at one time, have different truth-values in different contexts. Now when I say 'contexts', I mean 'contexts of ascription'. So the truth value of a sentence containing the knowledge predicate can vary depending on things like purposes, intentions, expectations, presuppositions, etc., of the speakers who utter these sentences" (Cohen 1999, 57).
D. "Suppose one speaker says about a subject *S* and a proposition *P*, '*S* knows *P*.' At the very same time, another speaker says of the very same subject and proposition, '*S* does not know *P*.' Must one of the two be speaking falsely? According to the view I will call 'contextualism', both speakers can be speaking the truth" (Cohen 1999, 57).
E. "...the truth value of an attribution of knowledge is determined relative to the context *of attribution*, i.e., relative to the speaker or the conversational context" (Cohen 1991, 22).

Linguistic Arguments against Contextualism

Cappelen and Lepore
I have rehearsed both the core aims of contextualism and its distinctive strategy for meeting them. The aims and the strategy taken together I call

"the spirit of contextualism." I now turn to syntactic and semantics arguments to the effect that 'know' is not a context-sensitive word. The arguments are by now fairly familiar. What's more, my central point will be that even if they work, the spirit of contextualism may be salvaged anyway. I will thus restrict myself to two illustrative linguistic arguments.

I begin with Cappelen and Lepore. They argue that we have been given no good reason to think that 'know' is a context-sensitive expression. Since the burden of proof is surely on those who take 'know' to be a context-sensitive word, Cappelen and Lepore conclude that 'know' is not context sensitive. They further point out that 'know' fails certain diagnostic tests for indexicality.

To illustrate, consider what I'll here call the *Can't Infer from Direct to Indirect Speech-Report* test. It has to do with indirect speech-reports of the form '*A* said that *p*'. When the complement of 'that' contains a paradigm indexical—such as 'I' or 'now' or 'here'—the whole sentence can easily be false even though speaker *A* really did token the sentence '*p*'. Put otherwise, when '*p*' contains an indexical, you cannot reliably go from the direct speech-report "*A* said '*p*'" to the indirect speech-report "*A* said that *p*," i.e., merely by disquoting.[2] To give an example, suppose Carlos once uttered 'I was born in Spain'. Hence, the reporting sentence (2) is true.

(2)   Carlos said, 'I was born in Spain'.

Suppose further that Carlos has never claimed, of anyone else, that they were born in Spain. In particular, he's never claimed of Daniela that she was born in Spain. If Daniela now indirectly reports Carlos' statement, by disquoting, saying:

(3)   Carlos said that I was born in Spain.

Daniela's report is false. (It's false precisely because 'I' is a speaker-world magnet. That is, it's a word that always "magnets back" to the speaker's context—here, to Daniela.) Say Cappelen and Lepore: If you *can* go from the direct-quotation version to the indirect-quotation version by disquoting, then the sentence in question is likely not context sensitive.

It's a related feature of speaker-world magnets that, no matter how deeply they are linguistically embedded, they take widest scope. That is, not only *can* they take widest scope, they *must* take widest scope. In particular, speaker-world magnets must take wide scope over temporal operators and modal operators. To use David Kaplan's examples, in (4), 'now' cannot refer to a proximal future time, but instead must refer to the time of utterance; and 'here' cannot refer to a non-actual Pakistan in (5), but instead must refer to the Pakistan of the context of utterance (Kaplan 1989, 498–499).

(4)   It will soon be the case that all that is now beautiful is faded.

(5)   It is possible that in Pakistan, in five years, only those who are actually here now are envied.

More to the point for present purposes, speaker-world magnets must also take scope over propositional attitude verbs and indirect speech reports. But one thing speaker-world magnets cannot scope out of is *direct* quotation. Even speaker-world magnets must take narrow scope, with respect to quotation marks. Applied to our example, this means that 'I' univocally takes wide scope with respect to 'Carlos' in the indirect speech report (3), with 'I' picking out Daniela. Contrast the direct speech report (2): in (2), 'I' may co-refer with 'Carlos'. Given their contrasting behavior vis-à-vis scope, it's no surprise that (2) does not entail (3). (This difference is what underlies the test, although talk of "scope" is a bit misplaced in examples in which there is no linguistic embedding.)

Contrast 'know'. Suppose Carlos says 'Keith knows that the bank is open'. Not only is sentence (6) true, but sentence (7) is true as well:

(6)   Carlos said 'Keith knows that the bank is open'.

(7)   Carlos said that Keith knows that the bank is open.

Indeed, ignoring tense and other context-sensitive elements, and the complexities about force and content described in note 2, (6) entails (7). Hence 'know' is unlike 'I', 'here', and 'now'. Thus 'I' passes the *Can't Infer from Direct to Indirect Speech-Report* test, but 'know' does not.

Cappelen and Lepore (2005a and elsewhere) offer further linguistic tests that all strongly suggest the same thing: As a matter of its standing semantics, 'know' does not behave like a speaker-world magnet. Since my central point will be that this may not matter to the spirit of contextualism, however, I rest content with this one test from them.

Stanley

Cappelen and Lepore take their arguments to show that 'know' isn't a context-sensitive term *at all*. Speaking for myself, I think that's somewhat hasty, since there is room to doubt whether their tests work for all subvarieties of context-sensitive terms. In particular, one might think that there are context-sensitive expressions that nevertheless are not "speaker-world magnets." What their various tests do establish, I think, is that 'know' isn't like 'I', 'here' or 'now'; if 'know' is context sensitive, it isn't context sensitive in that way.

But some contextualists will want to shrug this off as irrelevant. In particular, contextualists who are wont to insist that their model for 'know' is 'tall', 'flat', or 'rich' may be unimpressed. (See, e.g., Cohen 1999; Lewis 1996; Unger 1975.) This is where Jason Stanley's 2004 paper "On the Linguistic Basis for Contextualism" comes in. (See also his 2005 book.) Stanley has cogently argued that 'know' isn't like 'tall', 'flat', or 'rich' either—because whereas these words are gradable, 'know' is not.[3]

The basic point was stressed early on by Dretske. He writes:

> Knowing that something is so, unlike being wealthy or reasonable, is not a matter of degree. Two people can both be wealthy, yet one be wealthier than the other; both be reasonable, yet one be more reasonable than the other. When talking about people, places, or topics (*things* rather than *facts*), it also makes sense to say that one person knows something *better* than another... But *factual* knowledge, the knowledge *that s* is *F*, does not admit of such comparisons. If we both know that the ball is red, it makes no sense to say that you know this better than I. (Dretske 1981a, 107; see also Dretske 1981b, 363)

Stanley, building on these remarks, provides two linguistic tests for gradability. First, gradable expressions permit degree modifiers like 'really' and 'very':

(8)   Gradable Adjectives with Degree Modifiers
(a)   That is flat, though not very flat.
(b)   That is flat, though not really flat.
(c)   That is tall, though not very tall.
(d)   That is tall, though not really tall.

(That 'really' is a degree modifier here, and not merely a way of stressing that *in fact* the thing is tall/flat, is evidenced by (8b) and (8d) not being contradictions.)

Notice, however, that (9) and (10) are decidedly odd:

(9)   ?It is known, but it isn't very known.

(10)   ?It is known, but it isn't really known.

The only way to read (9) is not as a statement about the degree to which the proposition in question—say, that the bank is open—is known by a given person, but (at best) as a statement about how many people the proposition is known by (i.e., about how widely known it is). In particular, (9) doesn't speak to how high a standard is met. Similarly for (10). (The same holds for the more idiomatic, "It isn't very *well* known.") The problem is, it's a mystery why (9) and (10) do *not* have this reading, if 'know' is gradable. Nor should we be fooled by expressions like 'I know perfectly well that Felicidad didn't do her homework'. Granted, this *looks* like a statement of degree-of-knowledge. But it likely is not. For, as Stanley notes, if it were a statement of degree, we would expect the interrogative and negative form of the sentence to be fine as well. And they are quite odd:

(11) ??Do you know perfectly well that Felicidad didn't do her homework?

(12) ??I don't know perfectly well that Felicidad didn't do her homework.

Second, gradable expressions admit of comparative constructions: 'flatter than', 'taller than', 'richer than'. But there is no natural comparative for 'know'. Thus consider Stanley's examples:

(13) ??John knows that Bush is president more than Sally knows it.

(14) ??Hannah knows that Bush is president more than she knows that Clinton was president.

Both are peculiar. The closest we can come are things like (15):

(15) John knows better than anyone how much tax cuts hurt public education.

But, as Stanley also notes, it's doubtful that this is a genuine comparative—since 'John knows better than most politicians how much tax cuts hurt public education' is odd in a way that it should not be, if 'knows better than' really were a comparative in (15). Instead, 'knows better than anyone' seems to be an idiom.

It seems, on linguistic grounds, that 'know' is not gradable.[4] So 'know' isn't like 'tall', 'rich', or 'flat' after all. Stanley sums up as follows:

> Natural language expressions that are semantically linked to degrees on scales exploit this link in a variety of recognizable ways—by allowing for comparisons between degrees on the scale, and by allowing modifications of the contextually salient degree on the scale. If the semantic content of "know" were sensitive to contextually salient standards, and hence linked to a scale of epistemic strength (as "tall" is linked to a scale of height), then we should expect this link to be exploited in a host of different constructions, such as natural comparatives. The fact that we do not see such behavior should make us at the least very suspicious of the claim of such a semantic link. (2004, 130)

Three Cautions about Appeals to Context-Sensitivity

I have now presented two syntactico-semantic arguments against taking 'know' to be a context-sensitive word.[5] Before moving on to the main event—namely, of saving the spirit of contextualism, notwithstanding these and other quite compelling linguistic arguments—I want to raise three issues. They stand as cautions to anyone who wants to pursue the idea that, in spite of Cappelen and Lepore's and Stanley's arguments, 'know' is nevertheless a context-sensitive word.

First, one might hope that there is some other kind of context-sensitive word—neither of the 'I'/'here'/'now' variety, nor of the 'tall'/'rich' variety—which might serve as a better model for 'know'. In particular, there are words like 'foreigner', 'local', 'enemy', and 'home' whose referents seem to shift depending on who the speaker is, but which don't have to magnet out to the speaker's context of use. So, they are unlike 'I'/'now'/ 'here', yet they seem to be context-sensitive nonetheless. (To see how unlike 'I' they are, witness 'Every child went home early', or 'We are all foreigners when we travel'.) And some words of this kind aren't gradable. Truth be told, I think one could pursue this comparison, so that 'know' is likened to 'home'/'foreigner'. It's far from incoherent. But I also think that it's a risky choice to stake contextualism in epistemology on this or any other such comparison. For there exists the real threat that linguistic differences of the kind noted above will emerge, *mutatis mutandis*, for any model one picks. So rather than pursuing that path, I think it wiser to stress, as I will, that 'know' does not need to be *in any way* a context-sensitive word, in order to rescue contextualism.

A second caution. Having presented these tests, it might be asked why we need them at all. Can't we just tell, by consulting our intuitions, whether a word is context sensitive? Can't we tell, in particular, that 'know' is context sensitive just by considering contrasting situations in which a given sentence seems first true, and then false—though said of the very same situation, with only standards shifting? The answer is that we cannot, because such intuitions of shifting do not in general distinguish features of usage that come from the semantics of the type, from features which are pragmatic. (In fact, that is a central point of Cappelen and Lepore's recent work.) And for a word to be context sensitive is a semantic feature of the type *par excellence*. Put another way, such intuitions of truth-value shifting are patently an interaction effect, in just the way that a sentence "sounding bad" is an interaction effect. It is, therefore, a mistake to move quickly from intuitions about utterance-truth or falsehood, to conclusions about the nature of *one* of the contributing factors (namely, type semantics), unreflectively tracing the observed effects to that "cause." In sum, expression types can seem to be context sensitive to us, even though they are not actually context sensitive, because of pragmatic interference. So one should not assume, just because of our intuitions of context-shifting, that there *must* be some context-sensitive linguistic item that will provide our model for 'know'. Those intuitions could be misleading. (I here echo points made forcefully in Bach 2002.)

One last caution, about what might motivate one to pursue this route. Once the various tests are on the table, and we've noted that pragmatics can interfere with intuitions, one can *still* feel tempted to say that 'know' must be context sensitive. Why so? I wonder if we don't have an instance of what one might call "a perversion of the linguistic turn." There was this idea, muddy but deep, that answers to philosophical problems were somehow and to some extent encoded in our public languages. Let's not pause to decide whether this was a good idea; what matters is that embracing the linguistic turn in philosophy motivates, when doing epistemology, ethics, metaphysics, or what-have-you, very careful scrutiny of language and speech. What this methodology should not motivate, however, is deciding independently what the right answer to a philosophical problem is, and then insisting—since language reflects "philosophical reality"—that human tongues *must* have feature such-and-such. In particular, even granting the attractiveness of contextualism in epistemology, we should resist thinking that there simply *must* be a kind of context-sensitive word—whether 'I'/'now'/'here', or 'tall'/'rich', or 'enemy'/'home', or something else yet again—which can serve as a model for the context-sensitivity of 'know'. Even if you take the linguistic turn, this seems clearly the wrong direction to take it—not least because what features natural-language words have is, surely, very much a matter for empirical investigation.

Saving the Spirit of Contextualism

My main thesis, recall, is this: *If* there are pragmatic determinants of what is asserted/stated, *and* contextualism can overcome independent problems not having to do specifically with the context-sensitivity of the word 'know', *then* the spirit of contextualism can be salvaged. Even if 'know' isn't a context-sensitive word.

To give this a first-pass unpacking, I need to contrast two "tactics," each consistent with the broad contextualist strategy:

(16)   Two Versions of the Contextualist Strategy

(a)   *Type-semantics version*: The word 'know' is context sensitive. As a result, utterances of sentences containing 'know' have different truth conditions, depending on the context of utterance.

(b)   *Speech-act version*: Knowledge attributions are context sensitive. As a result, assertions made using 'know' have different truth conditions, depending on the context of utterance.

Proponents of contextualism typically run the two theses together. Recall, for instance, the quotations with which I began. Quotations (A)–(C) endorse the type semantics tactic. Quotations (D)–(E) endorse the speech act tactic. So far as I can see, the authors quoted don't distinguish between these: they write as if (A)–(C) and (D)–(E) are merely different ways of making the same point.[6] However, as will emerge in detail below, while both pursue the same basic strategy (which is what renders them contextualist in the first place), they employ quite different tools. One makes a claim about sentences, the other only makes claims about statements.

Notice too that the linguistic critiques given above are really directed at (16a): they all raise linguistic-style doubts about whether the word 'know' behaves syntactically and semantically the way some supposed model ('I' or 'tall') does. Thus, and this is the key idea, Cappelen and Lepore and Stanley's critical points *may well be consistent with (16b)*. And (16b) is all you need to save the spirit of contextualism in epistemology. (Assuming, to repeat, that there aren't reasons independent of the context-sensitivity of 'know' for rejecting contextualism in epistemology.[7]) Anyway, that's what I'll now try to argue.

There are two issues to deal with. First, how can the speech act version of contextualism be true, if the type semantics version is false? Second, does the speech act version on its own really save the spirit of contextualism (in the sense both of rescuing its three aims—splitting the difference between the skeptic and the ordinary attributor of knowledge without ambiguity, having attributor standards be sufficient for this, and saving deductive epistemic closure—and rescuing its distinctive strategy of appealing to sensitivity to the speaker's context)? I will take the two issues in turn.

To see how (16a) and (16b) can come apart, we need some terminology. There are at least three things that can help determine the content *conveyed*, literally or otherwise, by an utterance in context. Most obviously, what the (disambiguated) expression means in the shared language typically helps establish what an in-context utterance conveys. Call this first determinant of content the *disambiguated expression-meaning*. Another usual determinant is reference assignment, i.e., which non-linguistic objects are assigned, in context, to special context-sensitive items: at a minimum, to pronouns ('I', 'she', 'you'); to special time/place words like 'now', 'here', and 'today'; to tense markers ('lives' versus 'lived'), etc. These special context-sensitive "slots" must typically be filled in, from non-linguistic context, to arrive at what the utterance conveys. Call this second determinant of conveyed content *slot-filling*. It is widely, although not universally, agreed that pragmatics plays a part in helping to fix these first two determinants. But pragmatics can contribute to conveyed content in another way as well. This third determinant of conveyed content is more holistic, and is far less constrained by the syntactic form and conventional content of the sound-pattern uttered. It turns especially on things like what it would be reasonable and cooperative for the speaker to have intended to convey, in the situation. This third determinant is thought by many to play a large role in irony, sarcasm, conversational implicature, metaphor, and such. Call this third factor *free pragmatic enrichment*.

With that as background, I can now introduce three further bits of terminology. *Saturated expression meaning* is, by stipulative definition, the result of the first two determinants. That is, as I will use the term, saturated expression meaning just is what you get when you disambiguate, and fill in all resulting "slots." What is *asserted/stated/claimed*, in contrast, is what the speaker is strictly and literally committed to. It is, if you will, the literal truth conditions of the speech act. One way to get a grip on this latter notion is to think about the practical implications involved. Assertions/ statements, unlike merely conveyed thoughts, are lie-prone. And in contrast with merely misleading, a false assertion can (justly and correctly) get you convicted of perjury. Moreover assertions/statements are more easily subject to strict contractual obligations. (This isn't to say that merely conveyed propositions have no practical implications, of course; it's just to say that they seem to have different ones.) Or again, while conversational implicatures can easily be cancelled, asserted content is typically harder to cancel. (See the examples below for more on what the contrast comes to.)

Crucially for what's to come, it's not at all obvious that saturated expression meaning is the same thing as what is stated/asserted/claimed. Indeed, numerous authors have recently argued that free pragmatic enrichment plays a part in determining what is asserted/stated/claimed, i.e., the literal truth-conditional content of speech acts, though by definition they don't play a part in saturated expression meaning. Say these authors, not only does free pragmatic enrichment determine conversationally implicated propositions and the like ("non-literal truth conditions," if you will), it also determines which propositions are asserted/stated. Thus there are (and here is the final bit of terminology we'll need) *pragmatic determinants of what is asserted/stated/claimed*. (See, e.g., Carston 1988, 2002; Perry 1986; Récanati 2001, 2002; Searle 1978, 1980; Sperber and Wilson 1986. I return to this issue at length below.) So we have:

(17) Some Terminology
(a) Disambiguated expression meaning
(b) Slot filling
(c) Saturated expression meaning

(d)   Free pragmatic enrichment

(e)   What is asserted/stated/claimed

(f)   Pragmatic determinant of what is asserted/stated/claimed[8]

At last we can see how all of this relates to the two versions of the broad contextualist strategy. If there *aren't* pragmatic determinants of what is asserted/stated/claimed, then what is strictly and literally attributed would be the saturated expression meaning: the truth conditions of a knowledge attribution will be exhausted by the contributions of disambiguated expression meaning and slot filling. Since it's granted on all sides that 'know' isn't ambiguous, that would make (16a) and (16b) collapse into each other—because assertions made using 'know' would only vary according to context if 'know' were itself a context-sensitive word.

(16)   Two Versions of the Contextualist Strategy

(a)   *Type-semantics version*: The word 'know' is context sensitive. As a result, utterances of sentences containing 'know' have different truth conditions, depending on the context of utterance.

(b)   *Speech-act version*: Knowledge attributions are context sensitive. As a result, assertions made using 'know' have different truth conditions, depending on the context of utterance.

Thus, if there aren't pragmatic determinants of what is asserted/stated/claimed, then (16b) can only be true if (16a) is, because for saturated expression meaning to vary, 'know' must introduce a slot to be filled—that is, 'know' must be a context-sensitive word.

On the other hand, if there are pragmatic determinants of what is asserted/stated/claimed—if what is asserted/stated/claimed can exhibit more content than saturated expression meaning—then different assertions made using 'know' might well have different truth conditions even if 'know' isn't a context-sensitive word. This remains an open option. So (16b) could still be true even if, as Cappelen and Lepore and Stanley argue, (16a) is false on linguistic grounds.

Well but, are there pragmatic determinants of what is asserted/stated/claimed? I think so. Now, it would take me too far a field to mount a compelling defense, and my conclusion is conditional in any case. But let me rehearse some of the arguments in favor of pragmatic determinants. First, one can appeal to our intuitions about what is asserted. Here are a few examples. If I am at a party, and say of my friend, 'He can stick out his tongue and touch his nose' it's very tempting to think that what I asserted, of my friend, is that he can touch his nose *with his tongue*. And yet the saturated expression meaning, given the context, will contain no reference to this latter "means condition." It will have 'he' filled by my friend, and the time filled by when I spoke, with the rest of the saturated expression meaning coming directly from the type—which type makes no reference to what device he can touch his nose with. Thus in the case of this utterance of (18), saturated expression meaning is intuitively not the same as what is asserted/stated/claimed.

(18)   He can stick out his tongue and touch his nose.

Similarly, if I say in October 'I turned 21 in September', it does seem that I have asserted that I am now 21 years of age. But, in fact, the expression type doesn't contain any reference to which September it was that I turned 21 in, nor even to which calendar unit is such that I turned 21 of it. (21 years? 21 months? 21 days?) Here again, then, what is asserted/stated/ claimed intuitively goes beyond what is linguistically encoded, even after reference assignment to indexicals and such.

A second argument is a bit more theoretical, though it too relies on intuitions. There are many cases in which we identify something that is asserted, yet the saturated expression meaning is sub-propositional. Since nothing sub-propositional can be the thing asserted—an assertion is always of a proposition—what is asserted must be something more than saturated expression meaning. There are two kinds of examples. First, there are sentential cases where the complete sentence, even once all slots are filled, does not seem to express something that can be true or false *tout court*. Consider: 'I am ready' [for what?], 'It is raining' [where?], 'Jane can't continue' [what thing?], 'Aspirin is better' [than what?] or 'She will' [do what?]. In using these sentences, one can easily assert that one is ready for the race, that it's raining here, etc. But what is asserted goes beyond saturated expression meaning. Second, there are sub-sentential cases, in which an assertion is made with something whose semantics is patently sub-propositional. For instance, the prepositional phrase 'From Spain' expresses a property, not a proposition; yet one can use this very phrase to assert, of a demonstrated object, that it is from Spain. (The only sense in which this is "ellipsis" is that the speaker asserts more than what her words mean; and being "ellipsis" in that sense doesn't eliminate pragmatic determinants of what is asserted/stated/claimed. See Stainton 2005, 2006 for extended discussion. Notice, by the way, how hard it would be to cancel the inclusion of the demonstrated object within the proposition-meant. That said, cancellation certainly can take place in assertion: consider the 'He can stick out his tongue' case, where cancellation is relatively easy. Given present purposes, the details needn't detain us.)

A third argument goes like this. The standard view is that conversational implicatures are calculated on the basis of what is stated. But then where there is a conversational implicature calculated on the basis of content X, that content is stated. Now consider the following case, adapted from François Récanati. Jane asks Lewis, 'Are you hungry'. Lewis replies 'I've had breakfast'. Lewis thereby conversationally implicates that he isn't hungry. But to conversationally implicate *that*, Lewis must have stated that he has had breakfast today. The proposition that there exists some time prior to the present at which Lewis has had breakfast does not support the inference that he's not hungry. So, the latter is not what Lewis stated. However, that he's had breakfast today is not the saturated expression meaning of 'I've had breakfast': when he had breakfast is determined not by a slot, but by what I've called free pragmatic enrichment.

Finally, note how flexible we are in reporting what a person stated. Suppose Stephanie is on trial for embezzling. On May 22, I hear Stephanie say 'I bought an SUV and a Harley yesterday'. In July I can report this, in court, as follows: 'Stephanie claimed that she had purchased both an automobile and a motorcycle on the same day in May'. (Ignoring worries about hearsay being admissible, my report might support the prosecution's contention that Stephanie was spending a lot of money right about then.) Patently, the complement of my report is not semantically equivalent to the saturated expression meaning of Stephanie's 'I bought an SUV and a Harley yesterday'. We thus face a choice. Either my report is false, since what she claimed was that she bought an SUV and a Harley on May 21, or my report is true, and she stated something which goes well beyond the saturated expression meaning of her words.

There is much more to be said on this topic. (See Bach 1994a,b; Carston 1988, 2002; Perry 1986; Récanati 2001, 2002; Searle 1978, 1980; Sperber and Wilson 1986; Stainton 2006; and Travis 1985, 1991 for more.) In particular, it's clear that there are possible rejoinders. One might hold that, intuitions notwithstanding, what is asserted with 'I turned 21 in September' makes no reference to which year; and that 'I am ready' can be true without a specification of what one is ready for. See Borg 2004, 2005 and Cappelen and Lepore 2005a,b for such moves. One could also insist that there are more slots in the cases in play than what meets the eye. Stanley 2000 pursues this idea. Rather than trying to address all such replies, I rest content with the conditional claim: if there are pragmatic determinants of what is asserted, then one might well be able to save the spirit of contextualism, even if 'know' isn't a context-sensitive word.

Having drawn this contrast between two contextualist tactics (one pressing a claim about the semantics of types containing 'know', the other merely making a claim about variability in speech acts made using 'know'), and having provided a general motivation for believing in pragmatic determinants of what is asserted, let's consider a bit more at length how one tactic might be retained and deployed to good effect, even while the other is given up. The general point is clear enough: the truth-value of the sentence 'Keith knows that the bank is open', assuming its saturated expression meaning in a context *has* a truth value, does not vary according to context of use; but, given how ubiquitous pragmatic determinants are, what is stated/asserted/claimed using (19) can be expected to have different truth conditions, on different occasions, even though 'know' is no more a context-sensitive word than 'dog' is:

(19)   Keith knows that the bank is open.

The phenomenon occurs with clearly context insensitive words: what is asserted with 'There are no dogs in this building' can be falsified by wolves, or taxidermied poodles, or not...as the interests of the speaker and hearer vary. Given this, it would be surprising if 'know' were somehow exceptional.

So, it should be clear in broad outlines how to retain tactic (16b) in the face of syntactic and semantic results about 'know'. Still, it's worth revisiting the particular linguistic critiques of contextualism rehearsed above. Let's start with Cappelen and Lepore. Surprisingly, it turns out that they endorse pragmatic determinants of what is asserted/stated/claimed! More than that, the fourth argument for their existence, sketched above, was lifted more or less directly from them. What they maintain elsewhere (1997, 1998), put crudely, is that one cannot read off the type-semantics of an expression directly from perfectly correct reports of what the speaker asserted/stated/claimed. Put otherwise, Cappelen and Lepore agree that the correct description of assertion-content for an utterance—like the correct description of conversational implicature, metaphor, indirect speech act, and sarcastic content—draws on many interacting factors, hence assertion-content is not an especially safe guide to the contribution of type-semantics. Thus, despite the fact that Cappelen and Lepore describe their *opponents* as those who suggest "judgments," "claims," "knowledge attributions," and "speaker's attributions of knowledge" are made with 'know', I think their own take on pragmatic determinants of speech act content provides no grounds for disagreement. For all that is said in their "context-shifting arguments," for instance, they can endorse such suggestions, and still insist—like me—that 'know' is not a context-sensitive word.

As for Stanley's point that 'know' isn't gradable, if there are pragmatic determinants of what is asserted/stated/claimed then that's a bit of a red herring too, as far as the speech-act version of contextualism is concerned. For one can make *claims* that are subject to degrees using words that are not, in their syntactic and semantic behavior, themselves gradable. Take 'weighs 80 kg'. This patently isn't gradable. Sentences like (20a–c) are awful:

(20a)   Her weight is very 80 kg.

(20b)   Her weight is 80 kg, though her weight isn't really 80 kg.

(20c)   Hank's weight is more 80 kg than Ina's.

Still, what is required for the truth of an assertion, statement or claim of weighing 80 kg can vary. Or again, 'is vegetarian' isn't gradable either. ('John is very vegetarian' and 'John is more vegetarian than I am' can be used sensibly, but they are like 'Joan is very pregnant' and 'Joan is more pregnant than I am'.) Yet what degree of meat-abstinence a subject is claimed to be committed to can vary according to the situation, even though 'is vegetarian' is not like 'tall' or 'rich'. Thus 'John is a vegetarian' can be employed so as to require that John won't eat anything handled by someone who is also cooking meat; eschews all animal products, including eggs and milk; won't eat any animal products, but will wear leather; will not eat vegetables fried in animal fat; will eat eggs and milk, though not cheese having rennet in it; will eat insects, but not animal products. And, of course, we use 'vegetarian' to assert that someone will eat fish, but not red meat; etc. Similarly, then, there's no reason presented in Stanley's "On the Linguistic Basis for Contextualism" for denying that one can make knowledge-*claims* that are subject to degrees, even though 'know' isn't gradable.

Having seen how to save (16b) while rejecting (16a), the outstanding issue is whether (16b) alone is sufficient to rescue the spirit of contextualism in epistemology.[9] To see that it *ought* to be sufficient for what contextualists have always wanted, recall first of all that contextualists often enough state their view in terms of attributions, claims, and such. For instance, DeRose moves easily, in the pages immediately following those in which he talks of the variable truth conditions of sentences, to suggestions about "what I say in claiming," "my assertion," and "what I would be saying." He rightly notes that ordinary instances of *these* must be true, if contextual-

ism is to be interesting. Or again, he says: "One might think that requirements for making a knowledge *attribution* true go up as the stakes go up"
(1992, 110; my emphasis). Just to rub my interpretive point in, DeRose
himself describes the aim of contextualism as follows:

Contextualist theories of knowledge *attributions* have almost invariably been developed with an eye towards providing some kind of answer to philosophical scepticism. For some sceptical arguments threaten to show, not only that we fail to meet
very high requirements for knowledge of interest to philosophers seeking absolute
certainty, but also that we don't meet the truth conditions of ordinary, out-on-the-
street *claims to know*. They thus threaten to establish the startling result that we
never, or almost never, *truly ascribe* knowledge to ourselves or to other human
beings. According to contextual analysis, when the sceptic presents her arguments,
she manipulates various conversational mechanisms that raise the semantic standards for knowledge, and thereby creates a context in which she can *truly say* that
we know nothing or very little. But the fact that the sceptic can thus install very
high standards which we don't live up to has no tendency to show that we don't satisfy the more relaxed standards that are in place in ordinary conversation. Thus, it is
hoped, our *ordinary claims* to know will be safeguarded from the apparently powerful
attacks of the sceptic, while, at the same time, the persuasiveness of the sceptical
arguments is explained. (1992, 112; my emphases)

This passage illustrates, I think, that even DeRose implicitly realizes that
what he really needs, in order successfully to split the difference with the
skeptic, is that knowledge attributions, ascriptions, sayings, and claims—
all of which are speech-acts, notice—are affected by context. Which, if
there are pragmatic determinants of what is asserted/stated/claimed, does
not at all require that the truth conditions of sentences containing 'know'
be context sensitive.

That contextualists write this way highlights that they themselves recognize, at bottom, that all they really need is (16b), the thesis about speech-
acts, to pursue their strategy and achieve their aims. This is all to the good.
Still, it's worth the effort to see *precisely* how (16b), as opposed to (16a), can
save the spirit of contextualism. So, let's recall contextualism's three aims:

• to allow ordinary knowledge attributions to be literally true (and unam-
biguous), while also explaining the genuine pull of skeptical arguments,
by splitting the difference;
• to let attributor standards partly determine what is attributed;
• to save the principle of deductive epistemic closure.

It should be obvious how the first two aims can be achieved—and by
appeal to context shifting. The former is put in terms of attributions, that

is, assertions/statements of knowledge. But if pragmatic determinants of asserted content are ubiquitous, then of course they will show up in assertions/statements/claims about what is known. And, of course, this is done without positing ambiguity, and without resorting to making the anti-skeptic "merely convey a truth," or "assert something reasonable, though false." Turning to the second aim, the attributor's standards (e.g., the spouse's versus the skeptic's, both talking about Keith in the same "evaluation world") can alter what is stated/asserted/claimed—as could, of course, the attributee's standards, or even some third party's standards. Free pragmatic enrichment being abductive and holistic, a whole host of things could bear on what is asserted—so it's unsurprising, wholly expected in fact, that the attributor's standards could also impact on this. The issue of closure is more complicated.

The principle of epistemic closure can seem to be threatened by the following sort of *reductio*:

Assume: For any agent S, if S knows that p, and S knows that if p then q, then S knows that q. (Deductive epistemic closure principle)

(P1)   Keith knows that the bank is open.

(P2)   Since it's obvious that banks are objects in an external world, Keith knows that if the bank is open, then there exists an external world.

(C1)   Keith knows that the bank is open, and Keith knows that if the bank is open, then there exists an external world. (By conjunction of P1 and P2.)

(P3)   If Keith knows that the bank is open and Keith knows that if the bank is open, then there exists an external world, then Keith knows that there is an external world. (Instance of the deductive epistemic closure principle, assumed for *reductio*.)

(C2)   Keith knows that there is an external world. (By *modus ponens* on C1 and P3.)

(P4)   Because [FILL IN YOUR FAVORITE SKEPTICAL ARGUMENT], Keith does not know that there is an external world.

(C3)   The Assumption leads to a contradiction, hence it must be rejected.

Contextualists can resist this argument on many fronts, without taking 'know' to be a context-sensitive word. The key move is to reflect on the *claims/statements* made in producing the sentences above, and what they entail—rather than focusing on what the *sentences* entail. To give but a few examples:

• Contextualists can maintain that the claims made with C2 and P4 needn't actually contradict one another, since the standards that determine what one thereby states can surely be different in the two situations. In which case, there can be no *reductio*, there being no contradiction, when standards vary—which, adds the contextualist, they surely do.

• The contextualist can insist that as soon as talk of "knowing that there exists an external world" comes into it, at P2, the standards are pretty much bound to go up. Arguably this puts what one claims with C2 and P4 in conflict, since in uttering C2 what one states will now presumably exhibit the higher standard. But this move ends up blocking the argument *for C2*, as follows: Given the shift in standards at P2, what one asserts by P1 and what one asserts by P2 don't actually entail by conjunction what is claimed in C1, because there isn't a univocal knowledge claim in the two conjuncts.

• The contextualist may let the conjunctive assertion made with C1 exhibit different standards, between its two halves, so that the claims made with P1 and P2, even given different standards, still do support this conjunctive assertion; but she may then go on to deny that what one asserts with P3 is actually a (worrisome) instance of the Assumption at all, because the standards invoked must now vary, if the claims C1 and P3 are to entail the conclusion C2. So the argument as a whole cannot be a *reductio* of deductive epistemic closure, since that principle is never actually invoked in the argument.

One could go on. (See Stine 1976, 256ff., for related reflections.) What is clear is that a contextualist can hold onto the general principle of epistemic closure *where the standards relevant to knowledge attributions are held constant.* What the contextualist rescues is this: If S knows by $standard_1$ that p, and S knows by $standard_1$ that p entails q, then S knows by $standard_1$ that q. Crucially, that principle isn't at all threatened by the attempted *reductio* above.

Objections and Replies

I will end with three objections to my foregoing attempt to save the spirit of contextualism. First, even agreeing that there are pragmatic determinants of what is asserted/stated/claimed, and even agreeing that uses of 'know' could be subject to them, there remains a problem: How *exactly* do standards, including especially the attributor's standards, manage to have an impact on what is asserted/stated/claimed in attributions using 'know'? It's all well and good to say that this is possible in principle, on the grounds that it occurs with other words. But how *precisely* does it occur with 'know'? What are the specific mechanisms whereby standards manage to get in? This is a very good question. And it can indeed seem that until an answer is given, we cannot really feel sure that the spirit of contextualism can be saved. The question is also, however, one that I won't even attempt to address here. For it seems to me that this is a challenge that doesn't have anything specific to do with whether 'know' is a context-sensitive word: The problem of how exactly standards are set is just as hard for someone who thinks that 'know' affords a contextual slot to fill as it is for someone who thinks that standards get in directly via pragmatic determinants of what is asserted. For if you think there is a slot on 'know', you still need a story about what fixes its referent. And, I hazard, that story will be just as hard to tell. Put otherwise, I will treat this issue as falling under the conjunct, "contextualism can overcome independent problems not having to do specifically with the context-sensitivity of the word 'know'." *If* a plausible story can be told, then (16b) is adequately supported, and the spirit of contextualism might be salvaged.

Here is a second objection, and one that I won't just shunt aside. It might be suggested that I am merely making the familiar point that a person can convey different things with 'know' in different circumstances, even though the word isn't context sensitive. That is, what I'm proposing is just a "warranted assertibility maneuver" under a misleading name. I reject this accusation. Granted, this novel kind of shifting derives from pragmatics. But the ordinary knowledge attribution is not, for all that, merely a matter of saying something false, though reasonable, nor merely a matter of conveying a truth. What I'm suggesting, to repeat, is that if there are pragmatic determinants *of what is asserted/stated/claimed*, then knowledge attributors will make statements whose literal truth conditions vary, even though 'know' isn't context sensitive. And, unlike merely conveyed information, this content won't be easily cancelable, and it will be lie-prone, and so on.

One last worry. If 'know' is not a context-sensitive word, then saturated expression-meaning will be the same for the spouse's utterance of (19) and the skeptic's utterance of it.

(19)   Keith knows that the bank is open.

The slot for tense is filled in, and in just the same way for both utterances—and there is no other slot to fill, if 'know' isn't marked as context sensitive in the lexicon. This may seem to pose a problem for saving the spirit of contextualism in epistemology, since this means that there is *something* that the ordinary person and skeptic can't both be right about. In particular, they can't both be right about whether the saturated expression-meaning of (19) is true, since *it* does not vary with attributor standards. Only what is asserted does. Goes the objection: Either Keith's wife, who assigns TRUE to the saturated expression-meaning, is correct, or the skeptic, who assigns FALSE to the saturated expression-meaning, is correct. So we haven't successfully split the difference after all; the disagreement returns with full force.

Here is my reply. First, it's a bit fast to assume that the saturated expression-meaning of (19) in the skeptic's mouth and in the spouse's mouth really does get assigned different truth-values, not least because one might think that this sentence type does not yield something true/false even after disambiguation and slot-filling.[10] It's equally a bit fast to assume that both parties grasp the saturated expression-meaning, and assign a truth-value to it. But let's put those points aside, and suppose that either the saturated expression-meaning is true (and Keith's wife is right about it), or the saturated expression-meaning is false (and the skeptic is right about it). Even so, I don't think this would actually be worrisome, because the dispute between ordinary knowledge claims and what the skeptic maintains was never about some technical notion of theoretical semantics—which is what saturated expression-meaning patently is. Certain contextualists in epistemology, ill-advisedly in my view, managed to shift the emphasis onto this latter notion by comparing 'know' to indexical expressions like 'I' and 'now'. This has naturally led to linguistic objections like those canvassed above. But, their word-specific formulations of contextualism in epistemology notwithstanding, the original dispute was about, for instance, whether Joe Sixpack's statements/assertions about knowledge were true, whether Joe Sixpack's knowledge attributions were correct, etc.[11] And, regardless of whether 'know' is a context-sensitive word, if there exist pragmatic determinants of what is asserted/stated/claimed, then it might still turn out, just as the contextualist wishes, that *both* Joe's and the skeptic's assertions/statements are true. Because they are stating—not just non-literally conveying, but stating—different things, using the same words.

To sum up, there are two ways to spell out contextualism in epistemology. One tactic requires 'know' to be a context-sensitive word, as a matter of the semantics of the type. It is open to empirical objections of the kind raised by Cappelen and Lepore and by Stanley. Surprisingly, however, I have gone on to suggest that the falsehood of such semantic claims about the type 'know' may not matter with respect to rescuing the spirit of contextualism in epistemology—assuming any other problems with contextualism can be overcome. (See note 7.) That's because there is another way to spell out contextualism, such that all that's required is that there be pragmatic determinants of what is stated/claimed using 'know'—which do not occur via slot-filling or disambiguation. If there are such determinants, then it doesn't matter whether our intuitions of shifting-assertions-given-shifting-standards actually trace back to something semantic or not—that is, to something about the type 'know'.

To put the central result a bit polemically, suppose that linguistic considerations show that 'know' simply means know. (And note: 'I' does *not* simply mean I.) Suppose, indeed, that 'know' is no more context sensitive than 'dog' or 'weighs 80 kg'. The contextualist reaction can be "So what?"—if what is *stated* using the word 'know' can still vary in tune with the standards in place in the speaking context. For all Cappelen and Lepore and Stanley have shown, this option remains open to the contextualist.

My own view, for what it's worth, is that there *are* pragmatic determinants of what is asserted/stated/claimed. And I hazard to say that standards can pragmatically determine *what is asserted with 'know'*—though don't ask me just how. I also think, in light of this, that 'know' not being a context-sensitive word is not *per se* a worry. I remain agnostic, however, about whether the aims and strategy of contextualism can be rescued, since I recognize that contextualism in epistemology faces problems that do not have to do specifically with the syntax/semantics of the lexical item 'know'.

Acknowledgments

My thanks to Kent Bach, Ray Elugardo, David Hunter, Dave Matheson, Martin Montminy, Michael O'Rourke, Catherine Wearing, Juhani Yli-Vakkuri and two anonymous referees for comments on an earlier draft. Thanks also to the participants at the 2004 Inland Northwest Philosophy Conference for their input, and to Herman Cappelen, Ernie Lepore, Paul Pietroski, Jonathan Schaffer, and Robert Stalnaker for very useful discussion. Work on this essay was supported by the Canada Research Chairs program and by the Social Sciences and Humanities Research Council of Canada.

Notes

1. A word about notation. I employ single quotes for mention. I employ double quotes for shudder quotes, to cite material from other sources, and also in place of corner quotes.

2. There are some familiar reasons why "A said 'p'" doesn't entail "A said that p" that have to do not with context-sensitivity, but rather with indirect quotation track-

ing force and content. For instance, *A* might have uttered the sentence 'Romeo must die' while practicing his lines for a performance; because the utterance lacked the right force, this act would not entail that *A* said that Romeo must die. Or *A*, a unilingual Swahili speaker, might have uttered a string of sounds which happen to mean, in English, that Romeo must die. But, though *A* arguably said 'Romeo must die', even so it would nevertheless not be true that *A* said that Romeo must die, because *A* did not intend his utterance to exhibit that content. In light of such complexities, in the text it is assumed that *these* kinds of obstacles to the entailment do not hold. Yet, as will emerge, the entailment still sometimes won't go through.

3. Since the point is easy to miss, let me stress that Stanley thinks that being gradable is a necessary condition for being context sensitive in the way that 'tall' supposedly is. He does not think it sufficient.

4. Or more precisely, 'know' *in its propositional uses* is not gradable. One might, for all that has been said here, think that 'knows how' is gradable. Similarly, as Dretske points out, for 'knowing her/him'. That, however, is not obviously relevant to contextualism in epistemology.

5. I should mention that John Hawthorne (2003, 2004) has recently offered linguistically based arguments against contextualism as well. Since I'm granting the conclusion of such arguments, I won't discuss Hawthorne's points here. See also Douven 2004.

6. The same shift appears in contextualists about 'good'. At the beginning of "Contextual Analysis in Ethics," Peter Unger talks about contextual variability in *judgments* about whether something is permissible: "In many cases, the truth-value (or the acceptability) of a judgment about whether a person's behavior is morally permissible depends on the context in which the judgment is made" (1995, 2). Similarly, James Dreier (1990, 7) says that moral *claims* shift relative to context, and that people using "*x* is good" and "*x* is not good" may both *speak truly*. All of this is consistent with 'good', 'right', etc., *not* being context-sensitive words, if pragmatics can directly affect what is asserted. But a few pages later, Unger makes explicitly typesemantical claims to the effect that moral *terms* are indexical: "Because these terms are thus indexical, they can be sensitive to the contexts in which they are used or understood" (1995, 13). And Dreier also says that "the content of (what is expressed by) a sentence containing a moral term varies with (is a function of) the context in which it is used" (1990, 6). This, I think, is a rather different kettle of fish, and is subject to the kinds of linguistic criticism that Cappelen and Lepore provide.

7. It would take me too far afield to discuss these other problems in any detail. Simplifying greatly to give the flavor of the thing, however:

• in addition to assertions, there are skeptical-standard thoughts and ordinary-standard thoughts, and it's quite unclear how pragmatic determinants of *speech-act* content will split the difference between these (DeRose 1995);

- if I assert truly that S knows that p at t_1, it doesn't follow that I may assert truly at t_{1+n} that S knew at t_1 that p, which seems bizarre (Lewis 1996);
- if standards really are shifting, and especially if they are shifting because of varying speaker intentions, it's peculiar that people don't recognize that they are simply talking past one another (Schiffer 1996);
- genuine skepticism holds that by *ordinary* standards we do not know—skeptics don't grant that we have such-and-such evidence, and merely question whether that amount of evidence meets the standard for knowledge, they also question whether we have the evidence in question at all (Feldman 2001).

See Bach 2005 for discussion.

8. Just one more word about terminology; a word, in fact, about terminology that I *won't* employ. I here eschew use of the phrase 'what is said' for the following reason. Some people use 'what is said' as a synonym for (17e). Sperber and Wilson (1986) seemingly do, which is precisely why they have urged that there are "pragmatic determinants of what is said." Cappelen and Lepore in their various works on this topic also use it in this way. But others mean something more narrow by 'what is said'. Thus Bach distinguishes (17e) from his "what is said." (Indeed, he even denies that (17c), saturated expression-meaning, is what is said, since the latter includes reference assignment to expressions whose referent depends upon speakers' intentions. See Bach 1994a, 2001, and also Récanati 2001, 2002.) Given the variation in usage, it's best to just avoid the phrase.

9. Patrick Rysiew (2001) makes a related point about appealing to pragmatics to save the spirit of contextualism in epistemology, without granting that 'know' is indexical—though he does not think of pragmatics as affecting what is literally asserted. He writes: "There is no denying that epistemologists ought to 'take context into account'. Nor should we dispute the context-sensitivity of knowledge *attributions*. As for the idea that context plays an interesting role in determining the truth conditions of knowledge-attributing *sentences*, however, *that* is something which we need hardly accept" (Rysiew 2001, 507; only the last emphasis is original). What I would want to add is that the ordinary speaker does not assert falsely, though for an acceptable reason, in saying 'Keith knows that the bank is open'; nor does she merely convey something true; rather, she makes a statement that is strictly and literally true.

10. Charles Travis (1991), noting in effect that there are pragmatic determinants of what is asserted/stated/claimed, argues that Grice does not—simply by showing that Moore's utterance of 'I know I have hands' has (in my terms) a saturated expression-meaning—thereby win the day against Malcolm. For, the issue is surely whether Moore asserted truly in so speaking, and this requires something more than the existence of a saturated expression-meaning. See also Travis 1985.

11. My thanks to David Hunter for raising this point, and to Jonathan Schaffer and Robert Stalnaker for very useful discussion of it.

References

Bach, K. 1994a. "Semantic Slack: What Is Said and More." In S. Tsohatzidis, ed., *Foundations of Speech Act Theory*. London: Routledge.

Bach, K. 1994b. "Conversational Implicature." *Mind and Language* 9: 124–162.

Bach, K. 2001. "You Don't Say?" *Synthèse* 128: 15–44.

Bach, K. 2002. "Seemingly Semantic Intuitions." In J. Keim Campbell, M. O'Rourke, and D. Shier, eds., *Meaning and Truth: Investigations in Philosophical Semantics*. New York: Seven Bridges Press.

Bach, K. 2005. "The Emperor's New 'Knows'." In G. Preyer and G. Peter, eds., *Contextualism in Philosophy*. Oxford: Oxford University Press.

Borg, E. 2004. *Minimal Semantics*. Oxford: Oxford University Press.

Borg, E. 2005. "Saying What You Mean: Unarticulated Constituents and Communication." In R. Elugardo and R. Stainton, eds., *Ellipsis and Nonsentential Speech*. Dordrecht: Springer.

Cappelen, H., and E. Lepore. 1997. "On an Alleged Connection between Indirect Quotation and Semantic Theory." *Mind and Language* 12: 278–296.

Cappelen, H., and E. Lepore. 1998. "Reply to Richard and Reimer." *Mind and Language* 13: 617–621.

Cappelen, H., and E. Lepore. 2003. "Context Shifting Arguments." *Philosophical Perspectives* 17: 25–50.

Cappelen, H., and E. Lepore. 2005a. *Insensitive Semantics*. Oxford: Oxford University Press.

Cappelen, H., and E. Lepore. 2005b. "Radical and Moderate Pragmatics: Does Meaning Determine Truth Conditions?" In Z. Szabó, ed., *Semantics versus Pragmatics*. Oxford: Oxford University Press.

Carston, R. 1988. "Implicature, Explicature, and Truth-Theoretic Semantics." In R. Kempson, ed., *Mental Representations*. Cambridge: Cambridge University Press.

Carston, R. 2002. *Thoughts and Utterances*. Oxford: Blackwell.

Cohen, S. 1991. "Skepticism, Relevance, and Relativity." In B. McLaughlin, ed., *Dretske and His Critics*. Cambridge, Mass.: Blackwell.

Cohen, S. 1999. "Contextualism, Skepticism, and the Structure of Reasons." *Philosophical Perspectives* 13: 57–89.

DeRose, K. 1992. "Contextualism and Knowledge Attributions." *Philosophy and Phenomenological Research* 52: 913–929.

DeRose, K. 1995. "Solving the Skeptical Problem." *Philosophical Review* 104: 1–52.

DeRose, K. 1999. "Contextualism: An Explanation and Defense." In J. Greco and E. Sosa, eds., *The Blackwell Guide to Epistemology*. Oxford: Blackwell.

Douven, I. 2004. "The Context-Insensitivity of 'Knowing More' and 'Knowing Better'." *Canadian Journal of Philosophy* 34: 313–326.

Dreier, J. 1990. "Internalism and Speaker Relativism." *Ethics* 101: 6–26.

Dretske, F. 1981a. *Knowledge and the Flow of Information*. Cambridge, Mass.: MIT Press.

Dretske, F. 1981b. "The Pragmatic Dimension of Knowledge." *Synthèse* 40: 363–378.

Feldman, R. 2001. "Skeptical Problems, Contextualist Solutions." *Philosophical Studies* 103: 61–85.

Hawthorne, J. 2003. "Contextualism in Epistemology." Paper delivered to the American Philosophical Association Pacific Division, San Francisco, California, March 28, 2003.

Hawthorne, J. 2004. *Knowledge and Lotteries*. Oxford: Oxford University Press.

Kaplan, D. 1989. "Demonstratives." In J. Almog, J. Perry, and H. Wettstein, eds., *Themes from Kaplan*. Oxford: Oxford University Press.

Lewis, D. 1996. "Elusive Knowledge." *Australasian Journal of Philosophy* 74: 549–567.

Perry, J. 1986. "Thought without Representation." *Proceedings of the Aristotelian Society Supplementary Volume* 60: 263–283.

Récanati, F. 2001. "What Is Said." *Synthèse* 128: 75–91.

Récanati, F. 2002. "Unarticulated Constituents." *Linguistics and Philosophy* 25: 299–345.

Rysiew, P. 2001. "The Context-Sensitivity of Knowledge Attributions." *Noûs* 35: 477–514.

Schiffer, S. 1996. "Contextualist Solutions to Scepticism." *Proceedings of the Aristotelian Society* 96: 317–333.

Searle, J. 1978. "Literal Meaning." *Erkenntnis* 13: 207–224.

Searle, J. 1980. "The Background of Meaning." In J. Searle, F. Kiefer, and M. Bierwisch, eds., *Speech Act Theory and Pragmatics*. Dordrecht: Reidel.

Sperber, D., and D. Wilson. 1986. *Relevance*. Cambridge, Mass.: Harvard University Press.

Stainton, R. 2005. "In Defense of Nonsentential Assertion." In Z. Szabó, ed., *Semantics vs. Pragmatics*. Oxford: Oxford University Press.

Stainton, R. 2006. *Words and Thoughts*. Oxford: Oxford University Press.

Stanley, J. 2000. "Context and Logical Form." *Linguistics and Philosophy* 23: 391–434.

Stanley, J. 2004. "On the Linguistic Basis for Contextualism." *Philosophical Studies* 119: 119–146.

Stanley, J. 2005. *Knowledge and Practical Interests*. Oxford: Oxford University Press.

Stine, G. 1976. "Skepticism, Relevant Alternatives, and Deductive Closure." *Philosophical Studies* 29: 249–261.

Travis, C. 1985. "On What Is Strictly Speaking True." *Canadian Journal of Philosophy* 15: 187–229.

Travis, C. 1991. "Annals of Analysis." *Mind* 100: 237–264.

Unger, P. 1975. *Ignorance: A Case Study for Skepticism*. New York: Oxford University Press.

Unger, P. 1986. "The Cone Model of Knowledge." *Philosophical Topics* 14: 125–178.

Unger, P. 1995. "Contextual Analysis in Ethics." *Philosophy and Phenomenological Research* 55: 1–26.

7 Locke's Account of Sensitive Knowledge

George Pappas

Locke's epistemology, particularly as it concerns sensitive knowledge of external physical objects, is usually thought to suffer from both internal, textually supported difficulties, and also from powerful philosophical objections. The former difficulties concern Locke's apparent commitment, in Book IV of the *Essay*, to the thesis that all sensitive knowledge is *inferential*, and that a crucial step in any such inference will be a premise asserting a resemblance or conformity between currently experienced ideas and features of the object. Locke seems to assert that these inferences succeed only if one *knows* this premise with certainty. We are never in a position to have certain knowledge of that premise, according to Berkeley and a host of later writers, and so Locke is in the unfortunate position of having committed himself to an epistemological position that he lacks the resources to sustain.

There is also a philosophical objection to Locke's account of sensitive knowledge. The idea here is that Lockean sensitive knowledge must be inferential even if Locke's texts do not outright assert the view that these inferences move through a known-resemblance premise. Locke accepts an indirect realist account of perception, it is usually supposed, and it allows only for inferential knowledge of external bodies. Such knowledge would require a form of inductive inference that, so the argument goes, just does not work. So, independently of whether the texts actually show that Locke adopts this inferential account of sensitive knowledge, he is stuck with such an account and it ultimately fails. Locke may say that he thinks that there is sensitive knowledge, and even say that it is acquired without dependence on inference; but his theory of perception dictates otherwise and, indeed, leads directly to skepticism with regard to external objects.

In this essay, I look again at this twofold picture of Locke's epistemology which, I agree, makes Locke's theory of knowledge look quite unappealing. On the textual side, I try to show that Locke does not adopt the inferential picture about sensitive knowledge, both because the passages in which he is said to adopt that stance do not support that reading and also because other passages point in a different direction. I also try to show, on the philosophical side, that Locke's specific form of indirect realist theory is perfectly compatible with there being non-inferential sensitive knowledge.

Sensitive Knowledge in the *Essay*

At the outset I want to mention a number of interpretive problems that I will set aside. The first is what I call the "problem of the official definition," which seems to rule out sensitive knowledge from the start. Locke says that knowledge is perception of the agreement or disagreement of relations between ideas (IV, I, 1),[1] and this definition certainly seems to have the double consequence that all knowledge is between *pairs* or multiples of ideas, and that knowledge is had only of ideas and never of objects. The first consequence would rule out even knowledge of single, currently experienced ideas, along with knowledge of oneself; and the latter would rule out sensitive knowledge altogether. I will here assume that this problem can be solved and in a way that blocks both of these unwanted consequences.[2]

A second problem concerns certainty and the close tie this concept has, for Locke, to that of knowledge. Locke definitely seems to hold that all knowledge, and thus all sensitive knowledge, is also certain knowledge. Sensitive knowledge, if there is any, is surely not certain to the degree or in the manner of intuitive and demonstrative knowledge, so Locke would need a weaker concept of certainty to apply to sensitive knowledge. But it is hard to see what this might be, other than high probability—and *that*, Locke emphatically asserts, falls short of knowledge. I will take no stand on this issue but will set it to the side, thus tacitly assuming that Locke can provide for a concept of certainty that is stronger than high probability and still suitable for sensitive knowledge.

A third problem concerns the content of propositions sensitively known. Locke not only restricts sensitive knowledge to objects "presently perceived," but also seems to restrict sensitive knowledge to propositions expressed by sentences such as "Some object or other is causing my current ideas of sensation." This "restricted content problem," as we might call it, excludes simple propositions such as that expressed by "There is a spherical object before me," as items of sensitive knowledge, and if that cannot be allowed we might well wonder why anyone should care about the sensitive knowledge Locke does allow for. Again, I set this aside for present purposes, though a fuller treatment of sensitive knowledge in Locke will have to confront this issue.[3]

Connected to the restricted content problem is the matter of propositions asserting that some object has a secondary quality such as color. Locke famously holds that objects altogether lack colors as we perceive them in objects, and that colors in objects are merely powers to cause ideas of relevant sorts. So, on one account a proposition expressed by 'That spherical object before me is red' would just be *false*, and so unknowable even if the restricted content problem can be resolved in a liberating manner. In that case, while Locke might have a way to accommodate sensitive knowledge of an object's possession of a primary quality such as shape, he would have to rule out knowledge of all propositions asserting that this or that object has some secondary quality. Adequately dealing with this question of secondary quality propositions would take us far afield, and so will not be taken up here.

Textual Issues

In an account of real knowledge, that is, knowledge of actually existing bodies, Locke goes so far as to say that,

Where-ever we perceive the Agreement or Disagreement of any of our *Ideas*, there is certain Knowledge; and where-ever we are sure those *Ideas* agree with the reality of Things, there is certain real Knowledge. (IV, IV, 18)

In a related passage Locke seems to stress inference:

There can be nothing more certain, than that the *Idea* we receive from an external Object is in our Minds; this is intuitive Knowledge. But whether there be any thing more than barely that *Idea* in our Minds, whether we can thence certainly infer the existence of any thing without us, which corresponds to that *Idea*, is that, whereof some Men think there may be a question made... (IV, II, 14)

In this second passage Locke's stress is just on the need for inference if we are to have sensitive knowledge of bodies; in the first he is concerned to say something about the form of that inference.

In another part of the *Essay* Locke speaks of judgments that are made in perceiving objects, and if that is correct the road would be open to the further idea that knowledge of perceived objects depends on inference. He notes:

We are farther to consider concerning Perception, that the *Ideas we receive by Sensation*, are often in grown People *alter'd by the Judgement*, without our Taking any notice of it. When we set before our Eyes a round Globe, or any uniform Colour, *v.g.* Gold, Alabaster, or Jet, 'tis certain, that the *Idea* imprinted in our Mind, is of a flat Circle variously shadow'd, with several degrees of Light and Brightness coming to our Eyes. But we having by use been accustomed to perceive, what kind of appearance convex Bodies are wont to make in us; what alterations are made in the reflections of Light, by the difference of the sensible Figures of Bodies, the Judgement presently, by an habitual custom, alters the Appearances into their Causes: So that from that, which truly is variety of shadow or colour, collecting the Figure, it makes it pass for a mark of Figure, and frames to itself the perception of a convex Figure, and a uniform Colour; when the Idea we receive from thence, is only a Plain variously colour'd, as is evident in Painting. (II, IX, 8; emphases in original)

This passage presents just an example to illustrate a point; but if we generalize from it, as perhaps we can, we would reach the result that some judgment is present in all perception of bodies, though not necessarily a judgment that alters anything, as in the globe example.

Further, this passage makes clear that the judgment is in some way based on the appearances received. If we then think of the judgment as a perceptual belief, it would seem safe to say that Locke's point would be that this perceptual belief is based on and inferred from the beliefs one would initially have about the appearances.

Moreover, Locke seems to make this same point later in the *Essay*, and in a way that spells out the sorts of inferences he has in mind in more detail. He begins by saying this:

But besides the assurance we have from our Senses themselves, that they do not err in the Information they give us, of the Existence of Things without us, when we are affected by them, we are farther confirmed in this assurance, by other concurrent Reasons. (IV, XI, 3)

He then goes on to spell out these concurrent reasons, one of which is this:

...if I turn my Eyes at noon towards the Sun, I cannot avoid the *Ideas*, which the Light, or Sun, then produces in me. So that there is a manifest difference between the *Ideas* laid up in my Memory...and those which force themselves upon me, and I cannot avoid having. And therefore it must needs be some exterior cause, and the brisk acting of some Objects without me, whose efficacy I cannot resist, that produces those *Ideas* in my Mind, whether I will, or no. (IV, XI, 5)

In this case, Locke's point is that the inference is a causal one, based not just on the having of relevant ideas but also on their felt irresistibility. Since he is here expressly addressing the question of how we come to have sensitive knowledge, through these concurrent reasons, it again seems clear that Locke's overall point is that such sensitive knowledge as we may have derives from inferences from beliefs of one sort or another about experienced ideas.

Correcting Impressions

While these several texts may seem initially to be compelling, in fact closer scrutiny shows otherwise. In the first passage cited above, Locke seems to require that a cognizer be certain of a conformity between current ideas and objects or features of objects if that cognizer is to gain knowledge of the object through perception. We can think of this as strong conformity, because it demands knowledge that a conformity obtains. Whether Locke actually endorses this in the passage cited will depend on how we interpret his use of 'where-ever'. Strong endorsement would be there endorsed if that term was used by Locke to express a biconditional, of the form:

A person gains knowledge of objects via perception iff she is sure that her ideas conform to (agree with) the objects.

But it is also possible to interpret this passage as expressing merely a sufficient condition for knowledge of the object, and not a necessary condition; and if that is the correct reading, then the passage will not support the thesis that the knowledge one thereby gains is inferential.

To see that this alternative reading is not only possible but plausible, we can consider some other texts where Locke endorses a weaker form of conformity. He says at one point,

'Tis evident, the Mind knows not Things immediately, but only by the intervention of the *Ideas* it has of them. Our *Knowledge* therefore is *real*, only so far as there is a conformity between our *Ideas* and the reality of Things. (IV, IV, 3)

Further, Locke draws a parallel between the reality of knowledge and real truth. He says,

Though what has been said in the fore-going Chapter, to distinguish real from imaginary Knowledge, might suffice here, in answer to this Doubt, to distinguish *real Truth* from *chimerical*, or (if you please) *barely nominal*, they both depending on the same foundation. (IV, V, 8)

Slightly farther on in this passage Locke notes what this foundation is:

And therefore Truth, as well as Knowledge, may well come under the distinction of *Verbal* and *Real*; that being only *verbal Truth*, wherein terms are joined according to the agreement or disagreement of the *Ideas* they stand for, without regarding whether our *Ideas* are such, as really have, or are capable of having an Existence in Nature. But then it is they contain *real Truth*, when these signs are joined, as our

Ideas agree; and when our *Ideas* are such, we know are capable of having an Existence in Nature. (IV, V, 8)

In this passage the necessary condition for real truth is agreement of the ideas with things. And as this is claimed to be parallel with the case of real knowledge, Locke's point would have to be that one has real knowledge only if one's ideas conform or agree with things in nature. This is a weak form of conformity, one that does not require that one know that there is such a conformity in place. So the requirement of strong conformity cannot be used to support the thesis that sensitive knowledge is inferential because, as we here see, Locke does not require strong conformity.

These considerations affect only strong conformity, and the supposed inferences that would proceed through that step. Passages already quoted, however, at least suggest that inference of some sort is required by Locke, even if it has nothing to do with strong conformity. Two already-quoted passages bring this out:

There can be nothing more certain, than that the *Idea* we receive from an external Object is in our Minds; this is intuitive Knowledge. But whether there be any thing more than barely that *Idea* in our Minds, whether we can thence certainly infer the existence of any thing without us, which corresponds to that *Idea*, is that, whereof some Men think there may be a question made.... (IV, II, 14)

'Tis evident, the Mind knows not Things immediately, but only by the intervention of the *Ideas* it has of them. Our *Knowledge* therefore is *real*, only so far as there is a conformity between our *Ideas* and the reality of Things. (IV, IV, 3)

The first of these passages, it may be conceded, supports the need for some form of inference, as Locke sees it, if we are to have sensitive knowledge. Whether it counts as Locke's all-things-considered position, however, awaits the consideration of contrary passages to be taken up below. The second passage is less clear, however, for the intervention of ideas to which it refers can plausibly be interpreted as a claim about ideas being perceptual intermediaries whenever one acquires sensitive knowledge, rather than a claim about their also being epistemic intermediaries. An epistemic interpretation of this passage, therefore, according to which some inference is made from ideas to beliefs about objects, goes beyond what the text strictly allows.

Also overdrawn is the thesis that Locke requires an element of judgment in all perception. We can begin to see this once we notice that in the passage concerning judgment altering the appearances, Locke is merely claiming that one's unconscious judgment alters the original idea. He does not say that the judgment issues in or constitutes a belief to the effect that the object has the qualities correspondent to the altered ideas. On the contrary, Locke's point is that judgment enters to create new ideas, or to change existing ones, and in either case the result is ideas different from those given passively in sense. This seems to be the only role for judgment in the passage quoted above. In other words, judgment is not there claimed to be belief-productive, but rather idea-altering. While this role for judgment may compromise some of what Locke maintains about the passivity of perception for all simple ideas, it does not establish that judgment is present in all perception, and for that reason cannot be used to prop up the thesis that sensitive, perceptual knowledge of objects is inferential.

Lastly there are the passages on concurrent reasons from Book IV, chapter XI of the *Essay*. My sense of those passages is that Locke's aim in them is not to explain the sorts of inferences that are needed in connection with acquiring knowledge of bodies, but rather that he is defending the general reliability of the senses. To see this, it helps to look at the passage again in a slightly fuller context.

This is certain, the confidence that our faculties do not herein deceive us, is the greatest assurance we are capable of, concerning the existence of material beings. For we cannot act anything, but by our faculties; nor talk of knowledge itself, but by the help of those faculties, which are fitted to apprehend even what knowledge is. But besides the assurance we have from our senses themselves, that they do not err in the information they give us, of the existence of things without us, when they are affected by them, we are farther confirmed in this assurance, by other concurrent reasons. (IV, XI, 4)

This passage is then followed by a series of these concurrent reasons, including that alluded to earlier; and it should be clear from this context-setting passage which configures the whole discussion of concurrent reasons that Locke's aim is to bolster the idea that the senses are generally reliable. Since that is Locke's sole aim in that discussion, it is inappropriate to make use of the discussion of concurrent reasons as evidence of the thesis that sensitive knowledge is inferential.

So far the discussion has been negative, focusing on why the passages often adduced in favor of the inferential model of sensitive knowledge do not in the end support that reading. On the positive side, however, there are other passages that are most naturally read as supporting the view that sensitive knowledge is non-inferential. The first to be considered is this:

...I think we may add to the two former sorts of Knowledge (intuitive and demonstrative) this also, of the existence of particular external Objects, by that perception and Consciousness we have of the actual entrance of Ideas from them. (IV, II, 14)

Here Locke's point is that perception of the objects is sufficient to yield knowledge of the existence of the objects. A similar point is made elsewhere:

...we can have no knowledge, farther than we can have Perception of that Agreement or Disagreement: which Perception being, 1. Either by *Intuition*, or the immediate comparing any two Ideas; or, 2. By *Reason*, examining the agreement of the two Ideas, by the intervention of some others; or, 3. By *Sensation*, perceiving the Existence of particular things. (IV, III, 2)

Other passages support the same reading. For instance, in *Draft A* of the *Essay*, Locke speaks about our gaining knowledge of objects by the senses, or gaining knowledge by the sense alone:

The first & most natural predication or affirmation is of the existence not of the Idea but something without my minde answering that Idea, as having in my minde the Idea of white the question is whether any such quality i.e. that whose appearance before my eys always causes that Idea doth realy exist i.e. hath a being without me? & of this the greatest assureance I can possibly have & to which my faultys can atteine is the testimony of my eys, which are the proper & sole judges of this thing, & whose testimony I rely on as soe certaine, that I can noe more doubt whilst I write this that I see white & black & that they realy exist then that I write, which is a certainety as great as humane nature is capable of concerning the existence of any thing.... (1990, 20–21)

One point Locke is here stressing is that perception alone, without the need for added inference, suffices for one to gain knowledge of the features of external things. We may note, as well, that Locke also speaks here of knowledge of objects as *certain* knowledge, and this is some evidence, though not conclusive evidence, that he regards sensitive knowledge as non-inferential. The reason this is so derives from the fact that if sensitive knowledge were inferential, it would hardly ever be demonstrative, that is, based on deductively entailing evidence. Rather, it would be based on some inductive support, most likely of some explanatory causal sort. If *that* were the typical sort of evidence from which one gained sensitive knowledge, then it is hardly likely that it would qualify as certain. In fact, it would generate belief that is at best highly probable, and this is something Locke regards as falling short of knowledge.

In *Draft B* of the *Essay* Locke says something much weaker, namely that knowledge of objects is "founded on" the senses, a claim that is compatible with such knowledge being inferential (1990, 258). But elsewhere in the same draft Locke says that the simple regularity of the kinds of ideas suffices for certain knowledge of their causes and, as he takes these causes to be "without," we can interpret him as claiming that we have certain knowledge of objects that derives from the regularity of the ideas that they cause. Indeed, it is this sort of regularity, rather than inference from beliefs about current ideas, that Locke thinks underlies and is the explication of sensitive knowledge of bodies.[4]

So on balance, the chief passages where Locke seems to insist that sensitive knowledge *requires* inference from ideas, do not support such a reading; and there are collateral passages, both in the *Essay* and in two of the *Drafts*, where Locke stresses the very opposite—namely, that we gain knowledge of the existence of bodies by perception of those very bodies themselves. Inference from ideas, of course, *may* in rare cases operate to support a belief in bodies, but not in general, and typically Locke's view is that such inference is simply not needed.

Indirect Realism and Inference

The philosophical point noted at the outset is that indirect realism as a theory of perception is supposed to entail that any knowledge one acquires via perception be inferential knowledge. Locke is usually taken as having accepted a specific form of indirect realism, namely representative realism, and so his theory of perception would have the same entailment regarding perceptual knowledge of objects. Any such knowledge would be inferential, even if Locke himself did not realize this.

The indirect realist theory minimally maintains that in every perception, whether veridical or not, at least one phenomenal individual is immediately perceived. The physical objects that, in veridical cases, are the causes of these experiences of the phenomenal objects are not themselves immediately perceived. Rather, these physical objects are held to be only indirectly perceived. Their perception is said to be dependent upon and mediated by the immediate perception of the phenomenal objects.

Typically, it is held that more is involved. It is generally held, too, that an event of judging is involved in object-perception, either as a component of the perceptual event, or as actually making up the perception of the object. On the latter account, the event of immediately perceiving the phenomenal individual is not strictly a part of the event of perceiving the object. It is merely the causal antecedent to the event of judging, and it is this judging event that strictly speaking *is* the perception of the object. Seen in this way, the event of perceiving an object really does not have any sensory content. Whatever sensory content there may be is present simply as a causal and non-judgmental antecedent.[5]

Alternatively, one might construe the event of judging as just one component of a complex whole, and identify that complex with the perception of the object. All the elements of the first version are still in place: There is the event of immediate perception of some phenomenal individuals, itself standing in some causal relation to the object; experience of the phenomenal individuals, in turn, is a cause of an event of judging; and the complex ⟨immediate perception of phenomenal objects + judging that such-and-such⟩, construed as an organic whole with "fused" elements, is taken to *be* the event of perceiving the object. On this account, it is not judging alone that is the perception of the object. It is the complex event that contains an event of judging, related in just the right way to other elements, that is the event of perception of the object.

It is at least plausible that indirect realism, construed in either of these ways, will yield only inferential knowledge of perceived objects. Whether it does is apt to depend on what we take the content of the judgment made in a given perceptual context to be. Suppose that the content is always of a form that relates the current phenomenal objects to their likely causes, perhaps as given by "These visual sensa (phenomenal objects) of red are probably caused by a ripe tomato." In that case, due notice of the experienced phenomenal objects is taken in the very judgment, so it looks very much as if one is inferring that a tomato is present and causally effective from one's recognition of the visual sensa. And if this is general, being the form of the judgment in all cases of perception of objects, then the inferential character of perceptual knowledge of objects would seem an inevitable consequence of indirect realism.

If we think of the judgmental element in perception in a different way, however, matters are not as clear. For instance, if the judged content is merely that given by "There is a ripe tomato before me," so that no mention is made, in the perceptual judgment, of the currently experienced sensa, then knowledge that there is a ripe tomato present might qualify as non-inferential. The experienced sensa, in other words, might be merely the causally sufficient conditions for the judgment, not an epistemic basis for the judgment.

The point can best be seen if we think of a reliable-process theory of knowledge, adapted from the more familiar reliable-process theory of justified belief. So long as the process that takes experiences of phenomenal objects as inputs, and judgments (beliefs) that some object has this or that property as outputs, is a reliable process, the judgment or belief will qualify as knowledge. The event of experiencing phenomenal objects would function merely as the causal inputs to a process that generates beliefs as outputs, rather than as pieces of evidence from which the belief is inferred. In this way, even an indirect realist theory that finds an essential home for an element of judgment in all perceptual experiences would be perfectly compatible with knowledge of physical objects being non-inferential.

One might grant this point about the compatibility of indirect realism and non-inferential knowledge of objects, but go on to say that it is of no help in Locke's specific case. This is so, according to this line of argument, because Locke *does* accept the form of indirect realism that makes an essential place for judgment in all perception; *and because* the form-of-judgment ingredient in perception, for Locke, will always be one that takes the currently experienced phenomenal individuals (ideas, for Locke) to both represent and be caused by some physical object. The judgment, that is, will always be of the form, "The ideas I am currently experiencing represent and are likely caused by object *O*." Evidence that Locke accepted this view can be found in this passage:

'Tis therefore the actual receiving of *Ideas* from without, that gives us notice of the *Existence* of other Things, and makes us know, that something doth exist at that time without us, which causes that *Idea* in us, though perhaps we neither know nor consider how it does it. (IV, XI, 2)

This passage also bears on the restricted content problem that I mentioned at the outset, since here Locke seems to be saying that the content of propositions making up bits of sensitive knowledge will always be restricted to those asserting the simple existence and causal action of an object, but without further mention of any qualities that object might possess. Nor would any mention be made of the kind of object, say a table or an automobile, that was then present and exercising its causal power.

The plausibility of this line of reasoning in favor of the thesis that Locke's specific version of indirect realism leads to the view that sensitive knowledge is inferential depends squarely on the premise that all perception, for Locke, includes some element of judgment. In an earlier section, above, I briefly looked at the main text in favor of this "judgment version" of indirect realism to Locke and argued that the favored texts do not support that reading. Now we can look at additional texts that suggest that Locke understood his own theory of perception in a "non-judgment" way.

Early in Book II of the *Essay*, Locke says that perception is nothing more than the having of ideas. He writes:

To ask, *at what time a man has first any* Ideas, is to ask, when he begins to perceive; having *Ideas*, and Perception being the same thing. (II, I, 9; emphases in original.)

This passage suggests that Locke identifies the event of perceiving an object with the event of experiencing some ideas or, as we might also put it, he takes the sensory part of perception to be all there is to perception of objects. He makes essentially the same point elsewhere in a discussion of the perception of pain.

Fire may burn our Bodies, with no other effect, than it does a Billet, unless that motion be continued to the Brain, and there the sence of Heat, or *Idea* of Pain, be produced in the Mind, wherein consists *actual Perception.* (II, IX, 3; emphases in original)

In this case I take the phrase "wherein consists actual Perception" to be making a point about what perception *is* (namely the having of the relevant ideas), and not to be making a point about the location of the perception (namely, in the mind). On such a reading of this passage, Locke is repeating the point made earlier, namely, that there is nothing more to perception than the sensory element.

Of course, Locke's point cannot be taken in a thoroughly unrestricted manner. The *mere* having of ideas cannot be what perception amounts to, because one has ideas in dreams, hallucinations, illusions, and other sorts of experiences we would not want to take as perceptions of objects. His point has to be something more along the lines of this: Object-perception is nothing more than the experience of ideas of sensation that are brought about in the "right" way, that is, by causal action of the perceived body.

I will refer to this way of understanding indirect realism as the *constitution version*. This is because the theory maintains that each event of object-perception consists in, or is constituted by, an event of experiencing the "right sorts" of ideas, that is, ideas causally related to the object in just the right, non-deviant way. Such a theory would still count as indirect realism overall, because it would still be true that in every perception at least some ideas would be immediately perceived, and it would still be true as well that each event of object-perception would be dependent upon and mediated by an event of experiencing some ideas. Further, the dependence here would be asymmetric, just as we would expect. The experience of the ideas would not be dependent on or mediated by the perception of the object.

To get a sense of this version of indirect realism, we can briefly look at a related theory recently defended by Alston. Alston rejects Locke's account of sensation, couched as that is in terms of the immediate experience of phenomenal individuals (ideas). He rejects as well the so-called adverbial account of sensing, according to which sensations are adverbial events of sensing in certain ways. Instead, Alston adopts what Chisholm had years earlier labeled the "theory of appearing," which takes non-comparative events of appearing as primitive and then uses these events to devise a theory of perception. Here is Alston's take on his own theory:

the analysis of the concept of object perception given by the Theory of Appearing is of breathtaking simplicity. For S to perceive x is simply for x to appear to S as so-and-so. That is all there is to it. At least that is all there is to the *concept* of perception. Thus the Theory of Appearing is a form of "direct" realism, even "naïve" realism, in that it endorses our spontaneous, naïve way of taking sense experience as involving direct awareness of an object that is presented to consciousness, usually an external physical object. (1991, 55)

Alston thus identifies object-perception with the sensory element alone, just as Locke does, as indicated above. The difference is in their respective construals of this sensory element. For Locke, as we have been understanding him, the sensory element amounts to the immediate perception of one or more ideas of sensation, while in Alston the sensory component is just something's appearing as thus-and-so to an individual. Further, as Alston has no perceived intermediaries (something's appearing thus-and-so to an individual is not itself something the individual perceives), his theory allows for direct realism in a way that Locke's does not. In every other respect, their theories are the same. Events of object-perception are said to consist in nothing more than the sensory element, understood in the right way.

So far as I know, Alston does not adopt a reliable-process theory of *knowledge*, though he is well known for defending a reliable-process theory of epistemic justification. It is easy to see how the theory would work in many perceptual contexts. Events of something appearing a certain way to an individual would typically count as non-doxastic and non-epistemic inputs to processes that have beliefs about objects as outputs. When these processes are reliable, their doxastic outputs are justified, or at least prima facie justified, and outright justified provided there are no defeaters on hand. Alston's direct realist theory of perception, then, is perfectly compatible with a reliable-process theory of justified belief, and it should be clear that the justification involved is typically non-inferential in character. The relevant inputs in Alston's case are non-doxastic and non-epistemic, and so they do not function as elements of evidence from which beliefs derive their degree of justification.

In his discussion of sensitive knowledge, Locke is not talking about justified belief but instead about knowledge of objects. Nevertheless, it is easy to see that Locke's constitution version of indirect realism is compatible with a reliable-process theory knowledge. The events of immediately perceiving

one or more ideas of sensation would count as the relevant inputs, and
beliefs about objects would count both as causal products of the sensory
events and as outputs to the processes that take sensory events as inputs.
Processes of this sort that count as reliable, Locke can say, are those that
are productive of sensitive knowledge. The inputs to these processes, for
Locke, are akin to those in Alston in another manner, namely they are
non-doxastic, non-epistemic events. Thus, as in Alston, they do not count
as premises or items of evidence that provide support for the output beliefs.
Just as in the case of Alston's epistemically justified beliefs, Locke's output
beliefs would count as non-inferential items of knowledge, for the reliable
processes that yield such knowledge as outputs take non-evidential items as
inputs.

I have argued neither that the constitution version of indirect realism is
plausible nor that a reliable-process account of knowledge is; similarly, I
have not argued that their conjunction is plausible. Finally, I have not
argued that this conjunction avoids the charge that Locke's theory of perception leads to skepticism. I have only argued, instead, that something
like the constitution theory is found in Locke; that *it* consistently conjoins
with a reliable-process account of knowledge; and that this conjunction
escapes the charge that Locke's theory of perception requires that sensitive
knowledge be inferential. This conjunction of the constitution version of
indirect realism and the reliable-process theory of knowledge would allow
Locke to avoid skepticism *only* in the sense that it would avoid the usual
way in which skepticism is said to arise for Locke's theory of perception.
Whether it *really* avoids skepticism all things considered, of course, is another matter altogether.

Notes

1. This and all similar references in the text are to the book, chapter, and section of
Locke 1975.

2. This point is further discussed in Pappas 1998, 288ff.

3. Restricted content of just this sort seems to be endorsed in the *Essay*; see IV, XI, 2.
Note, though, that even in this section Locke seems to also say that we know that
the quality WHITE exists "without."

4. On the regularity of ideas underwriting and supporting beliefs about external
objects, see *Draft B* in Locke 1990, 142–144. For an insightful discussion of this
point, see Bolton 2004.

5. This fact is often taken as a major drawback to theories of this type. I discuss this
in connection with Reid's theory of perception in Pappas 1989.

References

Alston, W. 1991. *Perceiving God*. Ithaca: Cornell University Press.

Bolton, M. 2004. "Locke on the Semantic and Epistemic Role of Simple Ideas of Sensation." *Pacific Philosophical Quarterly* 85: 301–321.

Locke, J. 1975. *An Essay Concerning Human Understanding*. Peter Nidditch, ed. Oxford: Clarendon Press.

Locke, J. 1990. *Drafts for the Essay Concerning Human Understanding, and other Philosophical Writings*. P. Nidditch and G. A. J. Rogers, eds. Oxford: Clarendon Press.

Pappas, G. 1989. "Sensation and Perception in Reid." *Noûs* 23: 155–167.

Pappas, G. 1998. "Epistemology in the Empiricists." *History of Philosophy Quarterly* 15: 285–302.

8 Revelations: On What Is Manifest in Visual Experience

Joseph T. Tolliver

The Doctrine of Revelation for Colors

In "How to Speak of the Colors," Mark Johnston articulates several theses he takes to be part of our commonsense conception of color. They include:

Paradigms: Some of what we take to be paradigms of canary yellow things (e.g. some canaries) are canary yellow.

Explanation: The fact of a surface or volume or radiant source being canary yellow sometimes causally explains our visual experience as of canary yellow things.

Unity: Thanks to its nature and the nature of the other determinate shades, canary yellow, like the other shades, has its own unique place in the network of similarity, difference and exclusion relations exhibited by the whole family of shades. (Think of the relations exemplified along the axes of hue, saturation and brightness in the so-called color solid. The color solid captures central facts about the colors, e.g. that canary yellow is not as similar to the shades of blue as they are similar among themselves, i.e. that canary yellow is not a shade of blue.)

Perceptual availability: Justified belief about the canary yellowness of external things is available simply on the basis of visual perception. That is, if external things are canary yellow we are justified in believing this just on the basis of visual perception and the beliefs which typically inform it. (Further philosophical explication of this belief would come to something like this: if you are looking at a material object under what you take to be adequate conditions for perceiving its color and you take yourself to be an adequate perceiver of color then your visually acquired belief that the material object is canary yellow is justified simply on the strength of (i) the information available in the relevant visual experience and (ii) those general background beliefs about the external causes of visual experience which inform ordinary perception.)[1]

Figure 8.1
Goldfinch mule near clear canary. See plate 1.

My concern is with the last doctrine, namely, *Revelation*:

Revelation: The intrinsic nature of canary yellow is fully revealed by a standard visual experience as of a canary yellow thing.

For a yellow canary, see figure 8.1 (plate 1).

As an example of an endorsement of Revelation, Johnston quotes Russell's discussion of the knowledge of colors by acquaintance, in his *The Problems of Philosophy*.

The particular shade of colour that I am seeing may have many things said about it— I may say that it is brown, that it is rather dark, and so on. But such statements, though they make me know truths about the colour, do not make me know the colour itself any better than I did before: so far as concerns knowledge of the colour itself, as opposed to knowledge of truths about it, I know the colour perfectly and completely when I see it, and no further knowledge of it itself is even theoretically possible.[2]

Plate 1
Goldfinch mule near clear canary.

Plate 2
Salmon pink.

Plate 3
Salmon pink–red.

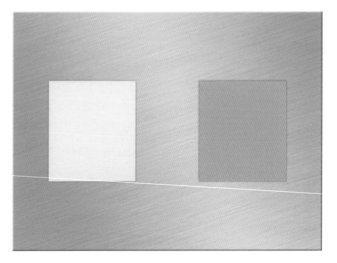

Plate 4
Manifest yellow and manifest orange.

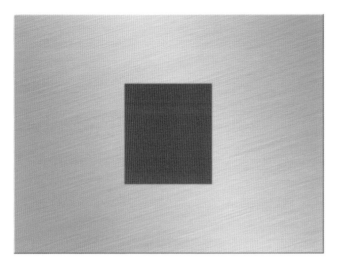

Plate 5
Manifest red.

Plate 6
The Sun Sphere.

Plate 7
The Sun Sphere.

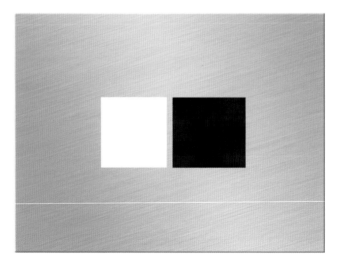

Plate 8
Two tiles from the Sun Sphere picture.

And this from Galen Strawson: "color words are words for properties which are of such a kind that their whole and essential nature as properties can be and is fully revealed in sensory-quality experience given only the qualitative character that that experience has."[3] Both of these statements of Revelation focus on color properties, but are clearly intended to capture a feature of a whole class of properties. A more general characterization of this idea might look like the following:

(Rev.)   There are perceivable qualities Q such that, a normal experience as of Q has a qualitative character C, such that, a subject's awareness of C is sufficient for the subject to fully know the intrinsic nature of a way a thing is when it is Q.

(Rev.) captures the idea that there are qualities in the world that have their intrinsic natures, what they are in themselves, fully revealed by the means of the qualitative character of normal experiences of them.

The force of the "fully" is given by the comparison to what science can tell us about the colors:

• The relationship between color and the underlying physical and chemical make-up of colored things;
• The psychophysics of the perception of color;
• The neurophysiology of the encoding and exploitation of color information in the brain;
• The semantics of color categorization and color naming systems.

Science delivers a variety of relational facts about the colors. These physical, psychophysical, neuropsychological, and semantic facts are interesting and important (to us), but are entirely beside the point of knowing what the colors are in and of themselves. What redness is in itself can only be learned in an experience as of a red thing. What is thus learned, what the quality is intrinsically, leaves nothing for a scientific theory to complete, revise, or even enhance. Or so Revelation says.

The Lockean Intuition

This conviction about the limits of a scientific theory of color and the Doctrine of Revelation are supported by a grounding intuition expressed by John Locke in his *Essay Concerning Human Understanding*: A man born blind who never receives sight can never know certain things about the nature of the colors that every normally sighted person comes to know in everyday visual experience. Here are some samples of Locke's expression of the Intuition.

The simple ideas we have are such as experience teaches them us, but if, beyond that, we endeavour by words to make them clearer in the mind, we shall succeed no better, than if we went about to clear up the darkness of a blind man's mind by talking; and to discourse into him the ideas of light and colours.[4]

The same inability will every one find in himself, who shall go about to fashion in his understanding any simple idea, not received in by his senses from external objects, or by reflection from the operations of his own mind about them. I would have any one try to fancy any taste, which had never affected his palate; or frame the idea of a scent he had never smelt: And when he can do this, I will also conclude that a blind man hath ideas of colours, and a deaf man true distinct notions of sounds.[5]

The Lockean Intuition and the Doctrine of Revelation combine to suggest that there is knowledge of the nature of color for which experiences as of colors is both necessary (the Intuition) and sufficient (the Doctrine).

Application of the Doctrine: Dispositional Theories of Color

Despite the motivation provided by the close fit between the doctrine and the intuition, it is not clear that there is a way to fit Revelation into a coherent total worldview, not even into that part of our worldview that concerns our perception of physical objects and their properties. As mentioned above, we appear to have every reason to accept a Doctrine of Explanation concerning the role of the colors in our perception of them: The fact of a surface or volume or radiant source being canary yellow sometimes causally explains our visual experience as of canary yellow things. At least part of our commonsense understanding of visual experience is that the distinctive chromatic character of that experience is causally explained by a correlated property of distal objects of visual perception. These explanatorily implicated properties of distal objects are their colors. Any property of distal objects not related in this way to the chromatic features of visual experience seems unqualified to be counted among the color properties.

The science of psychophysics collects, refines, and tests our best hypotheses about the causal explanation of experience, so candidates for the colors must come from the viable causal role-fillers it supplies. It can very well appear that the only viable candidates compatible with the requirements of Revelation are all response-dispositions, dispositional properties of parts of physical objects whose manifesting conditions are chromatic experiences of perceivers occurring as a response to visual receptivity to the occurrent basis of those dispositions. The dispositional properties that Revelation endorses are pure response-dispositions. These are properties that correspond to certain kinds of counterfactual conditionals. Corresponding to response-disposition D_r is the subjunctive conditional that has as its antecedent some condition of receptivity for a basis of D_r, and has as its consequent some experiential state of a person in that condition of receptivity. The antecedent of the dispositional conditional specifies the triggering condition for the manifestation of the disposition; the consequent specifies that manifestation-condition.

Pure response-dispositions are well suited to filling the color role because the manifestation-conditions of these properties can be plausibly regarded as displaying the intrinsic nature of the properties they manifest. Why is this? Because objects that share any pure dispositional properties (and not just response-dispositions), where those properties have similar manifestation-conditions, are rendered intrinsically similar by doing so. For example, the elasticity of two rubber bands that elongate to the same degree in response to an applied stretching force renders them more similar to each other, qua elastic objects, than either is to a rubber band that exhibits greater or less elongation when subjected to that force. If objects are rendered intrinsically similar by sharing certain properties, those properties must be intrinsically similar. Finally, in the case of pure response-dispositions, the mode of similarity of the properties is itself displayed in an experience of a subject. Such is the appeal, from the standpoint of Revelation, of a pure response-dispositional account of color.

The problem is that such a view does not slake our thirst for an account that answers to a doctrine of Explanation. Pure response-dispositions are not causes of the responses that manifest them, their occurrent bases are. From the standpoint of the need to accommodate both Revelation and Explanation, a Lockean secondary quality account of the colors looks very attractive. The pure response-dispositional properties are not identical to any physical property, and so they have no causal roles themselves; but perhaps, like mental properties, as a functionalist understands them, the colors are causal roles themselves. Maybe colors are higher-order properties, powers if you will, of physical states involving primary qualities, to cause certain types of responses in observers in certain circumstances of observation. The colors are involved in the explanation of chromatic experience, not as causes but as causal roles that the physical states fill. This a satisfying compromise.

It is an interesting aside to note that the Lockean secondary quality view of the colors does not fit very well with the Lockean Intuition, at least not insofar as the Intuition is understood as a thesis about physical-object color. This, of course, is the understanding that motivates color dispositionalism. Given this understanding of the Intuition and Locke's secondary quality account of the colors, the Lockean Intuition does not provide any reason to think that a blind man could not know all that there is to know about color. The reason is that on the Lockean account of physical-object color, and unlike the higher-order property account just considered, the knowledge he lacks of the content of normal visual experience contains no information about the nature of color in objects. This is because Locke is prepared to reduce powers to structures of primary qualities. The redness of the red apple just is the microphysical structure of its surface that causes ideas of red. It is nothing over and above that. Thus he writes,

such qualities which in truth are nothing in the objects themselves, but powers to produce various sensations in us by their primary qualities, i.e. by the bulk, figure, texture, and motion of their insensible parts, as colours, sounds, tastes, &c. these I call secondary qualities.[6]

So understood, the blind man who knows this structural property by description has all the knowledge there is to have of the redness of the red apple. The ideas of secondary qualities that those qualities play a role in causing contain no information about what those qualities are in themselves, and so, afford the sighted person no epistemic advantage concerning the nature of each secondary quality. For this very reason Locke's secondary quality account of the colors does not accord very well with Revelation either. The problem here is that colors, for Locke, are powers, and our ideas of these powers do not reveal these powers for what they are, for our ideas of them do not resemble them. Red things do not share the qualities that make up the content of our ideas of redness.

Is Revelation True of the Colors?

It is hard to say; for it's not clear what one knows in knowing what way a thing is when it is canary yellow. Unless we can clarify this notion we cannot know what constraint the truth of Revelation places upon our understanding of the nature of color. Revelation is understood by its advocates to entail that if the colors are dispositions, then the colors should look like dispositions (of colored surfaces and volumes) in a standard visual experiences as of a color. Here is an example of an understanding of what it would be for the colors to look like dispositions.

When one enters a dark room and switches on a light, the colours of surrounding objects look as if they have been revealed, not as if they have been activated. That is, the dispelling of darkness looks like the drawing of a curtain from the colours of the objects no less than from the objects themselves. If colours looked like dispositions, however, then they would seem to *come on* when illuminated, just as a lamp comes on when its switch is flipped. Turning on the light would seem, simultaneously, like turning on the colours; or perhaps it would seem like waking up the colours, just as it is seen to startle the cat. Conversely, when the light was extinguished, the colours would not look as if they were being concealed or shrouded in the surrounding darkness; rather, they would look as if they were becoming dormant, like the cat returning to sleep. But colours do not look like that; or not, at least, to us.[7]

Johnston observes that some colors *do* look like dispositions.

Contrast the highlights: a course of experience as of the highlights reveals their relational nature. They change as the observer changes position relative to the light source. They darken markedly as the light source darkens. With sufficiently dim light they disappear while the ordinary colors remain. They wear their light- and observer-dependent natures on their face. Thus there is some truth in the oft-made suggestion that (steady) colors don't look like dispositions; to which the natural reply is "Just how would they have to look if they were to look like dispositions?"; to which the correct response is that they would have to look like colored highlights or better, like shifting, unsteady colors, e.g. the swirling evanescent colors that one sees on the back of compact discs.[8]

Of course we could restrict the Doctrine of Revelation to a thesis about highlights and other unsteady colors. But this move would raise questions in our minds about the order of epistemic priority between experience and understanding in our acceptance of Revelation. Is it a priori evident that some version of Revelation for colors is true, and that this conviction motivates and directs a search for color properties that answer to it? Or rather do we have some knowledge of what we know about the nature of some color properties and the role of experience in acquiring it, such that this knowledge gets expressed in an appropriate doctrine? These questions just land us in the contrast between empiricist and rationalist approaches to the problems of inquiry. Let us hope that we do not have to settle our minds on these general matters to decide whether or not Revelation is true of the colors. Let us put aside the distinction between steady and unsteady colors and instead focus on what we come to know in a revelatory experience.

Is the knowledge we acquire in an experience as of canary yellow a concept of canary yellow that one would not have acquired but for a revelatory experience? Is this knowledge a collection of beliefs about canary yellow that one would not have accepted but for a revelatory experience? Since the content of the former (i.e., concepts) is exhausted, somehow surely, in the content of the latter (i.e., beliefs and dispositions to believe), I will, for the moment at least, consider Revelation as a doctrine about (explicit or tacit) beliefs about the nature of the colors that are acquired as a result of experiences as of those colors. Understood this way, Revelation entails that a person familiar with a color should have no false beliefs about what that color is in itself. Is this true?

Problems: Many have taken the colors to be simple qualities, but the colors are ordered in a three-dimensional structure of hue, saturation, and brightness. Since the structure is a similarity structure, and similarity requires shared properties, the colors must be complex. Clearly, then, one can be acquainted with canary yellow and yet come away from the acquainting experience with false beliefs about that color. Revelation also entails that a person familiar with a color ought not to be ignorant of any fact about the nature of that color as it is in itself, but this also appears to be false. There are no reddish greens; there are no greenish reds; but a person familiar with both colors could be ignorant of this fact. *Reply*: This is as it should be, for it is a contingent fact (if it is a fact)—a fact not dependent upon the nature of red or green in themselves—that there are no binaries of these colors.

Another problem: The browns are darkened reds and yellows, but someone could be familiar with a shade of brown, raw sienna brown say, and not know this. Likewise for salmon pink being a desaturated red; for a sample of salmon pink, see figure 8.2 (plate 2).

Figure 8.2
Salmon pink. See plate 2.

In figure 8.3 (plate 3) we can see that salmon pink is a desaturated red: The left side matches the salmon pink display, while the right side of the display is clearly an orangish red. Gradually reducing the percentage of white in the left side and replacing it with duplicates of the non-white constituents of the salmon pink region generates the intermediate colors.

Reply: These facts are relational facts of the shades in questions, and thus, not facts intrinsic to the nature of these colors. They are indeed facts that a person familiar with both salmon pink and this orangish red might fail to know, but in this they are like the facts in the earlier case, that there are no reddish greens or greenish reds, contingent facts about the shades that are not part of what these colors are in themselves. Just as it is a contingent fact about salmon pink that there is no transformation of it that generates a greenish red or a reddish green, so it is a contingent fact about salmon pink that there is a transformation of it that generates an orangish red.

Retort to reply: Surely some relational facts are essential to the colors. Reddish shades, such as salmon pink, are essentially so. The orangish red above is the only shade that can result from resaturating our pink shade. We can see that salmon pink is a reddish shade, and our transformation process shows that this reddish shade has a shade of orangish red as a component.[9] To be reddish is just to have a hue property that contains a shade of red as a

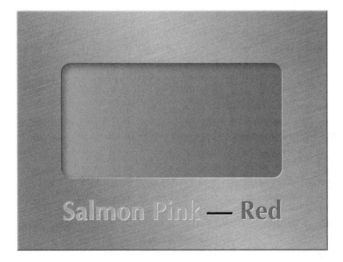

Figure 8.3
Salmon pink–red. See plate 3.

component. Since hue components are a part of what each color is in itself, a relation to an orangish red is part of what salmon pink is in itself. Every binary hue is reddish, yellowish, greenish or bluish. Therefore, relations to shades of red, yellow, green, and blue are part of the nature of binary hues.

I conclude, therefore, that construed as a doctrine about the beliefs, explicit and tacit, acquired as a result of experience in which one becomes acquainted with a color property, Revelation looks to be false. Indeed, Revelation is false—yet surely there is something right about it. The problem is to say what. It might help to get clear on what the doctrine is not. In particular it will help to distinguish Revelation from Presentation, to distinguish what can be revealed in an experience from what is presented in a revelatory experience. Revelation is not Presentation.

Presentation

Presentation: In a standard visual experience as of a canary yellow thing, one is presented with the property of being canary yellow and something that has it.[10]

In perceptual experience various objects, events, states of affairs, and properties seem to be present to us, given to us. In hearing the song of a songbird we seem to be affected by the sound of the song, and by its influencing us, we are placed in contact with the song. Our contact with the song brings with it a contact with the bird; song and bird are both present to us. The song sounds a certain way to us, sweet perhaps, and this way of sounding presents us with a quality of the song, its sweetness. The bird is a *concretum*, the song a somewhat more abstract repeatable type or kind; the sweetness of the sound of the song is a property or universal. All three sorts of things can be present to us in our auditory experience.

The characterization of Presentation offered above has two major shortcomings: (1) Clearly, it only applies to direct presentation, as it does not capture the indirect presentation of the songbird by means of its song; and (2) Presentation has not been defined above, because the undefined notion of being presented with a property is used in the characterization. I plan to do nothing about the first shortcoming, but here are a couple of substantive characterizations of Presentation, one suitable for objects, and the other equally suited to objects or properties.

Counterfactual Dependence (Chisholm): An object o is present to a person S in an experience E just in case some feature of the experience is counterfactually dependent upon some feature of o in such a way that were there to be continuous variation in that feature of o, there would be continuous variation in some feature of E.

Content Introduction/Original Aboutness (Johnston):   Presentation is a relation to a person sufficient for an object, kind, or property so related to become a content of thought.

Neither of these characterizations provides all that one might want out of an understanding of Presentation. The dependence-condition would seem to only permit particulars or states that involve some determinable quality to be presented in experience, for a completely determinate qualitative state cannot be subjected to continuous variation. The content-introduction idea is insightful, but provides only a necessary condition on Presentation.

Presentation is clearly related to Revelation. Since an experience can only be revealing of the nature of qualities present in that experience, Presentation is necessary for Revelation, but it is not sufficient. Dependence does not guarantee that a person will attend to that upon which his experience depends. A quality can be presented in a complex structure where, while the quality in question is attended to, its distinctive intrinsic character may be lost in the contribution it makes to a new organic whole, for instance, the character of a single note in a complex musical chord. Presentation is not Revelation. Revelation is an explicitly epistemic notion; Presentation is a non-epistemic notion. One can be completely ignorant of the nature of some object upon whose qualities some aspect of your experience is dependant, or of the nature of a quality that can find a place in one's thought and speech only because of the content of a grounding experience of it.

The Manifest Colors

In the case of color, the nature of what is presented is not revealed; but what might be revealed is the nature of its mode of presentation. Color qualities are present in experience, but their intrinsic nature is not therein revealed. Nevertheless the color qualities are plainly similar to and different from each other in a variety of ways, and this is made manifest in visual experience. What visual experience reveals is a way in which things can be presented as intrinsically similar to and different from each other, but it does so without revealing what features things similar in these ways share, or what features diverge in things that differ in these ways. While they are not revealed, these differentiative modes are nonetheless present in vision;

they are present in the form of simple intrinsic features of the objects of visual experience.

Corresponding to the ability to, for example, distinguish yellow things from orange things on the basis of the content of a visual experience as of yellow and as of orange, are the properties a possible state of affairs must have to be compatible with the way our experience of yellow and orange presents modes of similarity and difference among the yellow things and the orange things. One would have thought that these modes were being-yellow and being-orange, but yellow and orange are not mere differentiating features. These qualities have intrinsic natures beyond affording the presentation of a structure of differentiative features.[11] *There are, however, visual qualities whose nature is exhausted by their role in manifesting this differentiative function.* The role they fill is to be visually attributed to visual objects when they are represented as intrinsically similar to and dissimilar from other visual objects in certain distinctively chromatic ways. These are the visual qualities that are revealed, and not just presented, in experience.

Let us call these features that are revealed in color experience "manifest colors." Manifest red is a quality that, when present in experience, affords the possibility of differences in mode of presentation between, for example, lemons and oranges beyond their differences in shape and location. Each manifest color adds to an experience a distinct mode of differentiation anchored to a simple quality intrinsic to objects present in the visual scene. Consider the visual presentation in figure 8.4 (plate 4).

The yellow square on the left and the orange one on the right are plainly and evidently different, but they differ in a manner or mode that, while present in, is not itself revealed in an experience of this figure. It can be revealed in another experience; for this see figure 8.5 (plate 5).

Presented in figure 8.5 is the quality that defines one dimension along which the yellow and orange patches differ. The orange patch, in some sense, contains more of this quality than the yellow one does. The red quality is presented in the orange patch, albeit indirectly, much as a bird is presented in an auditory experience of its song.

The intrinsic nature of manifest red is fully revealed in an experience as of a manifestly red thing. What about the system of relational properties appealed to in the refutation of the Doctrine of Revelation for colors? Are these not also features of the manifest colors? Is not manifest red more similar to manifest orange than it is to manifest yellow? In a word, yes; but while these systematic relations are part of the essence of redness, they are not essential features of manifest red. Had the nature of the colors been

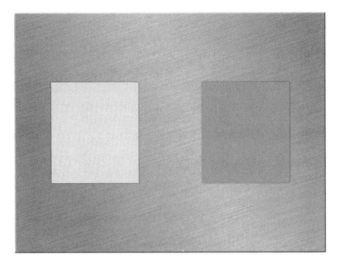

Figure 8.4
Manifest yellow and manifest orange. See plate 4.

Figure 8.5
Manifest red. See plate 5.

different, the relations among the manifest colors would have been different. If there had been more hues, there might have been another manifest
hue equally similar to both manifest red and manifest yellow; that is, manifest red might have stood in relations of similarity and difference to colors
to which it does not in fact bear any relation. This is not possible for the
colors. This is the major reason why the manifest colors are revealed in
visual experience while the colors are not.

If they differ in their intrinsic nature, what about the colors is made manifest in the manifest colors? One thing is the way the color of an object can
contribute to its visual differentiation from other objects in experience. The
colors of a collection of objects in the visual field of a perceiver, plus the
conditions of observation, explain the manifold structure of that part of
visual experience. This is one major role of the colors, to be the objective
intrinsic basis for a visual object's contribution to the chromatic content
and chromatic structure of visual experience. The manifest colors are simple qualities that manifest that content and present that structure.

Another thing revealed by the manifest colors is the way the colors look.
When viewed under standard conditions, the colors look like themselves.
Under standard conditions of observation, manifest red reveals the look of
a red object; the object looks the way it should. When viewed under abnor-
mal conditions, a white object might present a manifest red appearance,
and so not look like itself, not look the way it should. I have suggested
that manifest colors might be thought of as the mode of presentation of
the colors, as the way the colors are presented in visual experience. Since
the manifest colors are the look of the colors, they must always look like
themselves. In this sense, there can be no manifest color illusions.

What are the manifest colors? Epistemically, the manifest colors are what
we know about how things must be intrinsically similar to and different
from each other to conform to the distinctive character of our visual experience of the world. Visual experience reveals a distinctively chromatic
way that things must look in order for objects to be visually present to us.
The content of the knowledge is not a set of beliefs, but rather a visually
acquired concept of ways things can visually appear. The perceiver thereby
acquires the ability to see the canary, and other things, as manifestly
canary yellow. When the conditions of observation are favorable, the experience of a canary yellow thing contains a distinctive mode of the presentation of canary yellow, one wherein canary yellow things look like
themselves. This mode of presentation lets us know what canary yellow
and canary yellow things both look like. This is the knowledge acquired
in a revelatory experience.[12] While this knowledge exhausts what can be

known about the intrinsic nature of the manifest colors, we saw earlier that the intrinsic nature of the colors includes more than this. There is more to know about the intrinsic nature of canary yellow than the way canary yellow things look when seen under favorable conditions. Not so with manifest canary yellow.

Metaphysically, the manifest colors are role-fillers for differentiative roles of the colors—that is, they are properties the colors have in virtue of visually presenting objects in experience as intrinsically similar to and different from each other in certain ways. As such, the manifest colors are similar to functional properties. They are properties of properties of first-order things. They are properties of colors of things; properties the colors have in virtue of their capacity to afford chromatically structured visual representations. From the standpoint of role/occupant analysis, they are occupants of roles, but the roles are not causal roles. Rather than filling functional roles such as, tending to bring about x and tending to be brought about by y, manifest colors fill roles such as: x is intrinsically similar in way R_cO to y and intrinsically dissimilar in way $R/_cG$ from z, where "R_cO" is a way that red things appear similar in color to orange things in circumstances C, and "$R/_cG$" is a way that red things appear dissimilar in color to green things in circumstances C. While the manifest colors occupy differentiative roles, they are not definable in terms of the roles they occupy, for they might have occupied different roles had the nature of the colors been different—for instance, had there been more or fewer colors than there are, or had there been different, novel colors. Experience simultaneously presents us with things distinguished one from another in these and related ways, and presents the differentiative role properties themselves, but experience does not reveal any deeper nature to these properties. This last is because the only deeper nature to the manifest colors is the nature of the colors themselves, and we have seen that their nature is present in, but not revealed in, visual experience.

Consider first, the visual scene in figure 8.6 (plate 6); it is the famous Sun Sphere in Knoxville, Tennessee. Then consider the sphere alone, in figure 8.7 (plate 7). The tiles of the sphere all appear to be the same color, and yet they present different appearances. The reflective surfaces and their different angles of orientation afford the presentation of the tiles as varying in appearance while all appearing to be the same in color. The visual content of this scene includes that the immediate environment contains regions and objects that are intrinsically similar and different in respect of color. These respects of intrinsic color similarity and difference serve to structure the visual scene.

Figure 8.6
The Sun Sphere. See plate 6.

Figure 8.7
The Sun Sphere. See plate 7.

Figure 8.8
Two tiles from the Sun Sphere picture. See plate 8.

Figure 8.8 (plate 8) shows a pair of tiles from different parts of the sphere. These two tiles appear to be intrinsically different in just the way in which white and black are intrinsically different, and this despite the fact that, in the visual scene, they appear to be the same color. The tile on the left is manifest white despite being copper in color. It differs in manifest color from the tile on the right despite looking to be the same in color. These contrasts in manifest color are different ways in which the same color can be presented to a subject. Again we see the manifest colors as modes of presentation of the colors—the public face of the colors, if you will.

We now need to make more precise our understanding of what is involved in something being manifestly colored. I propose that we type-individuate manifest colors by means of their essential connection to the types of phenomenal properties involved in their perception. Sense impressions, as I understand them, are mental representations that employ phenomenal properties as constituents of sensory representations of objects and properties. A visual sense impression of a surface incorporates a chromatic phenomenal property produced while perceiving that surface. The sense impression represents the surface as possessing some intrinsic property relevantly similar to the chromatic phenomenal property it includes. Corresponding to the representational content of the sense impression of the surface is some objective property that would have to exist for the world to be as the visual sense impression represents it as being. This property is a manifest color. Two visual sense impressions represent the same manifest color if, and only if, they incorporate the same chromatic phenomenal property, so each manifest color is the objective property represented by all sense impressions that incorporate the same chromatic phenomenal property.

An object surface has a particular manifest color M at some time t by having some color property or other which is such that, in the circumstances, it plays a role[13] in producing a visual sense impression that is revelatory of M. In our illustration of the two tiles from the Sun Sphere, the tiles are the same copper color, but they manifest two different colors—white and black. Manifest colors are higher-order properties of object surfaces (and volumes), properties they have in virtue of having color properties that fill a certain role in visual perception. What role is this? Manifest colors render object-surfaces and volumes manifestly similar to and different from each other. Also, so understood, objects can have many manifest colors, one for every type of visual sense impression its color properties can play a role in producing. This will, in part, be a matter of the object being represented in a particular manner in a visual sense impression of the object.

Dispositionalism Reconsidered

Is canary yellow a disposition? Is manifest canary yellow a disposition? Manifest canary yellow does not appear to be a dispositional property of the manifestly canary yellow thing. It, like canary yellow, looks to be an intrinsic occurrent property of its bearer. We saw above that there is a way for colors to be dispositions, that is, if they are pure response-dispositional properties, which is compatible with Revelation being true of them. We also saw, however, that this is in tension with the demands of our commitment to Explanation, to the conviction that colors are involved in the explanation of our experience of them (we also saw that this tension can be ameliorated by adopting a functional understanding of the colors). There is no such tension in the case of the manifest colors, for all the work of explaining how the manifest colors fill the differentiative roles that they do falls entirely to the colors. The reason why manifest white and manifest black play their roles as structuring elements of the visual field in the way they do is explained by the nature of the colors white and black (and circumstances of observation). The color of the Sun Sphere's tiles and the circumstances of viewing them explain the manifest visual appearance of the sphere. So, there is not the same systematic reason to reject a dispositional account of the manifest colors as exists in the case of the colors.

Is manifest canary yellow a disposition? It does not appear to be. It appears to be a manifestation of the color of canary yellow things. Construed as a disposition, canary yellowness is equally well understood as a disposition of a thing to be manifest canary yellow under standard conditions of observation or as a disposition of such a thing to produce experiences as of a manifestly canary yellow thing under those same conditions. Of course the fact that manifest colors can fill the role of supplying the manifestation-conditions of a family of dispositional properties, does not settle the question of whether or not the manifest colors are themselves dispositions, for dispositions can be manifested by dispositional properties. Manifest colors might be dispositions, given all their apparent role in color experience tells us, but if they are, they are degenerate dispositions. Understood as pure response-dispositions, manifest canary yellow would be a disposition to look manifest canary yellow under all conditions of observation.

Conclusion

The Doctrine of Revelation is not true of the colors, but it is true of the manifest colors. The colors have a substantive nature that is too rich to be revealed by the content of visual experience. There is more to be known about the intrinsic nature of the colors than can be learned merely by having visual experiences of them. More is required; scientific inquiry is required. Not so with the manifest colors. They wear their intrinsic natures on their sleeves. And they must, for their role is to be our basic mode of visual access to the colors. Whatever fills this role must have its nature revealed in visual experience. If there were some unrevealed hidden nature to a putative filler of this role, this nature, and whatever revealed it, would supply the real mode of access to the colors. So, the colors, with their substantive intrinsic nature, cannot be self-revealing. They are not even self-presenting. The manifest colors present the colors to us, and reveal their essential nature in so doing—and sometimes look good doing it.

Acknowledgments

I presented a version of these ideas at talks delivered to the Center for Consciousness Studies at the University of Arizona and to the Department of

Philosophy of the University of Washington. Feedback during these presentations and during discussions with Keith Lehrer, Uriah Kriegel, Thomas Christiano, and Houston Smit revealed several shortcomings with those earlier views. I am entirely to blame for any shortcomings that still remain.

Notes

1. Johnston 1997.

2. Russell 1959, 47.

3. Strawson 1989, 224.

4. Locke 1975, Book 2, chapter 4, section 5. Note: subsequent references to the *Essay* follow this form of reference.

5. Locke 1975, 2, 2, 2.

6. Locke 1975, 2, 2, 10. Of course our concept of the corresponding response-disposition does essentially involve the feature of perceptual experiences that manifest the disposition. This means that if secondary qualities reduce to their occurrent basis, secondary qualities are not response-dispositions.

7. Boghossian and Velleman 1989, 85.

8. Johnston 1997, 141.

9. I have no substantive commitments in mind behind my use of the term "component" here. I do not intend to suggest that colors have components in anything like the way physical objects do, nor do I intend to endorse the interesting and useful understanding of this notion as a feature of our representation of colors, provided by Byrne and Hilbert (2003).

10. The talk of "something that has it" is intended to be neutral on the topic of the ontological status of the thing in question, that is, with regard to whether it is a physical object, a sense datum, or merely an intentional object.

11. Of course the colors have a differentiative function, but in addition to distinguishing red things from green things, red and green each distinguish the one from the other, only we cannot *sense* how this latter is done. This last is the point that Johnston is making when he says: "Sensible profiles are manners of presentation that are themselves presented in sensing. Indeed this is a distinctive aspect of sensory experience, one that marks it off from belief or thought. Sensory manners of presentation are themselves sensed" (2004, 141).

12. The conceptual role of experiences wherein canary yellow is made manifest, can be captured using the device of dot-quotation (•). Dot-quotes—for instance, •canary yellow•—create a sortal predicate expression that applies to everything relevantly

similar to what is inside the dot-quotes. In a cognitive system that has the ability to dot-quote its own visual experiences, and where the resulting sortal predicate applies to anything that causes experiences which have the same phenomenal character as the dot-quoted experience, an *experience* of a manifestly canary yellow thing can result in a way of *representing* visual objects as manifestly canary yellow.

13. The roles involved here are not causal roles. They are rather like the functional roles posited in a functional account of mental states, but do not essentially involve causal powers. I take functional roles to be an element of one form of role/occupant analysis, but there are others. What role/occupant analysis does is offer a characterization of a domain of things by describing some of those things in terms of the structure of relational properties of lower-level things. The lower-level things have some properties or other whose relational structure make them fit to fill the roles defined in terms of those relations. Money, as understood in standard economic analysis, is a role property, but not a functional role, since monetary value relations are not causal relations. This is compatible with money having a causal role in economic transactions; for the structure of those transactions might have been different, had the monetary value-relations been different.

References

Boghossian, P., and D. Velleman. 1989. "Colour as a Secondary Quality." *Mind* 98: 81–103.

Byrne, A., and D. Hilbert. 2003. "Color Realism and Color Science." *Behavioral and Brain Sciences* 26: 3–21.

Johnston, M. 1997. "How to Speak of the Colors." In A. Byrne and D. Hilbert, eds., *Readings on Color*, volume 1. Cambridge, Mass.: MIT Press.

Johnston, M. 2004. "The Obscure Object of Hallucination." *Philosophical Studies* 120: 113–183.

Locke, J. 1975. *An Essay Concerning Human Understanding*. Peter Nidditch, ed. Oxford: Clarendon Press.

Russell, B. 1959. *The Problems of Philosophy*. Oxford: Oxford University Press.

Strawson, G. 1989. "Red and 'Red'." *Synthèse* 78: 193–232.

9 Knowing It Hurts

Fred Dretske

When it hurts, you know it does because...well, because it hurts. Unlike envy, fear, and desire—feelings and emotions which, at least since Freud, can be unconscious—pain, at least physical pain, by its very nature is something you are aware of. If you don't feel it, it doesn't hurt. So if it hurts, you know it does.

Are things this simple? No. When it hurts, we certainly know it does, but if there is a way we know it, this can't be it (I'll say why in a moment). Maybe, as my Chapel Hill friends tell me, there is no *way* we know it. We just know it.

Sorting out the epistemology of pain—of sensations in general—is a tricky business. It leads directly into some of the most baffling problems of consciousness. What follows is an attempt to navigate some of these murky waters.

Awareness of Pain

Many people think of pain and other bodily sensations (e.g., tickles, itches, nausea) as feelings one is necessarily conscious of. Some think there can be pains one doesn't feel, pains one is (for a certain interval) not conscious of ("I was so distracted I forgot about my headache"), but others agree with Reid (1969, 1, 12) and Kripke (1980, 151) that unfelt pains are like invisible rainbows—they don't exist. If you are so distracted you aren't aware of your headache, then, for that period of time, you are not in pain. Your head doesn't hurt. It doesn't *ache*. For these people (and I'm one of them) you can't be in pain without feeling it, and feeling it is awareness of it.

Whether or not we are necessarily conscious of our own pains is relevant to the epistemology of pain. If there are—or if there could be—pains of which we are not aware, then there is obviously an epistemological problem about pain. How do we know we are not always in pain without being aware of it? In order to simplify things and minimize problems, therefore, I focus on pains (if there are any other kind) of which we are aware—pains, as I will say, that really hurt. For those who conceive of pain as something of which one is necessarily aware, then I am concerned, simply, with pain itself: When you are in pain, how do you know you are? For those who think that there are, or could be, pains one does not feel, I am concerned with a subset of pains—those you are aware of, the ones that really hurt. When it hurts, how do you know it does?

If this is the topic, what is the problem? If we are talking about things of which we are necessarily aware, the topic is things that, when they exist, we know they exist. There may be a question about *how* we know we are in pain, but that we know it is assumed at the outset. Isn't it?

No, it isn't. To suppose it is, is to confuse awareness of things[1] with awareness of facts. One can be aware of an armadillo, a thing, without being aware of the fact that it is an armadillo, without knowing or believing it is an armadillo—without, in fact, knowing what an armadillo is. There is a sensory, a phenomenal, form of awareness—experiencing armadillos (seeing or smelling them)—and a conceptual form of awareness—knowing that they are armadillos. We use the word 'awareness' (or 'consciousness') for both. We are aware *of* objects (and their properties) on the one hand, and we are aware *that* certain things are so on the other. If one fails to distinguish these two forms of awareness, awareness of *x* with awareness that it is *x*, one will mistakenly infer that simply being in pain (requiring, as I am assuming, awareness of the pain) requires awareness of the fact that one is in pain and, therefore, knowledge. Not so.[2] I am assuming that if it really hurts, you must feel the pain—yes, and feeling pain is awareness of it; but this is the kind of awareness (thing-awareness) one can have without fact-awareness of what it is that one is aware of—that is, that it is pain, or that one is aware of it. Chickens and maybe even fish, we may suppose, feel pain, but in supposing this we needn't suppose that these animals have the concept *pain*. We needn't suppose they understand what pain is sufficiently well to believe (hence know, hence be aware) that they are in pain. They are aware of their pain, yes. It really hurts. That is why they squawk, squirm, and wiggle. That is why they exhibit the behaviors we take to be symptomatic of pain. But this does not mean that they believe or know they are in pain. It is a chicken's feeling pain, its awareness *of* its pain— and not its belief or awareness *that* it is in pain—that explains its behavior. The same is true of human infants.[3] They cry when they are hungry not because they think (much less know) that they are hungry. They cry because they *are* hungry or, if you prefer, because they *feel* hungry. You can feel hungry without knowing that it is hunger you feel, or that you are feeling it.

So I do not begin by assuming that if it hurts, you know it does. In fact, as a general rule, this is false. Maybe adult human beings always know when it hurts, but chickens and fish (probably) don't, and human infants probably don't either. I'm asking, instead, why we, adult human beings, always seem to know it and if we really do know it, *how* we know it. What is it about pain—unlike, say, cancer—that confers epistemological authority on those who feel it?

Acts and Objects of Awareness

When I see a pencil, the pencil doesn't depend on my awareness of it. Its existence, and its existence as a pencil, does not depend on my seeing it. When I stop looking at it, the pencil continues to exist in much the way it did when I saw it. Pencils are indifferent to my attentions. There is the pencil, the (physical) object of awareness, on the one hand, and there is my awareness of it, a (mental) act of awareness, on the other. Remove awareness of the pencil, this relational property, from the pencil, and one is left with the pencil, an unchanged object of awareness.

This can't be the way it is with pains since pains, at least the ones I am concentrating on here, unlike pencils, are (see above) things we are necessarily conscious of. Remove the act of awareness from this object of awareness and this object ceases to be pain. It stops hurting.

So in this respect, pains are unlike pencils. Unlike a pencil, the stabbing sensation in your lower back cannot continue to exist, at least not as pain, when you cease to be aware of it. If it continues to exist at all, it continues to exist as something else. When the marital relation is removed (by divorce, say) from a man who is a husband, the relation that makes the man a husband disappears (legally, at least), and you are left with a single man—a man who is no longer a husband. If you remove the awareness-relation from a stabbing sensation in your lower back—the relation without which it doesn't hurt, without which it isn't painful—what are you left with? A stabbing event (?) in your lower back that doesn't hurt? That isn't painful? What sort of thing could this be?[4]

To understand the sort of thing it might be, think about something I will call a *crock*.[5] A crock (so I stipulate) is a rock you are visually aware of. It is a rock you see. A crock is a rock that stands in this perceptual relation to you. Remove that relation, as you do when you close your eyes or look elsewhere, and the crock ceases to be a crock. It remains a rock, but not a crock.

A crock is like a husband—a person whose existence as a husband, but not as a man, depends on the existence of a certain extrinsic relationship. Crocks are like that. They look just like rocks. They have all the same intrinsic (non-relational) properties of rocks. They look like rocks because they *are* rocks—a special kind of rock, to be sure (one you are aware of), but a rock nonetheless.

Should we think of pains like crocks? When you cease to be aware of it, does your pain cease to exist as pain, but continue to exist as something else? Something that has all the same intrinsic (and other relational) properties of pain but which requires your awareness of it to recover its status as pain, in the way a rock has all the same intrinsic (and most relational) properties of a crock and requires only your awareness of it to regain its status as a crock? Is there something—let us call it *protopain*—that stands to pain the way rocks stand to crocks? Is a stabbing pain in your lower back merely a protopain in your lower back that you happen to be aware of? Under anesthesia, is there still protopain in your lower back, something with all the same intrinsic properties you were aware of when feeling pain, but something that, thanks to the anesthetic, no longer hurts because you are no longer aware of it?[6]

Knowing One Is Aware of Something

If we understand pain on this model—the 'crock' model—we have a problem. How serious the problem is depends on how much of a problem it is to know one is aware of something. To appreciate the problem, or at least threat of a problem, think about how you might go about identifying crocks. When you see a crock, it is visually indistinguishable from an ordinary rock. Rocks and crocks look alike. They have the same intrinsic, the same observable properties. They differ only in one of their relational properties. They are, in this respect, like identical twins. This means that when you see a crock, there is nothing in what you are aware of, nothing in what you see, that tells you it is a crock you see and not just a rock. So how do you figure out whether the rock you see is a crock and not just a rock?

I expect you to say: I know the crocks I see are crocks because I know they are rocks (I can see this much), and I know I see them; so I know they are crocks. Assuming there is no problem about recognizing rocks, this will work as long as there is no problem in knowing that you see them. But how do you tell that you see, that you are visually aware of, a rock? There is, as already noted, nothing in what you see (the crock) that tells you that you see it. The crock would be exactly the same in all observable respects if you didn't see it—if it wasn't a crock. Just as husbands differ from non-husbands in having a certain hidden (to direct observation) quality, a quality one cannot observe by examining the husband, crocks differ from rocks in having a certain hidden quality, a quality that can't be observed by examining the crock. When you observe a crock, the relational property of being observed by you is not itself observed by you. Just as you must look elsewhere (marriage certificate, etc.) to find out whether a man you see is a husband, you must look elsewhere to find out whether the rock you see is a crock.

But where does one look? If one can't look at the crock to tell whether it is a crock, where does one look? Inward? Is introspection the answer? You look at the rock to see whether it is a rock, but you look inward, at yourself, so to speak, to find out whether it is that special kind of rock we are calling a crock. If we understand pain in your lower back on the crock model—as a condition (in the lower back?) you are aware of—we won't be able to say how you know you have lower back pain until we understand how you find out that this condition in your lower back is not just a condition in your lower back, but a condition in your lower back that really hurts, that is, a back-condition that you are aware of.

Self-Intimation

This is beginning to sound terribly strange. The reason it sounds so strange is that although awareness (at least awareness of objects) is a genuine relation between a person and an object, it is (we keep being told by philosophers) an epistemologically *transparent* or *self-intimating* relation. When S is aware of something, S knows automatically—without the need for evidence, reasons or justification—that he is aware of it. S can be married to someone and not realize he is (maybe he has amnesia or was drunk when he got married), but he can't be *aware* of something and not know that he is. If this were so, there would be no problem about knowing the rocks you see are crocks, since you can easily (let us pretend) see that they are rocks and so would know immediately, without need for additional evidence, in virtue of the transparency or self-intimation of awareness, that you see (are visually aware) of them. So anything one sees to be a rock is known, without further ado, to be a crock. The fact that makes a rock a crock—the fact that one is aware of it—is a self-intimating fact for the person who is aware of it. That is why there is no epistemological problem about pain beyond the familiar problem of distinguishing pain from nearby (but not quite painful) sensations—for example, aggressive itches. That is why we don't have a problem distinguishing pain from 'protopain'. Whatever it is, exactly, we are aware of when we are in pain, we always know, in virtue of the self-intimacy of awareness, that we are aware of it. When we have a pain in our back, therefore, we always know that it is real pain and not just protopain.

This nifty solution to our problem doesn't work, but it comes pretty close. It doesn't work because awareness is not self-intimating in this way. Animals and very young children are aware of things, but, lacking an understanding of what awareness is, they don't realize, they don't know, that they are aware of things. A chicken is visually aware of rocks and lots of other things without knowing it is. That is why animals and very young children—even if they know what rocks are (they probably don't even know this much)—don't know the rocks they see are crocks. They don't know they see these rocks. They don't know they are aware of them. If awareness is a self-intimating relation, it is so for only a select class of people. It certainly isn't so for infants and animals.

So if we are going to appeal to the intimacy of awareness in the epistemology of pain, we must be careful to restrict its intimacy to those who understand what awareness is, to those capable of holding beliefs and making judgments about their own (and, of course, others') awareness of things.[7] We need, that is, a principle something like:

(SI)   If S understands what awareness is (i.e., is capable of holding beliefs and making judgments to the effect that she is aware of things), and S is aware of x, S knows she is aware of x.

We have to be careful here with the variable 'x'. What, exactly, does it mean to say that S knows she is aware of x? If x is a rock, must S know she is aware of a rock? Clearly not. A person who knows what awareness is (and what rocks are), can perceive a rock and not know it is a rock and, therefore, not know she is aware of a rock. She thinks, mistakenly, it is a piece of cardboard. She might not even know it is a physical object. She thinks she is hallucinating. So what, exactly, does principle SI tell us a person automatically know about her awareness of things?

SI doesn't say that S must know anything about the x she is aware of except the fact that she is aware of it. Awareness of objects makes these objects available to the person who is aware of them as objects of belief, as *this*'s and *that*'s she can have (*de re*) beliefs about. If S has additional beliefs about x (i.e., beliefs in addition to the belief that she is aware of x), none of these other beliefs need be true. So, according to SI, S needn't know anything else about x—anything beyond the fact that she is aware of x.

To illustrate the way SI is to be understood and, at the same time, to neutralize a possible objection to it, consider the following example. *S* sees six rocks on a shelf. She sees them long enough and clearly enough to see all six. When *S* looks away for a moment, another rock is added. When *S* looks back she, once again, observes the rocks long enough and clearly enough to see all seven. She doesn't, however, notice the difference. She doesn't realize that there is an additional rock on the shelf. She sees—and is, therefore, aware of—an additional rock on the shelf, but she doesn't know she is.

Does this possibility show, contrary to SI, that one can be aware of an object and not know it? No it does not. It only shows that one can be aware of an additional rock without knowing that it is an additional rock and, therefore, without knowing one is aware of an additional rock. This, though, doesn't show that awareness is not self-intimating. It does not show that one can be aware of another rock without knowing one is aware of it; all it shows is that one can be aware of an additional rock without knowing one is aware of it under the description, 'an additional rock'. Maybe, though, one knows one is aware of the additional rock under the description 'the leftmost rock' or, simply, as 'one of the rocks I see' or, perhaps (if she doesn't know it is a rock), as 'one of the things I see'. If all seven rocks are really seen the second time, we can say the perceiver knows she is aware of each and every rock she sees. She just doesn't know they are rocks, how many there are, or that there are more of them this time than last time. But she does know, of each and every rock she sees, that she is aware of it.

If we accept this way of understanding '*S* knows she is aware of *x*' in the statement of SI, there may still be a problem about the intended reference of '*x*' in our formulation of the self-intimation principle. Suppose *S* hallucinates a talking rabbit with the conviction that she really sees and hears a talking rabbit. *S* mistakenly thinks she is aware of a talking white rabbit. She isn't. There are no white rabbits, let alone talking white rabbits, in *S*'s vicinity. What, then, is *S* aware of? More puzzling still (if we assume she is aware of something), what is it that (according to SI) *S knows* she is aware of? Is there a *that* she knows she is aware of? If so, what is it? A mental image? If so, does this image talk? Or does it merely appear to be talking? Does it have long ears? Or does it only appear to have long ears? Is *S*, then, aware of something (in her head?) that has or appears to have long white ears and that talks (or sounds like it is talking) like Bugs Bunny?

Knowing what lies ahead on this road (viz., sense data), many philosophers think the best way to understand hallucinations (dreams, etc.) is that in such experiences one is not aware of an object at all—certainly nothing that is white, rabbit-shaped, and talks like Bugs Bunny. Nor is one aware of something that only appears to have these properties. It only seems as though one is. Although there appears to be an object having these qualities, there actually is no object, certainly nothing in one's head, that has or even appears to have[8] the qualities one experiences something as having.[9]

This way of analyzing hallucination, however, seems to threaten SI. S thinks she is aware of something—a talking rabbit, in fact—but she isn't. She isn't aware of anything. So while hallucinating, S's belief that she is aware of something is false. Doesn't this show that—sometimes at least—S can't tell the difference between being aware and not being aware of something? Why, then, suppose, as SI directs, that S always knows when she is aware of something?

What we need to understand in order to sidestep this kind of objection to SI, is that the 'it' S knows she is aware of needs to be interpreted carefully. It needn't be a physical object. It needn't be a mental object (sense datum) either. It can be a property or a set of (appropriately 'bound'-together) properties which the subject experiences something as having. In hallucinating a talking white rabbit, S is conscious of various sensory qualities—colors, shapes, tones, movements, orientations, and textures. These are qualities S experiences (perceptually represents) something as having, qualities S is conscious of, in having this hallucinatory experience. According to the intended interpretation of SI, it is the qualities, and not some putative object that has (or appears to have) these qualities, that S is aware of, and (in accordance with SI) knows she is aware of. The difference between an hallucination of a talking white rabbit and a veridical perception of one isn't—or needn't be—the phenomenal (sensory) qualities one is aware of. These can be exactly the same. The experiences can be subjectively indistinguishable. In one case one is aware of something that has the qualities, in the other case not. But in both cases the subject is aware of, and in accordance with the intended interpretation of SI, knows she is aware of, the qualities that make the experiences that kind of experience.

So much by way of propping up SI. What we are left with may appear to be contrived and suspiciously *ad hoc*. Nonetheless, it or something close to it seems to do the job. It explains how one can, without additional epistemic effort (beyond what it takes to identify rocks), know that crocks are crocks. More significantly for present purposes, it also explains why someone who understands what awareness is, someone who is cognitively developed enough to *think* she is in pain, can't be aware of protopain without knowing she is aware of it and, therefore, without knowing she is in pain.

Explaining Self-Intimation

Is SI true? If it is, *why* is it true? What is it about awareness, or perhaps the concept of *awareness*, or perhaps the having of this concept, that yields these striking epistemological benefits?

The fact that, according to SI, S must not only be aware of x, but also understand what awareness is (an understanding animals and infants lack) in order to know—*gratis*, as it were—that she is aware of x, tells us something important. It tells us that the knowledge isn't constitutive of awareness. It tells us that awareness of x doesn't consist of knowing one is aware of it. The truth of SI—if indeed it is true—isn't what Fricker (1998) calls an Artifact of Grammar (and that used to be called an "analytic" truth). There are some relations we bear to objects in which knowledge is built into, is a component of, the relationship. Memory of persons, places, and things is like that.[10] For S to remember her cousin (an object), S must remember (hence, know) certain facts about her cousin (not necessarily that he is her cousin). Memory of objects, it seems reasonable to say, consists in the retention (and therefore, possession) of knowledge about them. Awareness of objects, though, isn't like that. You—or if not you, then chickens and children—can be aware objects without knowing they are. So the knowledge attributed in SI is not the result of some trivial, semantic fact about what it means to be aware of something. It isn't like the necessity of knowing something about the things you remember. If SI is true, it is true for some other, some deeper, reason.[11]

Perhaps, though, it goes the other way around. Although a (lower-level) awareness of something (a rock) doesn't have a (higher-level) belief that one is aware of it (the rock) as a constituent, maybe the higher-level belief that you are aware of it (a belief, again, that animals and young children lack) has awareness as a constituent. Maybe, that is, awareness is a relation that holds for whoever thinks it holds of him or herself.[12] If this were so, then the belief that you are aware of something would always be true. According to some theories of knowledge, then, such a belief would always count as knowledge. Whoever thinks they are aware of something knows they are because thinking it so makes it so. So they can't be wrong. So they know.

This possibility would be worth exploring if it really explained what we are trying to explain—namely, why, when we are aware of something, we know we are. But it doesn't. The fact (if it were a fact) that awareness of something is, somehow, a constituent of the (higher-order) belief that one is aware of something would explain why the higher-order belief, if we have it, is always true—why, if we believe we are aware of something, we are. But it would not explain what we are trying to explain, which is the converse—why, if we are aware of something, we always believe (thus, know) we are. The proffered explanation leaves open the possibility that, when we are aware of something, we seldom (if ever) believe we are and, therefore, the possibility that, when aware of something, we seldom (if ever) know we are.

So if SI is, somehow, an artifact of grammar—a truth vouchsafed in virtue of the concept of *awareness*—it is not in virtue of the belief being a constituent of the awareness. Or *vice versa*. If you always know when you are in pain, you know it for reasons other than the belief (that you are in pain) being a constituent of the pain or the pain a part of the belief. The pain and the belief that you are in pain are distinct existences. The problem is to understand why then, despite their distinctness, they are, for those who understand what pain is, apparently inseparable.

Chris Peacocke (1992; and earlier Evans 1982, 206) provides a way of understanding our possession of concepts in which the truth of SI can be understood as somehow (to use Fricker's language) an "artifact of grammar" without supposing that it is to be understood in terms of the knowledge being a constituent of the awareness or *vice versa*. Concepts not only have what Peacocke (1992, 29) calls attribution conditions—namely, conditions that must be satisfied for the concept to be correctly attributed to something. They also have possession-conditions, that is, conditions that must be satisfied for one to have the concept. To have a perceptual concept—or what Peacocke (1992, 7) calls a *sensational* concept—for the color red, for instance, he says that a person must, given normal circumstances, be able to tell, just by looking, that something is or isn't red. She must know that the concept applies, or doesn't apply, to the things she sees. Possessing the concept *red* requires this cognitive, this recognitional, ability. Those who lack this ability do not have the (perceptual) concept *red*.[13]

Adapting this idea to the case of awareness, it might be supposed that a comparable cognitive ability is part of the possession-conditions for *awareness*. Although (as the case of animals and young children indicate) knowledge isn't part of the attribution conditions (truth conditions) for awareness (*S* can be aware of something and not know she is), an ability to tell, in your own case, authoritatively, that you are aware of something may be a possession-condition for this concept. You don't really have the concept, you don't really understand what it means to be aware of something, if you can't tell, when you are aware of something, that you are aware of it. This is why, in the antecedent of SI, an understanding (of what awareness is) is required. Awareness is self-intimating for those who have the concept of *awareness*, because its self-intimation is a requirement for the ability to think one is aware of something. If you can think you are aware of something, then when you are aware of something, you know you are in that special authoritative way required for possession of the concept.

This strikes me as a plausible—if not the only possible—explanation of why SI is true. Regrettably, though, it doesn't take us very far. It is, in fact, simply a restatement of what we were hoping to explain—namely, SI: That those who understand what awareness is know, in virtue of having this understanding, when they are aware of something. It does not tell us what we were hoping to find out—the *source* of the epistemological ability required for possession of this concept. If, to have the concept *awareness*, I have to know I'm aware of everything I'm aware of, how do I manage to acquire this concept? What is it that gives me the infallible (or if not infallible, then near-infallible) powers needed to have this concept and, thereby, the capacity to *think* I'm aware of something?[14]

One doesn't explain the infallible—or if not infallible, then authoritative—application of a concept by saying that infallibility (or authoritativeness) in its application is a condition for possessing the concept. That might be so, but that doesn't help us understand the source of this authority. It merely transforms an epistemological question into a developmental question, a question about how we know into a question about how we manage to even believe. If we are, in our skeptical moods, suspicious about infallibility or first-person authority, then requiring it as a condition for possession of a concept does nothing to alleviate our skepticism. It merely displaces the skepticism to a question about whether we in fact have the concept—whether we ever, in fact, *believe* we are aware of something. It is like trying to solve an epistemological problem about knowing you are a husband by imposing infallibility in believing you are a husband as a requirement for possessing the concept *husband*. You can do this, I suppose, but all you really manage to achieve by this maneuver is a kind of conditional infallibility: If you think you are a husband, you know you are. But the old question remains in a modified form: Do you think you are? Given the beefed-up requirements on possessing the concept *husband*, it now becomes very hard—skeptics will say impossible—to think you are a husband.

We began by asking how one knows one is in pain. Since pain, at least the kind of pain we are here concerned with, is a feeling one is necessarily aware of (it doesn't hurt if you're not aware of it), this led us to ask how one knows one is aware of something. We concluded, tentatively, that the kind of reliability in telling you are aware of something required for knowledge (that you are aware of something) must be a precondition for possessing the concept *awareness*, a precondition, therefore, for thinking you are aware of something. That explains why those who think they are aware of something know they are. By making reliability of judgment a possession-condition for the concept *awareness*, we have transformed our epistemological problem into a developmental problem. How do we come to possess the concept *awareness* or, indeed, any concept (like pain) that requires awareness? How do we manage to *think* we are in pain?

This doesn't seem like much progress. If we don't understand how we can achieve reliable judgments on topic *T*, it doesn't help to be told that reliability is necessary for making judgments about topic *T*. But though it isn't *much* progress, it is, I think, *some* progress. If nothing else it reminds us that the solution to some of our epistemological problems, problems about how we know a so-and-so exists, await a better understanding of exactly what it is we are thinking when we think a so-and-so exists, how we acquired the resources needed for believing this. It reminds us that questions about how we know *P* are sometimes best approached by asking how we manage to believe *P*.[15] This is especially so when the topic is consciousness and, in particular, pain. Understanding how we know it hurts may await a better understanding of what, exactly, it is we think and how we came to think it when we think it hurts.

Notes

1. By 'things' I mean spatiotemporal particulars. This includes, besides ordinary objects (e.g., houses, trees, armadillos), such things as events (e.g., births, deaths, sunsets), processes (e.g., digestion, growth), conditions (e.g., the mess in his room), and states (e.g., Tom's being married). Events occur at a time and in or at a place (the place is usually the place of the objects to which the event occurs). Likewise for states, conditions, processes, and activities, although these are usually said to persist for a time, not to occur at a time. So if one doesn't like talking about pains as objects and prefers to think of them as events (conditions, activities, processes) in the nervous system, that is fine. They are still things in my sense of this word. For more on property-awareness and object-awareness as opposed to fact-awareness, see Dretske 1999.

2. This is the fallacy committed in the opening paragraph of this essay; and this is why I said in the second paragraph, that if there is a way we know we are in pain, this isn't it.

3. It is for this reason that I cannot accept Shoemaker's (1996) arguments for the 'transparency' of pain—the idea that pain is necessarily accompanied by knowledge that one is in pain. Even if it is true (as I'm willing to grant) that pains (at least the pains of which we are aware) necessarily motivate certain aversive behaviors, I think it is an over-intellectualization of this fact to *always* explain the pain-feeler's behavior in terms of a desire to be rid of her pain (a desire that, according to Shoemaker, implies a belief that one is in pain). I agree with Siewert (2003, 136–137) that the aversive or motivational aspect of pain needn't be described in terms of conceptually articulated beliefs (that you have it) and desires (to be rid of it). In the case of animals (and young children), it seems to me implausible to give it this gloss. Maybe you and I go to the medicine chest because of what we desire (viz., to lessen the pain) and think (viz., that the pain pills are there), but I doubt whether this is the right way to explain why an animal licks its wound or an infant cries and pulls back when poked with a pin.

4. Daniel Stoljar and Manuel Garcia-Carpintero have asked me why I think there is anything remaining when I subtract awareness from pain. Why isn't subtracting awareness from pain more like subtracting *oddness* from the number 3 rather than subtracting *being married* from a husband? My reason for thinking so is that when we are in pain there is obviously something we are aware of—for instance, the location, duration, and intensity of the pain. These are among the qualities that give pain its distinctive phenomenal character, the qualities that make one pain different from another. They are among the qualities that make it a splitting headache rather than a throbbing toothache. Take away awareness of these qualities and one is surely left with something—if nothing else, the qualities one was aware of.

5. I introduced crocks as an expository device in Dretske 2003.

6. This way of thinking about pain (and other bodily sensations) is one version of the perceptual model of pain (Armstrong 1961, 1962; Dretske 1995; Lycan 1996; Pitcher 1971; Tye 1995) according to which pain is to be identified with a perceived bodily condition (injury, stress, etc.). Under anesthesia the bodily injury, the object you are aware of when in pain, still exists, but since it is no longer being perceived it no longer hurts. It isn't pain. I say this is 'one version' of a perceptual theory, because a perceptual model of pain can identify pain not with the perceived *object* (bodily damage when it is being perceived), but the act of perceiving this object—not the bodily damage of which you are aware, but your awareness of this bodily damage. In the latter case, unlike the former, one does not perceive, one is not actually aware of, pain. When in pain, one is aware of the bodily injury, not the pain itself (which is one's awareness of the bodily injury). I do not here consider theories of this latter sort. I am concerned with the epistemology of pain (sensations in general) where these are understood to be *objects* of awareness, things of which one is consciously aware. If you aren't (or needn't be) aware of pain, there would appear to be an even greater problem than the one I am confronting here about how you know you are in pain.

7. For careful formulations along these lines see C. Wright 1998, Fricker 1998, and Shoemaker 1996. Chalmers (1996, 196–197) describes awareness as an epistemologically special relation in something like this sense, and Siewert (1998, 19–20, 39, 172) suggests that mere awareness of things (or failure to be aware of things) gives one first-person warrant for believing one is (or is not) aware of them. I take it that even animals and children have the warrant, they just don't have the (warranted) belief.

8. Nor *appears* to have these qualities, because to suppose that S was aware of something that merely appeared to have these qualities would be to introduce an appearance-reality distinction for mental images. What is it (a part of the brain?) that appears to be a talking white rabbit? This seems like a philosophically disastrous road to follow.

9. If this sounds paradoxical, compare: It can appear to S as though there is a fly in the ointment without there being a fly who appears to be in the ointment.

10. I do not argue for this. I'm not even sure it is true. I use it simply as a more or less plausible example of a relation we bear to objects that has, as a constituent, knowledge of that object.

11. This is why functionalism (about the mental) is of no help in explaining why SI is true. Even if awareness (of an object) is a functional state, one defined by its causal role, its role cannot include the causing of belief that one is aware of something.

12. This echoes a Burgian thesis about belief (Burge 1985, 1988)—that the higher-order belief that we believe p embodies, as a constituent, the lower-order belief (that p) that we believe we have. This echo is pretty faint though. The major difference is that awareness of an object is not (like a belief) an intentional state. It is a genuine relation between a conscious being, S, and whatever it is she is aware of. It may be that believing you believe p is, among other things, to believe p; but why should believing you are aware of something be, among other things, awareness of something? Can you make yourself stand in this relation to something merely by thinking you do? It is for this reason that Bilgrami (1998) thinks that the *constituency thesis* (as he calls it) is only plausible for intentional states like belief (desire, etc.) that have propositional 'objects'.

13. It isn't clear to me what concept they have—or even whether they have a concept—if they do not have this ability at the requisite (presumably high) level of reliability but are, nonetheless, more often right than wrong in describing something as red. If they don't have the concept *red*, what are they saying? What, if anything, are they thinking? Nothing? I take this to be the problem David Chalmers was raising in the discussion at the INPC conference. I ignore the problem here for the sake of seeing how far we can get in the epistemology of pain by requiring a level of reliability (of the sort needed to know) in the capacity to believe.

14. As I understand him, this is basically the same point Gallois (1996) is making against Peacocke's account of why (or perhaps, how) we (i.e., those of us who have

the concept of belief) are justified in believing that we believe the things we do. See, in particular, Gallois 1996, 56–60.

15. In Dretske 1983 I argued that the condition (relating to justification, evidence or information) required to promote a belief that x is F into knowledge that x is F is also operative in our coming to believe that x is F (in acquiring the concept F). Roughly, if something's being F isn't the sort of thing you can know, it isn't the sort of thing you can believe either. This, of course, is the same conclusion Putnam (1981) reaches by considering brains in a vat.

References

Armstrong, D. 1961. *Perception and the Physical World*. London: Routledge & Kegan Paul.

Armstrong, D. 1962. *Bodily Sensations*. London: Routledge & Kegan Paul.

Bilgrami, A. 1998. "Self-Knowledge and Resentment." In C. Wright, B. Smith, and C. Macdonald, eds., *Knowing Our Own Minds*. Oxford: Clarendon Press.

Burge, T. 1985. "Authoritative Self-Knowledge and Perceptual Individualism." In R. Grimm and D. Merrill, eds., *Contents of Thought*. Tucson: University of Arizona Press.

Burge, T. 1988. "Individualism and Self-Knowledge." *Journal of Philosophy* 85: 649–663.

Chalmers, D. 1996. *The Conscious Mind*. New York: Oxford University Press.

Dretske, F. 1983. "The Epistemology of Belief." *Synthèse* 55: 3–19.

Dretske, F. 1995. *Naturalizing the Mind*. Cambridge, Mass.: MIT Press.

Dretske, F. 1999. "The Mind's Awareness of Itself." *Philosophical Studies* 95(1–2): 103–124.

Dretske, F. 2003. "How Do You Know You Are Not a Zombie?" In B. Gertler, ed., *Privileged Access*. Aldershot: Ashgate.

Evans, G. 1982. *The Varieties of Reference*. Oxford: Oxford University Press.

Fricker, E. 1998. "Self-Knowledge: Special Access versus Artifact of Grammar—A Dichotomy Rejected." In C. Wright, B. Smith, and C. Macdonald, eds., *Knowing Our Own Minds*. Oxford: Clarendon Press.

Gallois, A. 1996. *The World Without, the Mind Within*. Cambridge: Cambridge University Press.

Kripke, S. 1980. *Naming and Necessity*. Cambridge, Mass.: Harvard University Press.

Lycan, W. 1996. *Consciousness and Experience*. Cambridge, Mass.: MIT Press.

Peacocke, C. 1992. *A Study of Concepts*. Cambridge, Mass.: MIT Press.

Pitcher, G. 1971. *A Theory of Perception*. Princeton: Princeton University Press.

Putnam, H. 1981. "Brains in a Vat." In *Truth and History*. Cambridge: Cambridge University Press.

Reid, T. 1969. *Essays on the Intellectual Powers*. B. Brody, ed. Cambridge, Mass.: MIT Press. (Originally published 1785.)

Shoemaker, S. 1996. "Self-Knowledge and 'Inner Sense'." In *The First Person Perspective and Other Essays*. Cambridge: Cambridge University Press.

Siewert, C. 1998. *The Significance of Consciousness*. Princeton: Princeton University Press.

Siewert, C. 2003. "Self-Knowledge and Rationality: Shoemaker on Self-Blindness." In B. Gertler, ed., *Privileged Access*. Aldershot: Ashgate.

Tye, M. 1995. *Ten Problems of Consciousness*. Cambridge, Mass.: MIT Press.

Wright, C. 1998. "Self-Knowledge: The Wittgensteinian Legacy." In C. Wright, B. Smith, and C. Macdonald, eds., *Knowing Our Own Minds*. Oxford: Clarendon Press.

Wright, C. 2003. "Some Reflections on the Acquisition of Warrant by Inference." In S. Nuccetelli, ed., *New Essays on Semantic Externalism and Self-Knowledge*. Cambridge, Mass.: MIT Press.

10 Reasoning Defeasibly about Probabilities

John L. Pollock

1 The Problem of Sparse Probability Knowledge

The use of probabilities is ubiquitous in philosophy, science, engineering, artificial intelligence, economics, and many other disciplines. It is generally supposed that the logical and mathematical structure of probabilities is well understood, and completely characterized by the probability calculus. The probability calculus is typically identified with some form of Kolmogoroff's axioms, often supplemented with an axiom of countable additivity. Mathematical probability theory is a mature subdiscipline of mathematics based on these axioms, and forms the mathematical basis for most applications of probabilities in the sciences.

There is, however, a problem with the supposition that this is all there is to the logical and mathematical structure of probabilities. The uninitiated often suppose that if we know a few basic probabilities, we can compute the values of many others just by applying the probability calculus. Thus it might be supposed that familiar sorts of statistical inference provide us with our basic knowledge of probabilities, and then recourse to the probability calculus enables us to compute other previously unknown probabilities. The picture is of a kind of foundations theory of the epistemology of probability, with the probability calculus providing the inference engine that enables us to get beyond whatever probabilities are discovered by direct statistical investigation.

Regrettably, this simple image of the epistemology of probability cannot be correct. The difficulty is that the probability calculus is not nearly so powerful as the uninitiated suppose. If we know the probabilities of some basic propositions $P, Q, R, S, \ldots$, it is rare that we will be able to compute, just by appeal to the probability calculus, a unique value for the probability of some logical compound like $((P \& Q) \vee (R \& S))$. To illustrate, suppose we know that $\text{PROB}(P) = .7$ and $\text{PROB}(Q) = .6$. What can we conclude about

PROB(P & Q)? All the probability calculus enables us to infer is that $.3 \leq$ PROB(P & Q) $\leq .6$. That does not tell us much. Similarly, all we can conclude about PROB($P \vee Q$) is that $.7 \leq$ PROB($P \vee Q$) ≤ 1.0. In general, the probability calculus imposes constraints on the probabilities of logical compounds, but it falls far short of enabling us to compute unique values.

Unless we come to a problem already knowing a great deal about the relevant probabilities, the probability calculus will not enable us to compute the values of unknown probabilities that subsequently become of interest to us. Suppose a problem is described by logical compounds of a set of simple propositions $P_1, \ldots, P_n$. Then to be able to compute the probabilities of all logical compounds of these simple propositions, what we must generally know is the probabilities of every conjunction of the form PROB($(\sim)P_1 \& \ldots \& (\sim)P_n$). The tildes enclosed in parentheses can be either present or absent. These n-fold conjunctions are called *Boolean conjunctions*, and jointly they constitute a "partition." Given fewer than all but one of them, the only constraint the probability calculus imposes on the probabilities of the remaining Boolean conjunctions is that the sum of all of them must be 1. Together, the probabilities of all the Boolean conjunctions determine a complete "probability distribution"—an assignment of unique probabilities to every logical compound of the simple propositions.

In theoretical accounts of the use of probabilities in any discipline, it is generally assumed that we come to a problem equipped with a complete probability distribution. However, in real life this assumption is totally unrealistic. In general, given n simple propositions, there will be 2^n logically independent probabilities of Boolean conjunctions. As Gilbert Harman (1986) observed years ago, for a rather small number of simple propositions, there is a completely intractable number of logically independent probabilities. For example, given just 300 simple propositions, a grossly inadequate number for describing many real-life problems, there will be 2^{300} logically independent probabilities of Boolean conjunctions. 2^{300} is approximately equal to 10^{90}. To illustrate what an immense number this is, recent estimates of the number of elementary particles in the universe put it at 10^{80}–10^{85}. Thus to know the probabilities of all the Boolean conjunctions, we would have to know 5–10 orders of magnitude more logically independent probabilities than the number of elementary particles in the universe.

Lest one think this is an unrealistic problem, consider a simple example. Pollock (2006a) describes a challenge problem for AI planners. This problem generalizes Kushmerick, Hanks, and Weld's (1995) "slippery gripper" problem. We are presented with a table on which there are 300 numbered blocks, and a panel of correspondingly numbered buttons. Pushing a button activates a robot arm which attempts to pick up the corresponding block and remove it from the table. We get 100 dollars for each block that is removed. Pushing a button costs two dollars. The hitch is that half of the blocks are greasy. If a block is not greasy, pushing the button will result in its being removed from the table with probability 1.0, but if it is greasy the probability is only 0.01. We are given exactly 300 opportunities to either push a button or do nothing. Between button pushes, we are given the opportunity to look at the table, which costs one dollar. Looking will reveal what blocks are still on the table, but will not reveal directly whether a block is greasy. What should we do? Humans find this problem terribly easy. An informal survey reveals that most people quickly produce the optimal plan—push each button once, and don't bother to look at the table. But when Pollock (2006a) surveyed AI planners, most could not even encode this problem, much less solve it. The difficulty is that there are too many logically independent probabilities. For every subset K of the 300 blocks, let $p_{K,i}$ be the probability that, when K is the set of blocks on the table, block i is still on the table after the button corresponding to block i is pushed. There are 2^{300} choices of K, so there are more than 2^{300} probabilities $p_{K,i}$ such that $i \in K$. Furthermore, none of them can be derived from any of the others. Thus they must each be encoded separately in describing a complete probability distribution for the problem. It seems to be impossible for a real cognitive agent to encode such a probability distribution.

Although we humans cannot encode a complete probability distribution for the preceding problem, we can deal with problems like the slippery blocks problem. How do we do that? It is, apparently, computationally impossible for the requisite probabilities to be stored in us from the start, so they must be produced one at a time as we need them. If they are produced as we need them, there must be some kind of inference mechanism that has the credentials to produce rationally acceptable estimates. We have seen that, unless we begin with more information than it is computationally possible for us to store, we cannot derive the new probability estimates from previously accepted probabilities by way of the probability calculus. So there must be some other rational inference procedures enabling us to generate new probability estimates that do not follow logically, via the probability calculus, from prior probability estimates. What might these rational inference procedures be?

I will call this *the problem of sparse probability knowledge*. It is computationally impossible for us to store explicit knowledge of a complete probability distribution. At any given time, our knowledge of probabilities is worse than just incomplete. The set of probabilities we know is many orders of magnitude smaller than the set of all true probabilities. How then can we be as successful as we are in applying probability to real-world problems?

It is noteworthy that in applying probabilities to concrete problems, probability practitioners commonly adopt undefended assumptions of statistical independence. The probabilities PROB(P) and PROB(Q) are *statistically independent* iff PROB($P\&Q$) = PROB(P) · PROB(Q). An equivalent definition is that PROB(P/Q) = PROB(P). In the practical use of probabilities it is almost universally assumed, often apologetically, that probabilities are independent unless we have some reason for thinking otherwise. In most real-world applications of probabilities, if we did not make such assumptions about independence we would not be able to compute any of the complex probabilities that interest us. Imagine a case in which we know that the probability is .3 of a Xian (a fictional Chinese car) having a defective door lock if it has power door locks and was manufactured in a certain plant, whereas the probability of its having a defective door lock otherwise is only .01. We also know that the probability of a Xian being manufactured in that plant is .33, and the probability of a Xian having power door locks is .85. If we know nothing else of relevance, we will normally assume that whether the car has power door locks is statistically independent of whether it was manufactured in that plant, and so compute

prob(power-locks & plant) = .33 × .85 = .28

Then we can compute the general probability of a Xian having defective door locks:

prob(defect) = prob(defect/power-locks & plant) · prob(power-locks &

plant) + prob(defect/~(power-locks & plant))

· (1 − prob(power-locks & plant))

= .3 × .28 + .01 × (1 − .28) = .09

We could not perform this, or similar computations, without the assumption of independence.

The independence assumption is a defeasible assumption, because obviously we can discover that conditions we thought were independent are unexpectedly correlated. The probability calculus can give us only necessary truths about probabilities, so the justification of such a defeasible assumption must have some other source.

If we have a problem in which we can assume that most propositions are statistically independent of one another, there are compact techniques for storing complete probability distributions using what are called "Bayesian nets" (Pearl 1988). The use of Bayesian nets allows us to explicitly store just that subset of probabilities that cannot be derived from each other by assuming statistical independence, and provides an efficient inference mechanism for recovering derivable probabilities from them. However, this is not the entire solution to the problem of sparse probability knowledge, because in the slippery blocks problem, none of the probabilities $p_{K,i}$ can be derived from others, so they would all have to be encoded separately in a Bayesian net, and that would make the Bayesian net impossibly large.

I will argue that a defeasible assumption of statistical independence is just the tip of the iceberg. There are multitudes of defeasible inferences that we can make about probabilities, and a very rich mathematical theory grounding them. It is these defeasible inferences that enable us to make practical use of probabilities without being able to deduce everything we need via the probability calculus. I will argue that, on a certain conception of probability, there are mathematically derivable second-order probabilities to the effect that various inferences about first-order probabilities, although not deductively valid, will nonetheless produce correct conclusions with probability 1, and this makes it reasonable to accept these inferences defeasibly. The second-order principles are principles of *probable probabilities*.

2 Two Kinds of Probability

No doubt the currently most popular theory of the foundations of probability is the subjectivist theory, originally put forward by Ramsey and Savage and developed at length by many more recent scholars. However, my solution to the problem of sparse probability knowledge requires that we start with objective probabilities. Historically, there have been two general approaches to probability theory. The most familiar takes "definite" or "single-case" probabilities to be basic. Definite probabilities attach to closed formulas or propositions. I write them using small capitals: PROB(P) and PROB(P/Q). To be contrasted with definite probabilities are "indefinite" or "general" probabilities (sometimes called "statistical probabilities"). The indefinite probability of *an A* being a *B* is not about any particular *A*, but rather about the *property* of being an *A*. In this respect, its logical form is the same as that of relative frequencies. I write indefinite probabilities using lower-case 'prob' and free variables: prob(Bx/Ax). For instance, in the fictional example above, in which we concluded that the probability of a Xian having defective door locks is .09, that conclusion was about Xians in general—not about individual cars. If we examine a particular car and determine conclusively that its door lock is defective, then the definite probability of its having defective door locks is 1.0, but that does not alter the indefinite probability of Xians in general having defective door locks.

The distinction between definite and indefinite probabilities is commonly overlooked by contemporary probability theorists, perhaps because of the popularity of subjective probability (which has no way to make sense of indefinite probabilities). But most objective approaches to probability tie probabilities to relative frequencies in some essential way, and the resulting probabilities have the same logical form as the relative frequencies. That is, they are indefinite probabilities. The simplest theories identify indefinite probabilities with relative frequencies (Russell 1948; Braithwaite 1953; Kyburg 1961, 1974a; Sklar 1970, 1973).[1] The simplest objection to such "finite frequency theories" is that we often make probability judgments that diverge from relative frequencies. For example, we can talk about a coin being fair (and so the indefinite probability of a flip landing heads is 0.5) even when it is flipped only once and then destroyed (in which case the relative frequency is either 1 or 0). For understanding such indefinite probabilities, we need a notion of probability that talks about *possible* instances of properties, as well as actual instances. Theories of this sort are sometimes called "hypothetical frequency theories." C. S. Peirce was perhaps the first to make a suggestion of this sort. Similarly, the statistician R. A. Fisher, regarded by many as "the father of modern statistics," identified probabilities with ratios in a "hypothetical infinite population, of which the actual data is regarded as constituting a random sample" (1922, 311). Karl Popper (1956, 1957, and 1959) endorsed a theory along these lines and called the resulting probabilities *propensities*. Henry Kyburg (1974b) was the first to construct a precise version of this theory (although he did not endorse the theory), and it is to him that we owe the name 'hypothetical frequency theories'. Kyburg (1974b) also insisted that von Mises should also be considered a hypothetical frequentist. There are obvious difficulties for spelling out the details of a hypothetical frequency theory. More recent attempts to formulate precise versions of what might be regarded as hypothetical frequency theories are van Fraassen (1981), Bacchus (1990), Halpern (1990), Pollock (1990), and Bacchus et al. (1996). I will take my jumping-off point to be the theory of Pollock (1990), which I will sketch briefly in section 3.

After brief thought, most philosophers find the distinction between definite and indefinite probabilities to be intuitively clear. However, this is a distinction that sometimes puzzles probability theorists, many of whom have been raised on an exclusive diet of definite probabilities. They are sometimes tempted to confuse indefinite probabilities with probability distributions over random variables. Although historically, most theories of objective probability were theories of indefinite probability, mathematical probability theory tends to focus exclusively on definite probabilities. When mathematicians talk about variables in connection with probability, they usually mean "random variables," which are not variables at all but functions assigning values to the different members of a population. Indefinite probabilities have single numbers as their values. Probability distributions over random variables are just what their name implies—distributions of definite probabilities rather than single numbers.

It has always been acknowledged that for practical decision-making we need definite probabilities rather than indefinite probabilities. For example, in deciding whether to trust the door locks on my Xian, I want to know the probability of *its* having defective locks, not the probability of Xians in general having defective locks. So theories that take indefinite probabilities as basic, need a way of deriving definite probabilities from them. Theories of how to do this are theories of *direct inference*. Theories of objective indefinite probability propose that statistical inference gives us knowledge of indefinite probabilities, and then direct inference gives us knowledge of definite probabilities. Reichenbach (1949) pioneered the theory of direct inference. The basic idea is that if we want to know the definite probability PROB(Fa), we look for the narrowest reference class (or 'reference property') G such that we know the indefinite probability prob(Fx/Gx) and we know Ga, and then we identify PROB(Fa) with prob(Fx/Gx). For example, actuarial reasoning aimed at setting insurance rates proceeds in roughly this fashion. Kyburg (1974a) was the first to attempt to provide firm logical foundations for direct inference. Pollock (1990) took that as its starting point, and constructed a modified theory with a more epistemological orientation. The present paper builds upon some of the basic ideas of the latter.

The appeal to indefinite probabilities and direct inference has seemed promising for avoiding the computational difficulties attendant on the need for a complete probability distribution. Instead of assuming that we come to a problem with an antecedently given complete probability distribution, one can assume more realistically that we come to the problem with some limited knowledge of indefinite probabilities and then infer definite probabilities from the latter as we need them. For example, I had no difficulty giving a description of the probabilities involved in the slippery blocks problem, but I did that by giving an informal description of the indefinite probabilities rather than the definite probabilities. We described it by reporting that the indefinite probability $\text{prob}(Gx/Bx)$ of a block being greasy is .5, and the indefinite probability $\text{prob}(\sim Tx(s+1)/Txs \text{ \& } Pxs \text{ \& } Gx)$ of a block being successfully removed from the table at step s if it is greasy is .01, but $\text{prob}(\sim Tx(s+1)/Txs \text{ \& } Pxs \text{ \& } \sim Gx) = 1.0$. We implicitly assumed that $\text{prob}(\sim Tx(s+1)/\sim Txs) = 1$. These probabilities completely describe the problem. For solving the decision-theoretic planning problem, we need definite probabilities rather than indefinite probabilities, but one might hope that these can be recovered by direct inference from this small set of indefinite probabilities as they are needed.

Unfortunately, I do not think that this hope will be realized. The appeal to indefinite probabilities and direct inference helps a bit with the problem of sparse probability knowledge, but it falls short of constituting a complete solution. The difficulty is that the problem recurs at the level of indefinite probabilities. Direct statistical investigation will apprise us of the values of some indefinite probabilities, and then others can be derived by appeal to the probability calculus. But just as for definite probabilities, the probability calculus is a weak crutch. We will rarely be able to derive more than rather broad constraints on unknown probabilities. A simple illustration of this difficulty arises when we know that $\text{prob}(Ax/Bx) = r$ and $\text{prob}(Ax/Cx) = s$, where $r \neq s$, and we know both that Ba and Ca. What should we conclude about the value of $\text{PROB}(Aa)$? Direct inference gives us defeasible reasons for drawing the conflicting conclusions that $\text{PROB}(Aa) = r$ and $\text{PROB}(Aa) = s$, and standard theories of direct inference give us no way to resolve the conflict, so they end up telling us that there is no conclusion we can justifiably draw about the value of $\text{PROB}(Aa)$. Is this reasonable? Suppose we have two unrelated diagnostic tests for some rare disease, and Bernard tests positive on both tests. Intuitively, it seems this should make it more probable that Bernard has the disease than if we only have the results of one of the tests. This suggests that, given the values of $\text{prob}(Ax/Bx)$ and $\text{prob}(Ax/Cx)$, there ought to be something useful we can say about the value of $\text{prob}(Ax/Bx \text{\&} Cx)$, and then we can apply direct inference to the latter to compute the definite probability that Bernard has the disease. Existing theories give us no way to do this, and the probability calculus imposes no constraint at all on the value of $\text{prob}(Ax/Bx \text{\&} Cx)$.

I believe that standard theories of direct inference are much too weak to solve the problem of sparse probability knowledge. What I will argue in this paper is that new mathematical results, coupled with ideas from the theory of nomic probability introduced in Pollock 1990, provide the justification for a wide range of new principles supporting defeasible inferences about the expectable values of unknown probabilities. These principles include familiar-looking principles of direct inference, but they include many new principles as well. For example, among them is a principle enabling us to defeasibly estimate the probability of Bernard having the disease when he tests positive on both tests. I believe that this broad collection of new defeasible inference schemes provides the solution to the problem of sparse probability knowledge, and explains how probabilities can be truly useful even when we are massively ignorant about most of them.

3   Nomic Probability

Pollock (1990) developed a possible-worlds semantics for objective indefinite probabilities,[2] and I will take that as my starting point for the present theory of probable probabilities. The proposal was that we can identify the *nomic probability* prob(Fx/Gx) with the proportion of physically possible Gs that are Fs. A *physically possible G* is defined to be an ordered pair $\langle w, x \rangle$ such that w is a physically possible world (one compatible with all of the physical laws obtaining in this world) and x has the property G at w. Let us define the *subproperty relation* as follows:

$F \leqslant G$ iff it is physically necessary (follows from true physical laws) that $(\forall x)(Fx \rightarrow Gx)$.

$F \approx G$ iff it is physically necessary (follows from true physical laws) that $(\forall x)(Fx \leftrightarrow Gx)$.

We can think of the subproperty relation as a kind of nomic entailment-relation (holding between properties rather than propositions). More generally, F and G can have any number of free variables (not necessarily the same number), in which case $F \leqslant G$ iff the universal closure of $(F \rightarrow G)$ is physically necessary.

Given a suitable proportion function ρ, we could stipulate that, where $\mathfrak{F}$ and $\mathfrak{G}$ are the sets of physically possible Fs and Gs respectively:

prob$_x$(Fx/Gx) $= \rho(\mathfrak{F}, \mathfrak{G})$.[3]

However, it is unlikely that we can pick out the right proportion function without appealing to prob itself, so the postulate is simply that *there is* some proportion function related to prob as above. This is merely taken to tell us something about the formal properties of prob. Rather than axiomatizing prob directly, it turns out to be more convenient to adopt axioms for the proportion function. Proportion functions are a generalization of measure functions, studied in mathematics in measure theory. Pollock (1990) showed that, given the assumptions adopted there, ρ and prob are interdefinable, so the same empirical considerations that enable us to evaluate prob inductively also determine p.

Note that prob_x is a variable-binding operator, binding the variable x. When there is no danger of confusion, I will omit the subscript 'x', but sometimes we will want to quantify into probability contexts, in which case it will be important to distinguish between the variables bound by 'prob' and those that are left free. To simplify expressions, I will often omit the variables, writing '$\text{prob}(F/G)$' for '$\text{prob}(Fx/Gx)$' when no confusion will result.

It is often convenient to write proportions in the same logical form as probabilities, so where φ and θ are open formulas with free variable x, let $\rho_x(\varphi/\theta) = \rho(\{x \mid \varphi \,\&\, \theta\}, \{x \mid \theta\})$. Note that ρ_x is a variable-binding operator, binding the variable x. Again, when there is no danger of confusion, I will typically omit the subscript 'x'.

I will make three classes of assumptions about the proportion function. Let $\#X$ be the cardinality of a set X. If Y is finite, I assume:

$$\rho(X, Y) = \frac{\#X \cap Y}{\#Y}.$$

However, for present purposes the proportion function is most useful in talking about proportions among infinite sets. The sets $\mathfrak{F}$ and $\mathfrak{G}$ will invariably be infinite, if for no other reason than that there are infinitely many physically possible worlds in which there are Fs and Gs.

My second set of assumptions is that the standard axioms for conditional probabilities hold for proportions. These axioms automatically hold for relative frequencies among finite sets, so the assumption is just that they also hold for proportions among infinite sets.

That further assumptions are needed derives from the fact that the standard probability calculus is a calculus of definite probabilities rather than indefinite probabilities. A calculus of indefinite probabilities is related to the calculus of definite probabilities in a manner roughly analogous to the relationship between the predicate calculus and the propositional calculus. Thus we get some principles pertaining specifically to relations that hold for indefinite probabilities but cannot even be formulated in the standard probability calculus. For instance, Pollock (1990) endorsed the following two principles:

Individuals
$\text{prob}(Fxy/Gxy \,\&\, y = a) = \text{prob}(Fxa/Gxa)$

PPROB
$\text{prob}(Fx/Gx \,\&\, \text{prob}(Fx/Gx) = r) = r.$

I will not assume either of these principles in this paper, but I mention them just to illustrate that there are reasonable-seeming principles governing indefinite probabilities that are not even well formed in the standard probability calculus.

What I do need in the present paper is three assumptions about proportions that go beyond merely imposing the standard axioms for the probability calculus. The three assumptions I will make are:

Finite Set Principle
For any $N > 0$,

$$\rho_X(\Phi(X)/X \subseteq B \ \& \ \#X = N) = \rho_{x_1,\ldots,x_N}(\Phi(\{x_1,\ldots,x_N\})/x_1,\ldots,x_N$$

$$\text{are pairwise distinct} \ \& \ x_1,\ldots,x_N \in B).$$

Projection Principle
If $0 \leq p, q \leq 1$ and $(\forall y)(Gy \to \rho_x(Fx/Rxy) \in [p,q])$,

then $\rho_{x,y}(Fx/Rxy \ \& \ Gy) \in [p,q]$.[4]

Crossproduct Principle
$\rho(A \times B, C \times D) = \rho(A,C) \cdot \rho(B,D).$

Note that these three principles are all theorems of elementary set theory when the sets in question are finite. For instance, the crossproduct principle holds for finite sets because $\#(A \times B) = (\#A) \cdot (\#B)$, and hence

$$\rho(A \times B, C \times D) = \frac{\#((A \times B) \cap (C \times D))}{\#(C \times D)} = \frac{\#((A \cap C) \times (B \cap D))}{\#(C \times D)}$$

$$= \frac{\#(A \cap C) \cdot \#(B \cap D)}{\#C \cdot \#D} = \frac{\#(A \cap C)}{\#C} \cdot \frac{\#(B \cap D)}{\#D}$$

$$= \rho(A,C) \cdot \rho(B,D).$$

My assumption is simply that ρ continues to have these algebraic properties even when applied to infinite sets. I take it that this is a fairly conservative set of assumptions.

I often hear the objection that in affirming the crossproduct principle, I must be making a hidden assumption of statistical independence. However, that is to confuse proportions with probabilities. The crossproduct principle is about proportions—not probabilities. For finite sets, proportions are computed by simply counting members and computing ratios of cardinalities. It makes no sense to talk about statistical independence in this context. For infinite sets we cannot just count members any more, but the algebra is the same. It is because the algebra of proportions is simpler than the algebra of probabilities that it is useful to axiomatize nomic probabilities indirectly by adopting axioms for proportions.

Pollock (1990) derived the entire epistemological theory of nomic probability from a single epistemological principle coupled with a mathematical theory that amounts to a calculus of nomic probabilities. The single epistemological principle that underlies probabilistic reasoning is the *statistical syllogism*, which can be formulated as follows:

Statistical Syllogism

If *F* is projectible with respect to *G* and $r > 0.5$, then $\ulcorner Gc$ & $\text{prob}(F/G) \geq r\urcorner$ is a defeasible reason for $\ulcorner Fc\urcorner$, the strength of the reason being a monotonic increasing function of *r*.

I take it that the statistical syllogism is a very intuitive principle, and it is clear that we employ it constantly in our everyday reasoning. For example, suppose you read in the newspaper that Barack Obama is visiting Guatemala, and you believe what you read. What justifies your belief? No one believes that everything printed in the newspaper is true. What you believe is that certain kinds of reports published in certain kinds of newspapers tend to be true, and this report is of that kind. It is the statistical syllogism that justifies your belief.

The projectibility constraint in the statistical syllogism is the familiar projectibility constraint on inductive reasoning, first noted by Goodman (1955). One might wonder what it is doing in the statistical syllogism. But it was argued by Pollock (1990), on the strength of what were taken to be intuitively compelling examples, that the statistical syllogism must be so constrained. Furthermore, it was shown that without a projectibility constraint, the statistical syllogism is self-defeating, because for any intuitively correct application of the statistical syllogism it is possible to construct a conflicting (but unintuitive) application to a contrary conclusion. This is the same problem that Goodman first noted in connection with induction. Pollock (1990) then went on to argue that the projectibility constraint on induction derives from that on the statistical syllogism.

The projectibility constraint is important, but also problematic, because no one has a good analysis of it. I will not discuss it further here. I will just assume, without argument, that the second-order probabilities employed below in the theory of probable probabilities satisfy the projectibility constraint, and hence can be used in the statistical syllogism.

The statistical syllogism is a defeasible inference scheme, so it is subject to defeat. I believe that the only primitive (underived) principle of defeat required for the statistical syllogism is that of subproperty defeat:

Subproperty Defeat for the Statistical Syllogism

If H is projectible, then $\ulcorner Hc$ & $\text{prob}(F/G\&H) < \text{prob}(F/G)\urcorner$ is an under-cutting defeater for the inference by the statistical syllogism from $\ulcorner Gc$ & $\text{prob}(F/G) \geq r\urcorner$ to $\ulcorner Fc\urcorner$.[5]

In other words, information about c that lowers the probability of its being F constitutes a defeater. Note that if $\text{prob}(Fx/G\&H)$ is high, one may still be able to make a weaker inference to the conclusion that Fc, but from the distinct premise $\ulcorner Gc$ & $\text{prob}(F/G\&H) = s\urcorner$.

Pollock (1990) argued that we need additional defeaters for the statistical syllogism besides subproperty defeaters, and formulated several candidates for such defeaters. But one of the conclusions of the research described in this paper is that the additional defeaters can all be viewed as derived defeaters, with subproperty defeaters being the only primitive defeaters for the statistical syllogism.

4 Indifference

Principles of probable probabilities are derived from combinatorial theorems about proportions in finite sets. I will begin with a very simple principle that is in fact not very useful, but will serve as a template for the discussion of more useful principles.

Suppose we have a set of 10,000,000 objects. I announce that I am going to select a subset, and ask you how many members it will have. Most people will protest that there is no way to answer this question. It could have any number of members from 0 to 10,000,000. However, if you answer, "Approximately 5,000,000," you will almost certainly be right. This is because, although there are subsets of all sizes from 0 to 10,000,000, there are many more subsets whose sizes are approximately 5,000,000 than there are of any other size. In fact, 99% of the subsets have cardinalities differing from 5,000,000 by less than .08%. If we let '$x \approx_\delta y$' mean "the difference between x and y is less than or equal to δ," the general theorem is:

Finite Indifference Principle

For every $\varepsilon, \delta > 0$ there is an N such that if U is finite and $\#U > N$ then

$$\rho_X(\rho(X, U) \approx_\delta 0.5/X \subseteq U) \geq 1 - \varepsilon.$$

In other words, the proportion of subsets of U which are such that $\rho(X, U)$ is approximately equal to .5, to any given degree of approximation, goes to 1 as the size of U goes to infinity. To see why this is true, suppose $\#U = n$. If $r \leq n$, the number of r-membered subsets of U is $C(n, r) = n!/(r!(n - r)!)$. It is

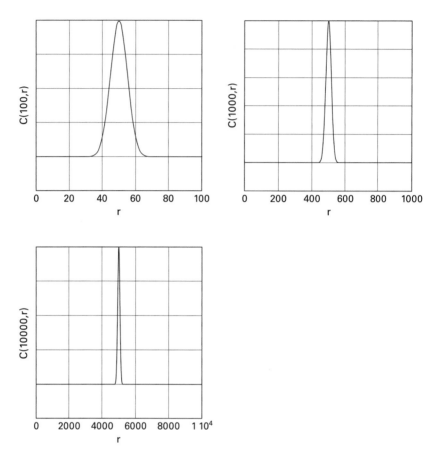

Figure 10.1
$C(n,r)$ for $n = 100$, $n = 1000$, and $n = 10000$.

illuminating to plot $C(n,r)$ for variable r and various fixed values of n.[6] See figure 10.1. This illustrates that the sizes of subsets of U will cluster around $n/2$, and they cluster more tightly as n increases. This is precisely what the indifference principle tells us.

The reason the indifference principle holds is that $C(n,r)$ becomes "needle-like" in the limit. As we proceed, I will state a number of similar combinatorial theorems, and in each case they have similar intuitive explanations. The cardinalities of relevant sets are products of terms of the form $C(n,r)$, and their distribution becomes needle-like in the limit. In this paper, I will omit the proofs of theorems. They will be presented elsewhere in detail, and can currently be found on my website.[7]

The finite indifference principle is a mathematical theorem about finite sets. It tells us that for fixed $\varepsilon, \delta > 0$, there is an N such that if U is finite but contains at least N members, then the proportion of subsets X of a set U which are such that $\rho(X, U) \underset{\delta}{\approx} 0.5$ is greater than $1 - \varepsilon$. This suggests that the proportion is also is greater than $1 - \varepsilon$ when U is infinite. But if the proportion is greater than $1 - \varepsilon$ for every $\varepsilon > 0$, it follows that the proportion is 1. In other words:

If U is infinite then for every $\delta > 0$, $\rho_X(\rho(X, U) \underset{\delta}{\approx} 0.5 / X \subseteq U) = 1$.

Given the rather simple assumptions I made about ρ in section 3, we can derive this infinitary principle from the finite principle. First, we can use familiar-looking mathematics to prove:

Law of Large Numbers for Proportions
If B is infinite and $\rho(A/B) = p$ then for every $\varepsilon, \delta > 0$, there is an N such that

$\rho_X(\rho(A/X) \underset{\delta}{\approx} p / X \subseteq B \ \& \ \#X \geq N) \geq 1 - \varepsilon$.

Note that unlike laws of large numbers for probabilities, the law of large numbers for proportions does not require an assumption of statistical independence. This is because it is derived from the crossproduct principle, and as remarked in section 3, no such assumption is required (or even intelligible) for the crossproduct principle.

Given the law of large numbers for proportions, the finite indifference principle can be shown to entail:

Infinitary Indifference Principle
If U is infinite then for every $\delta > 0$, $\rho_X(\rho(X, U) \underset{\delta}{\approx} 0.5 / X \subseteq U) = 1$.

Nomic probabilities are proportions among physically possible objects. For any property F that is not extraordinarily contrived, the set F of physically possible Fs will be infinite.[8] Thus the infinitary indifference principle for proportions implies an analogous principle for nomic probabilities:

Probabilistic Indifference Principle
For any property G and for every $\delta > 0$,

$\text{prob}_X(\text{prob}(X/G) \underset{\delta}{\approx} 0.5 / X \preccurlyeq G) = 1$.[9]

Next note that we can apply the statistical syllogism to the probability formulated in the probabilistic indifference principle. For every $\delta > 0$, this gives us a defeasible reason for expecting that if $F \preccurlyeq G$, then $\text{prob}(F/G) \underset{\delta}{\approx} 0.5$, and these conclusions jointly entail that $\text{prob}(F/G) = 0.5$. For any property F, $(F\&G) \preccurlyeq G$, and $\text{prob}(F/G) = \text{prob}(F\&G/G)$. Thus we are led to a defeasible inference scheme:

Indifference Principle
For any properties F and G, it is defeasibly reasonable to assume that $\text{prob}(F/G) = 0.5$.

The indifference principle is my first example of a principle of probable probabilities. We have a quadruple of principles that go together: (1) the finite indifference principle, which is a theorem of combinatorial mathematics; (2) the infinitary indifference principle, which follows from the finite principle, given the law of large numbers for proportions; (3) the probabilistic indifference principle, which is a theorem derived from (2); and (4) the indifference principle, which is a principle of defeasible reasoning that follows from (3) with the help of the statistical syllogism. All of the principles of probable probabilities that I will discuss have analogous quadruples of principles associated with them. Rather than tediously listing all four principles in each case, I will encapsulate the four principles in the simple form:

Expectable Indifference Principle
For any properties F and G, the expectable value of $\text{prob}(F/G) = 0.5$.

So in talking about expectable values, I am talking about this entire quadruple of principles.

I have chosen the indifference principle as my first example of a principle of probable probabilities because the argument for it is simple and easy to follow. However, as I indicated at the start, this principle is only occasionally useful. If we were choosing the properties F in some random way, it would be reasonable to expect that $\text{prob}(F/G) = 0.5$. However, pairs of properties F and G which are such that $\text{prob}(F/G) = 0.5$ are not very useful to us from a cognitive perspective, because knowing that something is a G then carries no information about whether it is an F. As a result, we usually only enquire about the value of $\text{prob}(F/G)$ when we have reason to believe there is a connection between F and G such that $\text{prob}(F/G) \neq 0.5$. Hence in actual practice, application of the indifference principle to cases that really interest us will almost invariably be defeated. This does not mean, however, that the indifference principle is never useful. For instance, if I give Jones the opportunity to pick either of two essentially identical balls, in the absence of information to the contrary it seems reasonable to take the probability of either choice to be .5. This can be justified as an application of either the indifference principle or the generalized indifference principle.

That applications of the indifference principle are often defeated illustrates an important point about nomic probability and principles of probable probabilities. The fact that a nomic probability is 1 does not mean that there are no counterinstances. In fact, there may be infinitely many counterinstances. Consider the probability of a real number being irrational. Plausibly, this probability is 1, because the cardinality of the set of irrationals is infinitely greater than the cardinality of the set of rationals. But there are still infinitely many rationals. The set of rationals is infinite, but it has measure 0 relative to the set of real numbers.

A second point is that in classical probability theory (which is about definite probabilities), conditional probabilities are defined as ratios of unconditional probabilities:

$$\text{PROB}(P/Q) = \frac{\text{PROB}(P\&Q)}{\text{PROB}(Q)}.$$

However, for indefinite probabilities, there are no unconditional probabilities, so conditional probabilities must be taken as primitive. These are sometimes called "Popper functions." The first people to investigate them were Karl Popper (1938, 1959) and the mathematician Alfred Renyi (1955). If conditional probabilities are defined as above, $\text{PROB}(P/Q)$ is undefined when $\text{PROB}(Q) = 0$. However, for nomic probabilities, $\text{prob}(F/G\&H)$ can be perfectly well-defined even when $\text{prob}(G/H) = 0$. One consequence of this is that, unlike in the standard probability calculus, if $\text{prob}(F/G) = 1$, it does not follow that $\text{prob}(F/G\&H) = 1$. Specifically, this can fail when $\text{prob}(H/G) = 0$. Thus, for example,

$\text{prob}(2x \text{ is irrational}/x \text{ is a real number}) = 1$

but

$\text{prob}(2x \text{ is irrational}/x \text{ is a real number } \& \ x \text{ is rational}) = 0$.

In the course of developing the theory of probable probabilities, we will find numerous examples of this phenomenon, and they will generate defeaters for the defeasible inferences licensed by our principles of probable probabilities.

5 Independence

Now let us turn to a truly useful principle of probable probabilities. It was remarked above that probability practitioners commonly assume statistical independence when they have no reason to think otherwise, and so compute that $\text{prob}(A\&B/C) = \text{prob}(A/C) \cdot \text{prob}(B/C)$. In other words, they assume that *A and B are statistically independent relative to C*. This assumption is ubiquitous in almost every application of probability to real-world problems. However, the justification for such an assumption has heretofore eluded probability theorists, and when they make such assumptions they tend to do so apologetically. We are now in a position to provide a justification for a general assumption of statistical independence.

Although it is harder to prove than the finite indifference principle, the following combinatorial principle holds in general:

Finite Independence Principle
For $0 \leq r, s \leq 1$ and for every $\varepsilon, \delta > 0$ there is an N such that if U is finite and $\#U > N$, then

$$\rho_{X,Y,Z}(\rho(X \cap Y, Z) \underset{\delta}{\approx} r \cdot s / X, Y, Z \subseteq U \;\&\; \rho(X, Z) = r \;\&\; \rho(Y, Z) = s) \geq 1 - \varepsilon.$$

In other words, for a large finite set U, subsets X, Y, and Z of U tend to be such that $\rho(X \cap Y, Z)$ is approximately equal to $\rho(X, Z) \cdot \rho(Y, Z)$, and for any fixed degree of approximation, the proportion of subsets of U satisfying this approximation goes to 1 as the size of U goes to infinity.

Given the law of large numbers for proportions, the finite independence principle entails:

Infinitary Independence Principle
For $0 \leq r, s \leq 1$, if U is infinite then for every $\delta > 0$:

$$\rho_{X,Y,Z}(\rho(X \cap Y, Z) \underset{\delta}{\approx} r \cdot s / X, Y, Z \subseteq U \;\&\; \rho(X, Z) = r \;\&\; \rho(Y, Z) = s) = 1.$$

As before, this entails:

Probabilistic Independence Principle
For $0 \leq r, s \leq 1$ and for any property U, for every $\delta > 0$:

$$\text{prob}_{X,Y,Z}(\text{prob}(X \;\&\; Y/Z) \underset{\delta}{\approx} r \cdot s / X, Y, Z \preccurlyeq U \;\&\; \text{prob}(X/Z) = r$$

$$\&\; \text{prob}(Y/Z) = s) = 1.$$

Again, applying the statistical syllogism to the second-order probability in the probabilistic independence principle, we get:

Principle of Statistical Independence
$\ulcorner \text{prob}(A/C) = r \;\&\; \text{prob}(B/C) = s \urcorner$ is a defeasible reason for $\ulcorner \text{prob}(A\&B/C) = r \cdot s \urcorner$.

Again, we can encapsulate these four principles in a single principle of expectable values:

Principle of Expectable Statistical Independence
If $\text{prob}(A/C) = r$ and $\text{prob}(B/C) = s$, the expectable value of $\text{prob}(A\&B/C)$
$= r \cdot s$.

So a provable combinatorial principle regarding finite sets ultimately makes
it reasonable to expect, in the absence of contrary information, that properties will be statistically independent of one another. This is the reason why,
when we see no connection between properties that would force them to
be statistically dependent, we can reasonably expect them to be statistically
independent.

The assumption of statistical independence sometimes fails. Clearly, this
can happen when there are causal connections between properties. But it
can also happen for purely logical reasons. For example, if $A = B$, A and B
cannot be independent unless $r = 1$. More general defeaters for the principle of statistical independence will emerge below.

6 The Probable Probabilities Theorem

Principles like that of statistical independence are supported by a general combinatorial theorem, which underlies the entire theory of probable probabilities. Given a list of variables $X_1, \ldots, X_n$ ranging over subsets
of a set U, Boolean compounds of these sets are compounds formed
by union, intersection, and set-complement. So, for example $(X \cup Y) - Z$
is a Boolean compound of X, Y, and Z. *Linear constraints* on the Boolean compounds either state the values of certain proportions (e.g., stipulating that $\rho(X, Y) = r$), or they relate proportions using linear equations.
For example, if we know that $X = Y \cup Z$, that generates the linear constraint

$$\rho(X, U) = \rho(Y, U) + \rho(Z, U) - \rho(X \cap Z, U).$$

Our general theorem is:

Probable Probabilities Theorem
Let $U, X_1, \ldots, X_n$ be a set of variables ranging over sets, and consider a finite
set LC of linear constraints on proportions between Boolean compounds of
those variables. If LC is consistent with the probability calculus, then for
any pair of Boolean compounds P, Q of $U, X_1, \ldots, X_n$ there is a real number
r between 0 and 1 such that for every $\varepsilon, \delta > 0$, there is an N such that if U is
finite and $\#U > N$, then

$$\rho_{X_1,\ldots,X_n}(\rho(P, Q) \underset{\delta}{\approx} r / LC \ \& \ X_1, \ldots, X_n \subseteq U) \geq 1 - \varepsilon.$$

This is the theorem that underlies all of the principles developed in this paper. Given the law of large numbers for proportions, we can prove:

Limit Principle for Proportions

Consider a finite set LC of linear constraints on proportions between Boolean compounds of a list of variables $U, X_1, \ldots, X_n$. For any real number r between 0 and 1 and for every $\varepsilon, \delta > 0$, if there is an N such that if U is finite and $\#U > N$, then

$$\rho_{X_1,\ldots,X_n}(\rho(P,Q) \underset{\delta}{\approx} r/LC \,\&\, X_1,\ldots,X_n \subseteq U) \geq 1 - \varepsilon,$$

then if U is infinite, for every $\delta > 0$:

$$\rho_{X_1,\ldots,X_n}(\rho(P,Q) \underset{\delta}{\approx} r/LC \,\&\, X_1,\ldots,X_n \subseteq U) = 1.$$

Given the limit principle for proportions, the probable probabilities theorem entails:

Expectable Probabilities Principle

Let $U, X_1, \ldots, X_n$ be a set of variables ranging over properties and relations, and consider a finite set LC of linear constraints on probabilities between truth-functional compounds of those variables. If LC is consistent with the probability calculus, then for any pair of truth-functional compounds P, Q of $U, X_1, \ldots, X_n$ there is a real number r between 0 and 1 such that for every $\delta > 0$,

$$\mathrm{prob}_{X_1,\ldots,X_n}(\mathrm{prob}(P/Q) \underset{\delta}{\approx} r/LC \,\&\, X_1,\ldots,X_n \preccurlyeq U) = 1.$$

In other words, given the constraints LC, the expectable value of $\mathrm{prob}(P/Q) = r$.

This establishes the existence of expectable values for probabilities under very general circumstances. The theorem can probably be generalized further—for example, to linear inequalities, or even to nonlinear constraints—but this is what I have established so far.

The expectable probabilities principle tells us that there are expectable values. It turns out that there is a general strategy for finding and proving theorems describing these expectable values, and I have written a computer program (in Common LISP) that will often do this automatically, both finding the theorems and producing human-readable proofs. This program can currently be downloaded from my website.[10]

I will go on to illustrate these general results with several interesting theorems about probable probabilities.

7   Nonclassical Direct Inference

Pollock (1984) noted (a restricted form of) the following limit principle:

Finite Principle of Agreement
For $0 \leq a, b, c, r \leq 1$ and for every $\varepsilon, \delta > 0$, there is an N such that if U is finite and $\#U > N$, then:

$$\rho_{X,Y}\left(\begin{array}{c} p(X, Y \cap Z) \approx_{\delta} r/X, Y, Z \subseteq U \ \& \ p(X, Y) = r \\ \& \ p(X, U) = a \ \& \ p(Y, U) = b \ \& \ p(Z, U) = c \end{array} \right) \geq 1 - \varepsilon.$$

In the theory of nomic probability (Pollock 1984, 1990), this was used to ground a theory of direct inference. We can now improve upon that theory. As above, the Finite Principle of Agreement yields a principle of expectable values:

Nonclassical Direct Inference
If $\text{prob}(A/B) = r$, the expectable value of $\text{prob}(A/B\&C) = r$.

This is a kind of "principle of insufficient reason". It tells us that if we have no reason for thinking otherwise, we should expect that strengthening the reference property in a nomic probability leaves the value of the probability unchanged. This is called "nonclassical direct inference" because, although it only licenses inferences from indefinite probabilities to other indefinite probabilities, it turns out to have strong formal similarities to classical direct inference (which licenses inferences from indefinite probabilities to definite probabilities), and as we will see in section 8, principles of classical direct inference can be derived from it.

It is important to realize that the principle of agreement, and the corresponding principle of nonclassical direct inference, are equivalent to the probabilistic product principle and the defeasible principle of statistical independence. This turns upon the following simple theorem of the probability calculus:

Independence and Agreement Theorem
$\text{prob}(A/B\&C) = \text{prob}(A/B)$ iff A and C are independent relative to B.

As a result, anyone who shares the commonly held intuition that we should be able to assume statistical independence in the absence of information to the contrary is also committed to endorsing nonclassical direct inference. This is important, because I have found that many people do have the former intuition but balk at the latter.

There is a variant of the principle of agreement that is equivalent to the first version but often more useful:

Finite Principle of Agreement II
For $0 \leq r \leq 1$ and for every $\varepsilon, \delta > 0$, there is an N such that if U is finite and $\#U > N$, then:

$$\rho_{X,Y}(\rho(X,Z) \underset{\delta}{\approx} r / X, Y \subseteq U \ \& \ Z \subseteq Y \ \& \ \rho(X,Y) = r) \geq 1 - \varepsilon.$$

This yields an equivalent variant of the principle of nonclassical direct inference:

Nonclassical Direct Inference II
If $C \leqslant B$ and $\text{prob}(A/B) = r$, the expectable value of $\text{prob}(A/C) = r$.

The principle of nonclassical direct inference supports many defeasible inferences that seem intuitively reasonable but are not licensed by the probability calculus. For example, suppose we know that the probability of a twenty-year-old male driver in Maryland having an auto accident over the course of a year is .07. If we add that his girlfriend's name is 'Martha', we do not expect this to alter the probability. There is no way to justify this assumption within a traditional probability framework, but it is justified by nonclassical direct inference.

Nonclassical direct inference is a principle of defeasible inference, so it is subject to defeat. The simplest and most important kind of defeater is a *subproperty defeater*. Suppose $C \leqslant D \leqslant B$ and we know that $\text{prob}(A/B) = r$, but $\text{prob}(A/D) = s$, where $s \neq r$. This gives us defeasible reasons for drawing two incompatible conclusions, namely, that $\text{prob}(A/C) = r$ and $\text{prob}(A/D) = s$. The *principle of subproperty defeat* tells us that because $D \leqslant B$, the latter inference takes precedence and defeats the inference to the conclusion that $\text{prob}(A/C) = r$:

Subproperty Defeat for Nonclassical Direct Inference
$\ulcorner C \leqslant D \leqslant B$ and $\text{prob}(A/D) = s \neq r \urcorner$ is an undercutting defeater for the inference by nonclassical direct inference from $\ulcorner C \leqslant B$ and $\text{prob}(A/B) = r \urcorner$ to $\ulcorner \text{prob}(A/C) = r \urcorner$.

We obtain this defeater by noting that the principle of nonclassical direct inference is licensed by an application of the statistical syllogism to the probability

(1)
$$\text{prob}_{A,B,C}(\text{prob}(A/C) \underset{\delta}{\approx} r / A, B, C \leqslant U \text{ and } C \leqslant B \text{ and } \text{prob}(A/B) = r) = 1.$$

We can easily establish the following principle, which appeals to a more comprehensive set of assumptions:

(2)
$$\text{prob}_{A,B,C}\left(\text{prob}(A/C) \underset{\delta}{\approx} s \Big/ \begin{array}{c} A,B,C,D \leqslant U \text{ and } C \leqslant D \text{ and } D \leqslant B \text{ and} \\ \text{prob}(A/B) = r \text{ and } \text{prob}(A/D) = s \end{array}\right) = 1.$$

If $r \neq s$ then (2) entails:

(3)
$$\text{prob}_{A,B,C}\left(\text{prob}(A/C) \underset{\delta}{\approx} r \Big/ \begin{array}{c} A,B,C,D \leqslant U \text{ and } C \leqslant D \text{ and } D \leqslant B \text{ and} \\ \text{prob}(A/B) = r \text{ and } \text{prob}(A/D) = s \end{array}\right) = 0.$$

The reference property in (3) is more specific than that in (1), so (3) gives us a subproperty defeater for the application of the statistical syllogism to (1).

A simpler way of putting all of this is that corresponding to (2) we have the following principle of expectable values:

Subproperty Defeat for Nonclassical Direct Inference

If $C \leqslant D \leqslant B$, $\text{prob}(A/D) = s$, $\text{prob}(A/B) = r$, $\text{prob}(A/U) = a$, $\text{prob}(B/U) = b$, $\text{prob}(C/U) = c$, $\text{prob}(D/U) = d$, then the expectable value of $\text{prob}(A/C) = s$ (rather than r).

As above, principles of expectable values that appeal to more information take precedence over (i.e., defeat the inferences from) principles that appeal to a subset of that information.

Because the principles of nonclassical direct inference and statistical independence are equivalent, subproperty defeaters for nonclassical direct inference generate analogous defeaters for the principle of statistical independence:

Subproperty Defeat for Statistical Independence

$\ulcorner (B\&C) \leqslant D \leqslant C$ and $\text{prob}(A/D) = p \neq r \urcorner$ is an undercutting defeater for the inference by the principle of statistical independence from $\ulcorner \text{prob}(A/C) = r \& \text{prob}(B/C) = s \urcorner$ to $\ulcorner \text{prob}(A\&B/C) = r \cdot s \urcorner$.

This is because $\text{prob}(A\&B/C) = r \cdot s$ only if $\text{prob}(A/B\&C) = \text{prob}(A/C)$, and this defeater makes it unreasonable to believe the former.

8 Classical Direct Inference

Direct inference is normally understood as being a form of inference from indefinite probabilities to definite probabilities, rather than from indefinite probabilities to other indefinite probabilities. However, I showed in Pollock 1990 that these inferences are derivable from nonclassical direct inference if we identify definite probabilities with a special class of indefinite probabilities. The present treatment is a generalization of that given in Pollock 1984, 1990.[11] Let **K** be the conjunction of all the propositions the agent knows to be true, and let $\Re$ be the set of all physically possible worlds at which **K** is true ("K-worlds"). I propose that we define the definite probability PROB(P) to be the proportion of K-worlds at which P is true. Where $\mathfrak{P}$ is the set of all P-worlds:

$$\text{PROB}(P) = \rho(\mathfrak{P}, \Re).$$

More generally, where $\mathfrak{Q}$ is the set of all Q-worlds, we can define:

$$\text{PROB}(P/Q) = \rho(\mathfrak{P}, \mathfrak{Q} \cap \Re).$$

Formally, this is analogous to Carnap's (1950, 1952) logical probability, with the important difference that Carnap took ρ to be logically specified, whereas I take the identity of ρ to be a contingent fact. ρ is determined by the values of contingently true nomic probabilities, and their values are discovered by various kinds of statistical induction.

It turns out that definite probabilities, so defined, can be identified with a special class of nomic probabilities:

Representation Theorem for Definite Probabilities
(1) PROB(Fa) = prob($Fx/x = a$ & **K**);

(2) If it is physically necessary that $[K \to (Q \leftrightarrow Sa_1 \ldots a_n)]$ and that $[(Q$ & $K) \to (P \leftrightarrow Ra_1 \ldots a_n)]$, and Q is consistent with **K**, then PROB(P/Q) = prob($Rx_1 \ldots x_n/Sx_1 \ldots x_n$ & $x_1 = a_1$ & $\ldots$ & $x_n = a_n$ & **K**).

(3) PROB(P) = prob(P & $x = x/x = x$ & **K**).

PROB(P) is a kind of "mixed physical/epistemic probability," because it combines background knowledge in the form of **K** with indefinite probabilities.[12]

The probability prob($Fx/x = a$ & **K**) is a peculiar-looking nomic probability. It is an indefinite probability, because 'x' is a free variable, but the probability is only about one object. As such it cannot be evaluated by statistical induction or other familiar forms of statistical reasoning. However, it can be evaluated using nonclassical direct inference. If **K** entails Ga, nonclassical direct inference gives us a defeasible reason for expecting that PROB(Fa) = prob($Fx/x = a$ & **K**) = prob(Fx/Gx). This is a familiar form of "classical" direct inference—that is, direct inference from nomic probabilities to definite probabilities. More generally, we can derive:

Classical Direct Inference
$\ulcorner Sa_1 \ldots a_n$ is known and prob($Rx_1 \ldots x_n/Sx_1 \ldots x_n$ & $Tx_1 \ldots x_n) = r \urcorner$ is a defeasible reason for $\ulcorner$PROB($Ra_1 \ldots a_n/Ta_1 \ldots a_n) = r \urcorner$.

Similarly, we get subproperty defeaters:

Subproperty Defeat for Classical Direct Inference

$\ulcorner S \leqslant V$, $Va_1 \ldots a_n$ is known, and $\mathrm{prob}(Rx_1 \ldots x_n/Vx_1 \ldots x_n$ & $Tx_1 \ldots x_n) \neq r \urcorner$ is an undercutting defeater for the inference by classical direct inference from $\ulcorner Sa_1 \ldots a_n$ is known and $\mathrm{prob}(Rx_1 \ldots x_n/Sx_1 \ldots x_n$ & $Tx_1 \ldots x_n) = r \urcorner$ to $\ulcorner \mathrm{PROB}(Ra_1 \ldots a_n/Ta_1 \ldots a_n) = r \urcorner$.

Because definite probabilities are indefinite probabilities in disguise, we can also use nonclassical direct inference to infer definite probabilities from definite probabilities. Thus $\ulcorner \mathrm{PROB}(P/Q) = r \urcorner$ gives us a defeasible reason for expecting that $\mathrm{PROB}(P/Q\&R) = r$. We can employ principles of statistical independence similarly. For example, $\ulcorner \mathrm{PROB}(P/R) = r$ & $\mathrm{PROB}(Q/R) = s \urcorner$ gives us a defeasible reason for expecting that $\mathrm{PROB}(P$ & $Q/R) = r \cdot s$.

9 Computational Inheritance

Suppose we have two seemingly unrelated diagnostic tests for a disease, and Bernard tests positive on both tests. We know that the probability of his having the disease if he tests positive on the first test is .8, and the probability if he tests positive on the second test is .75. But what should we conclude about the probability of his having the disease if he tests positive on both tests? The probability calculus gives us no guidance here. Nor does direct inference. Direct inference gives us one reason for thinking the probability of Bernard having the disease is .8, and it gives us a different reason for drawing the conflicting conclusion that the probability is .75. It gives us no way to combine the information. Intuitively, it seems that the probability of his having the disease should be higher if he tests positive on both tests. But how can we justify this?

This is a general problem for theories of direct inference. When we have some conjunction $\ulcorner G_1$ & $\ldots$ & $G_n \urcorner$ of properties and we want to know the value of $\mathrm{prob}(F/G_1$ & $\ldots$ & $G_n)$, if we know that $\mathrm{prob}(F/G_1) = r$ *and we don't know anything else of relevance*, we can infer defeasibly that $\mathrm{prob}(F/G_1$ & $\ldots$ & $G_n) = r$. Similarly, if we know that an object a has the properties $G_1, \ldots, G_n$ and we know that $\mathrm{prob}(F/G_1) = r$ *and we don't know anything else of relevance*, we can infer defeasibly that $\mathrm{PROB}(Fa) = r$. The difficulty is that we usually know more. We typically know the value of $\mathrm{prob}(F/G_i)$ for some $i \neq 1$. If $\mathrm{prob}(F/G_i) = s \neq r$, we have defeasible reasons for both $\ulcorner \mathrm{prob}(F/G_1$ & $\ldots$ & $G_n) = r \urcorner$ and $\ulcorner \mathrm{prob}(F/G_1$ & $\ldots$ & $G_n) = s \urcorner$, and also for both $\ulcorner \mathrm{PROB}(Fa) = r \urcorner$ and $\ulcorner \mathrm{PROB}(Fa) = s \urcorner$. As these conclusions are incompatible they all undergo collective defeat. Thus the standard theory of

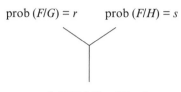

prob $(F/G) = r$ prob $(F/H) = s$

prob $(F/G\&H) = Y(r,s)$

Figure 10.2
The Y-function.

direct inference leaves us without a conclusion to draw. The upshot is that the earlier suggestion that direct inference can solve the computational problem of dealing with definite probabilities without having to have a complete probability distribution was premature. Direct inference will rarely give us the probabilities we need.

Knowledge of indefinite probabilities would be vastly more useful in real application if there were a function $Y(r,s)$ such that, in a case like the above, when $\text{prob}(F/G) = r$ and $\text{prob}(F/H) = s$, we could defeasibly expect that $\text{prob}(F/G\&H) = Y(r,s)$, and hence (by nonclassical direct inference) that $\text{PROB}(Fa) = Y(r,s)$. I call this *computational inheritance*, because it computes a new value for $\text{PROB}(Fa)$ from previously known indefinite probabilities. Direct inference, by contrast, is a kind of "noncomputational inheritance." It is *direct* in that $\text{PROB}(Fa)$ simply inherits a value from a known indefinite probability. I call the function used in computational inheritance "the Y-function" because its behavior would be as diagrammed in figure 10.2.

It has generally been assumed that there is no such function as the Y-function (Reichenbach 1949). Certainly, there is no function $Y(r,s)$ such that we can conclude *deductively* that if $\text{prob}(F/G) = r$ and $\text{prob}(F/H) = s$ then $\text{prob}(F/G\&H) = Y(r,s)$. For any r and s that are neither 0 nor 1, $\text{prob}(F/G\&H)$ can take any value between 0 and 1. However, that is equally true for nonclassical direct inference. That is, if $\text{prob}(F/G) = r$ we cannot conclude deductively that $\text{prob}(F/G\&H) = r$. Nevertheless, that will tend to be the case, and we can defeasibly expect it to be the case. Might something similar be true of the Y-function? That is, could there be a function $Y(r,s)$ such that we can defeasibly expect $\text{prob}(F/G\&H)$ to be $Y(r,s)$? It follows from the Probable Probabilities Theorem that the answer is "yes." It is more useful to begin by looking at a three-place function rather than a two-place function. Let us define:

$$Y(r, s \mid a) = \frac{rs(1 - a)}{a(1 - r - s) + rs}$$

I use the non-standard notation '$Y(r, s \mid a)$' rather than '$Y(r, s, a)$' because the first two variables will turn out to work differently than the last variable.

Let us define:

B and C are *Y-independent for A relative to U* iff $A, B, C \leqslant U$ and
(a) $\mathrm{prob}(C/B \ \& \ A) = \mathrm{prob}(C/A)$
(b) $\mathrm{prob}(C/B \ \& \sim A) = \mathrm{prob}(C/U \ \& \sim A)$.

The key theorem underlying computational inheritance is the following theorem of the probability calculus:

Y-Theorem

Let $r = \mathrm{prob}(A/B)$, $s = \mathrm{prob}(A/C)$, and $a = \mathrm{prob}(A/U)$. If B and C are Y-independent for A relative to U then $\mathrm{prob}(A/B\&C) = Y(r, s \mid a)$.

In light of the Y-theorem, we can think of Y-independence as formulating an independence condition for C and B which says that they make independent contributions to A—contributions that "add" in accordance with the Y-function, rather than "undermining" each other.

By virtue of the principle of statistical independence, we have a defeasible reason for expecting that the independence conditions (a) and (b) hold. Thus the Y-theorem supports the following principle of defeasible reasoning:

Computational Inheritance

$\ulcorner B, C \leqslant U \ \& \ \mathrm{prob}(A/B) = r \ \& \ \mathrm{prob}(A/C) = s \ \& \ \mathrm{prob}(A/U) = a \urcorner$ is a defeasible reason for $\ulcorner \mathrm{prob}(A/B \ \& \ C) = Y(r, s \mid a) \urcorner$.

It should be noted that we can prove analogues of computational inheritance for finite sets, infinite sets, and probabilities, in essentially the same way we prove the Y-theorem. This yields the following principle of expectable values:

Y-Principle

If $B, C \leqslant U$, $\mathrm{prob}(A/B) = r$, $\mathrm{prob}(A/C) = s$, and $\mathrm{prob}(A/U) = a$, then the expectable value of $\mathrm{prob}(A/B \ \& \ C) = Y(r, s \mid a)$.

In the corresponding quadruple of principles, the finite Y-principle can be proven directly, or derived from the finite principle of agreement. Similarly, the Y-principle is derivable from the principle of agreement. Then the Y-principle for probabilities is derivable from either the Y-principle or from the principle of agreement for probabilities.

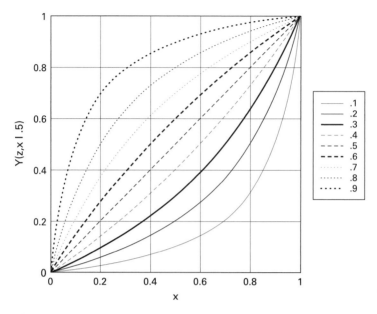

Figure 10.3

$Y(z, x | .5)$, holding z constant (for several choices of z as indicated in the key).

To get a better feel for what the principle of computational inheritance tells us, it is useful to examine plots of the Y-function. Figure 10.3 illustrates that $Y(r, s | .5)$ is symmetric around the right-leaning diagonal.

Varying a has the effect of warping the Y-function up or down relative to the right-leaning diagonal. This is illustrated in figure 10.4 for several choices of a.

The Y-function has a number of important properties.[13] In particular, it is important that the Y-function is associative and commutative in the first two variables:

Theorem 1: $Y(r, s | a) = Y(s, r | a)$.

Theorem 2: $Y(r, Y(s, t | a) | a) = Y(Y(r, s | a), t | a)$.

Theorems 1 and 2 are very important for the use of the Y-function in computing probabilities. Suppose we know that $\text{prob}(A/B) = .6$, $\text{prob}(A/C) = .7$, and $\text{prob}(A/D) = .75$, where $B, C, D \preccurlyeq U$ and $\text{prob}(A/U) = .3$. In light of theorems 1 and 2, we can combine the first three probabilities in any order and infer defeasibly that $\text{prob}(A/B\&C\&D) = Y(.6, Y(.7, .75 | .3) | .3) = Y(Y(.6, .7 | .3), .75 | .3) = .98$. This makes it convenient to extend the Y-function recursively so that it can be applied to an arbitrary number of arguments (greater than or equal to 3):

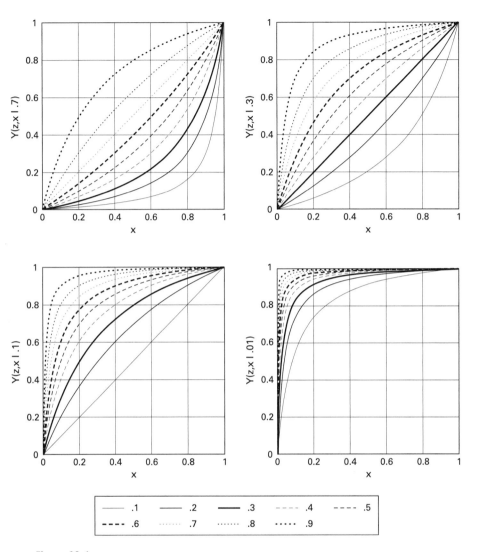

Figure 10.4

$Y(z, x \mid a)$ holding z constant (for several choices of z), for $a = .7$, $a = .3$, $a = .1$, and $a = .01$.

If $n \geq 3$, $Y(r_1, \ldots, r_n \mid a) = Y(r_1, Y(r_2, \ldots, r_n \mid a) \mid a)$.

Then we can then strengthen the Y-principle as follows:

Generalized Y-Principle:
If $B_1, \ldots, B_n \leqslant U$, $\mathrm{prob}(A/B_1) = r_1, \ldots, \mathrm{prob}(A/B_n) = r_n$, and $\mathrm{prob}(A/U) = a$, the expectable value of $\mathrm{prob}(A/B_1 \,\&\, \ldots \,\&\, B_n \,\&\, C) = Y(r_1, \ldots, r_n \mid a)$.

If we know that $\mathrm{prob}(A/B) = r$ and $\mathrm{prob}(A/C) = s$, we can also use non-classical direct inference to infer defeasibly that $\mathrm{prob}(A/B\&C) = r$. If $s \neq a$, $Y(r, s \mid a) \neq r$, so this conflicts with the conclusion that $\mathrm{prob}(A/B\&C) = Y(r, s \mid a)$. However, as above, the inference described by the Y-principle is based upon a probability with a more inclusive reference property than that underlying nonclassical direct inference (that is, it takes account of more information), so it takes precedence and yields an undercutting defeater for nonclassical direct inference:

Computational Defeat for Nonclassical Direct Inference
$\ulcorner A, B, C \leqslant U$ and $\mathrm{prob}(A/C) \neq \mathrm{prob}(A/U) \urcorner$ is an undercutting defeater for the inference from $\ulcorner \mathrm{prob}(A/B) = r \urcorner$ to $\ulcorner \mathrm{prob}(A/B\&C) = r \urcorner$ by Nonclassical Direct Inference.

It follows that we have a defeater for the principle of statistical independence:

Computational Defeat for Statistical Independence
$\ulcorner A, B, C \leqslant U$ and $\mathrm{prob}(A/B) \neq \mathrm{prob}(A/U) \urcorner$ is an undercutting defeater for the inference from $\ulcorner \mathrm{prob}(A/B) = r \,\&\, \mathrm{prob}(A/C) = s \urcorner$ to $\ulcorner \mathrm{prob}(A\&B/C) = r \cdot s \urcorner$ by statistical independence.

The phenomenon of computational inheritance makes knowledge of indefinite probabilities useful in ways it was never previously useful. It tells us how to combine different probabilities that would lead to conflicting direct inferences and still arrive at a univocal value. Consider Bernard again, who has symptoms suggesting a particular disease, and tests positive on two independent tests for the disease. Suppose the probability of a person with those symptoms having the disease is .6. Suppose the probability of such a person having the disease if they test positive on the first test is .7, and the probability of their having the disease if they test positive on the second test is .75. What is the probability of their having the disease if they test positive on both tests? We can infer defeasibly that it is $Y(.7, .75 \mid .6) = .875$. We can then apply classical direct inference to conclude that the probability of Bernard's having the disease is .875. This is a result that we could not have gotten from the probability calculus alone. Similar reasoning will have significant practical applications, for example in engineering, where we have multiple imperfect sensors sensing some phenomenon, and we want to arrive at a joint probability regarding the phenomenon that combines the information from all the sensors.

Again, because definite probabilities are indefinite probabilities in disguise, we can apply computational inheritance to them as well and infer defeasibly that if PROB$(P) = a$, PROB$(P/Q) = r$, and PROB$(P/R) = s$ then PROB$(P/Q\&R) = Y(r, s | a)$.

10   Inverse Probabilities and the Statistical Syllogism

All of the principles of probable probabilities that have been discussed so far are related to defeasible assumptions of statistical independence. As we have seen, nonclassical direct inference is equivalent to a defeasible assumption of statistical independence, and computational inheritance follows from a defeasible assumption of Y-independence. This might suggest that all principles of probable probabilities derive ultimately from various defeasible independence assumptions. However, this section turns to a set of principles that do not appear to be related to statistical independence in any way.

Where $A, B \leqslant U$, suppose we know the value of prob(A/B). If we know the base rates prob(A/U) and prob(B/U), the probability calculus enables us to compute the value of the *inverse probability* prob$(\sim B / \sim A \& U)$:

Theorem 3:   If $A, B \leqslant U$ then

$$\text{prob}(\sim B / \sim A \& U) = \frac{1 - \text{prob}(A/U) - \text{prob}(B/U) + \text{prob}(A/B) \cdot \text{prob}(B/U)}{1 - \text{prob}(A/U)}.$$

However, if we do not know the base rates then the probability calculus imposes no constraints on the value of the inverse probability. It can nevertheless be shown that there are expectable values for it, and generally, if prob(A/B) is high, so is prob$(\sim B / \sim A \& U)$.

Inverse Probabilities I
If $A, B \leqslant U$ and we know that prob$(A/B) = r$, but we do not know the base rates prob(A/U) and prob(B/U), the following values are expectable:

$$\text{prob}(B/U) = \frac{.5}{r^r (1-r)^{1-r} + .5};$$

$$\text{prob}(A/U) = .5 - \frac{.25 - .5r}{r^r (1-r)^{1-r} + .5};$$

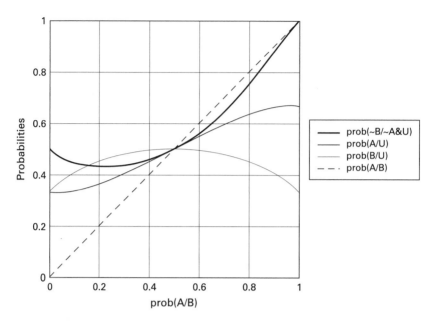

Figure 10.5
Expectable values of prob($\sim B/\sim A\&U$), prob(A/U), and prob(B/U), as a function of prob(A/B), when the base rates are unknown.

$$\text{prob}(\sim A/\sim B\&U) = .5;$$

$$\text{prob}(\sim B/\sim A\&U) = \frac{r^r}{(1-r)^r + r^r}.$$

These values are plotted in figure 10.5. Note that when prob(A/B) > prob(A/U), we can expect prob($\sim B/\sim A\&U$) to be almost as great as prob(A/B).

Sometimes we know one of the base rates but not both:

Inverse Probabilities II
If $A, B \leqslant U$ and we know that prob(A/B) = r and prob(B/U) = b, but we do not know the base rate prob(A/U), the following values are expectable:

$$\text{prob}(A/U) = .5(1 - (1 - 2r)b);$$

$$\text{prob}(\sim A/\sim B\&U) = \frac{.5 + b(.5 - r)}{1 + b(1 - r)};$$

$$\text{prob}(\sim B/\sim A\&U)) = \frac{1 - b}{1 + b(1 - 2r)}.$$

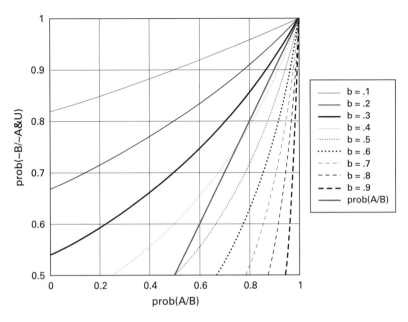

Figure 10.6
Expectable values of prob($\sim B/\sim A\&U$) as a function of prob(A/B), when prob(A/U) is unknown, for fixed values of prob(B/U).

Figure 10.6 plots the expectable values of prob($\sim B/\sim A\&U$) (when they are greater than .5) as a function of prob(A/B), for fixed values of prob(B/U). The diagonal line indicates the value of prob(A/B), for comparison. The upshot is that for low values of prob(B/U), prob($\sim B/\sim A\&U$) can be expected to be higher than prob(A/B), and for all values of prob(B/U), prob($\sim B/\sim A\&U$) will be fairly high if prob(A/B) is high. Furthermore, prob($\sim B/\sim A\&U$) > .5 iff prob(B/U) < $1/(3 - 2r)$.

The most complex case occurs when we know the base-rate prob(A/U), but we do not know the base-rate prob(B/U):

Inverse Probabilities III
If $A, B \leqslant U$ and we know that prob(A/B) = r and prob(A/U) = a, but we do not know the base rate prob(B/U), then:
(a) where b is the expectable value of prob(B/U), $(r \cdot b/(a - r \cdot b))^r \cdot ((1 - r)b/(1 - a - (1 - r)b))^{1-r} = 1$;
(b) the expectable value of prob($\sim B/\sim A\&U$) = $1 - ((1 - r)/(1 - a))b$.

The equation characterizing the expectable value of prob(B/U) does not have a closed-form solution. However, for specific values of a and r, the

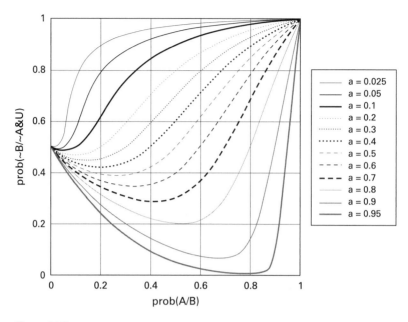

Figure 10.7
Expectable values of prob($\sim B/\sim A\&U$) as a function of prob(A/B), when prob(B/U) is unknown, for fixed values of prob(A/U).

solutions are easily computed using hill-climbing algorithms. The results are contained in figure 10.7. When prob(A/B) = prob(A/U), the expected value for prob($\sim B/\sim A$) is .5, and when prob(A/B) > prob(A/U), prob($\sim B/\sim A\&U$) > .5. If prob(A/U) < .5, the expected value of prob($\sim B/\sim A\&U$) is greater than prob(A/B).

The upshot is that even when we lack knowledge of the base rates, there is an expectable value for the inverse probability prob($\sim B/\sim A\&U$), and that expectable value tends to be high when prob(A/B) is high.

11   Meeting Some Objections

I have argued that mathematical results, coupled with the statistical syllogism, justify defeasible inferences about the values of unknown probabilities. Various worries arise regarding this conclusion. A few people are worried about any defeasible (non-deductive) inference, but I presume that the last half-century of epistemology has made it amply clear that, in the real world, cognitive agents cannot confine themselves to conclusions drawn deductively from their evidence. We employ multitudes of defeasible inference schemes in our everyday reasoning, and the statistical syllogism is one of them.

Granted that we have to reason defeasibly, we can still ask what justifies any particular defeasible inference scheme. At least in the case of the statistical syllogism, the answer seems clear. If $\text{prob}(A/B)$ is high, then if we reason defeasibly from things being B to their being A, we will generally get it right. That is the most we can require of a defeasible inference scheme. We cannot require that the inference scheme will always lead to true conclusions, because then it would not be defeasible. People sometimes protest at this point that they are not interested in the general case; they are concerned with some inference they are only going to make once. They want to know why they should reason this way in this single case. But all cases are single cases. If you reason in this way in single cases, you will tend to get them right. It does not seem that you can ask for any firmer guarantee than that; you cannot avoid defeasible reasoning.

But we can have a further worry. For any defeasible inference scheme, we know that there will be possible cases in which it gets things wrong. For each principle of probable probabilities, the possible exceptions constitute a set of measure 0, but it is still an infinite set. The cases that actually interest us tend to be highly structured, and perhaps they also constitute a set of measure 0. How do we know that the latter set is not contained in the former? Again, there can be no logical guarantee that this is not the case. However, the indefinite probability of an arbitrary set of cases falling in the set of possible exceptions is 0. So without further specification of the structure of the cases that interest us, the probability of the set of those cases all falling in the set of exceptions is 0. Where defeasible reasoning is concerned, we cannot ask for a better guarantee than that.

We should resist the temptation to think of the set of possible exceptions as an amorphous, unstructured set about which we cannot reason using principles of probable probabilities. The exceptions are exceptions to a single defeasible inference scheme. Many of the cases in which a particular inference fails will be cases in which there is a general defeater leading us to expect it to fail, and leading us to make a different inference in its place. For example, knowing that $\text{prob}(A/B) = r$ gives us a defeasible reason to expect that $\text{prob}(A/B\&C) = r$. But if we also know that $\text{prob}(A/C) = s$ and $\text{prob}(A/U) = a$, the original inference is defeated and we should expect instead that $prob(A/B\&C) = Y(r, s \mid a)$. So this is one of the cases in which an inference by nonclassical direct inference fails, but it is a defeasibly expectable case.

There will also be cases that are not defeasibly expectable. This follows from the simple fact that there are primitive nomic probabilities representing statistical laws of nature. These laws are novel, and cannot be predicted defeasibly by appealing to other nomic probabilities. Suppose $prob(A/B) = r$, but $\ulcorner prob(A/B\&C) = s \urcorner$ is a primitive law. The latter is an exception to nonclassical direct inference. Furthermore, we can expect that strengthening the reference property will result in nomic probabilities like $\ulcorner prob(A/B\&C\&D) = s \urcorner$, and these will also be cases in which the nonclassical direct inference from $\ulcorner prob(A/B) = r \urcorner$ fails. But, unlike the primitive law, the latter is a defeasibly expectable failure arising from subproperty defeat. So most of the cases in which a particular defeasible inference appealing to principles of probable probabilities fails will be cases in which the failure is defeasibly predictable by appealing to other principles of probable probabilities. This is an observation about how much structure the set of exceptions (of measure 0) must have. The set of exceptions is a set of exceptions just to a single rule, not to all principles of probable probabilities. The probable probabilities theorem implies that even within the set of exceptions to a particular defeasible inference scheme, most inferences that take account of the primitive nomic probabilities will get things right, with probability 1.

12 Conclusions

The problem of sparse probability knowledge results from the fact that in the real world we lack direct knowledge of most probabilities. If probabilities are to be useful, we must have ways of making defeasible estimates of their values even when those values are not computable from known probabilities using the probability calculus. Within the theory of nomic probability, limit theorems from combinatorial mathematics provide the necessary bridge for these inferences. It turns out that in very general circumstances, there will be expectable values for otherwise unknown probabilities. These are described by principles telling us that although certain inferences from probabilities to probabilities are not deductively valid, nevertheless the second-order probability of their yielding correct results is 1. This makes it defeasibly reasonable to make the inferences.

I illustrated this by looking at indifference, statistical independence, classical and nonclassical direct inference, computational inheritance, and inverse probabilities. But these are just illustrations. There are a huge number of useful principles of probable probabilities, some of which I have investigated, but most of which have yet to be discovered. I proved the first such principles laboriously by hand; it took me six months to find and prove the principle of computational inheritance. But it turns out that there is a uniform way of finding and proving these principles. I have written a computer program (in Common LISP) that analyzes the results of linear constraints and determines what the expectable values of the probabilities are. If desired, it will produce a human-readable proof. This makes it easy to find and investigate new principles.[14]

This profusion of principles of probable probability is reminiscent of Carnap's logical probabilities (Carnap 1950, 1952; Hintikka 1966; Bacchus et al. 1996). Historical theories of objective probability required probabilities to be assessed by empirical methods, and because of the weakness of the probability calculus, they tended to leave us in a badly impoverished epistemic state regarding probabilities. Carnap tried to define a kind of probability for which the values of probabilities were determined by logic alone, thus vitiating the need for empirical investigation. However, finding the right probability measure to employ in a theory of logical probabilities proved to be an insurmountable problem.

Nomic probability and the theory of probable probabilities lies between these two extremes. This theory still makes the values of probabilities contingent rather than logically necessary, but it makes our limited empirical investigations much more fruitful, by giving them the power to license defeasible, non-deductive inferences to a wide range of further probabilities that we have not investigated empirically. Furthermore, unlike logical probability, these defeasible inferences do not depend on *ad hoc* postulates. Instead, they derive directly from provable theorems of combinatorial mathematics. So even when we do not have sufficient empirical information to deductively determine the value of a probability, purely mathematical facts may be sufficient to make it reasonable, given what empirical information we do have, to expect the unknown probabilities to have specific and computable values. Where this differs from logical probability is (1) that the empirical values are an essential ingredient in the computation, and (2) that the inferences to these values are defeasible rather than deductive.

Acknowledgment

This work was supported by NSF grant no. IIS-0412791.

Notes

1. William Kneale (1949) traces the frequency theory to R. L. Ellis, writing in the 1840s, and John Venn (1888) and C. S. Peirce in the 1880s and 1890s.

2. Somewhat similar semantics were proposed by Halpern (1990) and Bacchus et al. (1996).

3. Probabilities relating n-place relations are treated similarly. I will generally just write the one-variable versions of various principles, but they generalize to n-variable versions in the obvious way.

4. Note that this is a different (and more conservative) principle than the one called "Projection" in Pollock 1990.

5. There are two kinds of defeaters. "Rebutting defeaters" attack the conclusion of an inference, and "undercutting defeaters" attack the inference itself without attacking the conclusion. Here I assume some form of the OSCAR theory of defeasible reasoning (Pollock 1995); for a sketch of that theory see Pollock 2006b.

6. Note that throughout this paper I employ the definition of '$n!$' in terms of the Euler gamma function. Specifically, $n! = \int_0^\infty t^n e^{-t}\, dt$. This has the result that $n!$ is defined for any positive real number n, not just for integers, but for integers the definition agrees with the ordinary recursive definition. This makes the mathematics more convenient.

7. See   http://oscarhome.soc-sci.arizona.edu/ftp/PAPERS/Probable%20Probabilities .pdf.

8. The following principles apply only to properties for which there are infinitely many physically possible instances, but I will not explicitly include the qualification 'non-contrived' in the principles.

9. If we could assume countable additivity for nomic probability, the indifference principle would imply that $\mathrm{prob}_X(\mathrm{prob}(X, G) = 0.5/X \leqslant G) = 1$. Countable additivity is generally assumed in mathematical probability theory, but most of the important writers in the foundations of probability theory, including de Finetti (1974), Reichenbach (1949), Jeffrey (1983), Skyrms (1980), Savage (1954), and Kyburg (1974a), have either questioned it or rejected it outright. Pollock (2006a) gives what I still consider to be a compelling counterexample to countable additivity. So I will have to remain content with the more complex formulation of the indifference principle.

10. See http://oscarhome.soc-sci.arizona.edu/ftp/OSCAR-web-page/CODE/Code for "probable probabilities.zip."

11. Bacchus (1990) gave a somewhat similar account of direct inference, drawing on Pollock 1983, 1984.

12. See chapter 6 of Pollock 2006a for further discussion of these mixed physical/epistemic probabilities.

13. It turns out that the Y-function has been studied for its desirable mathematical properties in the theory of associative compensatory aggregation operators in fuzzy logic (Dombi 1982; Klement, Mesiar, and Pap 1996; Fodor, Yager, and Rybalov 1997). $Y(r, s \mid a)$ is the function $D_\lambda(r, s)$ for $\lambda = (1 - a)/a$ (Klement, Mesiar, and Pap 1996). The Y-theorem may provide further justification for its use in that connection.

14. This program can be found at the link provided in note 7.

References

Bacchus, F. 1990. *Representing and Reasoning with Probabilistic Knowledge*. Cambridge, Mass.: MIT Press.

Bacchus, F., A. Grove, J. Halpern, and D. Koller. 1996. "From Statistical Knowledge Bases to Degrees of Belief." *Artificial Intelligence* 87: 75–143.

Braithwaite, R. B. 1953. *Scientific Explanation*. Cambridge: Cambridge University Press.

Carnap, R. 1950. *The Logical Foundations of Probability*. Chicago: University of Chicago Press.

Carnap, R. 1952. *The Continuum of Inductive Methods*. Chicago: University of Chicago Press.

de Finetti, B. 1974. *Theory of Probability*, vol. 1. New York: John Wiley.

Dombi, J. 1982. "Basic Concepts for a Theory of Evaluation: The Aggregative Operator." *European Journal of Operational Research* 10: 282–293.

Fisher, R. A. 1922. "On the Mathematical Foundations of Theoretical Statistics." *Philosophical Transactions of the Royal Society* A 222: 309–368.

Fodor, J., R. Yager, and A. Rybalov. 1997. "Structure of Uninorms." *International Journal of Uncertainty, Fuzziness, and Knowledge-Based Systems* 5: 411–427.

Goodman, N. 1955. *Fact, Fiction, and Forecast*. Cambridge, Mass.: Harvard University Press.

Halpern, J. Y. 1990. "An Analysis of First-Order Logics of Probability." *Artificial Intelligence* 46: 311–350.

Harman, G. 1986. *Change in View*. Cambridge, Mass.: MIT Press.

Hintikka, J. 1966. "A Two-Dimensional Continuum of Inductive Methods." In J. Hintikka and P. Suppes, eds., *Aspects of Inductive Logic*. Amsterdam: North Holland.

Jeffrey, R. 1983. *The Logic of Decision*, 2nd edition. Chicago: University of Chicago Press.

Klement, E. P., R. Mesiar, and E. Pap. 1996 ."On the Relationship of Associative Compensatory Operators to Triangular Norms and Conorms." *International Journal of Uncertainty, Fuzziness, and Knowledge-Based Systems* 4: 129–144.

Kneale, W. 1949. *Probability and Induction.* Oxford: Oxford University Press.

Kushmerick, N., S. Hanks, and D. Weld. 1995. "An Algorithm for Probabilistic Planning." *Artificial Intelligence* 76: 239–286.

Kyburg, Jr., H. 1961. *Probability and the Logic of Rational Belief.* Middletown, Conn.: Wesleyan University Press.

Kyburg, Jr., H. 1974a. *The Logical Foundations of Statistical Inference.* Dordrecht: Reidel.

Kyburg, Jr., H. 1974b. "Propensities and Probabilities." *British Journal for the Philosophy of Science* 25: 321–353.

Levi, I. 1980. *The Enterprise of Knowledge.* Cambridge, Mass.: MIT Press.

Pearl, J. 1988. *Probabilistic Reasoning in Intelligent Systems: Networks of Plausible Inference.* San Mateo, Calif.: Morgan Kaufmann.

Pollock, J. L. 1983. "A Theory of Direct Inference." *Theory and Decision* 15: 29–96.

Pollock, J. L. 1984. "Foundations for Direct Inference." *Theory and Decision* 17: 221–256.

Pollock, J. L. 1990. *Nomic Probability and the Foundations of Induction.* New York: Oxford University Press.

Pollock, J. L. 1995. *Cognitive Carpentry.* Cambridge, Mass.: MIT Press.

Pollock, J. L. 2006a. *Thinking about Acting: Logical Foundations for Rational Decision Making.* New York: Oxford University Press.

Pollock, J. L. 2006b. "Defeasible Reasoning." In J. Adler and L. Rips, eds., *Reasoning: Studies of Human Inference and its Foundations.* Cambridge: Cambridge University Press.

Popper, K. 1938. "A Set of Independent Axioms for Probability." *Mind* 47: 275–277.

Popper, K. 1956. "The Propensity Interpretation of Probability." *British Journal for the Philosophy of Science* 10: 25–42.

Popper, K. 1957. "The Propensity Interpretation of the Calculus of Probability, and the Quantum Theory." In S. Körner, ed., *Observation and Interpretation.* New York: Academic Press.

Popper, K. 1959. *The Logic of Scientific Discovery.* New York: Basic Books.

Reichenbach, H. 1949. *A Theory of Probability*. Berkeley: University of California Press.

Reiter, R., and G. Criscuolo. 1981. "On Interacting Defaults." In P. Hayes, ed., *Proceedings of the 7th International Joint Conference on Artificial Intelligence* (IJCAI'81). Los Altos, Calif.: William Kaufmann.

Renyi, A. 1955. "On a New Axiomatic Theory of Probability." *Acta Mathematica Academiae Scientiarum Hungaricae* 6: 285–333.

Russell, B. 1948. *Human Knowledge: Its Scope and Limits*. New York: Simon and Schuster.

Savage, L. 1954. *The Foundations of Statistics*. New York: Dover.

Shafer, G. 1976. *A Mathematical Theory of Evidence*. Princeton: Princeton University Press.

Sklar, L. 1970. "Is Propensity a Dispositional Concept?" *Journal of Philosophy* 67: 355–366.

Sklar, L. 1973. "Unfair to Frequencies." *Journal of Philosophy* 70: 41–52.

Skyrms, B. 1980. *Causal Necessity*. New Haven: Yale University Press.

van Fraassen, B. 1981. *The Scientific Image*. Oxford: Oxford University Press.

Venn, J. 1888. *The Logic of Chance*, 3rd ed. London: Macmillan.

II Skepticism

11 Anti-Individualism, Self-Knowledge, and Why Skepticism Cannot Be Cartesian

Leora Weitzman

Anti-individualism is often said to be at odds with the Cartesian view of the mind that grounds external-world skepticism. For according to the Cartesian view, it is coherent to doubt whether any of one's thoughts correspond to external objects, whereas anti-individualism says it is a conceptual truth that without objects external to an individual, that individual's purported thoughts would have no content at all.[1]

But what is external to an individual? Anti-individualist thought experiments often depict the individual as a physical creature bounded by its skin (or skull),[2] but this boundary cannot simply be assumed in an attempt to deploy anti-individualism against a serious Cartesian skeptic, since the existence of skin, skull, or anything physical at all is part of what's in question.

A well-known argument, originally due to McKinsey, seems to hold out the possibility of proving to skeptics that there are physical things (though that is not the lesson McKinsey draws from it). Such a proof would both reply to physical-object skepticism and restore the credibility of a physical boundary of the self. Much has been written about the McKinsey argument, but two things have been missing from the discussion. One is a thorough assessment of the extent to which the anti-individualism it relies on can be made compelling for the skeptic. Section 1 will undertake this task. The second missing element, taken up in section 2, is the application of a lesson that can be drawn from Wittgenstein to the Cartesian self-knowledge which is the other main component of the argument. When both of these elements are taken into account, it becomes clear that the McKinsey argument cannot justify a physical criterion for being outside the self. What notion of the self, then, can anti-individualist and Cartesian alike accept for the sake of argument until the issues between them are clarified?

The Cartesian skeptical notion of the self might at first seem more neutral. By the Cartesian skeptical notion of the self, I mean the notion of a mind that can introspect all its own conscious, occurrent thought-contents and in particular can know what its own concepts are. However, this notion cannot be simply assumed in an attempt to defend Cartesian skepticism against an anti-individualist, since some would argue—for reasons we shall encounter shortly—that anti-individualism is both a conceptual truth and incompatible with the Cartesian degree of self-knowledge just described.[3]

In the end, the Cartesian skeptical notion of the self is not available in any case, even to skeptics. For we are ultimately fallible about our own concepts, for reasons which have gone largely unmentioned in this debate, despite having arguably paved the way for it.[4] In brief, if it is to be an objective fact that my concepts mean something, then it must be possible that I have all the inward signs of meaning something by a given concept without actually doing so. This line of reasoning is more general than the anti-individualist views usually invoked—and it does not assume anything the skeptic questions. Section 2 will set out these reasons in detail.

The result is that neither the Cartesian skeptical notion of the self nor the anti-individualist physical notion of the self can play the needed neutral role in the debate. This leaves still unanswered the question of what counts as external to the self—so that the issue between Cartesian skeptics and their anti-individualist opponents remains crucially undefined.

What exactly are the implications for skepticism? Although the difficulties that will emerge with the McKinsey strategy for proving that there are physical objects are grist for skepticism in general, these difficulties do not vindicate *external-world* skepticism as such when the results of the first two sections are taken into account. Rather, as section 3 will explain, these difficulties point toward a broader skepticism—not the full-fledged Humean kind, yet one that still infiltrates the Cartesian realm.

1 Anti-Individualism

1.1 The McKinsey Argument

As mentioned above, an argument originally due to McKinsey seems to offer a strategy for showing, without illegitimate empirical assumptions, that there are physical objects outside oneself. This strategy is doubly relevant to this paper. First, it articulates the anti-individualist argument against skepticism about *external* objects. But second, if it works it gives reason to concede the existence of *physical* objects, so that the line between internal and external can be drawn on a physical basis. If it doesn't work, then neither goal will be met; and this, I shall argue, is what transpires. But first, a look at the argument.

On the Cartesian view, it is said, we have a priori knowledge of our own concepts. Anti-individualism, however, can also be established a priori, using the hypothetical reasoning of Twin Earth thought experiments.[5] These thought experiments are widely held to show that atomic concepts can acquire their contents only from their instances. This would mean that we can reason as follows, entirely a priori:[6]

1. I have atomic concept C.
2. I could not have any atomic concept unless there were instances of it.
3. Therefore there are instances of C.

If my atomic concepts include concepts of physical objects outside me, as seems plausible, then I can conclude that there are physical objects outside me.

Although to some writers, this strategy offers the prospect of a genuine reply to the skeptic,[7] others regard it as a *reductio*.[8] On the grounds that it would be absurd to achieve knowledge of the existence of physical objects a priori, McKinsey himself concludes that a priori knowledge of our own concepts is incompatible with there being an a priori derivation of the anti-individualistic second premise. This incompatibilist position, mentioned above in the introduction, is also held for another reason: Some hold that knowing what concepts one has requires knowing that the necessary conditions of having those concepts are satisfied. If anti-individualism is correct, one could not know a priori that the relevant conditions are satisfied, and thus could not know a priori what concepts one has.[9]

There is a small change to this argument that reduces the absurdity of reaching a conclusion like (3) on the basis of premises like (1) and (2): One can regard the self-knowledge of premise (1) as introspective but not a priori. Consider the situation envisaged by Cartesian and Humean skeptics. Initially we have knowledge only of how things appear to us—only of our Humean impressions, our sensations of hot, cold, bright, dark, and so forth. Although these impressions are in us, surely our knowledge of them is empirical if anything is; for they are our only epistemic link to the world, and we have no *other* direct knowledge that could count as more empirical. (Wouldn't it be absurd for a Cartesian or Humean to claim that our knowledge of chairs and tables is empirical, while claiming that our knowledge of the impressions that show us these chairs and tables is a priori? What else could be the empirical basis of our empirical knowledge?) Now, if knowledge of our own impressions is empirical *and* gives rise (as surely it does) to our empirical concepts, then knowledge of our own empirical *concepts* can reasonably be regarded as at least partly empirical as well. So I think it is justifiable to regard knowledge of our empirical concepts as *a posteriori*, even though introspective.[10]

If we thus revise the argument, it looks more capable of genuinely responding to skepticism. It then says that we know instances of premise (1), not a priori, but by empirical introspection. It continues to claim that we can know (2) a priori. It then draws a conclusion about what exists on the basis of the combination of an empirical premise with an a priori premise, which seems reasonable.

In this light, it does not seem so absurd to suggest that empirical introspective knowledge of one's own concepts could combine with a priori grounds for anti-individualism to yield proof of the existence of specific kinds of things. We can now ask more open-mindedly whether it works.

At first sight, the weakest link in this anti-skeptical strategy is premise 2, which the strategy requires to be demonstrable independently of any assumptions about what exists. The next two sections explore premises along the lines of (2) in light of their demonstrability to the skeptic. They conclude that at the very least, a skeptic who wants to reject everything in the vicinity of (2) has a significant burden of proof—although (2) probably does need to be weakened somewhat. Appropriately weakened versions of (2) are then considered.

1.2 Why Should a Skeptic Accept Premise 2?

The argument of this section turns on the assumption that whenever something—be it a brain state, mind state, tree ring, or what have you—has content, that is not a brute fact about it but holds in virtue of its non-semantic properties or relations. I shall not defend this assumption here, so the result will be conditional on it. What I shall focus on is the nature of the properties or relations that could explain a representation's having the content it has. Specifically, I shall examine whether a representation could derive its content solely from its own intrinsic properties, or whether it must be related to something outside itself in order to have content (and thus in order to be a representation). Let an account based purely on intrinsic properties be called internalist* and an account involving relations be called externalist*—somewhat revisionistically (hence the asterisk), since it is externality *to the representation* (and not to the individual) that will be at issue here. Then my argument has the following form. Every known internalist* attempt to explain content-possession fails, for reasons that do not depend on the kind of world that exists and that therefore cannot be shrugged off by the skeptic. Thus the skeptic who acknowledges a need to explain content-possession must either accept the truth of externalism* or offer a new, successful internalist* account. Pending the introduction of such an account, the skeptic must tentatively concede the truth of externalism*. But if externalism* is true, then so is something in the vicinity of (2)—though perhaps not as strong as (2) itself.

What is wrong with the existing internalist* accounts? These accounts fall into two categories, descriptivist/resemblance theories and conceptual-role theories. Let us begin with the former.

Descriptivist theories in the tradition of Frege and Russell[11] presuppose that the atomic components of descriptions already have meaning, thus assuming that *how* those atomic components get their meaning is either a brute fact or explained by some other theory. On the latter alternative, the atomic representations in turn receive meaning either from a causal relation to something outside themselves (e.g., Russellian acquaintance)—which would put these theories in the externalist* camp—or from their *resemblance* to some unique object or property. What makes the latter alternative internalist* is that the resemblance is wholly grounded in an intrinsic *property* of the representation. The representation purportedly signifies *all by itself* whatever object or property (if any) it uniquely resembles.[12]

The trouble with resemblance theories is that they depend on there being a determinate entity, actual or possible, that is uniquely resembled. As Putnam points out,[13] resemblance in itself is far too nonspecific a relation to determine content, since any two things resemble each other in some respect. Resemblance remains insufficient even if we insist, like the early Wittgenstein,[14] that the resemblance be structural. For, first of all, as Wittgenstein later argued in *Philosophical Investigations*,[15] anything that has structure at all has more than one structure. For example, a chessboard can be carved up into the sixty-four black and white squares; or into the rectangles or strips or pixels of color they're made up of; or into black, white, squareness, alternatingness, and eight-by-eight-ness (or components thereof)...In the same way, other would-be representations can be given more than one structural analysis. So a representation cannot be assumed to have a unique structure, as it would need to in order to have a unique signification in virtue of its structure.

Nor can it be assumed that if a representation *had* a unique structure, that would determine a unique signification for it, since there is no guarantee that the world contains only one or a few things with the appropriate corresponding structure. That is part of the point of 'twin'-type thought experiments[16] (and their forerunners[17]): The world may contain any number of things that are (at some level) qualitatively and structurally identical, in which case it will take more than resemblance (or isomorphism) to select one of those as the one meant. For this reason as well as the previous one, mere resemblance or isomorphism cannot in general specify a determinate content for a purported representation.

How this argument applies to general concepts, as opposed to singular ones, is perhaps worth special mention. For it might seem that the same issues don't arise with general terms, since there is no question of identifying which of many similar properties is the one meant; sufficiently similar properties are the same property. Still, one may fairly raise the question how a mental state gets to *signify* properties in the first place, as opposed to merely having properties itself. Putnam essentially shows us that a state's own properties (those in virtue of which it satisfies purely qualitative descriptions) are not enough to determine what descriptive *significance* it carries, if any. First of all there is the question of whether the state represents any of its own properties, and if so, which one(s). Then if it does not represent any of its own properties, but rather some *similar* property or properties, the trouble is that all kinds of properties can be seen as 'relevantly' similar to its own properties. So the descriptivist/resemblance model is no more adequate for general concepts than it is for singular ones.

Conceptual-role theories avoid these problems at first. According to inferential- or conceptual-role semantics, a representation (or "node") acquires content in virtue of belonging to a system of representations (or "network"), the mind, the content of each of whose member nodes is ontologically—not just epistemically—determined by its inferential or conceptual relations to the others. But what is the nature of these "inferential" or "conceptual" relations? If they consist of one node's implying another, for instance, it is hard to see how such a relation could hold prior to the nodes' having contents; how can one content-less thing imply another? Some content-independent relations are needed to ground the "inferential" or "conceptual" roles that the nodes play and receive their contents from.

But what could these content-independent relations be? They cannot be literally spatial relations, as is suggested by the claim that the nodes in such a system get their significance from their "places in the network" (even if we grant that there is physical place or something isomorphic to it). For what content is conveyed by place in a spatial network? Suppose a node in a network signifies all the entities, actual *or possible*, that occupy or would occupy corresponding places in isomorphic networks. Then even setting aside the above worries about the many kinds of isomorphism, that seems like potentially far too many contents to attribute to each representation, since there is no necessary restriction on the number of times the world copies a given structure. Suppose instead that a node simply represents its own relative location. Then nothing but relative locations can be signified—surely not what the conceptual-role theorist has in mind (since "getting its content from its relative location" would be misleading if its content just *were* its relative location). Finally, suppose that a node signifies just the *actual* corresponding entities, if any—or perhaps just a selected one of them. Then something *external to the network*—namely, what corresponding entities there actually are, and perhaps what picks one of them out as the unique one to be represented—is relevant to determining the node's content. That would yield a theory not merely externalist* but possibly even externalist.

It does not help internalism* to propose that the content-determining relations among nodes in the network are syntactic ones. For if they are really purely syntactic, entirely free of the semantic content they are to ground, then they must be capturable by mechanical rules that apply on the basis of form alone. These rules that determine which nodes trigger and are triggered by which other nodes cannot be rules created by stipulation, for to stipulate the rules would be to represent them, and we are looking for something that can serve as a *basis* for representation. But then the rules must be ones that apply without having been stipulated. This means they must be laws of nature—that is, they must be causal laws. So this sort of conceptual-role theory turns out to involve causal relations among nodes in the determination of content. That is, it says the content of any given node depends on its causal relations to nodes outside of itself. The theory is thus externalist*.

One way of looking at conceptual-role theories is to ask what the content-bearing units are. Theories that attribute content to individual nodes, we have just seen, are externalist*. If, however, one is tempted to save internalism* by proclaiming that it is holistic network states that carry meaning in virtue of their structures, then in effect one has gone back to a resemblance or isomorphism theory with its attendant problems of indefiniteness.

Resemblance and isomorphism, we have seen, are not sufficient to determine content. Something further is necessary. And that something appears to be causal. For in Twin Earth scenarios, the "twin" that is causally connected (in some appropriate way) to the utterance or thought is intuitively the one being spoken or thought of. This intuition can be elicited a priori by asking skeptics themselves which "twin" in a hypothetical scenario is being spoken or thought of. Skeptics' own intuitions would then support the *conditional* that *if* the relevant causal connection is present for just one of the twins, *then* that is the one that is meant. In fact, in the case of atomic concepts there is some hope that a sufficiently specific causal connection might *replace* all talk of resemblance, so that the problem of the too many kinds of resemblance would be eliminated altogether. And of course, if each atomic content-bearer is getting its content even partly from its causal connections to things outside itself, then the facts that ground semantic facts confirm externalism*.

We should remember at this point that the skeptics being cajoled into granting a role for *causation* in the determination of meaning do not necessarily assume that all causation is physical. (Remember Descartes and Berkeley. We may think we know better now—but have we really refuted them on their own terms? Are we even sufficiently clear about what it means for something to be physical? If we are tempted to reply in terms of physics, we should remember that the status and subject matter of physics are part of what's in question.) Nor have the arguments above done anything to support specifically physical causation. Skeptics who are moved by the foregoing considerations, then, may remain agnostic about the *nature* of the objects that play the causal roles in question. If there are arguments to persuade them that there is *physical* causality, those arguments are still ahead of us.

The considerations in this section so far constitute a strong a priori case for externalism*. It is not a deductive case; a skeptic still has the options of proposing an internalist* theory which is immune to the problems just canvassed, or maintaining that no theory is needed to explain a thought's possession of content because semantic facts do not hold in virtue of nonsemantic facts but rather are primitive. However, some skeptics may despair of internalism* and still find semantic facts mysterious enough to call for grounding in nonsemantic facts, thus finding themselves driven toward externalism*. It is to such skeptics and anyone interested in the fate of their position that the remainder of this essay is addressed.

1.3 In What Form Should a Skeptic Accept Premise 2?

We return now to the question of premise 2. Recall that it runs as follows:

2. I could not have any atomic concept unless there were instances of it.

What theoretical support can externalism* lend to something like (2)— something that ties a given concept to the existence of its instances?

Externalism* says that a representation gets its content at least in part from what it is appropriately related to. By far the simplest way for this to work is for the representation to *designate* the thing or property to which it is appropriately related. In particular, a *concept* would designate the *property* to which it is appropriately related. Since standing in the appropriate causal relation to a property requires standing in a causal relation to things that *have* the property, a concept's coming to signify a property would require the concept to have instances.

However, the accounts that have gained currency are more complicated than this, because they seek to allow for the possibility of misrepresentation even at the level of atomic concepts. They explain this possibility with the help of laws hypothesized to govern perceptual states (perceptual states being seen, in an empiricist spirit, as the original sources of all other concepts). The accounts typically run along the following lines:[18]

Perceptual states of type X represent property Y (perhaps if and) only if, under conditions C, nothing but a bearer of property Y would cause X to be tokened.

Notice that this doesn't require that the bearer of property Y be outside the thinker who is tokening X. So externalism*, as well as externalism in the sense of anti-individualism, is compatible with this statement. We shall return to the question whether either one is supported more than the other.

The idea behind the "conditions C" clause is to provide for hallucinations and other such errors: When conditions C fail, the perceptual state may be triggered in the absence of the type of thing that primarily causes it, producing an illusory representation.[19] The illusion's content is inherited from the veridical cases through the states' being of the same type. This appeal to sameness of type is backed up by the causal laws' own recognition of a relevant similarity. A particular state-type becomes relevant to content-determination only and precisely because causal laws correlate that state-type with something else.[20] So the similarities among state-tokens appealed to here are more determinate—independently of content—than are the purported similarities appealed to in resemblance theories.

It is true that what differentiates representations of different properties is difference in state-type—that is, difference in intrinsic properties of the representations. So these externalist* accounts share with internalist* accounts a reliance on intrinsic properties of representations. But in this case the intrinsic properties are, so to speak, identified extrinsically.

Candidates for filling in the "conditions C" clause include normal conditions,[21] ideal conditions,[22] or conditions obtaining during a training period.[23] Some of these (e.g., the last one) require the type of thing in question to have actually caused the state in question, at least in the past, and thus require the (at least past) existence of the type of thing being represented. Such candidates support premise 2 with only slight revision:

2'. I could not have any atomic concept unless there *had been* instances of it.

Here the content-bearing entity cannot bear the content it does unless there have really been instances of it. One might thus consider the (present or past) instances to be essential to or even part of the content-bearing entity itself, since without them in its history it would not have the content that it does (or, perhaps, any content at all). Thus the full content-bearing entity, instances included, would not even exist if it did not stand for some (once-)real things. This sort of view is associated with McDowell, among others,[24] and would, as mentioned above, support premise 2'.

If, however, the conditions C turn out to be ones that are not required by definition to have obtained (e.g., ideal conditions), then it becomes possible—at least so far as causal constraints on content are concerned—for a state to stand for things that have never existed. For example, suppose the relevant laws of optics, neurology, and so on, make it the case that under ideal conditions, a certain perceptual state would be caused only by the presence of a dragon in one's vicinity. That type of perceptual state then represents dragonhood. Now suppose that under some less-than-ideal conditions, I come to token that perceptual state repeatedly and form a concept from it in the usual way. I now have a concept of dragons without there having to have been any.[25]

In such a case it seems more dubious to define content-bearing entities so they cannot exist without the existence of the things they stand for; at least, some further reason for doing so is needed. Barring such a reason, we end up with a weaker version of premise 2':

2''. I could not have an atomic concept unless it were the case that, *under conditions C*, nothing but instances of that concept *would* cause the relevant perceptual state.

According to this version, concept-possession merely requires a causal context sufficient to guarantee that, *should* the specified conditions hold, only certain things *would* cause a particular state to be tokened. This gives only very general information about the causal context in question; the most salient implication is simply that concept-possession requires some causal context or other. And there has still been nothing to show that that causal context must be physical.

The above arguments for versions of premise 2 do not establish either version beyond doubt. But they do offer reasons for thinking that something in the vicinity is true, reasons that assume only (i) that there are appearances (and hence representation), and (ii) that representation requires grounding in nonsemantic facts (which then turn out to involve causation, according to both our twin-related intuitions and the externalist* way of accounting for semantic facts). These considerations are available, and even pressing, for skeptics and anti-skeptics alike.

So it is not unreasonable to expect a skeptic to accept something like premise 2. The question, then, is how far away from the original skeptical position (2) can lead.

Let us temporarily suppose, for the sake of argument, that it *were to turn out* that premise 2′ (and not just 2″) is defensible, even for the skeptic. *Would* that make it possible to argue for the existence of objects that are not merely *causes* of one's perceptual states, as Berkeley's God could be, but are specifically physical? The following argument suggests itself:

1*. I have atomic concepts of shape, size, and motion.

2′. I could not have any atomic concept unless there had been instances of it.

3*. Therefore there have been instances of shape, size, and motion.

But now we need to take a closer look at premise 1*.

2   Self-Knowledge

2.1   The Gap between Introspection and Meaning

As McLaughlin and Tye point out,[26] knowing by introspection which of my concepts are atomic is not clearly possible. However, we are about to see that matters are much worse: I cannot even be sure by introspection what concepts I have, let alone which of them are atomic. On the bright side, the argument will also have the consequence that there cannot even appear to be a meaningful thought unless there is also something to which the thinker (if there is one) lacks introspective access. This means that at least Humean present-moment skepticism is excluded.

The argument just ahead can be outlined as follows. Thought requires a modicum of consistency—of determinacy and stability of meaning. However, introspection is fallible about the presence of such consistency in any given case: It is logically possible to have all the inward signs of meaning something determinate, without actually doing so. Because of this possibility, introspection is fallible about the genuine occurrence of thought in any given case. So when thought does occur, it occurs partly in virtue of something not introspectable by the thinker. In other words, thought requires a non-introspectable context. This is the core of the anti-Humean point. Furthermore, since introspection is fallible about when thought is genuinely occurring, we are fallible about when we really have hold of a concept. For this reason, we are fallible about what concepts we have.

Why should thought require a modicum of consistency or stability? Couldn't there be a Humean momentary world containing nothing but a single momentary thought—and why should such a thought need "consistency" or "stability," whatever that would mean in such a world?

The answer is that for a thought to have any meaning at all and not be mere mental noise, it has to commit the thinker to at least minimal consequences. Something has to count as making a mistake, even about what one means: There have to be possible judgments about one's own thought that would count as incorrect, if that thought is to mean anything. If one is to count as having, say, a "red"-thought at a given moment, it must count as a mistake to think later that one is having the same thought as before but that it is not a "red"-thought. Without this potential for error, the supposition that one is having a "red"-thought is meaningless.

The implications of this point can be brought out with the help of Wittgenstein's discussion of following a rule. I am not primarily concerned with Wittgenstein interpretation, but my presentation of the next several points is indebted to him, and I shall indicate some details of this debt with footnotes. If I am reading him wrongly, however, that is not my present concern; my present concern is with the points themselves.

In his argument against the possibility of a private language, Wittgenstein asks us to consider the project of entering 'S' in a diary on each occasion of feeling a certain sensation. If what one means by 'S' is to be an objective fact, there must be a rule one is following in writing 'S'. There must be such a thing as using 'S' in the same way and using 'S' in a different way in the future. Similarly, if one is intending to use 'S' in the same way as in the *past*, there must be such a thing as failing to do so—on pain of 'S''s losing all meaning. So there must be something that can *make it the case* that one has failed to use S in the same way as before.

This means something must make it the case that one has been following a certain particular rule rather than other rules in one's uses of 'S'. Now, one's past uses of 'S' do not suffice to make this the case. For many mutually incompatible future uses of 'S' can be construed as consistent with all one's past uses, however many past uses there are.[27] Yet each of these incompatible future uses would, if construed as a continuation of the original rule, show one to have been following a different rule all along. Furthermore, even one's first-person experience and memory of these past uses can never fully determine which rule one has been following, since one cannot have thought ahead explicitly to every possible use—and thinking ahead to possible uses *implicitly* is, by definition, not something that falls fully within one's awareness.[28]

So whatever makes it the case that one is using 'S' in a particular way falls partly outside of what one can introspect. Now, I am not trying to create doubt about the existence of genuine rule-following on the grounds that one cannot introspect proof of following any particular rule. Rather, I am arguing that when one does actually follow a particular rule—when one does actually mean something determinate by 'S'—one does so *thanks to one or more factors that are not available to one's introspection*. When one does use 'S' in the same way as before, one is doing something more than merely thinking that one is using 'S' in the same way as before.[29] Precisely because meaning something is an objective matter, there is more to it than can be ascertained from one's own point of view.

Specifically, there needs to be something, independent of one's first-person impression of things, that can ground counterfactuals about present and future uses—such as, "If I were to use 'S' under conditions *A*, I would be using it in the same way that I am using it now," or, "If I were to use 'S' under conditions *B*, I would be using it in a different way from how I am using it now." To ground such counterfactuals I need a stable *disposition*, not constituted by anything transparent to me, to use 'S' under certain conditions and not others. In effect, an objective disposition to mean some particular thing in the future is a necessary condition of meaning something in the present. Without such a disposition, there is nothing to make it the case that some future uses of the representation would be right and others would be wrong. And without anything to make that the case, there is no determinate fact about which rule is being followed. Since first-person experience falls short of constituting such a disposition,[30] the ability to mean something even for a moment requires more than first-person experience—at or beyond that moment—can provide.

2.2 Implications for Humean Skeptics

What it takes to mean something, then, even just for a moment, goes beyond the scope of one's first-person experience. Facts beyond one's introspective reach are required to make it the case that any thoughts have meaning. Every thought, in other words, requires a non-introspectable context; a being consisting of just introspectable states could have no thoughts.

So contrary to present-moment skepticism, there cannot be a thought that really means something and is the only thing in the world. Still, could an *apparent* thought that only *seems* to mean something be the only thing in the world? Could skeptics still hold that, for all they can know, only what falls within reach of their introspection really exists—even though this would mean that they are not really thinking at all?[31]

That choice would cost skeptics dearly. For even the appearance of thinking entails some representational thought. Indeed, the appearance *of* anything does. For the appearance of any thing or event entails that that thing or event is being represented—otherwise, it is not an appearance of that thing or event. Even if something just *appears to appear* to be present, that apparent appearance is distinguished from the apparent appearances of other things *by its representational content*. (It is an apparent appearance of the one thing rather than of the others.) So any skeptic who wants to maintain that there is, at any level, so much as the appearance of anything (and surely this will include most skeptics, even most Humean ones) must admit that representational thought really occurs. But we have also just seen that if representational thought does really occur, then there is more in the world than just a thought; and indeed if the thought has a thinker, there is something outside the reach of that thinker's introspection.

2.3   Implications for Premise 1

We are thus in a quite interesting position with respect to our own thoughts. For on the one hand, even just the *appearance* of thought is enough to confirm for us that some representational thought does occur. Yet on the other hand, the objectivity of representational facts means that introspection cannot tell us for certain *which* of our subjective states actually involve(s) representational thought. Introspection thus cannot tell us for certain what concept(s) we actually have. For if I say to myself anything like, "I have concept *C*," or, "I have this concept"—mentally pointing as I do so—what guarantees that at the moment of my naming or my pointing, I am having a genuine thought? We saw above that nothing I can introspect guarantees that I am following a rule at any given moment; it is always possible that when I try to get hold of a concept to plug into premise 1, I lapse into mental gibberish without realizing it. Because of this, I cannot be sure of *what* concepts I have. Trying to catch a concept on the fly as I use it (rather than mention it) is subject to the same danger; I might in the crucial moment fail to be really using any concept at all, to be really following any rule at all in my purported application of a concept. So I cannot with certainty assert of any concept that I have it. And the reasons for this are much more general than any version of premise 2.

This uncertainty about our own concepts seems to fly in the face of compelling arguments by Burge and Davidson. Burge argues that just to believe, of a particular concept, that I have it, I must actually have it, for having the concept is an essential part of that belief.[32] Davidson argues that the same environmental factors that determine our concepts' contents necessarily also determine what we take their contents to be.[33] How, then, could we ever get our own concepts wrong?

It is important here to distinguish between the way in which we cannot mistake our own concepts, according to their arguments, and the way in which we can be mistaken, according to mine. It may well be, as they contend, a conceptual truth that whenever we are thinking that we have a certain concept, we do really have it. What I am arguing is that we are fallible about when the *antecedent* of this conditional holds: We have no way to tell in any given instance whether we really *are* thinking that we have a concept. For all that we can tell by introspection, we might fail at that particular moment to be having any meaningful thought at all.[34]

Although we may be wrong about *which* thoughts are genuine, we cannot be wrong that *some* thought is, and because of this we have reason to think that we have *some* concept(s). For, first, we saw above that if anything so much as appears to be the case, then at least one representational thought is occurring, since something's appearing to be the case is itself a representational phenomenon. Second, for something to appear to be the case arguably requires at least a rudimentary *concept* of the *way* things appear to be. For it requires being able to distinguish their appearing to be that *way* from their not appearing to be that way. And such an ability suffices for having a concept in the most rudimentary sense. Thus although we cannot be sure *what* concepts we have, we do have reason to believe that we have some.

This means that there is still a residual version of premise 1 available for attempted anti-skeptical argument. For possession of at least one concept entails possession of at least one *atomic* concept—either the first-mentioned concept itself, or others of which it is composed. It thus seems reasonable to hold onto a weakened premise,

1'. I have some atomic concept(s)—though I cannot be sure which one(s).[35]

3   Why Skepticism Cannot Be Cartesian

3.1   Physical-Object Skepticism

Where, then, do things stand with respect to the attempt to respond to physical-object skepticism? If we combine 1′ with premise 2′, we get

1′. I have some atomic concept(s);
2′. I could not have any atomic concept unless there had been instances of it;
3′. Therefore there have been instances of my atomic concept(s), whatever it (or they) may be.

For example, *if* I have atomic concepts of shape and size, then there have been things that had shape and size. However, we have seen that I cannot be sure that I *do* have atomic concepts of shape or size. So even with the strongest justifiable version of premise 2, I cannot be sure that there have been things that had shape and size. I can be sure only that there have been instances of whatever atomic concepts I do turn out to have.

Now, it is only to see how far we could get with the stronger premise 2′ that we have been focusing on that version of premise 2. If we instead combine 1′ with the weaker 2″, which remains a contender as well, what we get is

1″(= 1′). I have some atomic concept(s);
2″. I could not have any atomic concept unless it is the case that, *under conditions C*, nothing but instances of that concept *would* cause the associated perceptual state;
3″. Therefore there are sufficient causal forces in play to ensure that, *should* conditions C ever hold, nothing but instances of my atomic concept(s) *would* cause the perceptual states from which this (or those) concept(s) arose.

For example, if I have an atomic concept of size, then *if* on the one hand conditions C *have* held, *then* there have been things that had size—but if on the other hand conditions C have *never* held, then the world must simply be rich enough to ground the counterfactual that if conditions C *had* ever held, my perceptual experiences of size would have come from things that had size. The most natural candidate for such a world might be a physical world, but a Cartesian demon would do as well, giving me mental faculties suited to perceiving size under conditions C and then fooling those faculties.

Thus although there are weakened versions of premises 1 and 2 that the skeptic might accept, these versions can support only an extremely weak anti-skeptical conclusion, namely, the conclusion that there exists some thought occupying a context to which some causal laws apply. Because there has been no proof either that existing concepts represent physical things, or that the surrounding causal laws need be physical, we do not have the hoped-for proof of physical things.

3.2 External-World Skepticism

At the beginning of section 1, we noted that the McKinsey strategy is doubly relevant to this paper. First, it embodies the anti-individualist argument against skepticism about *external* objects. And second, it purports to give skeptics reason to concede the existence of *physical* objects, so that the line between internal and external can be drawn on a physical basis. We have just seen that the second goal is not met. It is time to turn to the first.

Do the arguments for anti-individualism or for a non-introspectable context at least show that *if* we have bodies and veridical physical concepts, *then* there are objects external to us? No. What these arguments show is only that there are causal conditions on representation: If a thing has meaning, it occupies *some* sort of causal context, perhaps (if 2' is vindicated) a causal context involving an instance of what it means. True, this causal context must be outside of the meaningful entity—say, the thought, the network node, or the brain state—and it must be outside the thinker's introspective reach, but it need not be outside the thinker as a physical whole. For example, on our everyday non-skeptical view of ourselves, a certain sort of brain-state means what it does because it is typically caused by an empty stomach—a state of the thinker's own body. Nothing in the foregoing arguments excludes the possibility that in the end *all* the representational states of, say, a thinker's brain and perceptual systems are typically caused by states of other parts of that thinker's body, receiving their meanings from those causal relations and not from relations to anything outside the body. What makes us reject this possibility out of hand is our everyday assumptions about the kind of world we live in and where, in this kind of world, a person's body begins and ends—but *these* assumptions have not yet been made compulsory for the skeptic. So the term 'anti-individualism' is misleading, at least as far as the present arguments are concerned. Arguments for a causation-invoking account of content-determination place the source of meaning outside the *representation*, but not necessarily outside the *individual* to whom the representation belongs.

The impression that the presence of content requires something outside the thinker as a whole may come from the Wittgenstein-inspired arguments of section 2. But these arguments show only that meaning requires something outside the thinker's introspective reach—not that meaning requires something outside the thinker as a whole.[36]

Indeed, the very dependence of meaning on facts outside one's introspective reach constitutes a reason for *not* setting the boundaries of even an immaterial self *at* the bounds of introspective reach. For, arguably, facts that help make it the case that I mean such-and-such are, at least in part, facts about me as a thinker. So if facts that help make it the case that I mean such-and-such are outside my introspective reach, then there are facts about me as a thinker that are outside my introspective reach. Such facts might include, for instance, the presence of some unconscious process that controls my use of my thought-symbols. I think that intuitively such a process should count as a part of my self.

An additional consideration arises from the question of whether an immaterial self should be thought to include that self's concepts. For we have seen that my concepts themselves fall outside my introspective reach, or at least that portion of my introspective reach (if there is one) about which I am infallible. Thus it makes sense to grant that there is more to me as a thinker than what falls within the bounds of my introspection, at least in the traditional sense. What exactly should be included remains an open question, but we cannot assume that what falls outside my introspection falls outside of me.

So the anti-skeptical strategy suggested by the McKinsey argument fails to show either that there are *physical* objects or that there are objects *outside* the thinker. If we revisit the lessons of section 2, we can see in a new light both why this anti-skeptical strategy has seemed promising to some and why it has elicited, for others, a sense of sleight-of-hand. Specifically, we need to remember that we are fallible about some of the very things Descartes taught us were most certain: Although we cannot doubt that representational thought occurs, we also cannot be sure of producing, when desired, a list of concepts or even a single particular concept that we certainly have. When we do succeed in using or thinking of a concept, we do so with the help of facts we cannot introspect and cannot guarantee. For all our introspection shows, we could be thinking nonsense at any given moment and not using or identifying a concept then at all.

So the first step in the McKinsey argument—the very one that seems friendly to skeptics because it evokes a realm we can know about without knowing about the outside world—is already loaded. Perhaps we should not be surprised, as if we had forgotten what comes after the Second Meditation. The strategy of using knowledge of our own concepts to prove the existence of "external" things is, after all, as Cartesian as the belief that we have knowledge of our concepts in the first place. The real point of segregating an alleged internal realm from things we are more obviously fallible about may have been to try to insulate our authority about the "inner" from our ignorance of the "outer." This in turn could have helped make it plausible that we have a foundation of authoritative knowledge from which to build up knowledge of the "external" world.

But in fact our fallibility is pervasive. The second step of the McKinsey-inspired argument cannot take us to certainty that particular kinds of things exist partly because the first step cannot start from certainty that we have particular concepts. And with the loss of certainty about our concepts we lose more than just a way of proving things to exist. We lose two ways of separating the outer from the inner. For the appeal to physical boundaries cannot be justified to a skeptic in the absence of a proof that physical things exist. And the appeal to Cartesian introspective boundaries cannot be justified *by* the skeptic, in the absence of introspective clarity about what and when we are thinking. The real skeptical challenge is not about the existence of a world outside a Cartesian mind, but about what goes on outside *and inside* the thinking self[37]—whatever that is.[38]

Acknowledgments

This essay has been brewing for a very long time and has accumulated a correspondingly long list of benefactors. Special thanks to Patricia Blanchette for showing me where clarification was most needed; to Paula Gottlieb and John Haldane for helping me see what this paper was really about; and to Lisa Warenski, my acute and helpful commentator at the 2004 Inland Northwest Philosophy Conference, who prompted many significant improvements. Thanks also go to many others, including Malcolm Forster, Ralph Kennedy, Win-chiat Lee, Genoveva Marti, Henry Newell, Michael O'Rourke, John Pollock, William Robinson, Anthony Rudd, Alan Sidelle, Dennis Stampe, Sergio Tenenbaum, Aladdin Yaqub, participants in the 2002 NEH Institute on Consciousness and Intentionality, and several anonymous referees.

Notes

1. See, e.g., Burge 1982, 1986, and McDowell 1986 for expressions of anti-individualism. Some writers call this view (semantic) externalism; see, for instance, Boghossian 1998, 271; or Gallois 1994, 49.

2. McDowell 1986, 167.

3. Woodfield 1982, vii; Brueckner 1986; McKinsey 1991, 16.

4. I have in mind arguments attributable to Wittgenstein (1958), which pioneered an anti-Cartesian view of the mind and gave some of the earliest motivations for the anti-individualist approach to reference.

5. See, e.g., Putnam 1975 and Burge 1982.

6. This way of putting (1)–(3) is essentially due to Boghossian (1998), 275. His version, like several others, omits 'atomic' from premises 1 and 2. Although that makes premise 1 more plausibly knowable by introspection, it makes premise 2 hopelessly implausible, for many concepts can be assembled from simpler concepts whether they themselves have instances or not. Compare McLaughlin and Tye 1998a, 369.

7. E.g., Brueckner 1993, Miller 1997, Sawyer 1998, and Warfield 1998.

8. See McKinsey 1991, Brown 1995, and Boghossian 1998.

9. McKinsey (1991), 15–16, discusses and criticizes this line of reasoning.

10. Sawyer (1998), 525, also questions the assumption that introspective knowledge of one's own concepts is a priori.

11. One recent example is Searle (1983). There has also been a resurgence of neo-Fregean and Russellian descriptivism.

12. What if there is no such object or property? If that makes the purported representation devoid of all content, then a representation must resemble something outside of itself in order to have meaning, and resemblance theories are externalist* after all. (I owe this point to Michael O'Rourke.) If this is correct, then the next few paragraphs, addressed to resemblance theories, can be considerably abbreviated. However, some resemblance theorists believe that an atomic representation that does not resemble any actual entity still has content and represents, for instance, any *possible* entity it uniquely resembles. On such a view, a representation *can* achieve content on its own. It is to such resemblance theorists that the next few paragraphs are particularly addressed.

13. Putnam 1981, especially the infamous chap. 1 ("Brains in a Vat") and, equally importantly, chap. 3.

14. Wittgenstein 1961 (written 1921).

15. Wittgenstein 1958, paras. 47–48.

16. See Putnam 1975 and Burge 1982, among many others.

17. Including—as should be more widely recognized—Strawson 1959, esp. 122–125.

18. Burge 1986, Dretske 1983, Putnam 1981, chap. 1, and Stampe 1979, 1986.

19. Here I am indebted to Stampe 1986.

20. These causal laws, by the way, still need not be physical for all the argument has shown so far.

21. Burge 1986, 131; and Putnam 1981, 14.

22. Stampe 1979, 1986.

23. Dretske 1983, esp. 7–12.

24. John Haldane, for one, reserves the term 'externalism' for this view that the content-bearing entity's very existence depends on the existence of some instance(s). See also Woodfield 1982, v.

25. For a detailed exploration of the different anti-skeptical implications of ideal-conditions theories and normal- or training-conditions theories, see Weitzman 1996.

26. McLaughlin and Tye 1998b, 298.

27. Wittgenstein 1958, paras. 146, 185–186.

28. Wittgenstein 1958, para. 187.

29. Wittgenstein 1958, paras. 202, 258–263.

30. Wittgenstein 1958, paras. 185, 187, 198.

31. This line is taken by Brueckner (1986), 155–156, 159; and Klein (1986), 384–386.

32. Burge 1988, 656, 662–663.

33. Davidson 1987.

34. I should note that my pessimism here about our self-knowledge represents a departure from my optimism about it in Weitzman 1996, 302. At the time I had not recognized the relevance of the Wittgensteinian argument above. I should also note that we may still be—for reasons not introspectable to us—*reliable*, even if not infallible, about when we are indeed thinking that we have a given concept. If this is so, then the Burge-Davidson model may be sufficient to ground ascription to us of a reliabilist kind of knowledge of our own thought-contents. This falls short, however, of the infallible knowledge initially sought by the skeptic and claimed by the Cartesian. For a detailed discussion of a reliabilist model of introspective knowledge, see Sawyer 1999.

35. Compare McLaughlin and Tye 1998a, 377, although there they do not give such a detailed argument for this premise.

36. Compare Wittgenstein 1958, para. 270, where the non-introspectable fact that gives the subject's uses of 'S' a meaning is a change in the subject's blood-pressure correlated with the subject's uses of 'S'.

37. Compare McDowell 1986, 164: "But in the different reading, scepticism about the objects of seeming singular thoughts is equally scepticism about the layout of the mental realm."

38. This is not to say that there are no responses to such a skeptical challenge. Rather, I am arguing that challenge and response alike must be careful to avoid framing themselves in terms of externality to the self, at least until a non-question-begging delineation of the self has been achieved and agreed upon.

References

Block, N., O. Flanagan, and G. Güzeldere, eds. 1997. *The Nature of Consciousness: Philosophical Debates*. Cambridge, Mass.: MIT Press.

Boghossian, P. 1989. "Content and Self-Knowledge." *Philosophical Topics* 17: 5–26.

Boghossian, P. 1998. "What the Externalist Can Know A Priori." In C. Wright, B. Smith, and C. Macdonald, eds., *Knowing Our Own Minds*. Oxford: Clarendon Press.

Brown, J. 1995. "The Incompatibility of Anti-Individualism and Privileged Access." *Analysis* 55: 149–156.

Brueckner, A. 1986. "Brains in a Vat." *Journal of Philosophy* 83: 148–167.

Brueckner, A. 1992. "Semantic Answers to Skepticism." *Pacific Philosophical Quarterly* 73: 200–219.

Brueckner, A. 1993. "What an Anti-Individualist Knows A Priori." *Analysis* 52: 111–118.

Burge, T. 1979. "Individualism and the Mental." In P. French, T. Uehling, and H. Wettstein, eds., *Midwest Studies in Philosophy IV: Studies in Metaphysics*. Minneapolis: University of Minnesota Press.

Burge, T. 1982. "Other Bodies." In A. Woodfield, ed., *Thought and Object: Essays on Intentionality*. Oxford: Oxford University Press.

Burge, T. 1986. "Cartesian Error and the Objectivity of Perception." In P. Pettit and J. McDowell, eds., *Subject, Thought, and Context*. Oxford: Clarendon Press.

Burge, T. 1988. "Individualism and Self-Knowledge." *Journal of Philosophy* 85: 649–663.

Davidson, D. 1984. "First Person Authority." *Dialectica* 38: 101–111.

Davidson, D. 1987. "Knowing One's Own Mind." *Proceedings and Addresses of the American Philosophical Association* 60: 441–458.

Davidson, D. 1988. "Reply to Burge." *Journal of Philosophy* 85: 664–665.

Dretske, F. 1983. "The Epistemology of Belief." *Synthèse* 55: 3–19.

Fricker, E. 1998. "Self-Knowledge: Special Access versus Artefact of Grammar—A Dichotomy Rejected." In C. Wright, B. Smith, and C. Macdonald, eds., *Knowing Our Own Minds*. Oxford: Clarendon Press.

Gallois, A. 1994. "Deflationary Self Knowledge." In M. Michael and J. O'Leary-Hawthorne, eds., *Philosophy in Mind*. Dordrecht: Kluwer.

Klein, P. 1986. "Radical Interpretation and Global Skepticism." In E. LePore, ed., *Truth and Interpretation: Perspectives on the Philosophy of Donald Davidson*. Oxford: Blackwell.

McDowell, J. 1986. "Singular Thought and the Extent of Inner Space." In P. Pettit and J. McDowell, eds., *Subject, Thought, and Context*. Oxford: Clarendon Press.

McKinsey, M. 1991. "Anti-Individualism and Privileged Access." *Analysis* 51: 9–16.

McLaughlin, B., and M. Tye. 1998a. "Is Content-Externalism Compatible with Privileged Access?" *Philosophical Review* 107: 349–380.

McLaughlin, B., and M. Tye. 1998b. "Externalism, Twin Earth, and Self-Knowledge." In C. Wright, B. Smith, and C. Macdonald, eds., *Knowing Our Own Minds*. Oxford: Clarendon Press.

Miller, R. 1997. "Externalist Self-Knowledge and the Scope of the A Priori." *Analysis* 57: 67–75.

Putnam, H. 1975. "The Meaning of 'Meaning'." *Mind, Language, and Reality*. Cambridge: Cambridge University Press.

Putnam, H. 1981. *Reason, Truth, and History*. Cambridge: Cambridge University Press.

Searle, J. 1983. *Intentionality: An Essay in the Philosophy of Mind*. Cambridge: Cambridge University Press.

Sawyer, S. 1998. "Privileged Access to the World." *Australasian Journal of Philosophy* 76: 523–533.

Sawyer, S. 1999. "An Externalist Account of Introspective Knowledge." *Pacific Philosophical Quarterly* 80: 358–378.

Stampe, D. 1979. "Toward a Causal Theory of Linguistic Representation." In P. French, T. Uehling, and H. Wettstein, eds., *Contemporary Perspectives in the Philosophy of Language*. Minneapolis: University of Minnesota Press.

Stampe, D. 1986. "Verificationism and a Causal Account of Meaning." *Synthèse* 69: 107–137.

Strawson, P. 1959. *Individuals: An Essay in Descriptive Metaphysics*. London: Methuen.

Warfield, T. 1998. "A Priori Knowledge of the World: Knowing the World by Knowing our Minds." *Philosophical Studies* 92: 127–147.

Weitzman, L. 1996. "What Makes a Causal Theory of Content Anti-Skeptical?" *Philosophy and Phenomenological Research* 56: 299–318.

Weitzman, L. 1998. "Is the Possibility of Massive Error Ruled Out by Semantic Holism?" *Journal of Philosophical Research* 23: 147–163.

Wittgenstein, L. 1958. *Philosophical Investigations.* G. E. M. Anscombe, trans. New York: Macmillan.

Wittgenstein, L. 1961. *Tractatus Logico-Philosophicus.* D. Pears and B. McGuinness, trans. London: Routledge & Kegan Paul.

Woodfield, A., ed. 1982. *Thought and Object: Essays on Intentionality.* Oxford: Oxford University Press.

12 Is There a Reason for Skepticism?

Joseph Cruz

1

Two compelling and persistent projects of contemporary epistemology are engaging skepticism and searching for adequate epistemic principles. The former project, of course, can be traced in various forms through the ancients and moderns, and the last decade has seen skepticism debated with renewed vigor. The centrality of skepticism in epistemology is manifest. It both presents a foil against which positive epistemic theses may be modified and tested, and offers powerful arguments that perhaps even lead to the conclusion that skepticism correctly captures our ultimate epistemic condition (Stroud 1984).

The latter project—generating and defending epistemic principles—arguably has a shorter history, but has been an extremely prominent and widely pursued research program for at least a half century. Sometimes it is overly associated with the important work of Chisholm, but this would be to underestimate the ubiquity of trying to make sense of epistemic achievement via principles that, taken together, allege to encode all cognitive transitions involving mental states where belief-output is of high epistemic quality (Cruz manuscript).

While these two projects have not always been specifically undertaken together, it is reasonably easy to see how the combination might go. That is, it is reasonably easy to see what principles the skeptic is deploying in skeptical arguments, and from there we may ask whether those principles are properly normative in reasoning. On first inspection, for most of us those principles appear unassailable. That is part of the explanation for why we take skepticism seriously.

The fact that skeptical arguments need to appeal to epistemic principles at all is not surprising. A series of *non sequiturs* leading up to the conclusion, "therefore you do not know you have hands," would not do. Skeptical arguments aim to be rationally persuasive, or at least to have enough of the trappings of rationality so as to be distinguishable from opining or uttering gibberish. In order to be compelling in this way, skeptical worries must be articulated or articulatable through principles of reason that lead us to the skeptical conclusion via our appreciation of the plausibility of the premises and of the rational irresistibility of the outcome. It has often been observed that this makes it so that the skeptic cannot be attempting to call into question all of our epistemic apparatus at once. Specifically, the skeptic cannot be calling into question the rational procedure, whatever it may be, that is being employed to yield the skeptical conclusion. According to the *principles approach* to epistemology, the skeptic needs to appeal to epistemic principles in order to make her alternative characterization of our epistemic situation a genuine competitor (i.e., something other than a series a *non sequiturs*) to non-skeptical conclusions. These principles will then remain undoubted, so that radical doubt reaches only so far.[1]

In spite of this limitation, skepticism seems to retain a potent arsenal of arguments that lead to startling conclusions. The claims that I might be a brain-in-a-vat, or that I have no evidence that the future will be like the past, or that there might be no past at all and that I came into being an instant ago with memories in place, still seem cogent and worrisome, even though in making them skeptical arguments follow epistemic principles. And these skeptical possibilities have been sufficient to vex generations of epistemologists with the threat that we are irrational to believe the things that we ordinarily believe.

My first aim in this essay is diagnostic. I will argue that skeptical arguments originate in a tension between our epistemic principles. Individual principles enjoy our endorsement both from the first-person perspective as well as from the perspective of understanding why our cognition operates according to those principles. Skepticism, I claim, arises from the unexpected *interaction* of some of those principles. From this diagnostic claim, I move to a more critical stance. We may ask after the epistemic credentials of the individual principles implicated in skeptical arguments. If the individual principles are genuinely constitutive of our epistemic cognition, then we may be led to a kind of pragmatic resignation with respect to skepticism. That pragmatic resignation would involve the insight that the principles involved in generating skeptical arguments are crucial to thought as we have it, but that their interaction leads to conclusions that are unexpected and (to some) odious. If, on the other hand, the very principles involved in skeptical arguments are suspect, then we have a way of addressing skepticism and perhaps of answering the skeptic. I scout this second line here and conclude that the particular principle used in generating (some) skeptical arguments is *not* one that we should view as normative with respect to our reasoning. I maintain that the skeptic must appeal to an especially strong epistemic principle of discriminating evidence for a belief, and that this principle is so demanding that it ultimately undermines skepticism itself.

2

The epistemological framework I am working in is cast in terms of epistemic principles, so I am anxious to ensure that they do not arouse undue suspicion. By *epistemic principle*, I have in mind a rule that states the conditions under which a set of inputs (typically mental states like beliefs or perceptions) yields epistemically high-quality output (typically a justified belief[2]). Epistemic principles do not merely describe the rules that people actually use. Rather, they prescribe rules. Descriptive details of how we come to believe what we do, originating in psychology or sociology, may be relevant to our understanding of epistemic principles, but they cannot tell us how we ought to form our beliefs. Epistemic principles are identified by the intuitive epistemic credentials of the output (Sosa 1980). If the output of a rule is non-accidentally epistemically laudable, then we have before us a plausible candidate for an epistemic principle.

Consider some examples: Some epistemologists have proposed that there is an epistemic principle regarding the good inferential relationship between perceptual states (or beliefs about perceptual states) and beliefs about the way the world is. One way of putting this perceptual principle is, "If a person has a clear sensory impression that *x is F* (or of *x's* being *F*) and on that basis believes that *x* is *F*, then this belief is prima facie justified" (Audi 2001, 43). Another way is: "If S believes that he perceives something to have a certain property *F*, then the proposition that he does perceive something to be *F*, as well as the proposition that there is something that is *F*, is one that is reasonable for S" (Chisholm 1966, 45). A third: "Having a percept at time t with the content P is a defeasible reason for the cognizer to believe *P-at-t*" (Pollock and Cruz 1999, 201). Other formulations of this principle can be found elsewhere and in quite diverse epistemologies (cf. Bonjour 2000, 30; Plantinga 1993, 99; Sosa 1980, 22). They all seem to be after the same thing, namely the claim that sensing that *p* is a fallible but good basis for an inference to the belief that *p*.

Similarly formulated principles abound with respect to, for instance, memory. When it appears to S that she remembers that *p*, then S is (highly defeasibly) justified in believing that p (cf. Audi 2001; Pollock and Cruz 1999). One can also find discussion of inductive principles. Induction is a particularly interesting case, because the principles involved in it are not so simple to state as those which are involved in perception and memory. Goodman (1954) taught us that we need to include a projectibility constraint in our inductive principles, so no simple rule of the form *discovering that most Fs are G is a prima facie reason for think that all F's are G* will be adequate (Pollock 1989).

We can isolate a generic schema for thinking about epistemic principles. The epistemologist claims that inferences are apropos when a mental state ψ_n (a belief) is based on the content of prior mental states $\psi_1, \ldots, \psi_{(n-1)}$:

Being in mental states $\psi_1, \ldots, \psi_{(n-1)}$ is a good (but defeasible) basis for an inference to mental state ψ_n in the cognizer.

We can say that the transitions captured by the generic principle schema are justification-preserving.[3] Justification-preservation names the capacity of a principle to ensure that "downstream" contentful states inherit the epistemic laudableness of the "upstream" contentful states.[4] The epistemologist is relying on the possibility of filling this schema for all the principles that we possess, and the result would be an abstract catalog of our capacity for good reasoning.

Viewed individually, the principles state what types of mental states are adequate starting points for generating particular high quality beliefs, but the principles are usually not content-specific. Presumably, this is because the principles that govern epistemically good cognition must be flexible enough to accommodate whatever content is delivered to the believer through her experiences in the world or as a result of her own thoughts. In my view, content-neutrality—that is, the property had by principles such that they can range over a variety of mental states with differing content—is one of the distinguishing features of epistemic principles. Principles that specify a narrow instance of reasoning—for instance, that it is reasonable to believe that there is an apple before you when confronted by the perceptual features of an apple—are not principles of reasoning as such. This represents a plausible explanatory scruple on the part of epistemologists. Epistemologists could in principle seek to enumerate all the instances of reasoning that start with particular mental states and lead to particular justified beliefs. It is obvious, however, that that strategy would fail to capture the phenomenon of rationality at the right level of abstraction.

For all their content-neutrality, however, the principles are usually *faculty-specific*, by which I mean there is a principle for each intuitively circumscribed cognitive faculty. Thus we have a principle for perception, a different principle for memory, a third principle for induction, and perhaps additional principles of abduction and other kinds of reasoning. This is due to a different kind of explanatory scruple. It looks to many epistemologists as if instances of epistemic achievement can be grouped into natural kinds and fruitfully tackled piecemeal. Those kinds map on to an intuitive carving-up of mental faculties. Indeed, it would not be surprising if one of the two derived from the other, but the priority here is obscure. At any rate, the epistemic principles to be found in the literature follow the contours of a mind divided into kinds of cognitive capacities.[5]

Some epistemic principles might be single-step imperatives, as are the ones governing perception and memory, above. I understand these one-step principles as limiting-case inferences that are justification-preserving. Epistemologists have carefully attended to these because they appear to be the likeliest candidates for being fundamental and basic to our cognition. When we move away from mundane cases of justified belief to rarified cases involved in, say, good scientific inference, the long chains of epistemic principles governing a conclusion may be quite complex.[6]

When epistemic principles are formulated, they are explicit to the philosopher doing the formulating. They may or may not have a psychological reality in the reasoner to whom the principles are attributed. Thus, epistemic principles need not be consciously or straightforwardly causally explicit in the epistemic agent. This keeps open the possibility that the underlying realization mechanism is the system of causes that can be understood normatively, which would be a kind of naturalism that I am sympathetic to (Pollock and Cruz 1999). Perhaps we would then be inclined to say that the epistemic principles supervene on the epistemic agent's psychology, but I take that to be a more partisan commitment than is necessary for present purposes.

Note, too, that the schema does not identify a relation that is *merely* causal in any straightforward sense. If ψ_n were merely causally related to $\psi_1, \ldots, \psi_{(n-1)}$, then principles would be instances of causal (perhaps counterfactual-supporting) analyses of the relations between mental states. This would leave out any role for the contents of the various mental states involved in the inference. Presumably it is the contents of the mental states that persuade us that the principles yield rational or justified beliefs.

3

Against the backdrop of this conception of epistemic principles, I am now able to say something about how we might understand certain kinds of skepticism. Here, I engage some familiar kinds, but I acknowledge that it would take some work to adapt the framework I am advocating to other kinds.

Consider the challenge that hackneyed external-world skepticism presents us with. Descartes believes that the world is more-or-less as he perceives it, but his perceptual evidence is wholly compatible with an alternative scenario where he is being deceived by an evil genius. After all, in the case where he is misled by a sufficiently powerful deceiver, there is simply no way he could ferret out the deception. Everything would seem to him as it would in the case with no evil genius and no villainous deceit. The combination of two factors—that the alternative hypothesis has nothing obviously wrong with it, and that the alternative hypothesis is completely at odds with what we believe—is devastatingly powerful in leading us to question whether our ordinary beliefs about the external world are justified (Stroud 1984; Greco 2000).

It appears that Descartes is appealing to a fairly agreeable consideration, namely something like: Evidence for the belief that p fails to adequately justify that p if the evidence is entirely equally compatible with some other belief that is in tension with that p. To be sure, there is need for refinement since, among other worries, the phrase "in tension with" is not at all clear. On some readings, this demand on reason or knowledge is completely dubious. My evidence for the belief that Earth is roughly spherical is completely compatible with the possibility that such claims are part of a massive and elaborate hoax played on me along with some bizarre optical illusions involving objects on the horizon. And it would appear that the hoax hypothesis is in tension with my actual belief. Is this enough to make the hoax hypothesis the basis for a skeptical argument? I do not think so, and that suggests that there must be other considerations at work that determine which "in tension" possibilities are the relevant ones. As a first pass, it looks very much as if the two alternatives need to belong to scaffoldings of evidence and belief that are sufficient to sustain them. An elaborate shape-of-Earth hoax would require massive effort and engineering. Maintaining the hoax would be daunting and overwhelming, as we could imagine a thousand simple ways that I might seek to expose the charade. The scaffolding of evidence for the hoax hypothesis is fragile and easily undermined, and thus insufficient to sustain the hypothesis as a viable skepticism-inducing competitor to my ordinary beliefs. There is no question that more imaginative accounts of the nature of the hoax might make it more and more difficult to uncover. At the limit we would be presented with something equivalent to an evil genius hypothesis. Still, for scenarios short of the evil genius hypothesis (or its equivalents), their mere possibility does not seem sufficient for compromising the rationality of my ordinary beliefs. This appears to be because those scenarios are subject to considerable evidential considerations—ones either already had at the time the scenario is proposed, or ones easily available once the scenario is a live possibility—against them.

As a general account of which possibilities create enough tension to generate skeptical arguments, this is far too vague to be anything more than a research-direction.[7] For our purposes here, though, it will do, since the external-world skeptic I have in mind has engineered a possibility where the collateral evidence *is* as durable as the evidence for the claim that the world is as it appears. This is because there is, by hypothesis, no collateral evidence that could have a bearing on the rival scenarios.

So, the external-world skeptic is offering a possibility that ought to at least make us nervous about the justificatory status of some of our ordinary beliefs. But what specific epistemic principle is at work here in the skeptical challenge? It seems that often, in the literature, this question has been dodged by attempting to capture skeptical claims via a theory of epistemic defeat. The way the account usually goes has it that the existence of alternative possibilities that undermine the connection from evidence to a belief, constitutes a defeater for that belief. The theory of defeat has, in turn, been treated as a part of the overall epistemic framework that is separate from particular epistemic principles. Sometimes this separation has been made explicit.[8] The idea is that we can see that the skeptical challenge ought to weaken our conviction with respect to our ordinary beliefs, and this weakening has been thought to take place at the pillar between evidence and belief. I now, however, think that treating the skeptical challenge as an instance of epistemic defeat separate from a framework of epistemic principles is a mistake, or at least a serious infelicity in nomenclature.

Think of it this way. Suppose someone fails to acknowledge that reasoning of Descartes's sort is cogent, and suppose that she does not have some account of why this is so. She simply shrugs and says that Cartesian reasoning does not undermine her ordinary beliefs. What we would want to say in response is that Descartes appears to be appealing to a manner of reasoning that surely we must all take seriously because there are many non-skeptical compelling applications of that reasoning. We might bolster our case through examples—by, for instance, offering a court case where the evidence is equally compatible with guilt or innocence, so that epistemically (though not legally, in the U.S. legal system) we should suspend judgment. Or we might rehearse live controversies in science where a rival theory of a phenomenon explains the data as well as the received view, and also does well on non-evidential scientific virtues. We would be inviting our reticent interlocutor to appreciate that there is a general strategy of reasoning that governs good cognition in the relevant circumstances. We are urging the normative status of a *principle*, and we are attributing to it the content-neutrality that seemed distinctive of principles. This is a more illuminating appraisal of what is going on than merely invoking epistemic defeat. In this case, claiming that the skeptical argument defeats the beliefs of the stubborn reader of Descartes says nothing of the manner of defeat or the power of the Cartesian strategy. This is why I prefer to attribute to the skeptic a specific principle of reasoning. The principle, I expect, is something like this:

(DE)   If *S* possesses total evidence *e*, and if *e* does not discriminate between two or more conflicting conclusions, then it is not rational for *S* to believe one of those conclusions.

Call this the *discriminating evidence principle*. The discriminating evidence principle is a powerful constraint on our reasoning, and is crucial in both rarified scientific and mundane reasoning. Should we understand DE as being content-neutral, like other principles? There are at least two reasons to do so. First, it seems that we can readily make DE consciously explicit in ourselves by reflecting on the intelligibility and plausibility of DE. Once we do that, many find DE unassailable in its content-neutral form. For any evidence and for any conclusion, if that evidence does not discriminate, then it is inadequate for drawing a conclusion. The second reason to think that DE is content-neutral is, again, the clear need for cognition to be sufficiently general. It might well be adaptive to be able to reason about anything at all, and a principle like DE might well need to be deployed with respect to any kind of evidence and belief. If DE were restricted in its content, we would be subject to determinate kinds of cognitive error where alternative possibilities, even when salient and reflectively considered, would mysteriously fail to undermine our beliefs.

Now, if we understand DE as content-neutral, then it seems even to apply to beliefs that are on first blush positively sustained by other principles. To illustrate, recall our perceptual principle (for convenience, I will take

Audi's as representative): "If a person has a clear sensory impression that x is F (or of x's being F) and on that basis believes that x is F, then this belief is prima facie justified." The perceptual principle serves us well in cognition. By and large, we believe and we are justified in believing that things are as they perceptually seem to us. We have at our disposal, then, an argument for commonsense realism that might go as follows:

(1)   I appear to have two hands.

(2)   Therefore, it is reasonable for me to believe that I have two hands.

The connection between (1) and (2) in the commonsense realist's argument is legitimated by the perceptual principle. Of course, the conclusion remains defeasible, but it strikes one as reasonable as far as it goes. The external-world skeptic, however, claims that any application of the perceptual principle can be undermined in light of the discriminating evidence principle. Thus, the skeptic points out that,

(3)   I may right now be subject to the deception of an evil genius; therefore it is not reasonable for me to believe that I have two hands.

And the connection between (1), (2), and (3) is legitimated by DE. Our perceptual evidence simply does not discriminate between the world being as we think it is and the world as a fabrication of an evil genius. Therefore, claims the skeptic, it is not epistemically reasonable for us to prefer one belief to the other, regardless of the apparent applicability of the perceptual principle. For the external-world skeptic, this is the end of the line, as there is no possible evidence available that would tip the balance back in favor of the perceptual principle. This reasoning can seemingly easily be applied to our memory principle or inductive principle or, perhaps, any other proper principle of epistemic justification. Through arguments like this, skepticism can seem to have a dramatic and crushing power over our pretensions to rationality. By pushing to the limit the application of a principle that is at the same time innocuous and crucial in our cognition, the skeptic has completely undermined our epistemic confidence. Can skepticism really be this potent so easily?[9]

It is illuminating here to deflect some anti-skeptical positions that I think go wrong. One way of resisting skepticism alleges that epistemic principles that articulate defeasible justification *already* address skepticism. Beliefs that are defeasibly justified are often viewed as *prima facie* justified. Their prima facie justifiedness, it is sometimes thought, itself constitutes additional justificatory power, so that the agent's evidence is precisely not equipoised in the way that is required by the skeptic's use of (DE). By this account, that a belief is prima facie justified is enough to tip the balance in favor of, for instance, the perceptual belief or the memory belief.[10] Indeed, some epistemologists might well think that the very point of the prima facie status had by the justifying power of epistemic principles is to break the deadlock between belief and non-belief.

It is not entirely clear what conception of prima facie justification is adequate to dispatch skepticism so readily, but one way to charitably reconstruct this view is as follows: Suppose that agents could entertain propositions without at all subjecting them to epistemic appraisal through the machinery of epistemic principles.[11] By this hypothesis, any proposition entertained by an epistemic agent initially enjoys full epistemic neutrality in the sense that it is neither justified nor unjustified, nor is mere suspension of judgment one way or the other the proper epistemic stance. From that condition of neutrality, an epistemic principle might then be deployed. For example, if the proposition is perceptual, then it might well enjoy a prima facie justified status in light of the perceptual principle. The anti-skeptical argument at hand wants to treat the skeptic's appeal to (DE) as applicable only to propositions in the state of full neutrality. Once the proposition gains some justificatory momentum through an epistemic principle, it can no longer be subject to the skeptical challenge.

I confess that I find this doctrine exceedingly strange. The prima facie justified status of beliefs that originate in genuine epistemic principles is first and fundamentally a recognition of fallibility. The mere recognition of fallibility, however, should not be conflated with a positive reply to skepticism. Two more specific worries about this conception of epistemic principles present themselves. The first is that this anti-skeptical response fails to make sense of the appeal of skepticism in the first place. It has been seen by many to be a desideratum of an account of skepticism, that it should explain skepticism's appeal and traditional role in our philosophical imagination. Treating the prima facie justificatory impetus of epistemic principles as *by itself* nullifying, for instance, external-world skepticism, leaves it mysterious as to why anyone would have been impressed with this kind of skepticism in the first place. All one would need in order to have an effective reply to Descartes in the Second Meditation would be to proclaim that epistemic principles offer prima facie justification, and that is enough to tip the balance in favor of perceptual beliefs even in the face of the proposal that we are being deceived by an evil genius. And that's it? It would not seem so, because it looks rather like the skeptic is taking into account the prima facie impetus of epistemic principles, and saying that, in spite of such prima facie justifiedness, there is yet an undefeated possibility that is equally adequate to the data of the senses but is incompatible with the beliefs that the agent maintains are justified.

Nor, incidentally, would an account that assigned a default positive epistemic status to a belief help here. It might be thought that the belief that p, when p is the output of perception, is justified until there is some defeater for it, because *all* beliefs are justified until there is some defeater. This can be understood as due to a kind of innocent-until-proven-guilty impulse.[12] This will not help in the skepticism case, though, because the external-world skeptic is offering a claim—that we are brains-in-vats or deceived by an evil genius—that we would not want to count as justified simply because we have no defeater for it. It is simply not the case that any belief that presents itself for reflection is justified until such time as a defeater for it is found. We instead wonder *whether* to accept as justified a belief that we entertain. But merely having some other mundane belief, like "there is a chair before me," is not enough to defeat the skeptic's claim. Again, this is because that ordinary belief is not incompatible with the skeptic's proposal. What seems to be needed is a solution to the skeptical problem that will allow us break the deadlock.

The second problem with this anti-skeptical response comes into stark relief when we attempt to makes sense of justified belief in cases where principles are in tension. Consider cases where the perceptual principle certifies a belief as prima facie justified, while the memory principle at the same time declares the same belief as unjustified. Perception delivers that p, while memory delivers that *not-p*. The Müller–Lyer illusion may well be a case of this sort. Familiarly, the illusion arises when looking at two lines of equal length where one is bounded by outward-pointing arrowheads and the other by inward-pointing arrowheads. The line with the outward-pointing arrowheads appears to be longer than the line with the inward-pointing arrowheads, so that the perceptual principle licenses the belief that they are *not* of equal length. But anyone who recalls having the illusion explained and recalls measuring the lines herself ought, it would seem, to believe that the lines *are* of equal length. And this memory-belief also enjoys a prima facie justified status. Which belief, then, is prima facie justified?

The question at hand is not one about which belief ultimately has the greater evidence in its favor, as I am imagining a case where we simply see the Müller–Lyer figure and simply remember that the lines are of equal length. The question being asked here is, at the moment that we look at the Müller–Lyer illusion, which belief is prima facie justified? Answering this question may appear to require developing a hierarchy of epistemic principles so that we might be able to judge which beliefs among those produced according to proper principles are more justified if they should be in tension. This, I submit, would be a misadventure. It is not the case that epistemic principles are somehow ordered in a way that makes some trump others in terms of prima facie justifiedness. Rather, epistemic principles generate beliefs that ought, with respect to the proposition in question, to move the epistemic agent away from a state of disbelief or neutrality to a state of belief pending more evidence. If two or more epistemic principles yield beliefs that are in tension, both or all of those beliefs are prima facie justified (Senor 1996). What is required is acquiring more evidence to resolve the tension between beliefs.

The case of illusory perceptual figures is such that more evidence is available, and with the Müller–Lyer figure the matter is settled once the lines are measured. (DE) is about evidence itself, though, and this is the important fact that the anti-skeptical position here fails to accommodate. (DE) makes a claim about what is reasonable to believe when there is no recourse to further evidence. In this way, it specifies what to believe in the case where there are two or more beliefs in tension, and where evidence does not help. The mandate of (DE) applies even when the beliefs are prima facie justified, and it can overcome prima facie justification. Cognition requires just such a principle if there are going to be times when the evidence remains resolutely equivocal. That is what makes the skeptic's use of (DE) legitimate.

To return, then, to my diagnosis of skepticism: I claim that the external-world skeptic is appealing, in her reasoning, to a perfectly intelligible epistemic principle; and this principle, when applied to instances of our perceptual principle, yields the skeptical result. My understanding of external-world skepticism, then, is different from most accounts of how such arguments work. I treat skepticism as showing that some of our epistemic principles are in tension in the sense that, when applied to one another, the outcome is a kind of cognitive breakdown. This understanding of skepticism might well lead us to a pragmatic resignation. The resignation is due to the fact that we can be brought to see what is going on in skeptical arguments, and we can see that their rational credentials are an inevitable result of the epistemic principles that we employ. We can see that the perceptual principle and (DE) usually only conflict locally and in a way that is important to our reasoning; we would be worse off as cognitive agents if these principles never conflicted locally. Only in the skeptical case, and when the principles involved are made consciously explicit (i.e., when we are doing philosophy that attends to skepticism), are our reasonings massively undermined.

Clearly the discriminating evidence principle is *most readily* activated with respect to ordinary empirical beliefs and requires some work to see that its content-neutrality makes it applicable to other epistemic principles. This is part of the explanation for why we must be brought around to seeing the force of skepticism, and why—as Hume artfully observed—it loses its grip on us so easily when we turn away from philosophy. Our perceptual principle is central to our cognition, so naturally there is some resistance to undermining it. We can thus conclude that our epistemic principles are shaped to accommodate our reasonings about ordinary beliefs. Indeed, we would not be able to reason in the way that we do without them. The value of our epistemic principles is not merely instrumental. Rather, we should think that the value is constitutive of the cognition itself. Recognition of that intrinsic value—our susceptibility to skeptical challenges notwithstanding—is the pragmatic element of our appreciation of skepticism in the framework I have offered.

4

I find the above pragmatic resignation appealing, in that it accounts both for the power of skepticism and for how tenuous and elusive it is. Moreover, it fits with a broader view of our cognitive lives as not smoothly integrated and unified but instead as a collection of epistemic processes that do not necessarily fully cohere, and that tend to break down when confronted with rarified reflection and speculation.[13]

In this final section, however, I want to advance a stance that is less defeatist with respect to skepticism. It is worth reflecting on the strategy of external-world skepticism in terms of what would be required for our ordinary beliefs to survive the challenge and be resolved as justified. The skeptic maintains that there can be no evidence in the sense of additional justified beliefs that can overturn the skeptical challenge, and in that regard I am inclined to agree with her. But, as the entire framework of epistemic principles suggests, acquiring evidence in the form of additional justified beliefs is not the only way that a belief can become justified. Indeed, this is a powerful virtue of the account because it is how the account avoids an infinite regress of justification, namely by having a belief justified if it answers to one of our epistemic principles, not all of which call for justified beliefs in their antecedents. We may wonder, then, whether there is any epistemic principle that we can apply to the output of the discriminating evidence principle in order to show that its application in skeptical arguments is illicit. Obviously there is no straightforward way of applying a principle like the perceptual principle to the output of (DE). We cannot literally perceive that the skeptic's application of (DE) is defective. We saw above, however, that (DE) could readily apply to the deliverances of other epistemic principles such as the perceptual principle. What happens when we apply (DE) to its own output? It would seem that the content-neutrality of (DE) allows for such an application. And if we can craft a case where the skeptic's use of (DE) is possibly defective, but where the skeptic's evidence with respect to the application of (DE) does not discriminate, then it would seem that the skeptical challenge is in substantial trouble.

Surely it is possible for an application of the discriminating evidence principle to be defective, and for it to be reasonable to believe that this is so. Imagine this: You firmly and clearly remember that your conscious and nonconscious applications of the discriminating evidence principle is defective. Make this scenario as vivid as you like, so that, perhaps, you have a clear recollection that a cognitive neuroscientist told you that have a rare brain defect that compromises your application of the discriminating evidence principle.[14] This would be an instance of invoking the memory principle in a scenario that undermines the (DE) principle. Now, you may well have reason to consider another explanation—namely, that you are misremembering this bizarre story of the defectiveness of your applications of the discriminating evidence principle. But this cannot be enough to cast doubt on this deployment of your memory principle, unless we simply stipulate the primacy of the discriminating evidence principle.

Or suppose that you have abundant inductive evidence that you chronically misapply the discriminating evidence principle. That is, suppose that you keep a careful log of all the times in the past year you have consciously or unconsciously applied (DE), and you discover while looking over it that you are mostly incorrect in its application (i.e., you think it applies when it does not, or vice versa). Here, an inductive principle appears in a scenario that undermines your (DE) principle. You may think that another explanation is that your inductive evidence is suspect; again, however, this appears to be begging the question in favor of the discriminating evidence principle.[15]

Likewise it is possible for (DE) to be defective without the skeptic or the skeptic's interlocutor knowing that it is or having any inkling that it is. When it seems to you that the discriminating evidence principle applies, it *might* well be the case that you are forgetting or are not in a position to appreciate the abundant evidence that your application of the discriminating evidence principle is completely defective.

In sum, one can seemingly be skeptical with respect to the discriminating evidence principle; and if one is, then most other kinds of skepticism—including those of the Cartesian or Humean or Russellian sort, relying as they do on the discriminating evidence principle—will be nullified, because the commonsense realist can marshal these observations to build a case against skepticism. The external-world skeptic argues that it is unreasonable to believe that the world is as our senses claim it is. The reasoning, recall, went like this:

(1) I appear to have two hands.

(2) Therefore, it is reasonable for me to believe that I have two hands.

(3) I may right now be subject to the deception of an evil genius; therefore it is not reasonable for me to believe that I have two hands.

Here the perceptual-principle connection between (1) and (2) was undermined by the (DE) principle, which led to (3). Now, another iteration of (DE) might offer

(4) I may be misapplying (DE); therefore it is not reasonable for me to retract my earlier argument (namely, 1 and 2).

(4) is again sustained by (DE). My claim is that this argument arises out the very content-neutrality of (DE) that the skeptic exploited in the first place. Here, (DE) is being used to neutralize an earlier instance of (DE), and it looks like the skeptical argument is undermined. The same strategy that the skeptic is using against commonsense beliefs is now being used against the skeptic. A merely possible epistemically defective condition is postulated, and this defective condition is being marshaled to discredit one of our beliefs. In this case, that belief is the belief that the skeptical challenge undermines our ordinary reasoning.

We are left with a kind of skepticism that is exotic and boggling, but it is not clear that anything is wrong with it. It is crucial to insist here that the fact that (DE) is being undermined cannot, by itself, constitute a victory for external-world skepticism. It is not as if the skeptic can accept that the content-neutral version of (DE) implodes, and treat that as showing that our reasoning is in general bollixed up. The ordinary reasoning that leads to the conclusion that the world is as it appears to be does not employ (DE), and stands on its own as yielding a prima facie justified belief. The initial argument for our commonsense beliefs employing the perceptual principle shows that.

Nor does the implosion of (DE) threaten to undermine its use in what appear to be legitimate contexts, such as reasoning in the law or in science, where some rival hypotheses really do appear to undermine the justified-ness of our beliefs. The discriminating evidence principle can be applied to itself, but that does not imply that it *must* be applied to itself in every context of reasoning. It is the skeptic who is insisting on a fully content-neutral understanding of (DE), and who is deploying (DE) in the case where no further evidence can be brought to bear. If the skeptic insists on her case, then the commonsense realist can deploy (DE) in the same fash-ion, but in ordinary reasoning (DE) yields to evidence that can make a dif-ference, if any can. The implosion of (DE) looks to be wholly the result of treating it as completely content-neutral. This implosion suggests that it is not content-neutral in the way that other epistemic principles are;[16] there are, after all, reasons to resist content-neutrality. For instance, one might be sufficiently impressed with work on the domain-specificity of cogni-tive capacities, such that claims to full generality even in central-system thought become suspect. Evolution may well have kludged together our reasoning system, and (DE) might have been selected for use only in mundane contexts. This, of course, is all wholly speculative, but the hand-waving is a gesture against the inevitability of the content-neutrality of (DE). I urge that we ought not to accept a content-neutral form of (DE) as a normative principle on reasoning.

The argument, recall, for (DE) being content-neutral was our tendency to reflectively endorse something like (DE) when it is made consciously ex-plicit, and the thought that cognition should be sufficiently general to in-sulate us from potentially dangerous cognitive illusions. There are now obvious replies to both arguments. First, it would seem that we can be wrong in what we endorse as a normative principle if the epistemic con-sequences are sufficiently intolerable. Becoming cognizant of the intoler-ability of the results of a principle constitutes further reflection on that principle. The commonsense realist does view the skeptical argument as in-tolerable, and the implosion of skepticism above ought to make the argu-ment (and the fully content-neutral version of the principle that generated it) intolerable to the skeptic, too. A different way of putting this is to claim that the content-neutral version of the (DE) is not one of our principles, though we can mistakenly think that it is. We had believed that a com-pletely content-neutral form of (DE) was one of our principles, but the only reason we thought that was because we thought that it had a legiti-mate role in compelling skeptical arguments. Once it is seen that it does not work in skeptical arguments, we have no reason to think that it is one of our principles. Epistemologists should instead hunt for more content-specific versions of (DE).

Perhaps the skeptic's best ploy is to resist the claim that we can be defective with respect to deploying (DE). In one respect this looks to be a hopeless gambit. Since epistemic principles operate through some portion of our psychology, it would be remarkable if this part of our psychology were immune from error. Still, matters would be clearer if we had a more specific articulation of (DE) going wrong. Consider two conflicting conclusions that are compatible with an agent's total evidence, and where the agent is on the brink of believing that the conclusions are compatible with her total evidence. To craft a scenario where (DE) is defective, we can appeal to the machinations of a discrimination demon. The discrimination demon maliciously switches an agent's belief that her total evidence fails to discriminate to the belief that her evidence *does* discriminate, and thus that one of two conclusions is to be preferred on the basis of this evidence. If the agent is pressed to reflect on the way in which her evidence discriminates, she may well detect that her evidence does not in fact discriminate. Unfortunately, when she is on the brink of forming the belief that (DE) has indeed been violated and that she should suspend belief in the conclusions, the discrimination demon again performs a switch. A parallel tale may be told regarding our belief that a particular conclusion is favored by our total evidence as against an alleged competitor. The discrimination demon will switch that belief to the belief that the total evidence fails to discriminate. Alas, this might be the condition that we are all in.

Given that it appears possible for us to be defective in deploying (DE), the skeptic may urge something more like a phenomenalist's analogue to (DE): If on our total evidence, an hypothesis *appears* not to discriminate, then it is irrational to prefer the original belief.[17] The thinking is, just as we cannot be wrong about how things visually appear to us, we cannot be wrong about it *seeming as if* a belief is subject to the discriminating evidence principle. The skeptic may insist that all that is required is that it appears to us "from the inside" that the skeptical challenge is an instance of the discriminating evidence principle being properly deployed.

I have some concerns about phenomenalism in general, as I am persuaded that we can be wrong about how things *appear* to us in the perceptual case.[18] I am therefore tempted to maintain that we can be wrong in whether it *seems* to us that our total evidence fails to discriminate. Even putting aside those doubts about phenomenalism, however, there is something suspicious about this move on the skeptic's part. Suppose the skeptic opts for a consistently phenomenal reading of (DE). That would mean that in the initial argument against commonsense realism, the skeptic is claiming that the skeptical challenge relies on the appearance of the applicability of the discriminating evidence principle. Skepticism would thereby show, not that we are *unjustified* in maintaining our ordinary beliefs, but that we *appear* to be unjustified in maintaining our beliefs. Admittedly, this appearance is according to our own lights, and that might be thought to be sufficient to secure the skeptical conclusion. Notice, though, that the parallel move in the perceptual argument is precisely what the skeptic is resisting. The commonsense realist employs the perceptual argument to draw the conclusion that the world *is* the way that it appears to be. The external-world skeptic is not (usually) denying that the commonsense realist is correct to think that the world appears a certain way. Rather, the skeptic is denying the realist's conclusion, namely that one can go from this claim about how the world appears, to a claim about how the world is. The way this inference is undermined, again, is to imagine a situation in which the appearance is consistent with a quite different state of affairs than the one that is proposed by the commonsense realist. If the skeptic insists on a phenomenal reading of the discriminating evidence principle, then she is claiming as legitimate an inference from the total evidence not *seeming* to discriminate, to a conclusion that the total evidence does not *actually* discriminate. The skeptic has helped herself to just the kind of inference that skepticism aims in general to reject.[19] The commonsense realist may object that, just as it is illegitimate by the skeptic's lights to draw a conclusion about how the world is from how it appears in the perceptual case, so too it is illegitimate to draw a conclusion about what is justified or unjustified from what appears to be justified or unjustified. The potential gap between appearance and reality in the realm of justification may be a difficult to appreciate, but all that is required to create that gap is a scenario in which the appearance is consistent with a quite different state of affairs than the one that is concluded by the skeptic. The anti-skeptical skeptical scenarios at the beginning of this section are just such scenarios.

I conclude that the dialectical strategy of skepticism can be used to undermine skepticism, by compromising the integrity of the discriminating evidence principle. Since it is possible that when confronted with skeptical arguments we are incompetently applying the discriminating evidence principle, it is unjustified for us to conclude that the skeptical challenge is successful in undermining our ordinary beliefs. What of skepticism, then, and its traditional command over the philosophical imagination? We can take on a pragmatic resignation with respect to the implosion of skepticism. That is, in the spirit of resignation we can see how we might have thought that (DE) could be deployed in a content-neutral form, because the content-neutral version of (DE) appears, on first inspection, to be reflectively pristine. The above considerations, however, show that the content-neutral version is untenable; and that, in turn, shows that the content-neutral version of (DE) is not one of our normative epistemic principles— and thus cannot be used in skeptical arguments. The skeptic's challenge is no less exotic than the troubling application of (DE) to itself. In both cases an esoteric mere possibility is employed to undermine a piece of reasoning that would appear to lead to an epistemically positive belief. On the other hand, there may yet remain considerations that urge pragmatism here. (DE) might be so very neutral that we can treat it as *almost* fully so, and that will tend to invite us to craft mistakenly anxiety-inducing skeptical arguments. Our temptation is so strong that perhaps we need not resist it all of the time. But is there really a reason for skepticism? The answer looks to be "no."

Acknowledgments

I am much indebted to Jonathan Vogel, Melissa Barry, Alan White, and Will Dudley for years of conversation on these and closely related issues. John Pollock's influence on my approach infuses the entire essay, and is much appreciated, and Jonathan Weinberg's comments on a version of this essay were invaluable. Thanks also to Michael Bergmann, John Greco, Tom Kelly, Brad Armour-Garb, Ron McClamrock, Youngshin Hahn, Joe Sheiber, P. J. Graham, Kris Kirby, Scott Sturgeon, and an anonymous referee for this volume, and to audiences at SUNY Albany, at Williams College, at the Canadian Symposium on Skepticism, and at the seventh Annual Inland Northwest Philosophy Conference.

Notes

1. This is not the same as saying that the skeptic must herself endorse the rational procedure or principles as rational. Some skeptics may well claim to merely take on the mantle of rationality in order to advance a skeptical claim. In this case, it is only the skeptic's interlocutor who needs to accept a framework of epistemic principles. I will neglect this subtlety in what follows, but it must be noted from the outset that these reflections on skepticism and skeptical arguments are aimed only at those who take reasons and reasoning seriously.

2. Justifiedness is the premiere epistemically positive property that philosophers focus on, but there are others. See, e.g., Goldman's (1986) discussion of *power* and *speed*.

3. See also Van Cleve's (1979) discussion of generation principles and transmission principles.

4. Sellars (1975) talks about this as *transmitting reasonableness*.

5. Two points: First, I do not mean to be committing to a historically accurate sense of faculty psychology. Rather, the phrase captures the typical principles approaches to epistemology. Second, the tidy identification of kinds of cognition suggested by the usual collection of epistemic principles strikes me as a glaring limitation of the literature on epistemic principles, especially given the attention to naturalized, i.e., more scientifically realistic, epistemology in the last thirty years. Here I am merely describing the literature's division of mental faculties, not endorsing it. See Sturgeon forthcoming for a nuanced discussion of this issue. My own more naturalistic approach to epistemic principles can be found in Cruz manuscript.

6. This observation is the basis of the liaison between epistemology and artificial intelligence research in Pollock's work (e.g., Pollock 1995). Since epistemologists will sometimes be incapable of following the complex interactions between principles, it is useful to encode the principles in an artificial reasoner. The epistemologist will then have a summary of the interaction of the principles that can be assessed for intuitive reasonableness. For the specific discussion of induction, see Pollock and Cruz 1999, 234–238.

7. For a different kind of theory of relevance, see Greco 2000, chap. 8.

8. For instance, Pollock and I talk of different levels of epistemic theorizing, and locate a theory of defeat at a higher level than theories of particular kinds of reasoning, in Pollock and Cruz 1999, 153.

9. One anti-skeptical reaction here maintains that, against appearances, the skeptical scenario *is* discriminable, and that, thus, the discriminating evidence principle cannot be used by the skeptic. For instance, Williamson (2000) claims that the intuitions that the skeptic exploits are part of a complex that cannot be readily made sense of as directly impugning our ordinary knowledge claims. Instead, he argues, our ordinary knowledge may be thought fundamental to the conceptual framework that we deploy in assessing skeptical scenarios. If that is so, then our worry that we do not know the things we ordinarily claim to know may be a kind of conceptual illusion. I am sympathetic with this strategy, very broadly conceived, in the sense that I will ultimately claim that skeptical scenarios can be discriminated from mundane ones; but my approach is quite different from Williamson's.

10. I thank Michael Bergmann and John Pollock for pressing this point.

11. This way of putting things casts the issue of how epistemic norms work in a more active, self-reflective way than I maintain. In my view, norms are deployed more or less automatically when a proposition is entertained. Or, even better, by the time a proposition is entertained, it has *already had* its epistemic status calculated,

and this calculation comes *along with* the proposition as it is entertained in consciousness. So, on my rendering, to entertain a proposition is to simultaneously entertain its content as well as its epistemic status for the agent at the moment of entertaining it. Of course, this epistemic status is defeasible and the act of entertaining the proposition explicitly might occasion a recalculation of the proposition's epistemic status. These niceties are set aside, above, to illustrate what I take to be going on in the way that some epistemologists understand prima facie justification.

12. Pollock calls theories of this sort, "negative coherence theories" (Pollock and Cruz 1999, 80–84). Harman (1986) offers a version of this kind of view, but his theory does not assign default justification to *all* beliefs. Instead, beliefs that we actually possess enjoy positive status.

13. I am reminded here of the enduring counter-intuitiveness of, for instance, quantum mechanics. The discomfort we feel when confronted with some of the ways of characterizing quantum-mechanical states could, I expect, be accommodated on an account that identifies a tension between the principles that govern our reasoning about middle-sized objects on the one hand, and scientist's massively complex and ramified reasoning about experimental results and scientific theories.

14. Or, as I would prefer, a defect that compromises the cognitive mechanism on which the (DE) principle supervenes.

15. Here it is being assumed that the begging-the-question principle has a kind of primacy over other principles, but that is also worrisome. What if you are forgetting the massive inductive evidence that you have to the effect that you tend to think you are begging the question when you are not? I will not pursue this possibility here.

16. I am attempting to be generous to content-neutrality here. I actually think that our epistemic principles are not generally fully content-neutral, but that they can mistakenly be taken for such when reflected on consciously.

17. Jonathan Weinberg suggested the phenomenal analogue to (DE) in defending skepticism.

18. For discussion, see Pollock and Cruz 1999, 56–59.

19. I thank Melissa Barry for helping me see the issues here.

References

Audi, R. 2001. *The Architecture of Reason*. Oxford: Oxford University Press.

Austin, J. L. 1961. "Other Minds." In G. Warnock and J. Urmson, eds., *Philosophical Papers*. Oxford: Oxford University Press.

Bonjour, L. 2000. "Toward a Defense of Empirical Foundationalism." In M. DePaul, ed., *Resurrecting Old-Fashioned Foundationalism*. Lanham, Md.: Rowman & Littlefield.

Chisholm, R. 1966. *Theory of Knowledge*. Englewood Cliffs, N.J.: Prentice-Hall.

Cruz, J. Manuscript. *Principles of Mind*.

Goldman, A. 1986. *Epistemology and Cognition*. Cambridge, Mass.: Harvard University Press.

Goodman, N. 1954. *Fact, Fiction, and Forecast*. London: Athlone Press.

Greco, J. 2000. *Putting Skeptics in Their Place*. Cambridge: Cambridge University Press.

Harman, G. 1986. *Change in View*. Cambridge, Mass.: MIT Press.

Plantinga, A. 1993. *Warrant: The Current Debate*. Oxford: Oxford University Press.

Pollock, J. 1989. *Nomic Probability and the Foundations of Induction*. Oxford: Oxford University Press.

Pollock, J. 1995. *Cognitive Carpentry*. Cambridge, Mass.: MIT Press.

Pollock, J., and J. Cruz. 1999. *Contemporary Theories of Knowledge*, 2nd ed. Lanham, Md.: Rowman & Littlefield.

Sellars, W. 1975. "The Structure of Knowledge: (1) Perception; (2) Minds; (3) Epistemic Principles." In H. Castañeda, ed., *Action, Knowledge and Reality*. Indianapolis: Bobbs-Merrill.

Senor, T. 1996. "The Prima/Ultima Facie Justification Distinction in Epistemology." *Philosophy and Phenomenological Research* 56: 551–566.

Sosa, E. 1980. "The Raft and the Pyramid." In P. French, T. E. Uehling, and H. Wettstein, eds., *Midwest Studies in Philosophy*, vol. 5: *Epistemology*. Minneapolis: University of Minnesota Press.

Stroud, B. 1984. *The Significance of Philosophical Skepticism*. Oxford: Clarendon Press.

Sturgeon, S. Forthcoming. *Epistemic Norms*. Oxford: Oxford University Press.

Van Cleve, J. 1979. "Foundationalism, Epistemic Principles, and the Cartesian Circle." *Philosophical Review* 88: 55–91.

Williamson, T. 2000. *Knowledge and Its Limits*. Oxford: Oxford University Press.

13   Skepticism Aside

Catherine Z. Elgin

My goal in this essay is not to defeat skepticism, but to articulate a reasonable epistemological basis for disregarding it. I argue that (1) skepticism is not continuous with ordinary epistemic practice. We do not, as it were, slide down a slippery slope to skepticism simply by raising our epistemic standards. (2) Skepticism is not a viable practical stance; in order to act, we must assume that skepticism is false. But (3) the practical is inseparable from the theoretical, so an assumption that is necessary for practice is at least not unreasonable for theory. The conclusion is not that skepticism is false, but that it can be epistemologically responsible to assume that skepticism is false. The fate of epistemology does not turn on defeating skepticism; for a variety of epistemological problems, we can simply set the skeptical challenge aside.

Descartes's demon is an irritatingly resilient little imp. Whenever a clever epistemologist threatens to disarm him, he feints, parries, and reappears seemingly unscathed. I have not devised a way to permanently squelch him. I doubt that it can be done. But I will not argue for or even exhibit my pessimism here. Rather, I will urge that skepticism should be set aside. That is, I will argue for the practical necessity and epistemological utility of assuming that no skeptical scenario obtains. As I use the term, to assume that p is to take it for granted that p. The point about practicality may seem obvious. Even Descartes (1955, part I, principle III) did not take skepticism to be a practical problem. But, I will suggest, the practical infiltrates the theoretical to a far greater extent than we standardly suppose. If my argument succeeds, it might be feasible to reconstrue epistemology as a branch of practical philosophy. Then the practical necessity would become an epistemological necessity. I shall make no such recommendation. I am content to leave skepticism as a legitimate epistemological concern, so long as we recognize that a variety of important epistemological issues can be fruitfully addressed by prescinding from skepticism, and that doing so is not always question-begging. Perhaps much of epistemology delivers only conditionals of the form, "If no skeptical scenario obtains, then..." But in the absence of reason to believe that its antecedent is false, such a conditional is often worth establishing. My point is that for a variety of important epistemological projects, all that is required is the *assumption* that no skeptical scenario obtains. If I am right, then rather than confronting the problem of skepticism, it is sometimes epistemologically reasonable and responsible simply to set it aside.

Skepticism is often treated as the endpoint of a continuum. As standards for epistemic acceptability rise, they become increasingly hard to satisfy. The higher the standards, the less we know. At the limit, epistemic standards are so demanding that we know (virtually) nothing. Skepticism results (Adler 1981; Lewis 1996). If this is so, skepticism can be blocked only by somehow stopping short of the limit; the tricky question is where to apply the brakes. I suggest, however, that this construal is incorrect. Skeptical scenarios differ significantly from ordinary high-standards scenarios. If I am right, skepticism is an isolated problem rather than being continuous with ordinary epistemic practice.

Let us begin with a familiar epistemological principle:

(R)   An epistemic agent S ought not believe or accept that p unless her evidence, reasons or other grounds rule out the relevant alternatives to p. If her resources do not equip her to rule out a relevant alternative, she should either (a) suspend judgment or (b) get the additional evidence or other support needed to settle the case.

Epistemologists disagree about what resources she can draw on. Empirical evidence, coherence considerations, reliable mechanisms, fit with past practice, and intuitions have been held to make a contribution. For my purposes, such disagreements are unimportant. Let us call the considerations that provide epistemic support for a belief, whatever they are, *reasons*. On this usage, an agent's reasons may include considerations that she is unaware of, such as the reliability of the mechanisms that generate her perceptual beliefs. Epistemologists also differ over the range of alternatives (R) requires ruling out. Since my goal is to investigate the differences between skeptical and nonskeptical scenarios, I shall take it that skeptical alternatives are neither always relevant nor always irrelevant.

My reason for formulating (R) in terms of relevant alternatives is strategic. This formulation provides a simple way to distinguish between skeptical and nonskeptical scenarios. In nonskeptical scenarios, we do not take all alternatives to be relevant. To arrive at a diagnosis, for example, a physician has to rule out all but one of the medical conditions that present a given cluster of symptoms. Those conditions are, in a clinical setting, the relevant alternatives. The physician need not, however, rule out skeptical possibilities since they are medically irrelevant. Were the scenario a skeptical one, both malevolent demons and vitamin deficiencies would need to be excluded before a diagnosis of adrenal malfunction could be made. The distinction between the two scenarios seems worth marking, and the device of relevant alternatives enables us to draw the line. Nothing directly follows about how the criterion of relevance that is operative in a given context bears on the epistemic standing of a claim.

Underlying principle (R) are the virtually platitudinous convictions that (1) epistemically justified or warranted commitments are supported by reasons, (2) the reasons offered in support of a commitment can be better or worse, and (3) a commitment backed by sufficiently good reasons is epistemically acceptable.

Consider an ordinary epistemic predicament: Inspector Hound wants to know who stole the spoons. Since the relevant alternatives are the people who had the motive, means, and opportunity to commit the crime, the only suspects are the scullery maid and the butler. The available evidence implicates them equally. As things stand, Hound cannot responsibly conclude that the butler did it. In his current epistemic circumstances, he should suspend judgment. To solve the case, he needs more evidence. It is in principle possible for him to get more evidence, and it is reasonably clear what sort of evidence he needs. So there seems to be no epistemological barrier to his eventually discovering the culprit. Once he learns, for example, that the maid has an unbreakable alibi, she is exonerated; he can then responsibly conclude that the butler stole the spoons.

Although they may initially seem to take the same form, skeptical arguments turn out to differ significantly from situations like Hound's. Consider a case where a skeptical alternative is relevant. Fox wants to know whether (p) Sam is playing a bassoon. He has what he and pretty much everyone take to be good reasons for thinking that p. He is inclined to believe or accept that p on the basis of those putative reasons. But Fox would be in exactly the same subjective state if q were the case, where q is the skeptical alternative that a malevolent demon is manipulating Fox's disembodied mind to produce in him the mental states he would have if he were an embodied person interacting with a material world as it seems to him that he does. That is why it seems to him that Sam is playing a bassoon.

By principle (R), if Fox is faced with incompatible alternatives p and q, and cannot rule out that q, he is not justified in believing that p. Standardly, an epistemic agent selects among competing alternatives by adducing reasons that support one over the others. If the reasons at hand are not sufficient, it is often open to him to get more. But faced with a skeptical alternative q, he can neither rely on the available reasons nor garner the additional reasons he needs. Since there is no possibility of coming up with such reasons, the availability of a skeptical alternative requires permanently suspending judgment.

By hypothesis, the skeptical alternative is, to *all* epistemically accessible appearances, indistinguishable from its nonskeptical counterpart; so it is pointless for Fox to adduce further reasons. No matter how good his reasons or how plentiful his evidence, it makes no difference. But if this is so, then no matter how bad his reasons or how sparse his evidence, it makes no difference either. Bad reasons are no worse than good ones. The epistemic situation of the scrupulous, meticulous investigator is no better than that of the careless, biased question-beggar.

This might be doubted. After all, one might think, the interconnected, systematically supported beliefs of a scrupulous investigator form a mutually reinforcing network which must make them better than the isolated, fragmentary beliefs of a cavalier question-beggar. Even if neither of them can know, one is inclined to think, surely the scrupulous investigator is epistemically better off. The problem is that the connections that allegedly enable the scrupulous investigator's beliefs to form a mutually supportive structure are suspect. Because a skeptical scenario is one of rampant, undetectable error, in such a scenario evidence must be considered misleading, seemingly secure connections unreliable, reasons spurious. Correlations are undependable, for generalizations hitherto borne out by experience must be considered accidental. The relations that apparently obtain among beliefs and other epistemic commitments within a subject's corpus are untrustworthy. A skeptical alternative thus neutralizes reasons. It renders them inert. With his reasons neutralized, Fox has no basis for believing that Sam is playing a bassoon. He also has no incentive to gather more data or improve his methods for determining such things. Indeed, whatever new information he comes up with, and whatever methods he uses to acquire it, he has no reason to think that he has more evidence or improved methods. By neutralizing reasons, a skeptical argument disengages the mechanisms of epistemic evaluation.

It is relatively easy to concede that the skeptical challenge demonstrates that Fox does not *know*, or is not justified in believing, that Sam is playing a bassoon. And it is relatively easy to concede that the argument generalizes, so that Fox does not know or reasonably believe (much of) anything. But suspending judgment—really suspending judgment—may be harder than it looks. For beliefs do more than represent the world; they also bear on and underwrite action.

Belief is complex. It involves both representing things to be a certain way, and taking that representation to afford a solid basis for inference and action. It is worth prizing these aspects apart. L. Jonathan Cohen does so by distinguishing between what he calls belief and acceptance. I want to use his distinction. But because epistemologists standardly use the term 'belief' for the entire complex (and because I have been using 'belief' in just that way), I shall label what Cohen calls belief *opinion*. So rather than distinguish between belief and acceptance, I shall characterize Cohen's distinction as holding between opinion and acceptance. Opining that *p* is, as he says, "a disposition, when one is attending to issues raised, or items referred to, by the proposition that *p*, normally to feel it true that *p* and false that *not-p*" (Cohen 1992). Opinion then is a psychological disposition to take things to be as the opinion-content says that they are. Acceptance is a willingness to use such a content as a premise in assertoric reasoning or as a basis for action. Acceptance is thus not a disposition to represent, but a disposition to act. To a large extent, of course, opinion and acceptance coincide. We opine much that we accept and accept much that we opine. Still, it pays to distinguish the two, not only because there are exceptions to this generalization (for example, we sometimes accept as a working hypothesis something we do not fully opine), but also because opinion and acceptance function differently. Acceptance is action-oriented in a way that opinion, per se, is not.

The question is whether the suspension of judgment that figures in (R) is a suspension of opinion or a suspension of acceptance. Construed as suspending opinion, suspending judgment is a matter of refraining from feeling that *p* is true and refraining from feeling that *not-p* is true. Construed as suspending acceptance, it is a matter of refraining from taking either *p* or *not-p* as a basis for assertoric inference or action. It is not clear that suspending opinion is something one can do at will (Adler 2002, 55–72). Even if I recognize that it is irrational for me to opine that crickets are dangerous, it may be that I cannot help but feel that they are. It seems that I cannot divest myself of this opinion merely by telling myself to do so. Perhaps by attending to the lack of warrant for my opinion, I can sow in myself seeds of doubt and gradually bring it about that I don't quite *opine* it any more; so even if a mere act of the will is insufficient, there may be a way for me to unseat my opinion. In any case, for my purposes it does no harm to assume that suspension of opinion is possible, so I shall make that assumption. Suspending acceptance is plainly under my voluntary control. If I recognize that my opinion is irrational or unfounded, I can refrain from accepting the opinion-content—that is, from acting on it and from using it in assertoric inferences.

In some cases, of course, both sorts of suspension are entirely reasonable. Since we will never be in a position to know, reasonably opine, or reasonably accept that

(v)   The number of stars is even,

we can and should suspend judgment over whether v is so. Doing this is unproblematic, since withholding opinion and acceptance is relatively uncostly here. Not much else that we are inclined to think or do is undermined by our refraining from feeling that or acting on v. In other cases, the price is higher. If Inspector Hound cannot eliminate either suspect, the case of the stolen spoons will never be solved, both parties will remain under suspicion, and the prospects of recovering the spoons will be considerably diminished. Moreover, our understanding of the theft—its causes, circumstances, and consequences—will remain sparser than we would like it to be. Unfortunate though this may be, it is epistemologically unproblematic. But to assume that such cases afford an avenue for generalizing to a global suspension of belief *is* problematic.

Both Pyrrhonian skeptics and Hume took it that skepticism involves globally suspending belief (Burnyeat 1980). The Pyrrhonists believed that doing so was possible. They took it that belief involves a commitment about how things really are. They maintained that one could forego beliefs entirely and live solely at the level of appearances. Hume (1993, 109–110) denied the possibility of living without belief. The skeptical stance, he maintained, is inherently precarious and short-lived. Insofar as the Pyrrhonist position concerns opinion, I am not at all confident that it can be sustained. But rather than argue against it directly, I want to look at the problem of acceptance. If we withhold acceptance of a contention, we refrain from incorporating it or its negation into our reasoning as an assertoric premise, and refrain from using it or its negation as a basis for action. Sometimes this is a good idea. But to do it across the board would be to forego reasoning and action entirely. Globally suspending acceptance is not just a bad idea, it is in practice impossible.

Action requires assuming that things are one way or another. An agent performs act a because she wants to get b and takes it that by a-ing she will get *b* or improve her prospects of getting *b*. Her taking need not be a matter of full-fledged opinion. She might not quite feel it to be true that by *a*-ing she will get *b* or improve her prospects of getting *b*; so she might not opine that by *a*-ing she will get *b* or improve her prospects of getting *b*. But she has a cognitively pro-attitude of some degree of strength in that direction. Her taking is, moreover, embedded in a background of opinions, acceptances, and perhaps other cognitively pro-attitudes having to do with the situation, her alternatives, and their foreseeable consequences. Her attitude toward the efficacy of *a*-ing is based on background opinions about the way things are, and background acceptances of these opinions as sound. If she wants to buy bread, she goes to the bakery, since she accepts that bakeries are the sorts of places that are likely to sell bread. This acceptance is sustained by a wide cluster of acceptances pertaining to stores, food, commercial transactions, past shopping experiences, and so on. If she were to suspend acceptance of the members of that cluster, she would have no more reason to go the store than she had, for example, to climb a tree, compose a fugue, or howl at the moon in order to get bread. If she were to globally suspend acceptance, she could not act. She would be bereft of agency; for reasons, beliefs, and inferences are integral to action. She would, of course, still be capable of responding to stimuli. But the explanation of her responses would be purely causal. She would be behaving, but not acting—for there would be no reason why she did whatever she did.

If the undefeated skeptical alternative *q* undermines Fox's grounds for accepting that *p*, why shouldn't Fox either accept the disjunction *p* or *q*, or simply opt for *q* rather than *p*? Hound might be remiss in concluding that the butler did it if the evidence tells equally against the maid, but he is certainly within his rights to conclude that either the butler or the maid did it, and hence to orient himself toward the future on the assumption that one of them is the culprit. This might, for example, involve being sensitive to suspicious behavior on the part of the butler and the maid but ignoring, as irrelevant, similar behavior on the part of the gardener, who has already been exonerated. Hound might also take each disjunct separately as a working hypothesis, and see, on further investigation, which hypothesis is more strongly supported. The problem for Fox is that a skeptical scenario provides no orientation toward the future. If a malevolent demon is manipulating his mind, there is no reason to suppose that the regularities he takes himself to have observed so far in fact obtain, or (if they do) that they will continue to obtain. So even if, for example, his past experience provides Fox with ample evidence that if Sam seems to blow, his bassoon will seem to emit a noise, the demon might decide henceforth at random intervals to make it seem to sprout flowers or recite the Gettysburg address or take on the appearance of a frog. In a skeptical scenario, all regularities must be deemed accidental. There is no reason to believe that they will continue to obtain.[1]

This means that Fox cannot feasibly take the skeptical scenario as a working hypothesis, not because the hypothesis is extreme, but because it is indefinite. It portends nothing in particular about the future. That being so, a skeptical scenario cannot provide a basis for action. Action involves a choice among alternatives; a skeptical scenario affords no basis for choice. So the effect of a skeptical argument is not to provide additional alternatives, as the introduction of the case against the maid provides an alternative to the hypothesis that the butler stole the spoons. It is rather to show that any choice is arbitrary. If we cannot accept causal inferences, inductive reasoning, the bearing of evidence on hypotheses, and so on, then *a*-ing in order to get *b* is arbitrary. We have no reason to think that it will work.

Ancient skeptics realized this. They did not think that one could live one's skepticism, if that meant suspending acceptance. Rather, they advised (as Descartes did later, and as Hume thought was inevitable) that we simply act on whatever it is we happen to believe, recognizing all the while that our beliefs are unjustified. If we cannot suspend acceptance, we can at least refrain from endorsing our acceptances. Our second-order attitudes will then have no bearing on our first-order ones. This makes skepticism idle—not in the sense of being trivial, but in the sense of being, like an idling engine, disengaged.

Disengagement, however, may be the least of our problems. Acting on whatever one happens to believe is not always a good policy; whether it is depends on what one happens to believe. Someone who believes that tobacco is not addictive, and therefore takes up smoking, acts unwisely. Even if undefeated skeptical alternatives show that she does not strictly *know* that her belief is false, this does little to mitigate the criticism of her. Nor is the Pyrrhonian policy of acting in accord with the practices of one's community, rather than on the basis of idiosyncratic beliefs, always an improvement. This too may be a good or bad policy, depending on the practices of the community. There are Ecuadorian Indians who, like generations of their forebears, cook in pots made of a clay that contains high levels of lead. This practice is deeply entrenched. Nevertheless, a member of the tribe who continues the practice on the grounds that undefeated skeptical alternatives show that she does not *know* that eating food cooked in these pots causes neurological damage, and that using such pots is a longstanding practice of her tribe, is making a tragic mistake. The problem is not that she is uninformed about the danger; we may suppose that the World Health Organization has provided her with reams of relevant information. But the undefeated skeptical alternative deprives that information of credibility. Having no reason to credit that information, she has no reason to cook any differently from the way her ancestors did.

The problem is vivid in cases of tragically mistaken acceptances and the practices that are based on them. But it also occurs in seemingly benign cases. The World Health Organization physicians can act on the basis of their data on the grounds that doing so accords with the practices of the medical community, but no more than the Ecuadorian Indians have they any reason to do so. As long as the skeptical alternative is relevant and undefeated, all acceptance is groundless.

Kant's (1969, 58–59) distinction between autonomy and heteronomy enables us to locate the source of the difficulty. An autonomous agent acts on laws that she gives to herself, and hence on laws that she can, on reflection, endorse.[2] A heteronomous subject acts on whatever inclinations she happens to have. She is, Kant contends, unfree, because she lives at the mercy of her inclinations. But if a subject is unfree because she acts on the basis of inclinations that she cannot on reflection endorse, she is equally unfree if she acts on the basis of beliefs that she cannot on reflection endorse, for beliefs and desires (or inclinations, as Kant calls them) jointly underwrite action. That is precisely the position the skeptical argument seems to leave her in. Because she has not eliminated the skeptical alternative, her beliefs are groundless. As a practical matter, she cannot globally suspend belief. So the epistemically heteronomous subject has factual beliefs that frame her choices and beliefs about the methods, powers, and resources at her disposal. But these beliefs are ones she just finds herself with, not ones she has any reason to trust. Although she finds herself believing that on previous occasions she has bought bread at the bakery, and finds herself inclined to go to the bakery to buy bread, she has no reason to accept that her beliefs about her past experience have any bearing on her current choice. She might, of course, go to the bakery anyway, since that is what she is most inclined to do. And her past experiences might influence her decision. But she can endorse neither her action nor the influence of her past experiences on her action; they are just things that happen to her. She is under the sway of whatever arbitrary choice-making mechanism happens to be in effect. She finds herself inclined to do this or that, and does whatever she is most inclined to do. But being at the mercy of her inclinations and their influences, she has no authority over the process or its outcome. Behaving in accord with whatever beliefs she happens to have, or living in accord with the practices of whatever community she happens to belong to, is epistemically on a par with flipping a coin.

Still, she accepts some second-order claims that bear on first-order views. To accept a second-order claim is to be disposed to treat it as a basis for assertoric inference or action—that is, to be disposed to think or do something about the first-order considerations it bears on. Suppose, she accepts the second-order contention

(S)   *r* is a reason for *t*.

Then she is disposed to treat *r* as a reason for *t*. This may involve being more inclined to believe, opine or accept *t* in view of her acceptance of *r* than she would be to accept *t* in the absence of any commitment to *r*. But this cannot be the whole story. For there is a difference between taking *r* as a *reason* for *t*, and merely taking *r* as a factor that increases one's inclination to accept that *t*. If she accepts that *r* is a reason for *t*, then she takes it that *ceteris paribus r should* weigh favorably in her epistemic assessment of *t*. Whether or not she is in fact more inclined to accept *t* in view of her acceptance of *r*, by her own lights she should be. Reasons for action are considerations that favor the actions they bear on, and not just influences that prompt one to act.

Perhaps our apparent reliance on reasons is a chimera. Perhaps we are merely self-deluded pawns in the hands of a malevolent demon. This could be so. Nonetheless, we think that we act, and indeed cannot do otherwise. Life presents itself as a series of choices—often forced choices. So whether or not we *really* act (in some metaphysically robust sense of 'really'), we accept that we act. That is, we take the contention that we act as a basis for assertoric inference and for action. In so doing, we accept that we have reasons; we act as if we do. But to treat something as a reason makes it, for all practical purposes, a reason.

Does this just push the difficulty up a level? If a subject's acceptance of (S) is heteronomous, she is still at the mercy of her inclinations—not her first-order inclinations, but her inclinations to treat some things as reasons for others. Clearly second-order heteronomy is no more palatable than first-order heteronomy. Seeking to solve the problem by appeal to third-order considerations, which give her reason to accept certain second-order considerations, which give her reason to accept certain first-order considerations, sets off a disastrous regress. So the question is whether there is any other way to vindicate second-order considerations.

Again, it pays to look to Kant. One formulation of the Categorical Imperative has it that those maxims are acceptable that an agent can endorse as a legislating member of the Kingdom of Ends. These maxims are not only laws that members of the Kingdom of Ends are subject to, they are laws that the members of the Kingdom of Ends *make themselves* subject to. On Kant's view, in the moral realm, legislators enact the laws that bind them. I suggest that the same holds in the epistemic realm. What gives certain second-order claims their authority is that they express standards, rules or principles that epistemic agents can on reflection endorse. Thinking of ourselves as reasonable and rational, we are prepared to accept those second-order considerations as specifying the constraints on what is good in the way of belief.

For our purposes, two aspects of the Kingdom of Ends formulation deserve notice. One is that there are multiple members of the Kingdom of Ends. The Kingdom of Ends is not really a kingdom; it is a commonwealth. Because legislation is enacted only with the agreement of other members of the legislature, the laws of the Kingdom of Ends must be laws that the members can justify to each other. Enacting the epistemic standards that bind us is a collective endeavor. The other is that maxims are accepted on reflection. Kant considers ethical reasoning largely a priori; that is no part of my position. As I see it, to determine whether a statement, rule, standard or method is epistemically acceptable is to assess it in light of relevant epistemic ends, means, resources, pitfalls, and so forth. The question is whether it is in reflective equilibrium with our other epistemic commitments. Whether a consideration is acceptable depends on what else is deemed acceptable. So acceptability is keyed to epistemic circumstances (Elgin 1996).

One might wonder why we should consider ourselves only *legislating* members of a commonwealth of cognitive ends rather than, as it might be, philosopher kings, each capable of issuing epistemic edicts on her own. Consider the situation of such a solitary legislator, Lex. Certain epistemic principles bind him because he considers it reasonable that he, as an epistemic agent, be bound by them. Lex has no grounds for thinking it reasonable for him to be bound by epistemic principles that it would not be reasonable for others to be bound by. And having no grounds for thinking that different principles should apply to different agents, he cannot, on reflection, think it. He thus believes that the principles that reasonably regulate his epistemic practice are suitable for regulating the epistemic practice of *others*. But other epistemic agents should be bound only by principles that they can, on reflection, endorse. So Lex's belief that the principles he endorses are suitable for regulating the epistemic practice of others is true only if those others can, on reflection, endorse those principles. By his own standards then, Lex ought to endorse only such principles as others can reflectively endorse as well. Even if he starts out aspiring to be a philosopher king, Lex turns out to be a legislating member of commonwealth of epistemic ends.

This has its benefits. Setting skepticism aside (or, indeed, refuting skepticism) does not determine what we should believe, or what criteria determine what we should believe. It merely enables us to assume that reasons are engaged, so that the epistemic situation of the scrupulous, meticulous investigator is better than that of the cavalier, biased question-beggar. This does not determine how we tell what makes for a scrupulous, meticulous investigation or how it differs from cavalier, biased question-begging. It notes that each of us has certain second-order commitments that she takes to bear on the acceptability of certain first-order views. But it does not say that these second-order commitments in fact constitute or define good reasons. Some of them probably do not. If reasons are engaged, we have both the opportunity and the responsibility to figure out which second-order considerations are, upon reflection, ones we should be prepared to endorse. By construing ourselves as joint legislators, we control for idiosyncrasy or bias, gain access to a wider range of perspectives and talents, and increase the possibility that unwise endorsements will be recognized, and revised or rescinded. That is, we considerably expand the range of epistemic resources we can draw on. The epistemic commonwealth is, in the end, more powerful than the philosopher king.

The first-person perspective is a perspective of agency. We act for what we take to be reasons, and we assess (or at least take ourselves to assess) both our actions and our reasons. Nor is this assessment idle. Sometimes, it seems, on the basis of our putative assessments we modify courses of action, reasoning strategies, or standards for how reasons should relate to choices. That is to say, we subject our actions to scrutiny, and act on considerations that on reflection we endorse. We do not, of course, subject every action to stringent tests. But in acting (even in acting unthinkingly) we take ourselves and our options to be located in a conceptual space where reasons are relevant, where considerations can be brought to bear to assess alternatives. Kant (1969, 59) maintains that action requires that we consider ourselves free, that is, capable of acting on laws we set for ourselves. His concern is the threat posed by determinism. But arbitrariness is equally threatening. If there are no stable connections between beliefs, desires, preferences, and actions—if we are pawns in the hands of a capricious demon—then no course of action is better than any other. If we believe that this is our situation, we have no basis for choice. But, Kant notes, we cannot help but act, cannot help but choose, hence cannot help but consider ourselves free.

To consider ourselves as free involves taking ourselves to have reasons for what we do. A reason for an action is a consideration that favors that action. To take a consideration to favor an action is to evaluate the action positively in light of that consideration. This requires thinking that the consideration is relevant to the action and that its holding increases the action's desirability or prospects of success. Acting for a reason thus involves being—and taking oneself to be—moved by a consideration because it favors the action. This is possible only if the consideration and its relation to the action are subject to assessment. Such an assessment requires that we have grounds, and requires that we think they are good grounds. That is to say, to act for a reason is to act on the basis of a consideration that we can, on reflection, endorse.

Drawing on Kant, I have argued that skepticism is antithetical to agency. We must assume that reasons are genuine in order to act, and we must act. Still, one might urge, skepticism is a theoretical problem, not a practical one; so the news that the skeptic can't live her skepticism is of limited interest. But action is not limited to things like buying bread. Reasoning, theorizing, deliberating, judging are actions. So if the argument shows that a denial of skepticism is a necessary assumption for action, it is a necessary assumption for theorizing, deliberating, and so forth. And if good theories are products of good theorizing, then good theories rest on the assumption that skepticism is false as well. Acceptance, as Cohen characterizes it, is a disposition to take a consideration as a premise in assertoric inference or as a basis for action. These are not separate things. Inferring is acting.

But the critical point of the argument is that all that is required is the *assumption* that no skeptical alternative obtains. (This is a necessary assumption for doing what we cannot help but do.) We need not demonstrate that this assumption is true; so we need not *prove* that skepticism is false, before getting on with the serious business of epistemology. We are entitled to assume it.

What does this assumption buy us? It puts us in a position to engage in second-order assessment. If we act on reasons that we can on reflection endorse, then the question arises, what sort of reasons should we endorse and why? Whether a consideration favors an action depends in part on the way the world is. So the assumption that we have reasons for action involves the assumption that we have access to the way the world is. This, as yet, says nothing about what affords the access. That is something we need to figure out. But if we set skepticism aside, we are in a position to investigate, to attempt to discover, what affords us access to things, what methods, mechanisms, and reasoning strategies are trustworthy, and how far our trust in such things should extend.

Earlier, I said that skepticism remains a legitimate, if somewhat isolated, epistemological problem. This contention may seem doubtful if theorizing is a form of practice, and practice requires setting skepticism aside. Such a doubt would be misplaced. In order to theorize, we must set skepticism aside—but we can theorize about anything we like, including skepticism. Skepticism thus remains a topic for epistemological investigation, even though it is not a viable stance.[3]

Very roughly the point is this: If a skeptical scenario obtains, all bets are off. Given what has happened so far, anything at all could happen next. If no skeptical scenario obtains, then it is not in principle impossible to figure out what the world is like, and not in principle impossible to act so as to improve our prospects of achieving our ends. We can begin to inquire systematically into questions about the nature and weight of evidence, the reliability of methods, the suitability of epistemic standards, and so forth. In view of the futility of accepting the skeptical scenario, we should simply suppose that it does not obtain.

This says nothing about how we should reason, but it connects second-order reflection with first-order views. It makes possible the assessment of inputs, reasoning strategies, and so forth. Among our beliefs, are beliefs about our epistemic resources. We have beliefs about evidence, methods, reasoning, epistemic standards, and the like. We are inclined to use them to assess our first-order beliefs. By setting skepticism aside, we can bring them on line. We can also evaluate them. We can ask whether our standards of evidence are reasonable and reliable, whether a revision would better accord with the data, would better promote our epistemic goals, and so forth.

A critical question for epistemology is: What is good in the way of belief? If a skeptical scenario obtains, the answer is *nothing*. But if no skeptical scenario obtains, some beliefs are better than others. To act, to reason, to make sense of our perspectives as perspectives on the world, we need to assume that no skeptical scenario obtains. With that assumption on line, reasons are engaged, and we can investigate which beliefs, strategies, and the like are in fact good in the way of belief. We can also investigate how to tell such things. That is, we can get on with epistemology. My point is that all we need to do to start this project, is assume; we need not prove. Moreover, there is no guarantee that the epistemological position which supplies the best answer to skepticism will also supply the best epistemology on the assumption that skepticism is false. That remains to be seen.

Acknowledgments

I am grateful to Jonathan Adler, Scott Brewer, Elizabeth Camp, Stephen Hetherington, Christine Korsgaard, Bradford Skow, Kenneth Walden, and participants in the 2004 Inland Northwest Philosophy Conference for comments on earlier drafts of this essay. I am grateful to the National Endowment for the Humanities for support.

Notes

1. In this way, Humean skepticism emerges from Cartesian skepticism. If Fox is utterly at a loss about how the world is, he has no basis for any particular expectations about the future. If, on the other hand, he is justified in believing that the future will be like the past in specifiable respects, he can evade skepticism. If everything is and always will be just as though he is a normal human being interacting with his environment in the ways he thinks he does, he need only interpret his beliefs as applying within his comprehensive, coherent worldview. Then, as Berkeley and Putnam have argued, his knowledge claims will in general be true. Only his views about their metaphysical underpinnings will be false. This is not a skeptical position. See Berkeley 1970 and Putnam 1981.

2. This is not to say that Kant's ethics is a reflective-endorsement theory. But it follows from the Kingdom of Ends formulation of the categorical imperative that the maxims that satisfy the categorical imperative are ones that the agent can on reflection endorse. My discussion of Kant is plainly indebted to Korsgaard 1996; Korsgaard is not, however, remotely responsible for the use I make of her work.

3. I am grateful to Peter Graham for raising the question discussed in this paragraph.

References

Adler, J. 1981. "Skepticism and Universalizability." *Journal of Philosophy* 78: 143–156.

Adler, J. 2002. *Belief's Own Ethics*. Cambridge, Mass.: MIT Press.

Berkeley, G. 1970. *Principles of Human Knowledge*. Indianapolis: Bobbs-Merrill.

Burnyeat, M. 1980. "Can the Skeptic Live His Skepticism?" In M. Schofield, M. Burnyeat, and J. Barnes, eds., *Doubt and Dogmatism: Studies in Hellenistic Epistemology*. Oxford: Clarendon Press.

Cohen, L. J. 1992. *An Essay on Belief and Acceptance*. Oxford: Clarendon Press.

Descartes, R. 1955. *Principles of Philosophy*. In E. S. Haldane and G. T. R. Ross, trans., *The Philosophical Works of Descartes*, vol. 1. New York: Dover Press.

Elgin, C. 1996. *Considered Judgment*. Princeton: Princeton University Press.

Hume, D. 1993. *An Enquiry Concerning Human Understanding*. Indianapolis: Hackett.

Kant, I. 1969. *Foundations of the Metaphysics of Morals*. Robert Paul Wolff, ed. Indianapolis: Bobbs-Merrill.

Korsgaard, C. 1996. *The Sources of Normativity*. Cambridge: Cambridge University Press.

Lewis, D. 1996. "Elusive Knowledge." *Australasian Journal of Philosophy* 74: 549–567.

Putnam, H. 1981. *Reason, Truth, and History*. Cambridge: Cambridge University Press.

14 Hume's Skeptical Naturalism

Peter S. Fosl

The task of this essay[1] is to describe the relationship between Hume's skepticism and his naturalism, and in doing so to demonstrate the way some of Hume's most important recent commentators have misunderstood both. It's not surprising that commentators have gotten things wrong, since both Hume's skepticism and his naturalism are complex and, perhaps more importantly, on the face of it inconsistent with one another. If one takes seriously the conclusions Hume reaches in those sections of his texts which address skepticism with regard to the senses and reason, it's easy to conclude that Hume can have no basis either for asserting claims about an independently and continuously existing natural reality, or for reasoning out the lines of any naturalistic theory of the world and the humans who inhabit it. To be consistently skeptical would seem to prohibit advancing any truth-claims or positive theories at all—especially those of the power and scope of Hume's naturalism. And yet, Hume does advance truth-claims—claims composing a positive, elaborate, naturalistic theory of the self, the world, and others. Is Hume's philosophical work then self-subverting?

Skirting this issue, some interpreters have ignored or demeaned Hume's naturalism and focused instead on his skepticism. Others have maintained that Hume's naturalism somehow defeats or expels his skepticism. The former holds for Hume's contemporaries—such as the ranting James Beattie (2004) or the Scottish Common Sense philosopher, Thomas Reid (1983a and 1983b)—who fretted over the skeptical implications of Hume's theory and ignored his naturalism with the exception, perhaps, of its threatening theological implications. More recent scholars, following an influential article by Norman Kemp Smith (1905), widely and stridently advanced the view that Hume's appeal to nature extinguishes his skeptical doubt. These interpretative lines have failed because they did not adequately describe the way Hume formulates a distinctive form of naturalism—what I wish to call here a 'skeptical naturalism'. It's high time to right the boat.

My argument will develop first by articulating the way in which Hume conceives of nature and natural philosophy in a way that differs from conceptions that prevailed among other early modern philosophers. Next I will fill out Hume's conception of *nature* by relating it to his conceptions of *convention* and *social artifice*, and the interpretation developed by Gilles Deleuze (1953). Having done this, the essay will then situate Hume's naturalism in the skeptical tradition, describing the manner in which he appropriates elements of both Pyrrhonian and Academic skepticism. Contextualizing Hume's thought in this way will set the stage for an understanding of Hume's distinctive, nondogmatic form of philosophical theory, and will subvert readings, such as Richard H. Popkin's (1951, 1979, 1980), that would render Hume a dogmatist.

1 Natural Science: Ancient, Modern, and Skeptical

Famously, Hume calls into doubt rationalistic pretensions concerning internal or logical connections between causes and effects, our reasons for believing in the very existence of that connection, and the uniform operations of nature—for example, the sun's rising or not rising tomorrow.[2] Hume's skepticism about causation, however, exhibits more than his assessment of an important metaphysical claim; it also points to the way in which his naturalism departs from the conceptions of *nature* and *scientific law* that were popular during his lifetime.

Hume shares with many early modern thinkers a rejection of what he understands to have been the project of ancient philosophy and science. Like Jean Buridan in the fourteenth century and those who followed him, Hume characterizes "ancient" philosophy as that which maintained the reality of substantial forms (1978, 221), as it did in the case of Platonic and Aristotelian science. For ancient traditions, independent reality is grounded in immaterial forms that give to things their specific unity and identity through qualitative change. Substantial forms structure rude matter into kinds or types of entities, and thereby endow them with being and intelligibility.

By contrast, for Hume substantial forms are not just superfluous and undetectable; they are, simply put, unintelligible. To the extent that we have an idea of them at all, we do so only through the activities of fanciful imagination and the habits that our minds develop in perceiving the way things change in continuous and gradual ways. Hume writes: "When we gradually follow an object in its successive changes, the smooth progress of the thought makes us ascribe an identity to the succession; because 'tis by a similar act of the mind we consider an unchangeable object" (1978, 220). If the term 'substance' is taken as referring to some sort of metaphysical ground or substrate, and not to some continuous collection of perceptions, it is literally senseless. Strictly speaking, we have no idea of transcendent reality at all. Metaphysicians' use of a term like 'substance' is nothing more than a linguistic deception that is made possible by the abbreviated way in which we often use meaningful terms.[3] Hume's critique of intelligibility, then, anticipates the terms of criticism that are central to much contemporary analytic philosophy.

Hume's rejection of ancient metaphysics is unsurprising. But Hume also explicitly and stunningly rejects what he regards as "modern" philosophy.[4] By implication, Hume declares that he does not regard himself as a modern philosopher. Modern philosophy, according to Hume, is a line of thought that traverses a course through the works of thinkers like Galileo, Gassendi, Descartes, Malebranche, Newton, and Locke.[5] Modern philosophy is characterized by its division of the perceptual order into two components, "primary qualities" and "secondary qualities." Secondary qualities (e.g., color, taste, smell, and texture) are those dimensions of perception that are held to be caused by independent reality, while they do not represent it. Primary qualities, on the other hand (e.g., extension, magnitude, spatial relation, and solidity), are supposed both to represent independently existing entities and to be caused by them. They are quantifiable, and as such primary qualities underwrite the claim of the new, modern, mathematical science to disclose the nature of independent reality.

Hume criticizes this form of philosophy on grounds analogous to those upon which he criticizes ancient philosophy, setting his own thought apart from both. Just as the supposition of imperceptible substantial forms is, for Hume, without philosophical warrant, so also is the supposition that primary qualities represent independent and imperceptible entities, while secondary qualities do not. It is impossible, according to Hume, to conceive of solidity without color. It is impossible to conceive of extension without texture. In short, it is unintelligible to conceive of primary qualities as distinct from secondary qualities. Upon the whole, writes Hume, we "must conclude, that after the exclusion of colours, sounds, heat and cold from the rank of external existences, there remains nothing, which can afford us a just and consistent idea of body" (1978, 229). "Our modern philosophy, therefore," says Hume, following George Berkeley in this, "leaves us no just nor satisfactory idea of solidity; nor consequently of matter" (1978, 229).[6]

Along with the doctrine of primary qualities falls the early modern justification for claiming to grasp the nature of an independent and continuously existing reality through our perception. Natural science cannot, therefore, claim to grasp nature where nature means something that exists either beyond or as a substrate to our experience. 'Science' and 'nature', if we are to continue to use these concepts, must be reconfigured to mean something else. This sort of reconfiguration—a skeptical reconfiguration of 'nature' and 'science'—is just what Hume undertakes.

We can observe Hume's labors in this project in his reconceiving the notion of *laws of nature* in a way that differs radically from the then-ascendant conceptions advanced by rationalistic philosophers and natural theologians. As is now well known, Hume maintained that our belief in necessary causal connections which are described by natural laws, can be justified neither by what we can strictly observe in experience, nor by demonstration or intuition; this belief and its certainty stem instead from specific processes in our minds.[7] Hume famously shows—against rationalists like Descartes, Leibniz, Toland, and Clarke—that we have no evidence of a logical or intrinsic connection between causes and their effects. All we experience are constant conjunctions and a feeling of necessity within our own breasts (1978, 73ff.). Correlatively, we cannot demonstrate that our perception or our reasonings based upon them represent the natural world as it is, independently of our experience of it. We cannot justify understanding scientific laws as formulations of divine ordinances or of the principles that govern an independent natural reality. If we formulate laws of nature, philosophical reflection demands that we restrain ourselves and understand them as something else.

Deists, by contrast, theorize without skeptical restraint and ground the worldly causal connection in the divine—a divinity to which they speciously claim to have achieved access. Natural laws, say deistic natural scientists and theologians, are divine commands; and the order and harmony of those laws is grounded in the order, harmony, and rectitude of God.[8] The necessities described by natural laws are rooted in the unchanging nature and power of God, and one's certainty in that necessity is established by a combination of observation and deductive reason. The discovery and formulation of natural law involves, therefore, the acquisition of metaphysical and theological knowledge. Natural science is, therefore, for the deists and other natural theologians, a species of natural religion.[9]

Hume's view of natural law, of course, is very different. Hume's skeptical conceptions of *science* and *scientific law* differ (1) from those based on ancient and medieval notions of form, as well as (2) from those based on the modern idea of primary qualities. Hume's conception differs, however, not only because of his skeptical rendering of our belief in the causal connection; it also differs because his conception of the *nature* it explains is different. Hume's conception of *nature* and *natural science* does not extend the modern scientific and philosophical project; nor does it retain the bankrupt metaphysics of ancient regimes. Rather, Hume's conception of *nature* and *natural law* is best understood as an attempt to recast philosophical and scientific theorizing in a skeptical way. But what was skepticism when Hume was writing?

The rediscovery of ancient skeptical texts in the fifteenth century provided Renaissance and early modern thinkers with conceptual instruments with which to dismantle Scholastic thought. It also, however, precipitated an intellectual crisis, as philosophers struggled to find ways to develop philosophical alternatives to Scholasticism that would not wither before the same skepticism they deployed against the Scholastics.[10] It wouldn't be much of an exaggeration to say that the project of modern philosophy may in large measure be defined as the project of trying both to enlist and to overcome the critical implications of skepticism.

Among the prominent movements in the modern struggle to overcome skepticism in new and defensible ways must be counted rationalism, primary-quality empiricism, and corpuscularism, as well as novel forms of natural and revealed theology. Because it rejects these movements and instead embraces skepticism, Hume's work may thus be understood as disengaged from the "modern" project. Hume's skepticism contributed to his twice failing to acquire an academic post—once at the University of Glasgow, once at the University of Edinburgh—and provoked floods of criticism and calumny. Among prominent philosophers, James Beattie (2004) produced perhaps the most dramatic instance of this invective. His "Castle of Skepticism" (1767) characterized Hume as the devious inhabitant of a dark fortress, bent upon luring unsuspecting travelers inside and then subjecting them to inhuman tortures.

It's ironic, however, that Beattie would attribute to Hume's thought consequences very similar to those that Hume attributes to modern dogmatism. It is not skepticism, for Hume, but misguided attempts to overcome skepticism—to establish divine, realistic, or rationalistic foundations for science and philosophy—that lead to suffering and philosophical captivity. Hume warns against these pathologies with his own cautionary images, comparing them to the torments of Tantalus and characterizing them as what he calls "false philosophy" (e.g., 1978, 223).[11]

The first part of my case, then, has been to argue that while within Hume's theoretical apparatus we find him appealing to human nature, natural laws, and natural principles, Hume distances himself from what he thinks of as the "modern" approach to natural philosophy and science—that is, the philosophical project of overcoming skepticism and representing the intrinsic qualities of an independently existing natural world. But there is more. In the last section of this essay, I will argue that Hume's much-neglected meta-theoretical reflections make abundantly clear that he regards nothing of his philosophical system as transcending, rebutting or defeating his skepticism.[12] Even in his naturalism, Hume remains a philosopher who acknowledges human finitude.

Commentators who read Hume as an anti-skeptical, modern naturalist miss this acknowledgment. Gilles Deleuze does not, and his commentary on Hume's empiricism (like the commentaries of continental philosophers who follow him[13]) orbits around it. But Deleuze—like Beattie, and others who would read Hume as a thoroughly destructive skeptic—misses something. For Deleuze, Hume is a philosopher who subverts naturalism; he is a philosopher, maintains Deleuze, of thoroughgoing contingency, artifice, and social constructivism. While there's something right in this, Deleuze—no less than those who read Hume as a modern naturalist—ignores something that is terribly important. In fact, he *misses* (or evades) just what the naturalists *notice*. As if embracing the other side of the tension I articulated at the beginning of this essay—namely, the tension between naturalism and skepticism—Deleuze cleaves to Hume's skepticism but denies his naturalism. Deleuze's avoidance of 'nature' is rooted, of course, in his own philosophical project; it also results, however, from his misconstruing the subtle and complex relationship that Hume articulates between nature and artifice. Understanding that relationship, then, will not only help us to see Deleuze's error. It will also fortify and deepen the rendering of Hume's skeptical naturalism I have so far advanced.

2   Natural Conventions and Conventional Nature

Consider the portrait Hume presents in this famous paragraph describing the relationship between nature and artifice, between necessity and contingency.

Our imagination has a great authority over our ideas; and there are no ideas that are different from each other, which it cannot separate, and join, and compose into all the varieties of fiction. But notwithstanding the empire of the imagination, there is a secret tie or union among particular ideas, which causes the mind to conjoin them more frequently together, and makes the one, upon its appearance, introduce the other.... 'Twill be easy to conceive of what vast consequence these principles must be in the science of human nature, if we consider, that so far as regards the mind, these are the only links that bind the parts of the universe together, or connect us with any person or object exterior to ourselves. For as it is by means of thought only that any thing operates upon our passions, and as these are the only ties of our thoughts, they are really to us the cement of the universe, and all the operations of the mind must, in a great measure, depend on them. (Hume 1978, 662)

The "empire of the imagination" is mighty, indeed. It can join and structure ideas into ever-changing combinations seemingly without end, giving rise to unicorns, phantoms, nations, abstract ideas, religions, and political parties. Imagination, of course, can also be a great destroyer, the force that not only combines but also disintegrates, that tears vast theories and systems and worlds of ideas asunder, rending them from top to bottom. What can be constructed can be deconstructed. Hume himself has seemed to many an agent of this sort of destruction, wielding with merciless power the great blade of skepticism, for as we have seen it is upon the shoals of Hume's skeptical philosophy that the rationalistic aspirations of Clarke, Descartes, Spinoza, and the natural theologians to deduce the nature of the self, the world, morals, and God crashed. And it is in this sense of the difference and otherness between ideas, together with the contingency of the relations among them that later Deleuze would find inspiration for his own form of "empiricism."

But as the preceding passage with which Hume closes the abstract to his *A Treatise of Human Nature* (1739–40; page numbers refer to the 1978 edition) indicates, there is something else here—some "secret union," almost a conspiracy, some countervailing force organizing around the banner of "human nature" that militates against the otherwise unchecked power of imagination and against the contingencies of skepticism. Hume calls these counter-revolutionaries the principles of the "association of ideas," and here we have played out in more theoretical form the tension between skepticism and naturalism. These principles signal a limit to the fragility of theory, a brake on the dizzying, delirious, and intoxicating sense of radical contingency skepticism and skeptical criticism can yield. It's this limit (this skepticism about skepticism) that Deleuze misses. It would be wrong, however, to construe the relationship between imagination and association, between skepticism and naturalism, as purely oppositional. For much of our theoretical and practical lives, and for what Hume calls our "common life," a more felicitous and convivial partnership is achieved.

There is a well-known paragraph describing the cooperation of two people rowing a boat that appears in Book III of Hume's *Treatise*.[14] It is a telling
image. The specific context of this passage is Hume's claim that the basis
and origin of conventions—in this case, the conventions of private property and possession—are not those of formal contract, of, that is, verbalized
agreement and commitment expressed in speech or writing. Earlier political philosophers like Thomas Hobbes and John Locke had argued that the
legitimacy of the state is grounded in a contractual agreement entered by
the members of the social order it governs. Hume, however, took a different
view, finding prevailing social contract theory philosophically baseless and
the politics it engendered not only distasteful but also, in too many cases,
downright dangerous. For Hume, the notion of contract—and the contingency it implies—presents an inadequate account of the bases of human
society and the legitimacy of the state. Contractual agreements are themselves, says Hume, only possible through the existence of something
deeper, something less contingent, namely the unreflective agreements
and alignments of what might be called human nature and sensibility.
Contracts and promises are, therefore, for Hume, derivative phenomena.
Contrary to the claims of social contract philosophers, they only "arise
from" prior "human conventions" and as such are insufficient, by themselves, to ground the political institutions that social contract philosophers
wished to legitimate with them.[15]

Deleuze's account of Hume as a social constructivist is shallow in the
same way as the social contract account of social order and state authority.
Yet, Deleuze (1953) does recognize the importance of what Hume calls
"general rules," and this is no small matter. General rules bring structure
and order to society as constituents of social institutions such as the law,
the state, family, and experimental science. General rules, may even, says
Hume, affect perception itself: "our adherence to *general rules* . . . has such a
mighty influence on the actions and understanding" that it "is able to impose on the very senses" (1978, 374) as well as the imagination (585). General rules articulate, modify, and channel sympathies and passions, thereby
developing and directing moral and aesthetic sensibilities.[16] Indeed, "We
can form no wish," Hume writes, "which has not a reference to society"
(363). So pervasive and important, in fact, are general rules that without
them human selves would lack integrity and human society would fail to
achieve the pleasant stability and consistency necessary for its coherence
and continued existence. Without general rules, therefore, neither human
selves nor the social orders that they compose would be possible. General
rules, then, are a necessary condition for the self, for science, for society,
and in a sense for the world as we know it. General rules structure our

ways of thinking, perceiving, and doing—even our ways of being, individually and together. Since they are socially constructed and since, for Hume, the relations among all ideas are external to them, these general rules together with all that depends upon them are contingent. It is the recognition of this radical contingency that inspired Deleuze to call himself an empiricist.

Deleuze, however, like the social contract philosophers, fails to grasp how these contingent, socially constructed cultural rules are themselves possible only through the prior possibility of human convention. Convention is contingent, but an account of this contingency tells only part of Hume's story. The genesis of "observations," "expectations," and calculations constitutive of convention formation requires, for Hume, much more than arbitrary choice or simple social construction or authority. Rather, conventions are generated principally through the complex educating, natural, and social processes Hume calls "experience." This process, unlike arbitrary contract or agreement, only "arises gradually," acquiring "force by a slow progression."

The experiences relevant to, for example, the conventions of justice include the experience of "inconveniences," such as the physical pain accompanied by the loss (or threat of loss) of one's own possessions likely to follow upon one's interference with another's. If I am right to discern a confrontation with skepticism animating Hume's thoughts on convention, then his referring to "inconveniences" may be read literally and thereby call our attention to something of the nature of convention itself.[17] What I wish to suggest is that Hume's mention of inconvenience as a crucial factor in the formation of convention resonates with a sense of those occasions when we are not able to con-vene with one another, when our desires and hopes and expectations of what others will or ought to do are thwarted, frustrated, or disappointed—when we are left at a loss in the face of others as other. When Hume writes about "convention," then, he is literally writing about people con-vening or coming together (or failing to come together), about their facing and surmounting in sustainable (though contingent) ways the otherness separating them, the gap of difference that skepticism exploits.

It is in working to overcome what I should like to call the friction, the resistance, the frustration with otherness and the world that humans produce convention. But, Hume argues, this overcoming is not simply a matter of calculative agreement. It also depends, more deeply, on certain possibilities we possess—among them possibilities for a kind of sentimental concord he calls in the paragraph to which I have referred a "general sense" of "common" interest (1978, 490).[18] This general sense may be the result but not the creation of deliberate calculation. Why not? Because calculative agreements are possible only on prior condition of what Hume calls our "common life." As there is, for Hume, something "natural" about our "common life," there is a natural basis to convention. Let's unpack this further.

Hume's position might be recast in this way: while common sensibility is modified, developed, and diversified through the course of contingent culture and history, no interest *could* become common, no culture and history *could* become operant, and no fellow-feeling *could* be produced without the antecedent, common capacities for achieving sentimental alignment that seem to be sensibly called "natural" to us, that seem natal to us, to which we seem fated.[19] Like the "secret union" of association that sets a check to the contingent empire of imagination, here too Hume signals that amid the contingency and artifice of convention formation we find ourselves depending on something apparently not contingent to bring us together—or, perhaps better, to make it possible in some contingent way to recognize what already binds us together—as we may engage in a shared world of meaning and practice.

In Hume's image, two people work together rowing a boat across a body of water. In such a context, he maintains, they "know" each other, their individual interests as well as their common interest in this shared situation; they possess and act on expectations of causal sequence, behavior, and character. Their shared situation is, I am tempted to say, following Wittgenstein, "shown" in their action, their *praxis*, in their working together. Through their shared work and perhaps through their own interpersonal histories, as well, they show a common experience and a common understanding of the nature and purpose of boats, of travel across water, of the structures of play and transportation and time. In short, they show that they have convened and have achieved a "common life."

For Hume this sort of activity—whether or not grounded in explicit agreement—depends on the prior condition of our naturally *being able* to row together—that is, on the human *possibility* of engaging in a world of common interests and practices. The existence of this possibility, in turn, depends on its being constitutive of what Hume calls our *nature*, of our natural capacity for having certain shared feelings and desires, for having complementary expectations that occurrences have consequences, for having mutually comprehensible pleasures and pains, attractions, interests, and revulsions. That the actual achievement of fellow feeling and common life may be the result of recognizing and conceptually formulating common interests does not render sentiment and shared action posterior to calculation, for no interest could produce fellow feeling and no practice could be shared were not the capacity for it already present; indeed, no calculations could take place without the prior sentimental alignments which underwrite the institutions of rationality.

Hume elaborates on this rendering of the intimate and inseparable connection between nature and convention, between the contingent and the natal, in discussing the conventions of justice. There Hume provocatively maintains not only that convention requires nature but also that nature actually completes itself in convention.[20] The development of rules governing the stability and transference of property (1978, 256) does not, therefore, entail the imposition of alien artifice upon the natural other. Rather, for Hume, the progress of convention (and with it the progress of sentiment) marks a change in nature itself—a change from an *"uncultivated"* human nature (1978, 488) to something "methodized" and "corrected" (1975, 130 [162]). Hume depicts this progressive continuity between the conventional and the natural more emphatically when he describes the achievement of certain "fundamental" (1978, 526) conventions as, in fact, the invention of new "laws of nature."

Tho' the rules of justice be *artificial*, they are not *arbitrary*. Nor is the expression improper to call them *Laws of Nature*; if by natural we understand what is common to any species, or even if we confine it to mean what is inseparable from the species. (1978, 484)

One might, therefore, upon Humean lines, distinguish (1) basic human nature from (2) artificial but non-arbitrary "laws of nature" and contrast these two against a third type: (3) more contingent arrangements made by human society. It is one thing, for example, to produce different conventions governing the proper manner of laying out silverware (perhaps, e.g., laying the knife at the bottom of the plate rather than to the right side). It is another to create different prohibitions governing sexual relationships and private property. It would be something else, yet again, as Stanley Cavell points out, to expect that our actions will not have consequences in the world, to count entirely different expressions (and not those we now count) as expressions of pain, or to "be bored by an earthquake or by the death of [one's] child or the declaration of martial law, or . . . quietly (but comfortably?) sit on a chair of nails."[21]

Echoing Wittgenstein, we might distinguish, then, in Hume, "basic" or fundamental agreements from those that are relatively "superficial."[22] Surface conventions, as opposed to those that are more basic, are agreements or alignments that are relatively contingent and revisable in ways that will not fundamentally disrupt what we recognize as our world and our selves. Distinguishing among conventions in this way need not depend on a purported grasp of metaphysical essences or of the intrinsic qualities of an independent natural order. The criteria for the more or less natural forms of human convention are to be found in the resistance, the friction, the frustration (something like what Sartre called the "coefficient of adversity") woven into different conventions—the extent to which we find and recognize that certain conventions, agreements, practices, or beliefs are or are not meaningfully plastic, revisable, or open to revision. Conversely, what is natural, when we do not resist or oppose or defy it, is easy and frictionless.[23]

This view of convention and nature, of course, together with our findings in section 1 of this essay, help us better to understand Hume's distinctive understanding of not only nature but also natural science. To understand this view more clearly, consider an analogy.[24] Grammarians formulate grammatical rules describing the practices of language. The practices of language were not originally produced by those rules. Language developed first; the rules were formulated later. Of course, in particular cases, the grammatical rules can subsequently be used to manipulate and discipline linguistic practices. Generally speaking, however, no one in particular invents language, and while we all have the power to change it in trivial or superficial ways (say, by speaking with one of various accents or refusing to use certain offensive words), no one individually has the power to change its deeper, more stable features. To the extent that (a) grammatical rules can be revised, the rules are contingent; and to the extent that they are (b) created through human artifice, the rules are conventional. But to the extent (a) none of us created and none of us can change linguistic practices and to the extent (b) those practices are grounded in the possibilities of our nature, the rules are not contingent.

From the point of view of someone we might call a grammatical Platonist or realist, there is an independent, external grammar, which it is the job of grammarians to discern and represent in their theories. For a Humean grammarian, by contrast, it seems impossible to know whether such a Platonic or independent grammar exists or, if it does exist, whether or not we can represent it. In fact, we are probably better off, from a Humean point of view, not pretending to having apprehended it.

Now, substitute 'nature' for 'practices of language' and 'natural law or philosophy' for 'grammatical rules'. Accordingly, for Hume nature is not produced by natural laws or philosophy—though we can manipulate nature by using them. Natural laws are contingent and conventional to the extent that we formulate them on the basis of empirical data we collect and organize with concepts we have created as well as to the extent we are able to revise those laws. Natural laws are, on the other hand, not contingent to the extent that we use them to describe features of the world we experience that appear to us to be beyond our control, not of our invention, and resistant to any attempts we might make to change them. Scientific laws are also natural to us in the sense that the very possibility of their formulation exhibits possibilities of our ways of being, of what it means to be the kind of entities we are.

For the Humean skeptic, then, while the natural laws we formulate may be useful and durable and satisfying to us, we should not pretend that they are able to represent an independent natural or a metaphysical order (though neither should we deny this). The theories and laws of philosophy and natural science are in Hume's view best conceived as the products of human convention, custom, history, culture, habit, invention, and imagination as well as what we might call the possibilities and imperatives of our nature, rather than as attempts to mirror the intrinsic nature of an independent natural world.

For Hume, then, the "natural" signals the easy, stable, useful, common, not easily revisable, compelling, and regular features we recognize in the world and ourselves; and what is natural to us can at least in part be artificial.[25] Hume's usage also suggests something of the natural as describing how we find ourselves, where we fit, what we appear to be born to, and what appears to be the way of things with us.

This way of reading Hume's conception of the natural and theorizing about the natural not only makes more comprehensive sense of Hume's texts than either the realistic or the social-constructivist accounts. It also points to the way Hume himself regards it as meaningful to be both a naturalist and a skeptic; for the conception of nature, convention, and natural science I have articulated here fits comfortably with the "mitigated" or "academical" skepticism to which Hume returns after "nature herself" breaks his foray into excessive, solitary, and uneasy skeptical doubts (1978, 269). To complete my portrait of Hume's skeptical naturalism, it will be useful to assess the way in which Hume's thought may be compared to the ancient forms of skepticism to which he himself appeals.

3 Implying "No Dogmatical Spirit"[26]

As we have seen, Hume's thoughts about nature are categorically different from those advanced by modern dogmatists like the Lockeans, Newtonians, Cartesians, deists, and commonsense theorists—all of whom make claim to various kinds of realism for their theories, realisms that Hume, as a skeptic, will not endorse. In refusing to endorse primary quality episte-mology, innate ideas, the notion of a substantial self, the disclosive power of reason, as well as both the epistemologies and the metaphysics of natu-ral religion, Hume excludes himself from the modern philosophical project, as he understands it. Refusing to assent to the existence of substantial forms, he rejects the ancient metaphysics and sciences flowing from Plato and Aristotle.

But Hume also explicitly aligns his work with another ancient stream of thought, Academic skepticism. Hume's designation of his own settled type of skepticism as "academical," of course, connects him to the Hellenistic school of skeptical philosophy led by Arcesilaus (315–240 BCE) and Car-neades (213–129 BCE), who each took the helm of Plato's Academy and whose legacy was transmitted to modernity largely through Cicero's ac-count of their thought in his *Academica* and *De natura deorum*.[27] Hume seems to have been well aware of these texts as his *Dialogues Concerning Natural Religion* (1777) is modeled on sections of both the *Academica* and *De natura deorum*, and in an autobiographical letter he reports having taken his "catalogue of Virtues" not from Christian sources, but rather "from *Cicero's Offices*" (Hume 1932, volume I: 34 [Letter 13]).

Hume characterizes his Academic skepticism as "durable and useful," and these attributes fit well with the conception of *nature* and *natural science* I have culled from his texts.[28] As Humean natural science and phi-losophy develop through conventions that answer what we find resistant and inconvenient, its propositions succeed when they are easy and "dura-ble," rather than representative. As Humean natural science and philoso-phy develop in practical ways that succeed in achieving or facilitating the satisfying, practical, conveniences of common life, they are "useful."

Hume's theory is not, however, Academic in the way that those like Peter Klein (2001, 2004, 337), following Sextus Empiricus (1933–49, 226–230), have defined it—that is, as denying theoretically the possibility of knowl-edge[29] (a denial that I think better called "nihilism") or as a dogmatic as-sertion of probabilism (which Sextus alternatively perhaps erroneously imputes to the Academics).[30] Rather, Hume's naturalistic philosophy is Academic in these two ways: (1) it comprises extensive theory (which the Pyrrhonians avoided, even for the sake of rhetorical gambit); and (2) it develops probabilistic criteria.

Of course, these criteria differ from the probabilistic criteria known as the *"pithanon"* and the *"eulogon"* developed by the ancient Academics. The ancients' criteria were generated in opposition to Stoic epistemic doctrines centered on "cataleptic impressions"—impressions, much like Descartes's "clear and distinct ideas," that are thought to be utterly indubitable and veridical. Against this Stoic doctrine of certain truth, Academic skeptics advanced a doctrine of probable truth. On this topic, Hume's skeptical theory of "impressions" follows the work of the ancient Academic skeptics, refusing and subverting clear and distinct ideas as well as cataleptic impressions.

Hume's probabilistic theory, however, differs from the probabilistic theories of the ancient Academics in this way: The ancient skeptics developed criteria for probable truth, where truth means dogmatically grasping the nature of independent reality and where probability means measuring that grasp in a probabilistic way. Hume's "proper *criteria* for truth and falsehood" (1975, 151), on the other hand, cannot be understood dogmatically as justified on rational grounds since the skeptical arguments remain unanswered. What makes them "proper" is not that we can justify, intuit, prove, or demonstrate their capacity to represent or correspond to an independent natural world accurately. What makes them proper is that, like any part of his philosophical work, they will lead us to beliefs which "if not true (for, perhaps, that is too much to be hop'd for) might at least be satisfactory to the human mind, and might stand the test of the most critical examination" (1978, 272).[31]

Hume's skepticism, then, is in limited ways rightly construed as having inherited Academicism. But what of Academic skepticism's less reputable twin, Pyrrhonian skepticism? During Hume's time the account of Pyrrhonian and Academic skepticism that Sextus presented became inverted. Pyrrhonism became identified with the nihilistic denial of the possibility of knowledge and with the attempt to abandon all (other) belief. It is an identification one still finds common among philosophers. Indeed, this way of conceiving Pyrrhonism has come to define skepticism per se.

In the *Enquiry concerning Human Understanding*, Hume derides Pyrrhonism for being, like the skepticism of Descartes's First Meditation (1984), "excessive" (1975, 158, 159, 161)—that is for rejecting all belief in lieu of "universal doubt" (1975, 149–161). Pyrrhonians, Hume says, claim to have discovered something absolute or at least universal; in particular, they claim to have "discovered, either the *absolute* fallaciousness of their mental faculties, or their unfitness to reach *any* fixed determination in all those curious subjects of speculation, about which they are commonly employed" (1975, 150, emphasis mine). Their skepticisms are probably impossible to enact in the practice of our lives (1975, 150). Moreover, they "*admit of no answer and produce no conviction*" (1975, 155 n. 1). Their "only effect is to cause…momentary amazement and irresolution and confusion" (1975, 155 n. 1). Similar remarks are to be found in the *Treatise*, Book I.

Could it be, though, that Hume's own remarks are misleading on this point? Perhaps the sort of Pyrrhonism he deplores is a caricature in the same way that, say, the socialism that is commonly criticized in popular circles today is a caricature. Perhaps, in an effort to diminish the backlash against his work by the religious conservatives or "high flyers" of his time, Hume wrote in measured but not entirely forthright terms about his own skepticism.[32] Perhaps there is more Pyrrhonism in Hume's work than first meets the eye.

Consider the similarities between some of the major features of Hume's work and a short but terribly important passage from the most significant vehicle of the transmission of Pyrrhonian ideas to modernity. In the *Outlines of Pyrrhonism*, Sextus Empiricus characterizes the skeptical "criterion" for living and thinking this way:[33]

Adhering, then, to appearances we live in accordance with the normal rules of life, *undogmatically*, seeing that we cannot remain wholly inactive. And it would seem that this regulation of life is fourfold, and that one part of it lies in the guidance of Nature, another in the constraint of the passions, another in the tradition of laws and customs, another in the instruction of the arts. Nature's guidance is that by which we are naturally capable of sensation and thought; constraint of the passions is that whereby hunger drives us to food and thirst to drink; tradition of customs and laws, that whereby we regard piety in the conduct of life as good, but impiety as evil; instruction of the arts, that whereby we are not inactive in such arts as we adopt. But we make all these statements *undogmatically*. (1933–49, Book I: 23–24, chapter XI, emphasis mine)

With the exception of the endorsement of piety, Hume's work resonates with remarkably similar enjoinders.[34] Exploring these similarities in depth lies beyond the scope of this essay; but we might briefly, using the fourfold and other defining features of Pyrrhonism, catalog them in this way.

1. The "guidance of nature": Hume's philosophical work is, of course, deeply naturalistic. Radicalizing the critical dimensions early modern philosophy enlisted to subvert medieval and religious theories, Hume's epistemology and metaphysics of mind is thoroughly grounded in what he describes as natural principles and natural processes, forgoing any appeal to revelation or doctrines associated with it, such as noetic intuition. Inspired by Joseph Butler's naturalism, Hume's moral and political theory refuses and, indeed, opposes appeals to divine or metaphysical grounds, such as divine command, natural law theory, natural rights, or transcending reason. Hume's moral theory turns from these to more secular natural

sentiment and sympathy, natural human conditions (such as scarcity), custom and tradition, and the actual social relations among people (rather than metaphysical hierarchies).

Moreover, Sextus describes the "guidance of nature," in a frustratingly circular way, as that by which we "are naturally capable of sensation and thought." In text that shortly follows this one, however, and many places elsewhere in the text, Sextus elaborates by associating skeptical yielding in general and sensation in particular to "things unavoidable" (e.g., 1933–49, I:29). This is a view of nature remarkably similar to the explication of Hume's conception of *nature*, in section 2 of this essay, as what offers resistance when defied and ease when we yield to it: "I may, nay I must yield to the current of nature...and in this blind submission I shew most perfectly my sceptical disposition and principles" (1978, 274). If for Sextus Empiricus, Pyrrhonism consists in adhering to nature in the sense of what is unavoidable, to which we must yield, and if Hume's work develops a consistent and similar conception, then we have grounds for holding, at least within the rubric of Pyrrhonism, that Hume may meaningfully be called both a skeptic and a naturalist.

2. The "constraint of the passions": The central thrust of Hume's moral and political theory involves moderating the passions, discovering more felicitous ways of thinking and acting, diffusing the "enthusiasms" (or what we might today call "fanaticisms") of religion, metaphysics, and false philosophy. "Generally speaking the errors of religion are dangerous," writes Hume in a famous remark, while "those in philosophy are only ridiculous" (1978, 272). But better than either religion or false philosophy is skeptical and naturalistic philosophy.

Pyrrhonian skeptics characteristically employ a strategy of producing moderate emotion (*metriopatheia*) and reflective balance (*isosthenia*) by setting opposing arguments against one another in order to create a liberating suspension of judgment (*epochē*) and thence undisturbed peace (*ataraxia*).[35] Hume often pursues a similar strategy, opposing not only arguments against one another, however, but also theoretical conclusions against what he calls natural and ordinary beliefs. In a typical and well-known passage, using the Pyrrhonian strategy, he writes: "Opposing one species of superstition to another, set them a-quarreling; while we ourselves, during their fury and contention, happily make our escape into the calm, though obscure, regions of philosophy" (1886: 362–363). If there is any single motive driving Hume's subversive criticism of metaphysical, religious, and realistic dogmatics in favor of skeptical naturalism, it is to be found in his engagement with this calming, moderating project.

3. Deference to "customs" and "tradition": Hume says this in section V of the first *Enquiry*, "Sceptical Solution to these Doubts": "Custom is the great guide of life. It is that principle alone which renders our experience useful to us" (1975, 36 [44]). In his account of our causal inferences and other associations of ideas, in his validation of tradition as a factor in justifying state authority, in his genetic account of religious belief, in his theory of the development of moral rules, in the sympathetic rendering of Charles I and other monarchs that alienated Whigs from his work, Hume consistently acknowledges the importance of custom, habit, and tradition in human life.[36]

4. "Instruction of the arts (*techne*)": While Hume is not by any means what we would today, even in the spirit of Francis Bacon, call a technocrat, he does reconfigure the projects of science and philosophy as projects aimed at producing beliefs and theories that are for us both "durable" but also "useful." That is, knowing (*episteme*) for Hume is very much bound up with "knowing how" (*techne*)—knowing how to think and believe and act in ways that are useful and agreeable and peaceful. It is for this reason that those with pragmatist proclivities have found antecedents for that view in Hume (see Randall 1962).

5. "Adhering to appearances": Hume writes at the opening of the *Treatise*, Book I:

I here make use of these terms, *impression and idea*, in a sense different from what is usual, and I hope this liberty will be allowed me. Perhaps I rather restore the word, idea, to its original sense, from which Mr. *Locke* had perverted it, in making it stand for all our perceptions. By the term of impression I would not be understood to express the manner, in which our lively perceptions are produced in the soul, but merely the perceptions themselves; for which there is no particular name either in the *English* or any other language, that I know of. (1978, 2 n. 1)

The "original sense" from which Locke et al. had "perverted it"? What could this "original" sense have been? Clearly, and contrary to John P. Wright, part of Hume's point in this passage is to indicate his bracketing (neither affirming nor denying) of the "manner" or processes that cause or result in perception (Wright 1983, 1986, 407–436). Instead, Hume wishes to attend simply to the impressions "themselves."[37] I myself find in this an alignment between Hume's concept of *impression* and the more original concept, *phenomenon* or *appearance*, deployed by ancient skeptics.

Like the ancient Pyrrhonians who preceded him and the phenomenologists who would later follow him, Hume at least initially in the *Treatise* endeavors to "adhere to appearances" (*phainomena*) and resist speculating about unobservable entities, such as substantial forms or material objects and the way they might cause or produce appearances. Ancient skeptics recommended a similar kind resistance to speculating about this kind of thing, what they called "hidden things" (*adela*); their recommendation was simply to keep a "silence" (*aphasia*). Moreover, it's crucial to see that while Hume does write about nature breaking his skeptical doubts, the skeptical arguments remain unanswered in any rational or argumentative sense. That is, Hume never finds the skeptical arguments to be unsound. As far as his texts are concerned, no rational justification for any belief has been found: "'Tis impossible upon any system to defend either our understanding or senses; and we but expose them farther when we endeavor to justify them in that manner" (1978, 218). Epistemologically he remains a thoroughgoing Pyrrhonian—having failed to find a rational basis for any belief. But his assertion of this position should not, appearances at *Treatise* 218 to the contrary, be read in a dogmatic manner, as if Hume has committed himself to belief in the nihilistic conclusions that either (1) no basis for knowledge can possibly found be found or, as in Descartes's First Meditation (1984), that (2) all beliefs are false (Laird 1932). Hume writes later, in the penultimate paragraph of the *Treatise*, book I: "A true sceptic will be diffident of his philosophical doubts, as well as of his philosophical conviction" (1978, 273). Hume's willingness to continue theorizing must not be read as the consequence of his having defeated skepticism with either nihilism or realism, or of his avoidance of them. Rather it should be understood as a willingness to continue inquiring and philosophizing in a new way, a way that includes engaging a silence or *aphasia* about dogmatic alternatives.[38] Hume's silence about dogmatism makes it possible for him to develop naturalistic theories. Hume's acknowledgment of the skeptical arguments remaining unanswered and the possibility of dogmatism remaining open exhibits itself in his abandonment of dogmatic naturalisms and his developing an alternative, skeptical naturalism.[39]

6. "Acknowledging common life" (*ho bios ho koinos*): A central feature of Hume's philosophy is the notion of *common life* and his contention that true philosophy refuses attempts to transcend it (Livingston 1983, 1998; Fosl 1999a,b). Hume subverts specious false philosophies and religious dogmas, thoroughly rooting philosophical reflection in a public world of common interests, agreements, sentimental concord, and shared capacities. Sextus, too, recommends as much in chapter 34 of book I of the *Outlines* when he holds that while skeptics will have no part of dogmatism, they yield to *ho bios ho koinos* or "common life" (1933–49, I:237). For Hume neither natural science nor philosophy should be conceived in the way of realists and metaphysicians—that is, as attempts to transcend common human

perception, opinion, custom, and nature to grasp something beyond us, in some heavenly, hyperuranian realm or simply somewhere beyond or beneath our perception.

Whether or not Hume actually read Sextus and this particular passage or the passage describing the fourfold, however, is of little philosophical import. In either case, what remains true is that central features of Hume's work bear remarkable similarities to the features of Pyrrhonian skepticism presented by Sextus Empiricus. By showing that Hume's skepticism is in important ways consistent with ancient Pyrrhonism as well as ancient Academicism, these similarities reinforce my contention that his naturalism may be read as consistent with his skepticism.

Perhaps, however, the most dramatic and the most decisive way in which Hume's work follows along Pyrrhonian lines is to be found in his metatheoretical remarks—that is, his self-reflective remarks about the character of his own philosophical (and nonphilosophical) assertions. Hume's metatheory shows that he thought of his naturalism as itself Pyrrhonian through and through. This is crucial, because while at first glance Hume's theory appears to be naturalistic in a realistic, early modern sense, Hume's metatheory discloses its nonmodern, skeptical cast. Among the most telling of Hume's remarks on this score, and among those I wish to emphasize most, are these words with which Hume closes the whole of Book I of the *Treatise*, proclaiming that he, like Sextus, "makes all" of his "statements undogmatically":

I here enter a *caveat* against any objections, which may be offer'd on that head [i.e. the charge of dogmatism]; and declare that such expressions were extorted from me by the present view of the object, and imply no dogmatical spirit, nor conceited idea of my own judgment, which are sentiments that I am sensible can become no body, and a sceptic still less than any other. (1978, 274)

Hence we may add to our catalog of the Pyrrhonian features of Humean philosophy:

7. Living and theorizing "undogmatically." As he clearly states it, Hume's theory, including his theories of nature and his naturalistic moral prescriptions, are advanced "undogmatically." Popkin is therefore in error when he writes: "if one is really Pyrrhonian, as Hume was, one will be as dogmatic and as opinionated as one is naturally inclined to be" (1951, 406). The notion that Hume embraces dogmatic philosophy is simply contradicted by the above passage. Not only does Hume explicitly reject dogmatism and a naturalistic refutation of skepticism. Hume actually uses skepticism to order and define just what ought properly to be by meant by "nature" and the

"natural." The result is a nondogmatic concept of both. Popkin, in short, like many others, has put the cart before the horse, as it is not, for Hume, "nature" that justifies engaging in skeptical philosophy; rather, it is skeptical philosophizing that defines the sort of "nature" that makes a proper sort of naturalism possible—that is, the sort of naturalism proper to "true" philosophy.

From this point of view, then, part IV of Book I of the *Treatise* is the true philosophical beginning of Hume's *Treatise*, for it is from the peculiar metatheoretical vantage point Hume reaches there, after struggling with skeptical arguments and acknowledging their implications, that he *then* goes on to develop his philosophical theories. It is a philosophical standpoint from which Hume has come to acknowledge the finitude of theory and yet has chosen nevertheless to go on theorizing.[40]

This is what nearly all of Hume's commentators have missed. Popkin would have us believe that Hume's willingness to embrace philosophical theory despite having failed to expurgate skepticism is a sign of his willingness to be "dogmatic"—just as dogmatic as any other philosopher—when the "mood" strikes him to be so. Don Garrett (2002, 20) reads Hume as a dogmatic but somehow skeptically chastened naturalist.[41] Donald W. Livingston has moved from regarding Hume's return to common life as a rejection of skepticism to acknowledging it; but rather than understanding common life as a place of skeptical finitude and contingency as well as what appears to be natural to us, Livingston has enthusiastically fetishized tradition and custom; he has thereby through a perverse alchemy transformed Hume into Burke.[42] John P. Wright recognizes that Hume never banishes skepticism, but oddly suggests that he remains a realist. William E. Morris would have us believe that the voice of part IV is not Hume's at all but that of some sort of imagined metaphysician. Because Morris altogether fails not only to grasp the possibility of nondogmatic philosophy but also to acknowledge Hume's skepticism, it seems to him a "complete mystery" that Hume should go on philosophizing and accept the skeptical conclusions (Morris 2000, 96).

As we have seen, however, Hume's text is clear that although he continues to philosophize—to make assertions, to form concepts, to develop theories and beliefs, even about nature—he does so without *any* "dogmatic spirit." That is to say, the sort of theorizing in which Hume engages is a different sort of theorizing than that of the dogmatist. As his conception of *nature* is a central element of his philosophical-theoretical apparatus, it too must be presented in a manner different from the manner in which dogmatists of his time (and ours) present their naturalisms.[43] In a passage closely tied to Hume's advocacy of the "science of man," he continues describing this manner of skeptical theorizing:

The conduct of a man, who studies philosophy in this careless manner, is more truly sceptical than that of one, who feeling in himself an inclination to it, is yet so over-whelm'd with doubts and scruples, as totally to reject it. (1978, 273)

Returning to common life and engaging in naturalistic theorizing dispels Hume's skeptical doubt, but it does not dispel his skepticism. It permits, in addition to the doubt, a form of nondogmatic belief that allows Hume to remain "truly sceptical." Hume's conception of *nature* does not represent his refutation or overcoming or lapse from skepticism; rather, it is itself skeptical. While it would be wrong, therefore, to say that Hume wishes readers to take his claims dogmatically, it would not be wrong to take his contentions (including those about nature) philosophically and seriously, so long as we read them skeptically.

How is it, then, that Hume develops a philosophy of nature while also developing profoundly skeptical arguments? He does so by recasting 'nature' in a distinctive, nondogmatic way, a way suggested by Pyrrhonian as well as Academic skepticism, a way that honors both the apparent contingencies and the apparent necessities of our existence, both the finitude and the aspiration to theory found in human life.

Notes

1. Portions of this essay also appear in Fosl 2004.

2. Hume 1978, 77, 89, 124. Books I and II were published in 1739, Book III in 1740; the "Advertisement" was prefixed to Book III.

3. Along these lines, Hume writes:

For it being usual, after the frequent use of terms, which are really significant and intelligible, to omit the idea, which we wou'd express by them, and to preserve only the custom by which we recal the idea at pleasure; so it naturally happens that after the frequent use of terms, which are wholly insignificant and unintelligible, we fancy them to be on the same footing with the prece-dent, and to have a secret meaning, which we might discover by reflection. The resemblance of their appearance deceives the mind, as is usual, and makes us imagine a thorough resemblance and conformity. By this means the philosophers set themselves at ease, and arrive at last, by an illusion, at the same indifference, which the people attain by their stupidity, and true philoso-phers by their scepticism. (1978, 224)

4. I wish to thank my friend and teacher Donald W. Livingston for this line of inter-pretation, which has deeply influenced my own views of Hume and modernity.

5. Galileo 1967; Descartes 1984, 1985; Gassendi 1964; Newton 1999; Malebranche 1997; Locke 1975. This form of modern thought, of course, has its antecedents in the ancient atomism developed by Democritus and the Epicureans.

6. Berkeley (1948–57a and 1948–57b) had leveled similar criticisms of materialism. In this sort of critique, Hume anticipates the critical strategy of analytic philosophers such as Wittgenstein, Austin, Ryle, and Quine, who would dismiss philosophical claims not because they are false but because they are senseless. Hume's scrutiny not only, however, undermines modern philosophy's claims to knowledge of external, extra-perceptual posits. Hume surpasses Berkeley in the very next section of the *Treatise* (Bk. I, pt. IV, sec. 5) by also subverting the doctrine of an immaterial soul, a dogma that was particularly dear to the bishop. In the well-known sec. 6 of Book I, part IV of the *Treatise*, Hume also untangles the misguided doctrine of a substantial "self" which is said to remain constant through the course of "internal" experience, replacing it with the now familiar "bundle" theory of the self. According to the bundle theory, the self is a composite, a continuously changing aggregate, an event with no non-arbitrary principle of order and no fundamental "I" beyond the accidental collocation of perceptions composing any particular set of experiences. Hume writes:

setting aside some metaphysicians...I may venture to affirm of the rest of mankind, that they are nothing but a bundle or collection of different perceptions, which succeed each other with an inconceivable rapidity, and are in a perpetual flux and movement.... There is properly no *simplicity* in it at one time, nor *identity* in different; whatever natural propension we may have to imagine that simplicity and identity. (1978, 253)

The self, for Hume, is in other words an event, and not an entity. "Our self," writes Hume, "independent of the perception of every other object, is in reality nothing" (1978, 340). This lays the groundwork for Kant's stringent analysis of rationalism's metaphysics of the self in the "Postulates of Pure Reason" of the first *Critique* (1781). It is worth mentioning, however, that Hume was not entirely comfortable with his bundle theory. In an appendix Hume attached to the *Treatise*, he confessed,

I had entertain'd some hopes, that however deficient our theory of the intellectual world might be, it wou'd be free from those contradictions, and absurdities, which seem to attend every explication, that human reason can give of the material world. But upon a more strict review of the section concerning *personal identity*, I find myself involv'd in such a labyrinth, that, I must confess, I neither know how to correct my former opinions, nor how to render them consistent. If this be not a good *general* reason for scepticism, 'tis at least a sufficient one... for me to entertain a diffidence and modesty in all my decisions. (1978, 633ff.)

7. Many have falsely maintained that Hume denies the existence of necessary causal connections. He does not. His concern is not with the metaphysical question regarding whether or not such a connection exists; rather, he is concerned with how we develop that belief and whether we can justify it. See Hume's letter to John Stewart in 1754:

I never asserted so absurd a Proposition as *that any thing might arise without a Cause*: I only maintain'd, that our Certainty of the Falshood of that Proposition proceeded neither from Intuition or Demonstration; but from another Source. *That Caesar existed, that there is such an Island as Sicily*; for these propositions, I affirm, we have no demonstrative nor intuitive Proof. Woud you infer that I deny their Truth, or even their Certainty? There are many different kinds of Certainty; and some of them as satisfactory to the Mind, tho perhaps not so regular, as the demonstrative kind. (1932, vol. 1, 187; Letter 91. See also 1978, 124)

8. On the deists' conception of God consult Gilson 1941, chap. 3, "God and Modern Philosophy," 74–108, esp. 104ff. See also Fosl 1999a, where I discuss this issue at greater length.

9. Thomas Paine, for example, refers to the discovery of the principles of natural science—which was then called "natural philosophy"—as "the true theology" (1945, 487–488). Indeed, for Paine the only true Scripture is the "Bible of Creation": "THE WORD OF GOD," he writes, "IS THE CREATION WE BEHOLD" (1945, 482).

10. See Popkin 1979, 1980, as well as the detailed and comprehensive Floridi 2002.

11. But is it anything more than an empirical—and therefore a merely probable—claim that Tantalus will never reach the fruit he desires? Or, for that matter, that Sisyphus will never succeed in raising his rock to a permanent place on the top of the hill? What grounds do we have for thinking so? For an expansive articulation of Hume's theory of true and false philosophy, see Livingston 1998.

12. This is not to say that Hume's view of natural law is utterly different from conceptions that have been developed more recently. The claims Hume associates with natural law are true, non-analytic, universal generalizations, whose subject-terms are unrestricted, which sustain counterfactual conditionals, and which may be used to formulate explanations and predictions of events in nature. These features of Hume's claims are standard characteristics of natural laws that have been developed by regularist philosophers of science. See Ayer 1956, and Popper 1959, chap. 3. Other supporters of this view include Carl Hempel, J. L. Mackie, Ernest Nagel, Arthur Pap, and Bertrand Russell. One may wish to add the phrase, "expressing a necessary relation," to the list of features characteristic of law-like statements; Hume would, no doubt, assent.

13. For example, Michaud 1983.

14. Bk. III, pt. II, sec. 2: "Of the origin of justice and property." The paragraph, in its entirety, runs as follows:

This convention [i.e., respect for possessions and property] is not of the nature of a *promise*: For even promises themselves, as we shall see afterwards, arise from human conventions. It is only a general sense of common interest; which sense all the members of the society express to one another, and which induces them to regulate their conduct by certain rules. I observe, that it will be for my interest to leave another in the possession of his goods, *provided* he will act in the same manner with regard to me. He is sensible of a like interest in the regulation of his conduct. When this common sense of interest is mutually express'd, and is known to both, it produces a suitable resolution and behaviour. And this may properly enough be call'd a convention or agreement betwixt us, tho' without the interposition of a promise; since the actions of each of us have a reference to those of the other, and are perform'd upon the supposition, that something is to be perform'd on the other part. Two men, who pull the oars of a boat, do it by an agreement or convention, tho' they have never given promises to each other. Nor is the rule concerning the stability of possession the less deriv'd from human conventions, that it arises gradually, and acquires force by a slow progression, and by our repeated experience of the inconveniences of transgressing it. On the contrary, this experience assures us still more, that the sense of interest has become common to all our fellows, and gives us a confidence of the future regularity of their conduct: And 'tis only on the expectation of this, that our moderation and abstinence are founded. In like manner are languages gradually establish'd by human conventions without any promise. In like manner do gold and silver become the common measures of exchange, and are esteem'd sufficient payment for what is of a hundred times their value. (1978, 490)

15. See Hume's "Of the Original Contract" (1985, 465ff.). See also Hume 1978, 516–525.

16. Hume acknowledges this in the provocative text, "A Dialogue," that he attaches to the *Enquiry concerning the Principles of Morals* (1751). This is collected, along with the *Enquiry concerning Human Understanding* (1748) in Hume 1975. In the course of this dialogue, Hume maintains that what eighteenth-century Britons would count as vicious parricide and incest, passed readily among the ancient Romans as permissible, desirable, and even honorable behavior.

17. If one is to look for Hume's reflections on skepticism with regard to other minds (as opposed to skepticism with regard to the external world) it is here, in his thoughts on convention, to which one should turn. Moreover, although his "Abstract" or "Advertisement" might seem to suggest otherwise, the importance of general rules shows that Book III of the *Treatise* is not extraneous to the philosophical project he had taken up in Books I and II. The "Advertisement" describes it as a text that can be considered independently of the two prior books; but of course, this is not to say that it must be considered in this way, or that considering it independently suffices to understand Hume's philosophical position.

18. Plato's Socrates offers a remark which is consonant with Hume's sense of what transpires in convention/community-formation:

[In] our community, then, above all others, when things go well or ill with any individual everyone will use that word 'mine' in the same sense and say that all is going well or ill with him and his.... And, as we said, this way of speaking and thinking goes with fellow-feeling; so that our citizens, sharing as they do in a common interest which each will call his own, will have all their feelings of pleasure or pain in common. (Plato 1941, vol. 5, 463c–464a)

This image may also be taken as an extreme form of the sympathetic identification of one's own interest with the interests of the community that constitutes Hume's reply to Hobbes, Mandeville, and other neo-Augustinian moralists. Plato's Socrates sees in this communion "the greatest good." (See also Plato 1941, vol. 3, 412b.)

19. Heraclitus is reported to have remarked, "Man's *ethos* is his *daimon*" (Kahn 1979, 206; D. 119)—that is, something contingent (i.e., character) is his spirit or divinity (i.e., fate); and see also Heidegger 1998. The Latin *natura* is related to *nasci*, to be born, and hence 'nature' bears the sense of what one is born to, what is natal—i.e., one's fate. In addition, the *Oxford English Dictionary* tells us that the Latin *natura*, from which 'nature' is derived, refers to the character, constitution or course of things.

20. About the partiality and selfishness of humanity, Hume writes, for example: "The remedy, then, is not deriv'd from nature, but from *artifice*; or more properly

speaking, nature provides a remedy in the judgment and understanding, for what is irregular and incommodious in the affections" (1978, 489).

21. Cavell 1980, 111. Concerning such fantastic revisions of human convention, Cavell observes in a way that follows Hume:

That human beings on the whole do not respond in these ways is, therefore, seriously referred to as conventional; but now we are thinking of convention not as the arrangements a particular culture has found convenient, in terms of its history and geography, for effecting the necessities of human existence, but as those forms of life which are normal to any group of creatures we call human, any group about which we will say, for example, that they *have* a past to which they respond, or a geographical environment which they manipulate or exploit in certain ways for certain humanly comprehensible motives. Here the array of "conventions" are not patterns of life which differentiate human beings from one another, but those exigencies of conduct and feeling which all humans share. (1980, 111)

I also take it that this is the type of convention or agreement to which Wittgenstein refers: "the point here is not that our sense-impressions can lie, but that we understand their language. (And this language like any other is founded on convention [*Übereinkunft*])" (1953, no. 355).

22. Wittgenstein distinguishes "surface grammar" from deeper "grammatical" propositions; see Wittgenstein 1953, nos. 232, 251, 293, 295, 371, 373, 458, 496, 497, and 664. So he writes, "Essence is expressed by grammar" (1953, no. 371). Along these lines, one might say that for Hume these sorts of deeper agreements or conventions are also "natural" in the sense of being definitive of human ways of being, definitive such that they could not be altered without altering the very character of what we recognize or what appears to us as "human" life.

23. See related ideas in my interview with Richard Rorty, on the topic of realism (Fosl 1999c).

24. I am extremely grateful to Prof. Rollin Workman of the Philosophy Department of the University of Cincinnati, for his offering me the core of this analogy as a way of clarifying my thoughts on this matter.

25. For more on the meanings of 'nature' as Hume uses it, see McCormick 1993.

26. On the back of one of the sheets of his memoranda, Hume wrote a remark which may be translated as: "Keep sober and remember to be skeptical" (Mossner 1948, 503 n. 17).

27. About the influence of these on Hume, see Fosl (1994) and Neto (1997).

28. In the *Enquiry concerning Human Understanding*, Hume describes his skeptical mode of philosophy as "durable" and "useful," rather than "true" in the sense of accurately corresponding to some independent reality (1975, 161).

29. See also the entry on the "New Academy" in Audi 1999. More specifically, Klein follows one of the descriptions of the Academics from Book I of Sextus' *Outlines of*

Pyrrhonism (*Pyrrhonian hypostases*). The *Outlines* are composed of three books, the first outlining the Pyrrhonian skeptics' views and the latter two attacking various forms of what appeared to them as "dogmatism." Sextus produced four other books: *Against the Professors, Against the Logicians, Against the Ethicists,* and *Against the Physicists.*

30. In addition to describing the Academics as affirming that "all things are non-apprehensible," Sextus Empiricus also described the Academic doctrines of probability as being still too dogmatic (1933, vol. 1, 230ff.). Their doctrines of probability, however, may have been developed simply as devices to oppose the Stoics, and not as doctrines that they dogmatically advanced.

31. Hume's skillful use of 'perhaps' here exhibits an important feature of skepticism; as a consistent skeptic, Hume will neither affirm nor deny the veracity of his "proper" criteria.

32. We know that Hume was concerned by the backlash he foresaw for some of his works—for example, the *Dialogues concerning Natural Religion* (1935), and his essays on suicide and immortality (1985). His concerns were not baseless. Not only was Hume twice denied academic posts on the basis of his anti-religious views; he was also in the early 1750s brought up for prosecution by the General Assembly of the Presbyterian Church. Hume's views were commonly castigated in Britain and the American colonies for their anti-religious import, with sec. 10 of the first *Enquiry* (1748), "On Miracles," becoming especially notorious.

33. The use of '*kriterion*' here is probably an ironic device used in controversies with opponents to skepticism, such as the Stoics, concerning whether or not there are any criteria for distinguishing veridical from false perceptions.

34. The spirit of the passage is so similar to Hume's that one may easily wonder whether he read and absorbed it; see Fosl 1998a.

35. See 1933, vol. 1, 26–31. For example:

Now that we have been saying that tranquility [*ataraxia*] follows on suspension [*epochē*] of judgement, it will be our next task to explain how we arrive at this suspension. Speaking generally, one may say that it is the result of setting things in opposition [*antithesis*]. We oppose either appearances [*phainomena*] to appearances or objects of thought [*noumena*] to objects of thought or *alternando*. (1933, vol. 1, 31)

36. Unlike Edmund Burke (1993), Hume does not fetishize tradition, rendering it unassailable and immune to revision. Because he understands the contingency of tradition and the pathologies that it may nourish, Hume is able to sketch out a position that appreciates and supports the emerging modern political order, and simultaneously appreciates tradition and custom—with the exception, of course, of traditional metaphysics and religion. This difference regarding tradition perhaps in part explains why Hume and Adam Smith were close, but Hume and Burke remained virtual strangers, though all were contemporaries.

37. Hume's phrasing here anticipates the motto later phenomenologists would adopt, following Husserl, in bracketing theories about the causes, nature, and origins of phenomena: "Zu den Sachen selbst!" Regarding Hume's relationship to phenomenology, see Davie 1977.

38. Of course, Wittgenstein also famously recommended keeping silent about what cannot be said clearly (1974, no. 7).

39. Hume, then, is Pyrrhonian in the sense in which Rutgers philosopher Peter Klein (2001, 2004) defines the term.

40. "Methinks," Hume writes, "I am like a man, who having struck on many shoals, and having narrowly escap'd ship-wreck in passing a small frith, has yet the temerity to put out to sea in the same leaky weather-beaten vessel, and even carries his ambition so far as to think of compassing the globe under these disadvantageous circumstances" (1978, 263–264).

41. Garrett (2002) responds to Robert J. Fogelin (1985, 1998).

42. Livingston (1983) argues that in Hume the return to common life overcomes skepticism, clearing a basis for a "post-Pyrrhonian" philosophy. Later (1998), however, Livingston shifts his position to mine, holding that Hume's return to common life, after following out the radical implications of the skeptical arguments, remains part of his skepticism. My position here is that since Hume's metatheory of nature and naturalistic philosophy is formed only through facing those implications, one might say that the meta-theory as well as the theory are the fruit of his skepticism. Regarding Livingston's fetishization of Burke, see Fosl 1998b and Livingston 2000. Livingston writes:

> Edmund Burke's *Reflections on the Revolution in France* is commonly viewed as the origin of the modern conservative intellectual tradition, because he deemed the French Revolution to be an event unique to modern times: not at all an effort at reform but the hubristic attempt to transform the whole of society in accord with an ideology. But Hume before Burke had attached essentially this interpretation to the Puritan revolution in England. Additionally, if the intellectual core of conservatism is a critique of ideology in politics, then Hume's *History* and not Burke's *Reflections* would appear to be the primal source of modern conservatism. (2000, viii)

43. Again, as we saw in the case of Hume's "proper *criteria* for truth and falsehood," Hume distills his thoughts on the standing of theory this way: "we might hope to establish a system or set of opinions, which if not true (for, perhaps, that is too much to be hop'd for) might at least be satisfactory to the human mind, and might stand the test of the most critical examination" (1978, 272).

References

Audi, R., ed. 1999. *The Cambridge Dictionary of Philosophy*, 2nd ed. Cambridge: Cambridge University Press.

Ayer, A. J. 1956. "What Is a Law of Nature?" *Revue internationale de philosophie* 36: 144–165.

Beattie, J. 2004. "Castle of Skepticism." In J. Fieser, ed., *Early Responses to Hume's Life and Reputation*. Bristol: Thoemmes Press. (Originally published 1767.)

Berkeley, G. 1948–57a. *A Treatise concerning the Principles of Human Knowledge*. In A. A. Luce and T. E. Jessop, eds., *The Works of George Berkeley, Bishop of Cloyne*. London: Thomas Nelson and Sons. 9 vols. (Originally published 1710.)

Berkeley, G. 1948–57b. *Three Dialogues between Hylas and Philonous*. In A. A. Luce and T. E. Jessop, eds., *The Works of George Berkeley, Bishop of Cloyne*. 9 vols. London: Thomas Nelson and Sons. (Originally published 1713.)

Burke, E. 1993. *Reflections on the Revolution in France*. L. G. Mitchell, ed. Oxford: Oxford University Press. (Originally published 1790.)

Cavell, S. 1980. *The Claim of Reason: Wittgenstein, Skepticism, Morality, and Tragedy*. Oxford: Clarendon Press.

Davie, G. 1977. "Edmund Husserl and 'The as yet, in its most important respect, unrecognized greatness of Hume.'" In G. P. Morice, ed., *David Hume: Bicentenary Papers*. Edinburgh: Edinburgh University Press.

Deleuze, G. 1953. *Empiricisme et subjectivité*. Paris: Presses Universitaires de France.

Descartes, R. 1984. *Meditations on First Philosophy*. In J. Cottingham, R. Stoothoff, and D. Murdoch, eds. and trans., *The Philosophical Writings of Descartes*, vol. II. Cambridge: Cambridge University Press. (Originally published 1640.)

Descartes, R. 1985. *Principles of Philosophy*. In J. Cottingham, R. Stoothoff, and D. Murdoch, eds. and trans., *The Philosophical Writings of Descartes*, vol. I. Cambridge: Cambridge University Press. (Originally published 1644.)

Floridi, L. 2002. *Sextus Empiricus: The Transmission and Recovery of Pyrrhonism*. Oxford: Oxford University Press.

Fogelin, R. 1985. *Hume's Skepticism in the Treatise of Human Nature*. London: Routledge & Kegan Paul.

Fogelin, R. 1998. "Garrett on the Consistency of Hume's Philosophy." *Hume Studies* 24: 161–169.

Fosl, P. 1994. "Doubt and Divinity: Cicero's Influence on Hume's Religious Skepticism." *Hume Studies* 20: 103–120.

Fosl, P. 1998a. "The Bibliographic Bases of Hume's Understanding of Sextus Empiricus and Pyrrhonism." *Journal of the History of Philosophy* 36: 261–278.

Fosl, P. 1998b. Review. *Hume Studies* 24: 355–366.

Fosl, P. 1999a. "Hume, Skepticism, and Early American Deism." *Hume Studies* 25: 171–192.

Fosl, P. 1999b. "Animality and Common Life in Hume." *1650–1850: Ideas, Aesthetics, and Inquiries in the Early Modern Era* 4: 93–120.

Fosl, P. 1999c. "Note to Realists: Grow Up." *Philosophers' Magazine* 8: 40–42.

Fosl, P. 2004. "Cracks in the Cement of the Universe: Hume, Science, and Skepticism." In K. L. Cope and R. C. Leitz, eds., *Imagining Science: Expressions of New Knowledge in the "Long" Eighteenth-Century*. New York: AMS Press.

Galileo, G. 1967. *Dialogue Concerning the Two Chief World Systems: Ptolemaic & Copernican*. S. Drake, trans. University of California Press, Berkeley. (Originally published 1632.)

Garrett, D. 2002. "'A Small Tincture of Pyrrhonism': Skepticism and Naturalism in Hume's Science of Man." Paper delivered at the Boston Colloquium for Philosophy of Science.

Gassendi, P. 1964. *Syntagma philosophicum*. In *Opera Omnia*, a reproduction of 1658 Edition. Stuttgart-Bad Cannstatt: Friedrich Frommann Verlag. (Originally published 1649.)

Gilson, É. 1941. *God and Philosophy*. New Haven: Yale University Press.

Heidegger, M. 1998. "Letter on Humanism." F. A. Capuzzi, trans. In W. McNeill, ed., *Pathmarks*, Cambridge: Cambridge University Press. (Originally published 1946.)

Hume, D. 1886. *A Natural History of Religion*. In T. H. Green and T. H. Grose, eds., *David Hume: The Philosophical Works*, vol. 4. London: Longman's.

Hume, D. 1932. *The Letters of David Hume*, 2 vols. J. Y. T. Greig, ed. Oxford: Clarendon Press.

Hume, D. 1935. *Dialogues Concerning Natural Religion*. N. K. Smith, ed. New York: Oxford Press.

Hume, D. 1975. *Enquiries Concerning Human Understanding and Concerning the Principles of Morals*, 3rd ed., L. A. Selby-Bigge and P. H. Nidditch, eds. Oxford: Clarendon Press. (Originally published 1748.)

Hume, D. 1978. *A Treatise of Human Nature*, 2nd ed. L. A. Selby-Bigge and P. H. Nidditch, eds. Oxford: Clarendon Press.

Hume, D. 1985. *Essays: Moral, Political, and Literary*. E. Miller, ed. Indianapolis: Liberty Classics.

Kahn, C., ed. and trans. 1979. *The Art and Thought of Heraclitus: An Edition of the Fragments and Commentary*. Cambridge: Cambridge University Press.

Klein, P. 2004. "Skepticism." *Oxford Handbook of Epistemology*. Oxford: Oxford University Press.

Klein, P. 2005. "Skepticism." In E. N. Zalta, ed. *Stanford Encyclopedia of Philosophy*. http://plato.stanford.edu/entries/skepticism/

Laird, J. 1932. *Hume's Philosophy of Human Nature*. London: Methuen.

Livingston, D. 1983. *Hume's Philosophy of Common Life*. Chicago: University of Chicago Press.

Livingston, D. 1998. *Philosophical Melancholy and Delirium: Hume's Pathology of Philosophy*. Chicago: University of Chicago Press.

Livingston, D. 2000. "Forward." In L. L. Bongie, *David Hume: Prophet of the Counter-Revolution* (1965), 2nd ed. Indianapolis: Liberty Fund.

Locke, J. 1975. *Essay Concerning Human Understanding*. Peter Nidditch, ed. Oxford University Press. (Originally published 1689.)

Malebranche, N. 1997. *The Search after Truth*. T. M. Lennon and P. J. Olscamp, Trans. Cambridge: Cambridge University Press. (Originally published 1674–1675.)

McCormick, M. 1993. "Hume on Natural Belief and Original Principles." *Hume Studies* 19: 103–116.

Michaud, Y. 1983. *Hume et la fin de la philosophie*. Paris: Presses Universitaires de France.

Morris, W. 2000. "Hume's Conclusion." *Philosophical Studies* 99: 89–110.

Mossner, E. 1948. "Hume's Early Memoranda, 1729–40: The Complete Text." *Journal of the History of Ideas* 9: 492–518.

Neto, J. 1997. "Academic Skepticism in Early Modern Philosophy." *Journal of the History of Ideas* 58: 199–220.

Newton, I. 1999. *The Principia: Mathematical Principles of Natural Philosophy*. I. B. Cohen and A. Whitman, trans. Berkeley: University of California Press. (Originally published 1667.)

Paine, T. 1945. *The Age of Reason*. In P. S. Foner, ed., *The Complete Writings of Thomas Paine*. New York: Citadel Press. (Originally published 1794, 1795, and 1807.)

Plato. 1941. *Republic*. F. M. Cornford, trans. London: Oxford University Press.

Popkin, R. 1951. "David Hume: His Pyrrhonism and His Critique of Pyrrhonism." *Philosophical Quarterly* 1: 385–407.

Popkin, R. 1979. *The History of Scepticism from Erasmus to Spinoza*. Berkeley: University of California Press.

Popkin, R. 1980. *The High Road to Pyrrhonism*. R. A. Watson and J. E. Force, eds. San Diego: Austin Hill Press.

Popper, K. 1959. *The Logic of Scientific Discovery*. London: Hutchinson.

Randall, J. 1962. *The Career of Philosophy*, vol. 1. New York: Columbia University Press.

Reid, T. 1983a. *Essays on the Intellectual Powers of Man*. In W. Hamilton, ed., *The Works of Thomas Reid, D.D.* Hildesheim: G. Olms Verlagsbuchhandlung. (Originally published 1785.)

Reid, T. 1983b. *Essays on the Active Powers of Man*. In W. Hamilton, ed., *The Works of Thomas Reid, D.D.* Hildesheim: G. Olms Verlagsbuchhandlung. (Originally published 1788.)

Sextus Empiricus. 1933–1949. *Outlines of Pyrrhonism*. R. G. Bury, trans. Cambridge, Mass. and London: Harvard University Press.

Smith, N. K. 1905. "The Naturalism of Hume, I and II." *Mind* 14: 149–173; 335–347.

Wittgenstein, L. 1953. *Philosophical Investigations*. G. E. M. Anscombe, trans. Oxford: Blackwell.

Wittgenstein, L. 1974. *Tractatus Logico-Philosophicus*. D. Pears and B. McGuiness, trans. London: Routledge & Kegan Paul.

Wright, J. 1983. *The Skeptical Realism of David Hume*. Minneapolis: University of Minnesota Press.

Wright, J. 1986. "Hume's Academic Skepticism: A Reappraisal of His Philosophy of Human Understanding." *Canadian Journal of Philosophy* 16: 407–436.

Contributors

Kent Bach   San Francisco State University

Joseph Keim Campbell   Washington State University

Joseph Cruz   Williams College

Fred Dretske   Duke University

Catherine Z. Elgin   Harvard University

Peter S. Fosl   Transylvania University

Peter J. Graham   University of California, Riverside

David Hemp   London, England

Michael O'Rourke   University of Idaho

George Pappas   The Ohio State University

John L. Pollock   University of Arizona

Duncan Pritchard   University of Edinburgh

Joe Salerno   Saint Louis University and Australian National University

Harry S. Silverstein   Washington State University

Robert J. Stainton   University of Western Ontario

Joseph T. Tolliver   University of Arizona

Leora Weitzman   Madison, Wisconsin

Index